GOD AND
HUMAN DIGNITY

God AND HUMAN DIGNITY

The Personalism, Theology, and Ethics
of Martin Luther King, Jr.

RUFUS BURROW, JR.

Foreword by Lewis V. Baldwin and Walter G. Muelder

University of Notre Dame Press
Notre Dame, Indiana

Library of Congress Cataloging-in-Publication Data
Burrow, Rufus, 1951–
    God and human dignity : the personalism, theology, and ethics of
Martin Luther King, Jr. / by Rufus Burrow, Jr.
        p.   cm.
    Includes bibliographical references (p.   ) and index.
    ISBN-13: 978-0-268-02194-8 (cloth : alk. paper)
    ISBN-10: 0-268-02194-5 (cloth : alk. paper)
    ISBN-13: 978-0-268-02195-5 (pbk. : alk. paper)
    ISBN-10: 0-268-02195-3 (pbk. : alk. paper)
    1. Personalism.   2. King, Martin Luther, Jr., 1929–1968.   I. Title.
    B828.5.B86   2006
    230'.61092—dc22
                                                    2006001562

∞ *This book is printed on acid-free paper.*

For Sheronn Lynn (*Juris Doctor*), beloved daughter.

In the hope that you will retain your sense of dignity and self as you navigate the boundaries of law, ethics, and religion; and that your decision making, application of the law, and your daily living will always be guided by the highest estimate of the worth of persons as such and the conviction that the universe itself is founded on justice and morality.

CONTENTS

To understand Martin Luther King, Jr.'s commanding position in American religious, cultural, and intellectual history, it is crucial to recall his influence in the realm of ideas. After all, King was as much *a man of ideas* as he was a practitioner of creative nonviolent dissent and a crusader for freedom, justice, and equality of opportunity. Moreover, he profoundly influenced the intellectual climate of his times, for he wrote books and essays and inspired academics even as his ideas became the anvil upon which his crusade was shaped and launched. This is the message coursing through Rufus Burrow, Jr.'s painstaking, balanced, and probing treatment of King's intellectual sources, categories, and contributions.

Burrow reminds us that King was an *intellectual* before he was a *social activist,* a point often overlooked even by the most established King scholars. King's intellectual odyssey, Burrow concludes, began at Atlanta's Morehouse College (1944–48), where he was exposed to black preacher-scholars who combined a deep appreciation for trends in modern thinking with a keen sense of social responsibility, and extended through his years at Crozer Theological Seminary (1948–51) and Boston University (1951–55), where he studied theology, philosophy, and ethics. Burrow's attention to Morehouse is highly commendable, because that historically black institution is too often ignored or slighted in treatments of King's intellectual pilgrimage. Morehouse is rarely mentioned even in the best and most widely read intellectual biographies of King.

Equally praiseworthy is Burrow's insistence that King's pervasive power and influence as a thinker and idealist cannot be explained solely from the standpoint of his studies at Morehouse, Crozer, and Boston—that those institutions merely provided King with an intellectual structure and conceptual framework to articulate ideas that he initially inherited from his family background, church upbringing, and exposure to Jim Crowism. Thus, King's intellectual formation, and indeed his intellectual life as a whole, were complex and many-sided. Aside from the theological liberalism of

Benjamin E. Mays, George D. Kelsey, and others at Morehouse, the Christian theology and ethics of George W. Davis and others at Crozer, and the idealistic personalism of Edgar S. Brightman and L. Harold DeWolf at Boston, King had the traditions of his extended family, the inheritance of the black church, and the racial conflicts of the South. Apparently, Burrow has a genuine appreciation for the synthesis that exists in King's thought between his cultural-experiential sources and his academic-intellectual sources, a point that cannot be made regarding other intellectual biographers of King.

Burrow provides a rich and thorough examination of King's philosophical personalism, Christian theology, and ethical system, devoting special attention to his ethic of the beloved community and bringing out emphatically such ideas as: (1) God is personal; (2) freedomism; (3) reverence for persons; and (4) the communal nature of reality. The personalist tradition in philosophy, with which such ideas are largely associated, is the longest-lived school of thought continuously associated with one American university; namely, Boston University. Borden P. Bowne, the founder of Boston personalism, began his career there in 1876, and his influence on King, which was quite indirect, was filtered through subsequent generations of personalist thinkers. The second generation of that philosophy was dominated by Edgar S. Brightman, a prolific writer and lecturer, who became King's first Ph.D. advisor at Boston University.

Brightman died in 1953, and L. Harold DeWolf, one of his students, advised King through the completion of his doctoral work two years later. Burrow's treatment of King in relation to Brightman and DeWolf is quite definitive, covering the range of King's studies and also DeWolf's directorship of King's dissertation, which made a strong personalist critique of Paul Tillich's and Henry N. Wieman's ideas concerning God. Interestingly enough, Burrow has an advantage in dealing with King's personalism, theology, and ethics, in as much as he did his own doctoral studies at Boston University under Peter A. Bertocci and Walter G. Muelder, who belong to the third generation in the Boston personalist tradition. Burrow places himself in the fifth generation of that philosophical tradition, and he brings to his analysis a knowledge of black scholarly leaders who have dealt critically and constructively with the King materials.

While viewing personalism as King's conceptual framework and his way of understanding and relating to God and the universe, Burrow does not mean to suggest that the civil rights leader's prophetic utterances and social protest were rooted in white Western theological, philosophical, and ethical sources. Burrow refers to "a homespun Personalism" that King learned through his family and church traditions, a phenomenon in which the sacredness of human personality, the reality of the moral order, and the idea of a personal, loving, and rational God have always been affirmed. Also, while acknowledging King's indebtedness to Boston personalists like Bowne, Brightman, and DeWolf, Burrow boldly and rightly contends that King, by taking to the streets and translating personalist ideas into practical action and reality, contributed essentially as much to personalism as personalism gave him. Some King scholars might find this contention problematic. Even so, Burrow substantially builds on the analyses provided by scholars such as John J. Ansbro and Kenneth L. Smith and Ira G. Zepp, Jr., all of whom fail to note in their otherwise rich scholarship the vitality of King's contributions to personalism's deeper meaning and significance. Burrow's point is that when it comes to personalistic thought, King was as much a critical-creative contributor of ideas as he was an uncritical-prosaic recipient of ideas.

Burrow reminds us that during King's years as a leader in the civil rights movement, he matured in his understanding and appreciation of Boston personalism, and particularly the communitarian dimensions of the human person and how this related to his practice of nonviolence as a social ethic. King himself spoke to this in his *Stride Toward Freedom* (1958), which was written two years after he was catapulted to national and international fame due to his leadership in the Montgomery bus boycott. King wrote:

> The next stage of my intellectual pilgrimage to nonviolence came during my doctoral studies at Boston University. Here I had the opportunity to talk to many exponents of nonviolence, both students and visitors to the campus. Boston University, under the influence of Dean Walter Muelder and Professor Allen Knight Chalmers, had a deep sympathy for pacifism. Both Dean Muelder and Dr. Chalmers had a passion for social justice that stemmed not from a superficial optimism, but from a deep faith in the possibilities of human beings when they allowed themselves to become co-workers with God.

Dr. Burrow's analysis of King's adoption of philosophical personalism, his conception of God, his personal communitarianism, his goal of "the beloved community," his belief in an objective moral order with moral laws, and his presentation of the socio-ethical implications of the faith in a universe that is friendly to these values—all demonstrate various dimensions of the nonviolent convictions which King developed.

Burrow's insights concerning King's relationship to the social gospel tradition are equally important. In his estimation, the benefits King derived from his exposure to the works of Walter Rauschenbusch and other social gospel thinkers were clearly matched by King's own amazing tendency to address prophetically issues like racism, which earlier social gospelers either virtually ignored or spoke to mildly. Burrow also shows clearly how King, inspired by the social gospel, sought to meet the urban prejudices of the North and to embrace the economic challenges which the economic class conflicts gave to his nonviolent communitarian ethic. Similarly, King did not hesitate, when the time came, to oppose the Vietnam War. To be sure, King, as Burrow demonstrates, had a practical problem of deciding when he should break silence, because to oppose the war might detract from or compromise the struggle regarding civil rights. The decision to oppose the war was partly a matter of strategy and timing, not a failure to apply nonviolence internationally.

Much of the strength of this volume lies in Burrow's willingness to raise the difficult questions and to challenge some of the widely accepted conclusions of other King scholars. He exhibits a most thorough knowledge of both the primary sources on King and the critical literature that has been published by his interpreters, and his familiarity with developing trends in King scholarship is first-rate. Furthermore, Burrow challenges, directly and indirectly, those works which fail to emphasize King's enormous significance for a proper understanding of America's intellectual and literary history. Burrow's analysis at this level is strikingly relevant and timely in view of King's booming attraction for intellectual historians, theologians, ethicists, psychoanalysts, and other audiences today.

Burrow tells us that those who wish to truly understand King as an intellectual must look not only at what he wrote and said but what he did as well. He presents to us, in a splendidly balanced way, King's struggle at the level of ideas and how his thought was incarnated in his activities. Both the intellectual environments and the sociopolitical contexts in which particular facets of King's thought were shaped and applied are taken seriously. Thus, King emerges as not only one of the most influential interpreters of ideas in his generation, but also as a pivotal example of that black intellectual-activist tradition which figures like W. E. B. DuBois so strongly represented.

Burrow contributes immensely to the timely and challenging enterprise of taking King seriously as a thinker and idealist. He is not deterred by those who would argue that scholarship on King has been exhausted—that there are no new angles to explore and develop. Moreover, Burrow's examination of King's struggles and contributions as a thinker and personal idealist serve not only as a provocative challenge to a society that has not yet learned how to think critically and prophetically about what it is and what it should become, but also to a world that has inherited the tragic legacy of the most violent of all centuries, and is embroiled in numerous wars and military encounters as it begins its new century and millennium.

In conclusion, Burrow shows why King deserves a special place in the pantheon of gifted Christian thinkers. This is not claiming too much for this prophet of love and creative nonviolent action, for one who speaks to the present in surprising, imaginative, and invigorating ways, and whose intellectual legacy will be richer as time passes.

Lewis V. Baldwin
Professor of Religious Studies, Vanderbilt University

Walter G. Muelder
Dean Emeritus and Professor of Social Ethics Emeritus, Boston University

ACKNOWLEDGMENTS

I had my first encounter with the life, ministry, and writings of Martin Luther King, Jr., in a guided research project supervised by Dean Gene Newberry at the Anderson School of Theology in Anderson, Indiana, in 1975. Although the project focused on King's doctrine of nonviolent resistance to evil, I recall a fascination with his convictions that God is personal, and that each person possesses an inviolable sacredness by virtue of being called into existence and sustained by God. I wanted to know more about what King referred to as "personal idealism" or "personalism," but was not able to make much headway at the time. Upon completion of the project I decided to study under the teachers who taught King the philosophy of personalism at Boston University. Investigation revealed that only two of the personalists with whom King was affiliated were still teaching at Boston University: Peter A. Bertocci and Walter G. Muelder. By the time I was admitted to the graduate school there, both men were in semiretirement, teaching one or two courses a year. Bertocci assumed leadership of the seminar on Hegel that King was enrolled in when Edgar S. Brightman died suddenly in 1953. Muelder was dean of the School of Theology and had many conversations with King about Reinhold Niebuhr's critique of Gandhi's pacifism, among other things. King himself paid tribute to Muelder and Allan Knight Chalmers for their "passion for social justice that stemmed, not from a superficial optimism, but from a deep faith in the possibilities of human beings when they allowed themselves to become co-workers with God."

When I applied for the graduate program in social ethics at Boston, I was informed (in a telephone conversation) by Paul Deats, Jr., chairman of the Division of Theological and Religious Studies, that since I had only taken one course in ethics I would not likely be granted admission. Rather than close and bolt the door to admission, however, Deats made a move that was consistent with the spirit of personalism and Boston University School of Theology's reputation (under Muelder's leadership) of leading all graduate schools in admitting and graduating Afrikan Americans with doctoral degrees in religious studies. His proposal was that I forego completion of the requirements for the Master of Arts degree in religious studies at Anderson, and come to the School of Theology to complete requirements for the Master of Theological Studies degree in social ethics. I was to take six courses in ethics and one course each in two other disciplines. Deats informed me that if I earned a B or better in each course I would be admitted into the Ph.D. program in social ethics the following year. I did and I was.

I am deeply indebted to Paul Deats, Jr., a personalist social ethicist, and I am pleased to have this opportunity to express it in a more public way. I knew I had the ability to do well in graduate school. Had it not been for Dr. Deats, however, I would not have had the chance to try (at least at Boston University). Because of his willingness and courage to risk on my behalf, I had the very good fortune to do much of my graduate work under two of the most knowledgeable, caring, and generous personalist teachers during the third quarter of the twentieth century: Walter G. Muelder and Peter A. Bertocci. Dr. Muelder honored me by reading and providing critical comments on every major manuscript I have written, including the present work (which he read at age 95!) for which he has co-written the Foreword. Dr. Muelder died on June 12, 2004, at the age of 97, and thus did not live to see this book published. His passing ends a significant era in the history of the theistic, idealistic personalism that so deeply influenced and was influenced by Martin Luther King, Jr. Walter Muelder was the last survivor of the famed third generation of Boston University personalists frequently referred to as "the heavyweights."

I am convinced that had Dr. Deats not stepped up to the plate I would not likely have written this book. Thanks to him I was able to study the philosophy of personalism under two third-generation giants of that school of thought. In addition, I was able to take my first real course on King's life and teachings under the sometimes eccentric, but always brilliant and passionate John H. Cartwright, then the newly appointed Martin Luther King, Jr. Professor of Social Ethics. I quickly became what Afrikan American male graduate students under Cartwright affectionately referred to as "a son of John" (and every one of John's sons *and* daughters, all over the country, know what this means). At any rate, Cartwright was very knowledgeable about the field of Christian social ethics and the sociology of religion. It was in his course that I got my first opportunity to delve into King's understanding of personalism, as well as the influence of Walter Rauschenbusch and how King went beyond his social gospelism. It seemed to me at the time that Dr. Cartwright's knowledge and understanding of the philosophical and theological roots of King's thought was second to none. I continue to be grateful for all that he taught me about King, as well as his modeling for me what it means to be a serious teacher and careful scholar.

The Rev. Dr. Conley Hughes, now senior pastor of the Concord Baptist Church in Boston, was a beloved classmate during the Boston days. Over seemingly endless cups of coffee at the Martin Luther King, Jr. Center on campus, we had numerous passionate conversations about King and the great theological, philosophical, and social problems that he grappled with throughout seminary, graduate school, and his ministry. When I heard Conley preach in Boston one night two years ago, I remembered why it was so easy for me to respect, admire, and befriend him when we were in school together. He always exhibited a passion for the least. That same passion and appreciation for the prophetic elements of the Jewish and Christian faiths was evident in his sermon that night as he preached the roof off the sanctuary. He is a powerful, wise, and eloquent master of the pulpit who is making King's dream of the beloved community a reality in the spaces where he does ministry with people. Conley believed in me at times when I momentarily lost my way.

I would be remiss if I did not salute my good friend and classmate the Rev. Dr. Walter Chun. Walter and I took several ethics courses together at BU and became fast friends. In addition to the good-spirited conversations, we shared many Korean delicacies prepared by him and his dear wife, Grace. When my daughter, Sheronn Lynn, was born in 1977, Walter met us at the hospital and transported us home. Moreover, he was our most dependable babysitter when Sheronn Lynn's mother had to work and I had to be in class. Walter always believed I would "someday write a great work on Personalism" and that I would be devoted to keeping this philosophy and way of living in the world alive for yet another generation of students. I have written many articles on personalism, wrote a book on it that was published in 1999, and regularly teach a course on it. I continue to be driven to write "a great work on Personalism."

My three best conversation partners on matters pertaining to King and personalism are Lewis V. Baldwin (Vanderbilt University), Gary Dorrien (Union Theological Seminary in New York), and Jimmy L. Kirby (Lexington Theological Seminary). Baldwin, one of the top five King scholars in the world, has been both unselfish and even gracious in sharing with me his own research into the unpublished papers of King. He has also been both diplomatic and critical in the reading of my work on black theology, ethical prophecy, personalism, and King. What is more, he has shown his appreciation for my research, thinking, and writing about King by inviting me to contribute a chapter to his fine book, *The Legacy of Martin Luther King, Jr.: The Boundaries of Law, Politics, and Religion.* Indeed, were it not for Lewis Baldwin, his witness, and uncommon generosity regarding the work of other Afrikan American scholars, I would not have written a single article, let alone a book, on King. But that is a story to be told on another occasion. Presently, suffice it to say that I am deeply indebted to and grateful to him for the type of collegiality that makes sense to me. He keeps reminding me that I can.

With the death of Walter Muelder, Dorrien arguably possesses the broadest knowledge and understanding of the theological contributions of the Boston personalist tradition of anyone now living, as evidenced by his extensive and meticulous treatment of it in nearly 100 pages in the first two volumes of his massive trilogy, *The Making of American Liberal Theology* (2001, 2003). A white scholar, Dorrien seems to possess a level of sensitivity and appreciation for racial-ethnic and cultural differences that makes for good in racial and cultural relations. Kirby, my beloved former student, who followed in my footsteps by earning his doctorate at Boston University (and also became a son of John!), has been confidant, friend, and cheerleader. I continue to be hopeful that his interest in and knowledge of King, especially in relation to the likes of Bishop Reverdy C. Ransom of the A. M. E. Church and the personalist George A. Coe, will some day fill volumes. For now it is enough to know that he cares deeply about it all.

I have taught theological social ethics for a little over twenty years at Christian Theological Seminary in Indianapolis, Indiana. I have always felt at liberty to pursue my scholarly research and writing interests here. Although a freestanding seminary, without the financial resources of the divinity school that is affiliated with a large research university, the trustees and administration have been generous and supportive of my research and writing.

I simply must acknowledge the contributions and patience of my students who, I am sure, suffered as I sometimes argued openly with myself and with them as I struggled to work out many of the ideas in this book. I am particularly grateful to those Afrikan American, Latina, and white women students who persisted over the years (and some were downright adamant!) in urging me to be forthright about King's sexism and not to sugarcoat or pretend that it did not exist, or to argue that there was some "good" reason for it, e.g., "that he was a man of his time." Generally I have found students in my course on King's theological ethics to be eager to learn about him as person, his ideas and contributions, as well as the cultures and ideas that helped shape his thinking and ministry. Minister Preston Adams, recipient of the Doctor of Ministry degree at the seminary, had the task of reading the manuscript version of this book and providing two lectures in the King class (during school year 2003–4) based on his understanding and application of the argument. His discussions, criticisms, suggestions, and application to his work with *at risk* young Afrikan American males were particularly helpful as I completed the final draft. I am hopeful that this book will be a valuable resource for all who wish to make constructive contributions toward making better persons and establishing the community of love that was the central focus of King's life and ministry.

I am thankful for the efforts of Linda Sue Hewitt, educator of scores of youths at the middle school level in Rochester, Indiana, and witness to the truth and richness of multiculturalism in education, and close friend. More than any other person, Linda has seen to it that I have awareness of and access to the most recent scholarship on King as I researched and worked through various drafts of the manuscript. A former student, she has cheered my work in theological social ethics and has made much of it a part of her own efforts to make better persons and communities.

Last but not least, there is no way to adequately describe the skill of my editor, Mr. Jack Kirshbaum. His careful eye and commitment to this project are evident on every page. The success of this book will be due in a significant way to this outstanding editor.

GOD AND
HUMAN DIGNITY

INTRODUCTION

Dozens of dissertations, articles, and books have been written on various aspects of the life and work of Martin Luther King, Jr., and yet there are many areas of his thought that still merit attention. A published Princeton Theological Seminary master's thesis written by Ernest Shaw Lyght is the earliest book-length examination of the philosophical and religious roots of King's thought.[1] Kenneth Smith and Ira Zepp, Jr., provided a vastly more informed scholarly treatment of intellectual influences on King's thought, including the philosophy of personalism.[2] This philosophy was developed and taught at Boston University from 1876 to roughly the end of the 1960s. I date the decline of the influence of personalism to about the time of King's assassination and the retirement of third-generation personalists under whom he studied. In a 1981 book, Ervin Smith also addresses some of the intellectual influences and includes a fine chapter on the significance of a personal God as the source of King's ethics.[3] Smith does an admirable job of discussing the personalistic foundations of King's ethics. Also, unlike other King scholars, Smith includes a chapter which suggests implications of his personalistic ethics for specific social problems such as racism, economic exploitation, war, marriage, and family. In addition, Smith begins his book by discussing the importance of King's religious and family upbringing. The discussion is only a couple of pages long, but in them Smith provides important context. He knew that by the time King attended college, seminary, and graduate school some of his most important religious and ethical convictions—e.g., that God is personal and persons are sacred—had already been shaped through the influence of his family and black church upbringing.

Of the earlier texts, the best and most comprehensive book addressing the formal intellectual influences on King, as well as why he addressed social problems as he did and proposed the solutions he did, was published by John J. Ansbro in 1982.[4] Ansbro essentially shows King to be a consistent social personalist in the way he

1

developed and implemented his doctrine of nonviolence, inasmuch as he tried to live the meaning of personalism's two fundamental dicta: ultimate reality is personal and loving; and persons are the highest intrinsic values and thus are inherently precious.

The chief criticism that has been made against the work by Smith and Zepp, as well as Ansbro, is that they failed to acknowledge the black cultural, familial, and church influences on King's intellectual development. This criticism, made by black liberation theologians such as James H. Cone and church historian and King scholar Lewis V. Baldwin, is quite legitimate and needed to be made. Until the mid-1980s, white scholars were notorious for either excluding Afrikan Americans' contributions to whatever subject they were writing or teaching on, or for including one or more Afrikan Americans while treating only white western influences on their thought development.* Indeed, King scholars, regardless of race, tended to be guilty of this practice prior to the early- to mid-1980s. One need merely recall the otherwise fine work by the Afrikan American scholar David L. Lewis, *King: A Critical Biography* (1970). Afrikan American scholars were quite right to critique this tendency. Of course, since the Lewis text appeared barely two years after King was assassinated, he did not have access to King's unpublished papers at Boston University and the SCLC collections at the King Center for Nonviolent Social Change in Atlanta. Nor did he have access to a host of other resources that would later be available to historian Stephen B. Oates when he did the research for what is arguably the best biography on King at present: *Let the Trumpet Sound* (1982).[5]

In fairness to Ansbro, however, we should be clear about what he sought to do in his work. He acknowledged that his book focused on providing a systematic discussion of King's doctrine of nonviolence. To get at this, he sought to examine "central insights from ancient, medieval, modern, and contemporary thinkers who moved [King] to construct his own strategy."[6] Acknowledging that a number of scholars had already addressed the influence that Mahatma Gandhi, Walter Rauschenbusch, and Reinhold Niebuhr had on King's intellectual development, Ansbro felt that not nearly enough attention had been given the influence of personalism. He also believed that

---

* The use of "c" in the spelling of "Africa" is the Anglicized spelling; that letter does not exist in West Afrikan languages. I use the "k" out of respect and in honor of those who struggled for liberation in the 1960s. During the Black Consciousness movement of this period, a number of proponents adopted the use of "k" in the spelling of "Afrika," which was consistent with the usage of many groups on the Afrikan continent as well. The spelling is still prevalent among some Afrikans on the continent and in diaspora. For example, this is the preferred spelling in a publication I received from Accra, Ghana (*The Afrikan Crusader*), where on every page the spelling is "Afrikan". I adopted this spelling for my own writing after the publication of my first book in 1994 and consistently use it in my writing.

more attention needed to be given to other philosophers and theologians whose ideas influenced King's philosophy of nonviolence. The vast majority of those included in Ansbro's otherwise excellent book are Europeans and Euro-Americans. Although he did not examine the more formative black church and familial contributions to King's intellectual development, Ansbro included some of King's reactions to Afrikan American thinkers and leaders such as Booker T. Washington, W. E. B. DuBois, Marcus Garvey, Stokely Carmichael, Elijah Muhammad, and Malcolm X. Yet, one wonders why Ansbro did not think it important to include even a discussion of the obvious nonviolent stance of King's parents and maternal grandparents. The same cannot be said about his paternal grandparents James and Delia King who, respectively, threatened a white mill owner with a shotgun and physically fought with him for hitting their son (Daddy King).[7] The point is that the nonviolent approach to addressing social ills had been modeled for King by maternal family members, as well as local black pastors such as William Holmes Borders, long before he was introduced to the work of Henry David Thoreau in college and Gandhi in seminary.

At a time (the mid-1980s) when black liberation theologians and religious scholars were highly vocal and critical of the failure of white scholars to address the cultural, family, and black church influences on King and other major Afrikan American personalities, it could be argued that Ansbro's failure in this regard was simply inexcusable. One wonders whether he was even listening to the voices of these critics, and if he was, why did he not heed their advice and reflect it in his work? Indeed, after the Black Consciousness movement of the 1960s, one could also argue similarly regarding the publication of Smith and Zepp's book in 1974. These scholars, including Ansbro, should have—at the very least—included a brief statement noting the significance of the critique of black scholars, while declaring that they themselves would be focusing on the European and Euro-American influences on King's thought. That they did not do this might be indicative of white male arrogance, as well as the continued presence and influence of racism and unearned white privilege.

There is presently no better systematic treatment of King's theory of dignity than Garth Baker-Fletcher's book on the subject.[8] Baker-Fletcher gets at some of the important family and church roots of King's doctrine of "somebodyness." He then proceeds to address the philosophical underpinnings. Although the study leaves something to be desired in terms of accuracy of interpretation of personalist ideas, it clearly provides important foundation for future exploration of the theme of dignity in King's thought and work.

At any rate, although much has been written about King, there are many aspects of his thought that have been ignored or insufficiently addressed. The doctrine of God, the chief tenets of personalism, moral laws, and the objectivity of reality are some of the many specific topics that deserve far more attention. My book seeks to address a number of these and related matters, and how they played out in King's thought and ministry.

My discussion is informed by my intensive study of personalism at Boston University with two third-generation giants in that tradition, Peter A. Bertocci (1910–89) and Walter G. Muelder (1907–2004). In addition to being taught by these two men— who did not simply teach personalistic ideas, but consciously lived these ideas and their deepest meaning—I had the good fortune to be tutored by each of them for a two-week period during the summer of 1989, after I had been a seminary professor for six years. Bertocci tutored me in the metaphysics and epistemology of Borden Parker Bowne (1847–1910), who systematized American personalism and developed it into a philosophical method. After my time with Bertocci, Muelder gave me two fascinating weeks of instruction in Bowne's ethics. The quintessential teacher, Muelder, then in his early eighties, was simply incredible in his recall of the basic ideas of Bowne's ethics, reciting a number of long passages from the text verbatim. This was an invaluable and memorable month of study and tutorials that continue to affect my scholarly development in ways I could not then have imagined.

I also regularly teach a course on personalism at Christian Theological Seminary in Indianapolis. Since I long ago adopted personalism as my fundamental philosophical stance, I intentionally include its basic principles in all courses that I teach. In addition, I have written many articles and a book on the subject.[9]

There is yet another important reason why my discussion on these influences on King's thought is not a mere duplication of what has already been written. As an Afrikan American, my own familiarity with black family, cultural, and church values— and my application of these values—positions me to provide a richer examination of such topics as the doctrine of God and the objectivity of moral laws, how they influenced King, and how King influenced them in turn. White scholars who have written on King and personalism have read much of the basic literature on personalism, but they were either not able, or quite possibly not willing, to filter the meaning of this literature through the Afrikan American experience (if only vicariously). On the other hand, most Afrikan Americans who have written on King's thought have done little more than read secondary sources on personalism. Moreover, some of those who have in fact read some of the primary sources misread or misunderstood the texts. This is my judgment of Garth Baker-Fletcher's discussion of personalistic influences on King in his otherwise fine book, *Somebodyness: Martin Luther King, Jr.'s Theory of Dignity.*[10] In addition, although his book does not specifically address King, the late Major J. Jones erred frequently in his discussion of personalistic ideas about God in *The Color of God: The Concept of God in Afro-American Thought.*[11]

I bring to this study an interpretation of personalistic and other influences on King's thought and ministry that is different from others who have written on him.

For example, I discuss what I call King's "homespun personalism." This, I argue, is what caused him to gravitate so easily to the formal study of personalism in seminary and graduate school, for its basic tenets had been instilled in him through his black church and family socialization. The formal instruction he received in the academy simply provided him a reasonable philosophical framework on which to ground his boyhood convictions that the universe is fundamentally good, God is personal, and persons possess infinite worth as beings imbued with the image of God.

King's Published and Unpublished Writings

The claim of King scholars such as James H. Cone and David J. Garrow that the most reliable view of King's thoughts and ideas are found in his many extemporaneous unpublished speeches and writings no longer applies.[12] Much careful archival research and scholarly writing has been done, especially since the 1980s, so that now one can get as clear a picture of the authentic King in his published writings and speeches.[13] The first five volumes of the King papers have appeared, which make available skillfully edited versions of the previously unpublished writings, sermons, and speeches of King. The King Papers Project has also produced *The Autobiography of Martin Luther King, Jr.*, edited by Clayborne Carson (1998); a volume of sermons by King, *A Knock at Midnight* (1998), edited by Carson and Peter Holloran; and a volume of "landmark speeches," *A Call to Conscience* (2001), edited by Carson and Kris Shephard. More speeches, sermons, and writings are forthcoming. Therefore, anybody who reads King's previously unpublished works, as well as the writings of scholars such as Cone, Baldwin, Oates, Garrow, Baker-Fletcher, Taylor Branch, and Stewart Burns, will get an authentic sense of King's ideas.

A number of King's writings and speeches were ghostwritten. How well do these works represent King's thoughts? Baldwin and Baker-Fletcher make the convincing case that even those speeches were written with King's approval, "and there is no evidence that he disclaimed any of these texts." Furthermore, Baldwin contends that his own archival research reveals "no important discrepancies between what appears in King's edited and sometimes ghostwritten works and what is included in his extemporaneous, unpublished texts. King's personality and the basic outlines of his thought are evident in both."[14] The ghostwriters did not so much put words into King's mind and mouth, he says, as "they took words out of his mouth." These ghostwritten statements are more reliably King than Garrow thinks.[15] By all accounts, King was a man of tremendous intellectual acumen and could be sharply analytical. Surely had he disagreed with the ghostwriters he would have taken issue with what they wrote, rather than uncritically accept their ideas as his own.

The foregoing discussion is important because much of my own work on King primarily reflects my reading and study of his published works, as well as what I consider to be the best published scholarship on his life, thought, and work, most of which is based on thorough and painstaking archival research by the authors consulted. It is also true, however, that my work is based on a critical reading of many of King's unpublished papers, speeches, and sermons. Here I owe a huge debt of gratitude to Lewis V. Baldwin, a most astute, careful, and thorough King scholar, whose work on the cultural roots of King's thought and ministry is surpassed by no other.

A Preliminary Word on personalism

Long before King heard the term "personalism," he had been introduced to the idea of a personal God and the concept of the absolute dignity of persons through his family upbringing and teachings at Ebenezer Baptist Church, where his father was pastor.[16] King implied in his first book that by the time he studied the philosophy of personalism in a formal systematic way at Boston University, he already possessed a deep faith in two of its fundamental tenets: the infinite, inviolable worth of persons as such, and a personal God to whom people are of supreme value. This is why I argue for the idea of King's "homespun personalism," which stresses the family and black church roots and which made it easy for him to embrace the more formal, academic personalism he encountered in seminary and graduate school.[17] There is indication that even as a student at Morehouse College, King was introduced—however casually—to the work of the outstanding personalist, Edgar S. Brightman.[18] This introduction may have taken place in one of two philosophy classes taught by Samuel Williams during the 1947–48 school year,[19] or the previous year in his Bible course with George Kelsey.[20] In any case, it is more important for our purpose that we remember what Lewis Baldwin has said about the influence of King's sociocultural and familial roots on his speaking and writing. "When he spoke, he was speaking not only his own words but also the words of his parents and grandparents. Their dream became his dream, and their struggle, his struggle."[21] By the time King finished graduate school, his words and dreams were an amalgam of his familial and cultural roots as well as the more formal teachings of Morehouse College, Crozer Theological Seminary, and Boston University Graduate School. These would be refined and filtered through King's own personality and cultural lens during the civil and human rights movements.

When telling the story of the Montgomery struggle, King wrote that "personalism strengthened me in two convictions: it gave me metaphysical and philosophical grounding for the idea of a personal God, and it gave me a metaphysical basis for the dignity and worth of all human personality."[22] The phrase "strengthened me in two convictions" is an important reminder that these were already deeply ingrained in King even before he studied the metaphysical, epistemological, and ethical foundations of personalism in seminary and graduate school. Therefore, personalism primarily provided for King a philosophical framework for his long-held beliefs, ones instilled in him by his maternal grandmother, parents, the black church, and teachers at Morehouse College. Once introduced to systematic personalism in graduate school, however, King found himself "wholeheartedly committed" to it.[23] The basic principles of personalism were therefore indelibly etched into his being.

Personalism teaches that persons are the highest intrinsic values, and ultimate reality is personal. If one is also a theist, as King was, it means, further, that God is both personal and is that Being on which all other beings depend for their existence. God is the fundamental source of the whole of reality as well as the ground of human dignity. King is not selective in this regard. That is, his conviction is that *every* person, regardless of race, gender, class, ability, age, health, or sexuality is a being of absolute worth, because every person is created and loved by a supremely personal God. Each person is infinitely valuable to God, and therefore should be treated as such.

There are at least a dozen types of personalisms. I enumerate and discuss eight of these in *Personalism: A Critical Introduction* (1999).[24] Theistic personalism, which influenced King, is represented in the work of a number of philosophers and theologians who taught or studied at Boston University. These include Bowne; John Wesley Edward Bowen (1855–1933), the first Afrikan American academic personalist, and a student of Bowne's (although there is no indication that King knew of Bowen); Edgar Sheffield Brightman (1884–1953), the first Borden Parker Bowne Professor of Philosophy at Boston University, chief expositor and interpreter of Bowne's personalism, academic advisor to King, and the reason that King desired to earn his doctorate at Boston University; and L. Harold DeWolf (1905–86), theologian and Christian ethicist who became King's academic advisor when Brightman suddenly died, and who was King's mentor, confidant, and friend throughout his leadership in the civil and human rights movements.

INCONSISTENCIES IN KING'S PRACTICE OF PERSONALISM

The argument of this book is that King was generally a thoroughgoing personalist in both theory and practice. One of his distinctive contributions was his application of basic principles of personalism to major social problems of his day. In this regard he played second fiddle to no one, including his teachers at Boston University. Nonetheless, chapter 5, "Dignity of Being and Sexism," focuses on one significant area where King's practice was not consistent with his personalism—more specifically his doctrine of human dignity. One could rightly argue that there were at least two other areas of King's practice that were inconsistent with his ethical personalism: the plagiarism in many of his writings and speeches, and his extramarital relations throughout much of his leadership in the civil rights movement. Because of the sheer volume of scholarly and popular works that have been published on these two matters, I do not discuss them in the body of this book. It does seem reasonable, however, to devote brief attention to them here.

King's Appropriation of Sources

Concerns about King's footnote style—not plagiarism—were raised as far back as courses he took with Walter Chivers at Morehouse College. Chivers noted in one of King's papers that he needed to learn acceptable footnote style.[25] We know from reports of Clayborne Carson and other staff of the King Papers Project at Stanford University that King's pattern of "selective use of appropriated passages dates from the Crozer period."[26] The same practice is evident in the sermons, speeches, and writings during his public ministry. It would therefore be ludicrous to pretend that this did not happen, or that King was not aware that failure to give attribution for the use of sources was wrong. Many scholars have sought to determine why King engaged in such practices. The truth, however, is that *all* responses can only end in speculation.

Although the plagiarism story broke in late 1990, it is also known that King was chided periodically by some seminary and graduate school professors for failing to properly attribute appropriated sources. While in graduate school I recall reading an article that DeWolf wrote in 1977: "Martin Luther King, Jr., as Theologian." DeWolf implied that some of King's theological ideas were similar to his own and stated, "occasionally I find his language following closely the special terms of my own lectures and writings."[27]

Although DeWolf did not expressly accuse King of plagiarism, this is an issue that has received a tremendous amount of press and energy since 1990. Considering the amount of attention already given this subject by Carson and Garrow, as well as Theodore Pappas, Michael Eric Dyson, Richard Lischer, Keith D. Miller[28]—and the more than 100 pages devoted to the subject in the June 1991 issue of the *Journal of American History*[29]—I see no need to duplicate what has already been done.

A pattern of the appropriation of the written work of others is an important challenge to King's ethical personalism. This entire book is based on substantiating the significance of personalism for King—homespun, academic, and his own modifications of it—and how he *lived* it in the face of degrading social problems. Deviations from the standards of the personalism that King forged should not be relegated to a footnote. There is no question that King's plagiarism is inconsistent with his personalism and doctrine of dignity. Garrow, a member of the advisory board for the King Papers Project under Carson's direction, claims to have been so distraught over the discovery that King persistently plagiarized that his view of King as person has changed. Moreover, Garrow is quoted as saying that the discovery "had a tremendous shaking, emotional impact on me." He said further: "It's disconcerting, because it is fundamentally, phenomenally out of character with my entire sense of the man."[30] This reaction notwithstanding, Garrow claimed to retain his sense of high regard and respect for King's courage and commitment to the struggle for civil and human rights.

Dyson addresses this topic in *I May Not Get There with You*, written primarily for a more popular audience, with a strong appeal to the sensational. There is not much that I disagree with regarding his discussion of King's plagiarism, but I do find it both problematic and interesting that Dyson seems eager to remind his readers over and over that *he* recognizes King's moral failure regarding plagiarism.[31] It is as if Dyson felt the need to impress this point upon establishment readers of his book, as if to say: *This is one Afrikan American scholar who is critical of King's plagiarism!* What is more, Dyson makes unsubstantiated claims about plagiarism and other Afrikan Americans who earned academic doctorates at Boston University. He claims for example, that, "the wonder is not that King cheated" under some rather tough conditions, "but that C. Eric Lincoln, Samuel Proctor, Evans Crawford, Cornish Rogers, Major Jones, and thousands of other blacks did not."[32] While I concur that vast numbers of blacks did not, and do not, cheat in this way, the problem arises when Dyson names individual Afrikan Americans. To put it the way Dyson does merely sensationalizes the matter where King is concerned.

David Bundy is a white theological librarian and early church historian. He was librarian and professor of church history at Christian Theological Seminary where I teach. In September 1991, I wrote Bundy to thank him for the use of his personal copy of the issue of the *Journal of American History* devoted to the plagiarism matter. In his handwritten response Bundy put his finger on the issue that concerned me most: that the discovery of plagiarism in King's work will make it too easy for King detractors to dismiss the many very important things that he accomplished in the area of human rights. Without minimizing the gravity of the plagiarism issue, I close this part of the discussion on limitations in the practice of King's ethical personalism with Bundy's response.

> I suspect King was a graduate student in a hurry. A Ford Foundation study indicated only 5% of dissertations were free of problems. I personally have found five other plagiarized Harvard Ph.D. dissertations—two of which were written by people who have become productive contributing, *even original* scholars.

Knowing that, when I heard King's story, I was not so much shocked as sad-
dened that many would use this lamentable behavior to undermine *all* of what
King stood for and-or use it as an excuse to dismiss his own original contributions. My admiration for King remains untarnished . . . from my Holiness background I suppose I'm more keen to see a whole life rather than a single moment
of either brilliance or defect. Faithfulness to God . . . is a long term project! I see
King as a faithful person.[33]

Alleged Extramarital Affairs

For reasons similar to those noted regarding the plagiarism issue, I choose not to
include a discussion in the body of this book on King's philanderering. My reason has
little to do with personal discomfort. Rather, it has to do with my distrust of the powers responsible for FBI surveillance reports on Afrikan American leaders (especially
preceding and during the civil rights and Black Consciousness movements of the
1960s and 1970s), as well as my skepticism of claims made by some of those close
to King, in particular, by his best friend, Ralph Abernathy.[34] The racism of FBI director J. Edgar Hoover and his vicious vendetta against King are and were well known.
Andrew Young, a close confidant and advisor to King, was absolutely convinced that
Hoover was out to destroy King emotionally and psychologically through disinforma-
tion, lies, and intimidation. In addition, Hoover and the White House seemed to pull
out all stops to destroy the planning of the Poor People's Campaign.[35] Then there is the
matter of Abernathy's desire to capitalize financially on his longtime close relationship with King in his *And the Walls Came Tumbling Down* (1989). Abernathy has written
that King was with a close female companion at her home in Memphis past 1:00 A.M.
When they returned to the Lorraine Motel, Abernathy writes, King then spent the remainder of the night with a female member of the Kentucky legislature (Senator Georgia Davis Powers) who "had clearly come to see Martin."[36] This all allegedly occurred
the night before King was assassinated, which makes the philandering charge all the
more sensational. Surely one's best friend, one's "alter ego,"[37] would not lie about such
a thing. But sensationalistic literature often brings the writer huge royalties. Indeed,
had not Abernathy himself written: "Sexual sins are by no means the worst. Hatred
and a cold disregard for others are the besetting sins of our time, but they don't sell
books or tabloid newspapers. . . ."[38] In any case, there is so much smoke and circum-
stantial evidence regarding the charge of philandering that there is surely truth in it.
    My chief discomfort about discussing King's extramarital relationships is based
on the tendency of many who placed him on a moral pedestal, and then utterly condemned him when he failed to live up to *their* moral standards, whether regarding extramarital relations or plagiarism. I have argued in articles and lectures on King that

if we are to truly understand his life, ideas, and ministry it is absolutely essential to understand that he was first and last a human being who possessed all the possibilities and limitations that every person possesses. As we will see, King was quite aware that his personal life was not spotless and without blemish. Failure to acknowledge King's humanity makes it too easy to condemn him as person, as Garrow did upon discovering that he plagiarized. Others, because of King's personal moral failures, have sought to minimize his contributions to the struggle for civil and human rights. This has been the reaction of many conservative and fundamentalist white racists when allegations about King's moral character surfaced. Of course, for this group the allegations themselves only confirmed what they had already conjured up about King.

Much scholarly and journalistic attention has already been devoted to King's alleged sexual escapades. Those who wrote books on King shortly after his assassination— e.g., John A. Williams, Jim Bishop, and David L. Lewis[39]—could only write of *rumors* of extramarital affairs. Lewis's was the best of the early biographies. He was careful to make it clear that these were nothing more than rumors, since FBI tapes that allegedly substantiated them were at the time sealed. Innuendos in the books by Bishop and Williams imply that they knew more about the *rumors* than they probably did. Stephen B. Oates was among the first of the scholars on King to obtain the previously sealed FBI files. He wrote about the contents of some of these files and tapes in *Let the Trumpet Sound*.[40] Once the floodgates opened, Garrow, Taylor Branch, Dyson, and a few other writers on King earned huge book royalties, in part, for focusing heavily on the alleged sex tapes and files.[41] Not all King scholars (including James H. Cone, Lewis V. Baldwin, and Garth Baker-Fletcher) have chosen to devote much energy and attention to this issue. They wonder, as I do, about the racist element embedded in the tendency (especially among white male scholars) to devote so much attention to King's personal moral shortcomings. In my judgment former Kentucky state Senator Georgia Davis Powers, King's close friend, confidant, and acknowledged lover during the last year of his life, asks an important question: "Why is the dedication that brings people together, the goals we shared, the work we did, less important than the fact that Dr. King and I had an intimate relationship?"[42] That vast numbers of people are less concerned about the former is a sad commentary on the moral status of this nation.

Martin Luther King, Jr. literally gave his life because of his faithfulness and commitment to eradicating human oppression, despite his human limitations. In the end, notwithstanding his personal moral failures, King was faithful to God's call to set at liberty the oppressed. Precisely here I second the words of David Bundy quoted above: "My admiration for King remains untarnished. . . . I suppose I'm more keen to see a whole life rather than a single moment of either brilliance or defect. Faithfulness to God . . . is a long term project! I see King as a faithful person." This general sentiment has also been echoed by a number of King scholars, not least the recently emerging voice of Michael G. Long who, in his reflections on King's legacy had this to say in light of charges of plagiarism and philandering.

> Recent years have proven difficult for the legacy of Martin Luther King, Jr. Heavily documented studies of King's practice of plagiarism, in addition to loosely documented, indeed sensational, reports of his alleged womanizing, have saturated much of the recent mass media coverage of his life. In offering this brief study, I seek not to ignore or dismiss these charges and allegations, but rather to suggest that King's legacy, just like his moral character, can never be reduced to such matters as plagiarism and intimate behavior. The whole King is greater, far greater, than the man who borrowed words without attribution or who expressed interest in women other than his wife. In my estimation, the whole King includes not only those actions, real or imagined, but also his willingness to suffer for the God-given dignity of his brothers and sisters, his courage to stand against a government that sought to degrade him, his abiding love for his family and friends, his deep faith in the Anchor—and, of course, his compelling vision of creative living. Like each of us, the whole King is both sinner and saint.[43]

Such behavior on King's part, regardless of rationales for his motives, was also a breakdown in his practice of personalism. Although King was a thoroughgoing personalist in theory, there are points at which his actual practice contradicted his fundamental personalistic ideas.

The first chapter of this book focuses on King's intellectual journey, beginning with his matriculation at Morehouse College. It examines some of his experiences there, how his religious thinking was shaken up and transformed, the type of student he was, and what led to his decision to enter ministry in order to help his people. There is also a consideration of King's experience in seminary, including his social life and adjustments he had to make at the predominantly white Crozer Theological Seminary, his studiousness and zeal to make a good impression and to be an excellent student, and his determination to find both a reasonable theological rationale for his social conscience and a method to help his people. This chapter also discusses the influence of George Washington Davis, under whom King did approximately one-third of his course work. Davis formally introduced King to the basic ideas of liberal theology and the philosophy of personalism—ideas King had grown up with in more informal ways through his family and his experiences in the black church.

Chapter 2 examines additional intellectual influences from King's seminary experience, more specifically the influence of the social gospel movement, and distinguishes between the black social gospel and the white social gospel. King was not first introduced to the existence and importance of social Christianity during his studies at Crozer, but grew up being told about the social ministry of his maternal grandfather. He also witnessed it in the ministry of his father and other black preachers (e.g., William Holmes Borders). What is more, as a college student King was exposed on a regular basis to the liberal social gospel preaching of Benjamin E. Mays and George Kelsey at Morehouse College. The case will therefore be made that King was quite familiar with social gospel Christianity long before he matriculated at Crozer. In addition, attention is given the issue of racism and the response of white social gospel leaders such as Walter Rauschenbusch, Washington Gladden, Lyman Abbott, and Josiah Strong. This discussion is influenced both by the more traditional works on the social gospel by early scholars such as Robert T. Handy, Thomas Gossett, and C. Howard Hopkins, as well as the more recent revisionist and provocative discussions of Ronald White and Ralph Luker. The chapter prompts one to ask: Was King aware of the racism of the white social gospelers, and most particularly Rauschenbusch's long silence on that issue, since he was most influenced by him? Did King respond to this? Special attention is given Rauschenbusch and racism, as well as his first major text, *Christianity and the Social Crisis*, which provided King with the formal theological rationale he sought in order to ground his social conscience. This chapter also considers the influence of Rauschenbusch's ideas on King and how he adapted them, as well as King's critique of various social gospel ideas, and how his own social gospelism transcended that of Rauschenbusch.

The task of the third chapter is to clarify the meaning and significance of King's fundamental philosophical point of departure: personalism. What is it, and what was King's experience with it at Boston University? How did it play out in his ministry? What did King's family and church upbringing contribute to his personalism, and how deeply rooted are these contributions in Afrikan American culture and history? The chapter also revisits attempts by some scholars to undermine the importance of personalism for King.

Chapter 4 examines King's doctrine of God. I argue that this is crucial for understanding his beloved community ethic, his doctrine of nonviolent resistance to evil, his emphasis on the sacredness of persons, and his conviction that the universe is friendly to value, that is, to the achievement of good. King's beloved community ethic, and his conviction that the universe hinges on a moral foundation, is grounded in his conception of God. Steering away from the stance of mainstream King scholars, this chapter introduces and examines the hypothesis that King was not a rigid, traditional theistic absolutist, and suggests that while he frequently used terms like "omnipotent" and "almighty" to characterize God, he did not mean that God possesses absolute power. It is quite possible that King meant something similar to what

Edgar S. Brightman (his teacher) and Charles Hartshorne expressed when they characterized God as *the most powerful being in the universe* and *a being of unsurpassable power,* respectively. Attention is also given to Brightman's doctrine of the finite-infinite God, as well as to black liberation theologians such as James Cone and J. DeOtis Roberts, who uncritically place King in the traditional camp of theistic absolutism. How did King respond to the doctrine of divine omnipotence in seminary and graduate school and during his ministry? What is the most reasonable way to characterize his conception of God? To get at these questions, the chapter examines various papers that King wrote in seminary and graduate school, as well as postgraduate school sermons and speeches. Because King was adamant that God is personal, the chapter devotes attention to the meaning of this concept and why it was important to him. I also try to make the case that in many of King's writings and speeches we frequently find openings for a version of theistic finitism.

Chapter 5 focuses on King's theory of dignity and the mutual influence of personalism. King had a strong sense that all being has dignity because God is the source. King focused primarily on the dignity of persons, most especially that of his own people. Considerable attention is given what may be the most glaring contradiction in King's doctrine of the dignity of being as such, namely sexism. Was King in fact sexist, and if so, how do we make sense of this in light of his personalism? What was Coretta Scott King's reaction to her husband's chauvinism? What was King's relationship with movement women such as Ella Baker? The chapter also considers the stance of several King scholars regarding his sexism.

The sixth chapter introduces the concept of personal-communitarianism, which represents King's and personalism's fundamental emphasis on the person *and* the community, as well as their interrelatedness. This idea is then connected to the achievement of the beloved community, a term whose origin is discussed along with how and when King became familiar with it at Boston University. King frequently used "Kingdom of God" and "beloved community" interchangeably, and we will examine interpretations of the beloved community and its influence on King as found in the work of Kenneth Smith and Ira Zepp and of Lewis V. Baldwin. Because the beloved community was not simply an ideal for King, but something he clearly expected would take place, the chapter discusses the role of freedom and moral agency, as well as cooperative endeavor between persons and God in this process.

Chapter 7 aims to clarify the significance of the idea of the objective moral order, and what it meant for King's dream of actualizing the beloved community. King often spoke and wrote about there being something in the nature of the universe itself that makes for goodness and justice and ultimately the achievement of the beloved community. Because of King's conviction that in order to achieve and live well in the beloved community one would have to abide by certain objective moral laws, the chapter also lists and discusses the nature of such laws.

Chapter 8 shows how King used the personalistic moral law system to decide whether to break silence on the war in Vietnam. It will be seen that King's ultimate reason for speaking out against the war on April 4, 1967, was primarily moral and theological rather than political. He was enough of a hardheaded realist to know that the political dimension had to be taken into consideration, but his faith and commitment to the God of the Hebrew prophets was such that he *chose* to be morally correct rather than politically correct.

The final chapter focuses on the socioethical significance of King's doctrine that the universe is friendly to value. Much of the discussion is in the form of a prophetic challenge to religious persons, particularly Christians and the ecclesial community. King's was, after all, a social personalism whose basic principles he sought to apply to solving social problems in order to make the world a more gentle place, one in which moral agents could be encouraged about the possibility of achieving a community of love. It is precisely here that King made his most significant contribution to personalism.

Four cornerstones distinguish King's personalism: God as personal, freedomism, reverence for persons, and the communal nature of reality. Because he was a thoroughgoing or systematic, theistic-creationist personalist, these cornerstones must be seen in their interrelatedness if one hopes to grasp the full meaning and socioethical challenge of King's personalism for the twenty-first century and beyond. Only as we see the integral connection among these four tenets will we also understand the full significance of King's ethic of the beloved community.

King's Intellectual Odyssey

From Morehouse to Crozer

Born on January 15, 1929, King entered the public school system of Atlanta in 1935. By the time he enrolled at Booker T. Washington High School, he was known to be studious. Almost immediately he exhibited signs of intellectual promise, and as a result, he was allowed to skip both the ninth and twelfth grades. Upon completion of high school in 1944 at the age of fifteen, he entered Morehouse College in September. In part, King was able to attend at such an early age because enrollment at Morehouse, as in other colleges throughout the United States, was quite low as a result of World War II. The idea to lower some of the entrance requirements was proposed by Benjamin Mays, president of Morehouse. Mays saw this as a temporary measure to raise and stabilize enrollment. King graduated high school at the right time to take advantage of this decision.

As a college student, King was impressed by the sense of freedom that he found on the Morehouse campus. For example, he engaged in candid, open discussions about a number of sensitive social issues. Looking back on the Morehouse experience he wrote, "[I]t was there that I had my first frank discussion on race. The professors were not caught up in the clutches of state funds and could teach what they wanted with academic freedom. They encouraged us in a positive quest for a salvation to racial ills and for the first time in my life, I realized that nobody there was afraid."[1] This experience made a strong impression on the young King. He majored in sociology under Walter Chivers, and joined several clubs on campus. In addition, King worked relentlessly at sharpening his oratorical skills, a practice he would continue in seminary.

King was neither an A student nor a consistent B student at Morehouse. He was, rather, an average student, one whose ability to perform well was not always displayed in his academic work. What we need to remember, however, is that he was quite young—emotionally and psychologically—and had much growing and maturing to do when he entered college. He was at best an academic "underachiever." According to Dean B. R. Brazeal, King had a "comparatively weak high school background." Looking back, King recalled that by the time he matriculated at Morehouse he was only reading on an eighth-grade level.[2] One can easily see how this alone made for tough times for the fifteen-year-old college student. Even President Mays said that King was "capable of 'substantial B work' but 'not brilliant.'" This is borne out by the fact that King earned one A, 20 B's, 18 C's, and one D during his years at Morehouse. He also earned a number of P's for pass.[3] It may be that George Kelsey, his teacher in religion, gave the most accurate and prophetic assessment of King's time at Morehouse. "Professor Kelsey termed King's record 'short of what may be called "good,"' but designated him '*one of those boys who came to realize the value of scholarship late in his college career. His ability exceeds his record at Morehouse.*'"[4] Nevertheless, even late in King's college career he earned mostly B's and a few C's.

Early in his college career, King had made the decision to become an attorney or a doctor. Like many Morehouse men, he took seriously the challenge extended by professors and administrators to prepare himself to contribute to the uplift of the race. His parents had impressed this point upon him and his siblings from the time they were young children. However, the courses he took in the biological sciences, for which he earned C's, convinced him that whatever contribution he would make toward the liberation of his people would not be in the area of medicine. For a longer period of time, however, King trained for a career in law. Having grown up in the South, and having witnessed firsthand the way blacks were mistreated in its criminal justice and judicial system, King believed that becoming a lawyer was the best way he could address its injustices and help create better living conditions for his people.

This early choice of a career in law is quite interesting in light of the fact that King grew up a preacher's son and was also the grandson and great-grandson of Baptist preachers. He was initially dissuaded from the possibility of becoming a minister because of his embarrassment that so many black preachers and churchgoers had a propensity to become (in his view) unduly emotional in church. The young King understood and appreciated the value and need for passion and liveliness in sermon delivery and the worship service. He understood that in light of what his people endured during the week, it was necessary for the church to deliver comfort, encouragement, and hope on Sunday morning. Nevertheless, the frequent practice of shouting, stomping, and walking the pews, which black Baptist preachers frequently did (including his father), was too much for him.

This early indecision about ministry was quite real. During his first two years at Morehouse, he and a number of other preachers' sons were in active rebellion against ministry and had no desire to follow in their fathers' footsteps.[5] What is most important is that even as a young college student, King was clear about his responsibility to help his people. Later, as it turned out, King was so impressed and inspired by the sermons preached by Mays and Kelsey at Morehouse, for example, that he decided in his junior year to answer the call to ministry. Although he reported that he experienced no abrupt religious conversion, religion had been central in his life from the time he was a young boy. He asserted that "religion for me is life."[6] As for his call to ministry, King said that it "was not a miraculous or supernatural something. On the contrary it was an inner urge calling me to serve humanity."[7]

At the age of six, King had promised his father that he would help him eradicate segregation and related evils.[8] His sense of social responsibility grew increasingly stronger as he progressed through college. He knew even then that he had to do something to help end racial discrimination in the United States. In this regard, King's father was an excellent role model for him. Daddy King, who had been dirt poor growing up in Stockbridge, Georgia, insisted that blacks should be self-determined in their quest for equality, and that from those who have much, much is expected. By the time his own children were born, he and his wife were members of the black elite in Atlanta. They were not rich, but were better off financially than most blacks in the South. Daddy King had learned from his father-in-law, A. D. Williams, that the black preacher was morally obligated to champion the cause of blacks for justice.[9] In addition, he believed that black pastors were less vulnerable than most of their people because they did not have to depend on whites for their livelihood. They therefore had no excuse for being fearful of white retaliation or for holding back in the struggle.[10] Martin shared this view and uttered it frequently during his ministry. During the Birmingham, Alabama, campaign, for example, he lectured black ministers on the "need for a social gospel" that addresses the social, economic, and political needs of oppressed blacks. Furthermore he said, in language quite characteristic of his maternal grandfather and Daddy King: "I pleaded for the projections of strong, firm leadership by the Negro minister, pointing out that he is freer, more independent, than any other person in the community."[11] According to King, the minister must always attend to the needs of the soul as well as the body. Reflecting on the meaning of the preaching ministry during his student days at Crozer Seminary, King said: "On one hand I must attempt to change the soul of individuals so that their societies may be changed. On the other I must attempt to change the societies so that the individual soul will have a chance."[12] The minister must therefore be concerned about any and all conditions that maim and devalue the worth of persons.

King's goal was to position himself to help his people. When he considered becoming a lawyer, it was not for the purpose of lining his own pockets but rather as the best means to make it possible to eradicate the injustices in the legal system that harassed and hounded his people. The family and church values that were instilled in him and reinforced at Morehouse served as a reminder of the obligation to contribute toward the survival, liberation, and empowerment of his people. As a child, King was taught the value of sharing as well as serving others,[13] of being responsible for himself and for the society in which he lived, and of having a healthy sense of self as well as individual responsibility. King's parents modeled for him the importance of giving back to the community and championing the poor and oppressed.

During the summer months of his college days, King worked labor-intensive jobs, much to the chagrin of his father, who desired to spare him this experience. King clearly had a choice in this, for by virtue of his parents' financial status and social standing he did not have to work such jobs. Nevertheless, he *chose* to work with those who were less fortunate than he, in order to learn firsthand their plight and what they thought about it. Although Daddy King preferred that he do other work during the summers, King's decision was actually consistent with the values instilled in him by his parents.

The choice to do hard labor during the summers was probably also fueled by the influence of King's sociology adviser, Walter Chivers.[14] King's transcript from Morehouse reveals that he took no fewer than eight courses under Chivers, a sign that he was probably making a significant impression on the young student. It was also during the Morehouse years that King gained an appreciation for social science methodology, which would serve him well in the civil and human rights movements. This method stresses the importance of collecting facts in order to know the actual state of affairs regarding specific social ills. This approach remained of great importance to King in the struggle from Montgomery to Memphis. Each nonviolent campaign was preceded by gathering the pertinent facts to determine whether injustice existed and whether negotiation or direct action was needed.[15]

When King worked those labor-intensive summer jobs, he came face to face with the evils of the capitalist economic system in a way he had not previously experienced. He saw for himself how black workers were paid less, and treated worse, than white workers who performed the same jobs. He also saw poor whites misused on the job, and thus had his eyes opened to the problem of economic class. There were poor whites as well as poor blacks, and both were severely mistreated and dehumanized. The race factor exacerbated the mistreatment of blacks. In his sociology classes, King learned that money was the root of much of the social evil and racism that was so prevalent in the United States. The experience affected him deeply, and he never forgot it. It surely influenced his level of sensitivity to the plight of the nation and the world's poor throughout the duration of his ministry. Working with the poor during those summers helped to pave the way for King's later ministry.

It is important to observe that by the time King decided to go to Crozer his mission in life was clear. He was now poised to find both a more sophisticated theological rationale for his still-growing social conscience, as well as a method for the elimination of racism and economic exploitation. Having grown up in the black church, King knew instinctively that Christianity required that one exhibit strong social concern for working to eradicate injustice and other social ills. Indeed, King reflected that by the time he entered Morehouse College his concern for racial and economic justice and political matters was already substantial,[16] and it had intensified by the time he enrolled at Crozer. King knew just as instinctively that as a Christian it was necessary to develop a sound theological rationale to support his social conscience. This, in part, was King's reason for wanting to go to seminary. As an average, "not brilliant" student, King earned college grades that were sufficient to allow him a place in the entering class of 1948 at Crozer Theological Seminary in Chester, Pennsylvania. Since Professor Kelsey said that King learned late in his college days the importance of scholarship and academic achievement, one might expect a better performance in his work at the next academic level, despite the fact that he would have to leave his beloved South and a loving family, and for the first time would be in an academic setting where the majority of the students and professors were white. He was ordained on February 25, 1948, and was named assistant pastor under his father at Ebenezer Baptist Church.

CROZER THEOLOGICAL SEMINARY

Looking back, King said that his experience at Morehouse College provided the key that unlocked the chain of fundamentalism that threatened to choke both reason and freedom.[17] In the fall of 1948, he matriculated in the Bachelor of Divinity degree program at Crozer Theological Seminary in Chester, Pennsylvania, not far from Philadelphia. Away from home for an extended period for the first time (and in the North!), King was happily surprised to find that in an entering class of thirty-two he was one of eleven black students (by the beginning of second semester).[18] The total student body numbered nearly one hundred. Only half of the entering class, including six of the black students, would graduate three years later.

Crozer was a remarkably different experience for King, primarily because he was a black southerner in a predominantly white academic setting. King had grown up under fundamentalist teachings such as belief in the absolute infallibility of the Bible, although at the age of thirteen he began to question this as well as the bodily resurrection of Jesus.[19] Because his conversion from black church fundamentalism had taken place under liberal black preacher intellectuals such as Mays and Kelsey at Morehouse, he did not, like many of his classmates from conservative southern Baptist churches, experience difficulty with Crozer's liberalism in theology and biblical interpretation. King was more challenged by the cultural differences, and was especially sensitive to the fact that there were certain practices in black schools and the black community that simply embarrassed him. Consequently, when King went to the predominantly white Crozer Seminary, he was conscious of these tendencies, and of the tendency of many whites to stereotype all blacks as behaving in these ways. "I was well aware of the typical white stereotype of the Negro, that he is always late, that he's loud and always laughing, that he's dirty and messy, and for a while I was terribly conscious of trying to avoid identification with it. If I were a minute late to class, I was almost morbidly conscious of it and sure that everyone else noticed it. Rather than be thought of as always laughing, I'm afraid I was grimly serious for a time. I had a tendency to overdress, to keep my room spotless, my shoes perfectly shined, and my clothes immaculately pressed."[20]

King was no doubt also burdened by the idea, pressed upon him by whites, of having always to represent his entire race. This was a burden that individual whites seldom if ever experienced. King knew that his people did not expect individual whites to represent their entire race. He reasoned that because persons are autonomous beings the individual (generally) cannot act for the entire race. What the individual does is generally a reflection on that person alone.

It mattered to King—perhaps too much—what his white peers and professors thought of him and his people. It was indeed a tremendous burden, to feel the sense that he essentially had to represent his entire race in all that he did. It meant having to live constantly on a kind of moral tightrope on which he must always be steady. To show up late for an appointment, for example, did not mean, "Martin Luther King is always late," but that "*those* people are always late."

Although King refined his "political and social graces" while at Crozer, he also acquired some behaviors that caused his fundamentalist preacher father grave concern. Taylor Branch has written about this:

> By the second year, King was so imbued with the Social Gospel that he dared to drink beer, smoke cigarettes, and play pool openly in the presence of his father, whenever Reverend King visited Crozer. He went so far as to usher his father into the poolroom beneath the chapel, inviting him to play, trying to act as though it were perfectly normal, taking pride in his hard-earned skill as a player. He knew Reverend King would object violently, which he did, but he trusted excessively in the persuasive powers of the liberal Christian teachings that defilement comes only from within (as in Matthew 15:11).[21]

It is not difficult to see that some of this was merely acting out, and thus was a case of strong parent-child rivalry. Whatever else may have been involved in those displays of rebelliousness, King was also trying to find his own self and voice amid the many new ideas and experiences he was encountering at Crozer. There would be more times during his days at Crozer that he and his father would have ideological and other clashes. One such time was when he decided to spend Christmas break of 1949 dividing his time between preaching at Ebenezer and reading the communist doctrines of Karl Marx. However, there was another incident that would surely have caused fireworks between King and his father, had the latter known of it at the time.

During his second year at Crozer, King fell in love with a young German immigrant named Betty. She was "evidently the daughter of Crozer's superintendent of buildings and grounds."[22] Her mother was the cook in the seminary cafeteria.[23] In fact, King competed with Kenneth Lee Smith, a young white professor, for her affection. King got the better of the competition. Prior to this he and Smith, who was only a few years older than King, had become good friends. But after King's coup, "tempers flared," for it was not long before King and Betty were discussing marriage. Obviously confused and not a little distressed over the jokes of his friends and their tendency to dismiss as mere infatuation what was to him true love, King sought the advice of several close friends. One of these, Joseph Kirkland, was critical of the relationship on social class grounds. Betty was, after all, the daughter of a cook and a glorified janitor. What mattered, according to Kirkland, was not her race, but her social and economic class. Another friend, Marcus Wood, reminded King of the difficulty that an interracial couple would have in finding a church to pastor, especially in his native South. "Horace Whitaker, older and perhaps wiser than the others, let King talk himself out. He listened as King resolved several times over the next few months to marry Betty, railing out in anger at the cruel and silly forces in life that were keeping two people from doing what they most wanted to do."[24]

King was also given advice by Reverend J. Pius Barbour, a local black pastor and longtime close friend of Daddy King. King had become a regular at the Barbour home and often enjoyed Mrs. Barbour's "down-home" cooking. In any event, Barbour had a long fatherly talk with King "about the terrible problems intermarriage would create for him in this country."[25] King later confided in Whitaker that he could take anything his father might throw at him about his love for Betty, but that he could not bear the pain it might cause his mother. We do not know for certain that this was the real reason that King essentially conceded defeat, or whether it was simply the only way he could bear breaking off the relationship with Betty. In any case, he was deeply angered that church and society in this country were so narrow and out of step with God's expectation regarding human relations. However, he did what is now called the "politically correct thing," and he did so despite the fact that his love for Betty was a matter of the heart. Slowly, he resigned himself to the view that the price of marriage to a white woman in the 1940s was too high. Therefore, King "forced himself to retreat, and struggled against bitterness."

Perhaps this disappointing, heartrending experience, contributed to King immersing himself in his studies for the duration of his time at Crozer. It might be that this too was an example of overcompensation. However, the decision to lose himself in his studies might also have contributed to his having never lost track of his boyhood desire to find a reasonable theological rationale to support his social justice convictions, as well as a method to eradicate the social problems that hounded his people. By the time King got to Crozer, and later to Boston University, the passion to help his people was already etched into his being.[26] The initiative and effort to find a method to do so were mostly his own. Neither Crozer nor Boston University even had a curriculum and a faculty expressly geared to what King was seeking. In a sense, then, and especially in seminary, King had to do some creative reinventing of the curriculum in order to get the information and knowledge that he thought would be most helpful. More than this, we should not forget the King family emphasis on the value of service and giving back to the community. No one modeled this better than King's parents, and it clearly left an indelible impression on him.

It was evident to King that his formal studies must be aimed at finding solutions to racism, discrimination, and economic exploitation, each of which caused his people tremendous suffering in an ostensibly free and democratic society. Knowledge and truth must be for the purpose of enhancing persons and communities. King came to think of personalism in the same way. It was not just a philosophy to discuss and debate. King was more concerned about what personalism could contribute to the uplift of his people and the achievement of the beloved community. He read voraciously, searching for the most reasonable philosophical and theological grounds for his deepening social conscience. The burning issue for King at Crozer was whether theologians acknowledged that Christianity had anything relevant and significant to say about the social crises that crushed the humanity and dignity of his people. He wanted to know whether Christianity had anything to say about otherwise Christian people who believed that their faith primarily required that they focus on spiritual matters, which ostensibly lead to the "saving" of the soul. King knew the Bible well enough, and had heard enough sermons preached by his father, and by William Holmes Borders and other black preachers, to know what the Bible and the best in the Jewish and Christian traditions required of Christians. What he so desperately sought at Crozer, then, was a formal theological basis on which to ground the strong social conscience and conviction he had grown up with from childhood.[27]

From the beginning of his seminary experience, King read many of the great Western theologians and philosophers in an effort to satisfy his quest. Of these he was most impressed with the philosopher Georg W. F. Hegel and his dialectical method of thesis, antithesis, and synthesis. The truth, Hegel maintained, is found in the ongoing synthesis of opposites. In addition, King was fascinated with Hegel's doctrine that growth comes through struggle and suffering,[28] an idea that was also articulated by his maternal grandfather, and adopted by Daddy King.[29] During his doctoral studies at Boston University, King again studied Hegel, this time in a year-long seminar taught by his advisor, Edgar S. Brightman. We will return to a brief discussion of the Hegelian influence in chapter 3.

The other person who most influenced King during this period was church historian and Christian ethicist Walter Rauschenbusch, the chief theologian of the white social gospel movement[30] during the first two decades of the twentieth century. King's reading and study of Rauschenbusch and the social gospel movement fulfilled one of his two aspirations regarding theological study: he found in Rauschenbusch, especially, a sound theological foundation to support his social conscience. As significant as Rauschenbusch and his Kingdom of God ideal was for King, I want to postpone fuller discussion of him until the next chapter. For now, however, I briefly consider several other influences on King while he was at Crozer.

OTHER INFLUENCES AT CROZER

As a seminary student, King took thirty-four of the required one hundred ten hours for the B. D. degree under George Washington Davis, a Yale Ph.D. recipient who joined the Crozer faculty in 1938. Davis was influenced by the personalism of both Bowne and Brightman.[31] "The personalism of Brightman . . . was by far the single most important philosophical influence upon Davis."[32] Brightman was important not only to Davis but "was held in high esteem by the Crozer community. This affection and regard is reflected in a statement by Morton Scott Enslin, who introduced him to Crozer Quarterly readers as 'a frequent and ever-welcome contributor.'"[33] Through Davis, King was also exposed to the broader evangelical liberal tradition. "King inherited from Davis the best of the Anglo liberal tradition—Friedrich S. Schleiermacher, Albrecht R. Ritschl, Horace Bushnell, William Newton Clarke, Walter Rauschenbusch, Edgar S. Brightman, and a host of others."[34]

Under Davis, King was able to grapple with many of his most important philosophical and theological concerns: the nature of God, the problem of evil, and the role of religion in the world. King did not by any means "solve" all or even most of his pressing theological issues, but Davis provided for him an atmosphere (in which) to work at it. In addition, Davis was both understanding and encouraging to his eager student.[35] Much of the encouragement came in the form of strong grades and brief comments on assigned papers ("Well done" or "Very well done," and occasionally, "Excellent").

Under Davis, King was able to continue honing the critical and analytical skills he learned under Kelsey, Williams, and others at Morehouse. As a seminary student, King was eclectic. His study habits and strong sense of wonder were second to none. It is also significant that it was under Davis that King got his first introduction to the theology of L. Harold DeWolf (a student of Brightman's), who would become his doctoral academic advisor and mentor when Brightman became ill and died during King's second year at Boston University.

In Davis's courses, King closely scrutinized and wrote essays on Brightman's text, *A Philosophy of Religion.* Also under Davis, in a paper entitled "A View of the Cross Possessing Biblical and Spiritual Justification," King cited at least two works—one of which he did not name—by Albert C. Knudson, a personalist theologian and dean of Boston University's School of Theology before King matriculated there.[36] In Kenneth L. Smith's course on Christianity and society, a paper attributed to King, "War and Pacifism," acknowledged his familiarity with Nels F. S. Ferré,[37] a "neo-personalist theologian."[38] Although King did not mention it in the paper, Ferré also studied under Brightman as an undergraduate student at Boston University. Ferré did not name himself a disciple of personalism, though one might consider him a friendly critic. He taught at Andover Newton Theological School, then spent "a few stormy years at Vanderbilt," before returning to Andover.[39]

Many of Davis's theological tenets—e.g., the existence of a moral order in the universe; the activity of God in history; the value of the personal; the social character of human existence; the ethical nature of Christianity—were evident in King's own thinking in his seminary and doctoral studies, as well as during his leadership in the civil and human rights movements.[40] His formal study of personalism at Boston University, for which he received more than adequate preparation under Davis, solidified for King the theological and philosophical foundations for these fundamental doctrines that became his own. In chapter 8, I examine more explicitly two of Davis's basic principles that deeply influenced King, especially as he engaged in moral deliberation to determine whether he should break silence on the war in Vietnam.

During the spring of his senior year at Crozer in 1950, King drove to nearby Philadelphia where he heard two fascinating lectures on Gandhi and the philosophy and practice of nonviolence. At the time, he was more impressed with what was said about Gandhi than about nonviolence as such. In addition, he was stirred by the passion of the lecturer, Mordecai Johnson, president of Howard University in Washington, D.C. Johnson had made a recent trip to India, where he learned of Gandhi's principles. Johnson was convinced that these principles were applicable to the elimination of racial discrimination in the United States. He was much influenced by "nonviolence and the redemptive power of love and unmerited suffering."[41] King's immediate reaction to Johnson's lectures was to rush out to purchase "a half dozen books on Gandhi's life and works."[42] An early King biographer reminds us that while King "found all this extremely enlightening and spiritually exalting," he was not at the time convinced that Gandhi's method of nonviolence would work if applied to race relations in the United States.[43] King liked Gandhi's concept of nonviolence, but several years would pass before he finally adopted and adapted it for use in the struggle for civil rights.

It should also be noted that while a student at Morehouse College, King read Henry David Thoreau's essay "On Civil Disobedience."[44] Gandhi himself was familiar with, and influenced by, Thoreau's famous essay.[45] When King found himself providing leadership for the civil rights movement, he also periodically quoted the thoroughgoing pacifist, Leo Tolstoi,[46] who based his pacifism on Jesus' saying in the Sermon on the Mount: "Resist not evil."

In addition to seeking a more formal theological foundation for his social conscience and a method to effectively address racism and economic exploitation, King was also interested in perfecting his oratorical and pulpit skills in seminary. In this, King knew what most seminary students do not know today, namely that good preaching is frequently seen by parishioners to be the bread and butter of parish ministry. Right or wrong, what most congregations desire is that their pastor be a very good preacher. At any rate, Taylor Branch writes that King's oratory was "among his chief distinctions at Crozer," noting that the chapel would generally be packed to capacity when it was known ahead of time that he was the student preacher.[47] In addition, when it was known that he would be at the practice podium in preaching classes, students who were not enrolled would show up to observe his technique. Preaching was for him an art, which also meant displaying some entertainment value as well. He "perfected minute details of showmanship, such as tucking away his notes at the podium in a manner just unsubtle enough to be noticed, and his general style was extremely formal."[48] He worked just as hard on the content of his sermons to ensure that what was being preached actually addressed the people at the point of greatest need. He believed "that preaching should grow out of the experiences of the people," and that the minister should work hard to become familiar with the problems that adversely affect them.[49]

Even as a student, King understood the importance of maintaining a good balance between showmanship and substance in preaching. If one could appeal to the intellect as well as the emotions and passions of congregants, the message, he believed, would more likely be heard and understood. According to the Afrikan American preaching tradition, finding just the right balance was an art in itself. It meant that one had to be able to size up an audience quickly. The preacher had to know how to get the congregation on board so that they could mutually feed and fuel each other during the sermon delivery.

When considering King's interest in the art of preaching while he was in seminary, it should be remembered that his oratorical skills were already superior to most students (and professors) by the time he arrived at Crozer. He had won oratorical contests in high school and at Morehouse. He had been exposed to good preaching styles and techniques from the time he was a boy. Although King did not care for some of the theology and pulpit antics of his father and other well-known, black, southern Baptist preachers, there was much about their humor, their application of the gospel to the plight of their people, and their overall manner and showmanship that profoundly impressed him. King learned much about homiletical theory and theology of preaching at Crozer. King took a total of nine courses in public speaking, homiletics, and pulpit oratory at Crozer.[50] His own preaching style, however, was patterned after those of good black preachers. Lewis Baldwin is careful to point to the dual influence of white and Afrikan American influences on King's preaching style. Baldwin is just as quick to remind us, however, that King's actual style was more influenced by the black preaching tradition from slavery onward. "When it came to the preaching art, the influence of King's father and that of [Vernon] Johns, [Benjamin] Mays, [Howard] Thurman, [Sandy] Ray, and others came together in his consciousness, and the ideals and examples of each reinforced those of the others in King's life."[51] Indeed, during his junior and senior year of college, King and two of his best friends frequented the Sunday worship services at the Wheat Street Baptist Church in Atlanta, pastored by William Holmes Borders. They were interested to learn all they could about the preaching styles of different black preachers and their ways of doing ministry that addressed the needs of the whole person.

As to King's own style, although King did not consider himself a whooper, he had the capacity to whoop, and did so on rare occasion. He did not resort to this style when preaching in the unemotional, more intellectual congregation in New England (e.g., Harvard's Memorial Church, where he preached not long after receiving the Nobel Peace Prize), but he did sometimes whoop when preaching in the more emotional southern black churches. Coretta Scott King recalled, "He responded to their expectations by rousing oratory; and as they were moved, he would react to their excitement, their rising emotions exalting his own. The first thunderous 'Amen' from the people would set him off in the old-fashioned preaching style. We called it 'whooping.' Sometimes, after we were married, I would tease him by saying, 'Martin, you were whooping today.' He would be a little embarrassed. But it was very exciting, Martin's whooping."[52]

The capacity to whoop linked King to an art form dating back to "slave preachers like Harry Hoosier and John Jasper."[53] Is it any wonder that King, surrounded from the time he was a boy by trained preachers whose preaching "had a strong theological and hermeneutical base as well as a social and prophetic character,"[54] would ultimately develop into a powerful, effective preacher with a profound oratorical flair, coupled with the propensity for prophetic pronouncements? Furthermore, when King became the pastor of Dexter Avenue Baptist Church in Montgomery, Alabama, he was an excellent, but generally restrained preacher. "King was controlled. He never shouted," writes Taylor Branch. "*But he preached like someone who wanted to shout,* and this gave him an electrifying hold over the congregation."[55]

KING'S ACADEMIC ACHIEVEMENTS

King was an excellent student in seminary, although not quite a "straight A" student, as some biographers have maintained.[56] He did perform much better at Crozer than he had at Morehouse. He would become valedictorian and was awarded a scholarship to do two additional years of graduate work at a school of his choosing. As to the question of why King performed so much better at Crozer, Lawrence D. Reddick wrote: "Possibly it was the interracial situation, more than any other factor, that had stimulated him to do his best. He felt a compulsion to do well, for whatever he did, he felt sure, would be accredited not just to him as a person but to the Negro people as a whole."[57]

James B. Pritchard, who taught Old Testament studies, was "surprised to find that a Southern Baptist like King adjusted so quickly to Crozer."[58] For Crozer was a very liberal, social gospel seminary by comparison with many others. Most Southern Baptists, white as well as black, tended to be fundamentalist and rigid in theological outlook. Such a perspective generally made it difficult for them to do well at places like Crozer. This was not the case for the young, searching, perspicacious King, who actually began questioning some of his fundamentalist beliefs by the age of thirteen.[59] He had been taught the value of thinking and critical reflection at Morehouse College, and was introduced to many liberal theological ideas by Mays and Kelsey. This served him very well indeed in seminary, and later in graduate school. Therefore, unlike many of his southern Baptist classmates at Crozer, King was not troubled by "the skeptical rigor of Pritchard and [Morton Scott] Enslin."[60] The latter taught New Testament studies and was considered "a radical biblical critic" who did not hesitate to question the factuality of more traditional biblical claims. For example, Enslin rejected the claim that Jesus and John the Baptist ever met.

It was also Enslin who wrote in his confidential evaluation of King that he was "a very able man," and made a prediction that later came to fruition: "He will probably become a big strong man among his people."[61] Dean Charles E. Batten wrote even more laudably about him: "King is one of the most brilliant students we have had at Crozer. He has a keen mind which is both analytical and constructively creative. While interested in social action, he has a fine theological and philosophical basis on which to promulgate his ideas and activities."[62] Batten went on to praise the quality of King's academic work at the University of Pennsylvania, where he took one course on aesthetics and another on Kant. He added that King's peers thought highly of him, as evidenced by his election as president of the student body in his senior year. Moreover, Batten wrote that King was the only student to be granted honors in the comprehensive examinations. In addition, he wrote: "He is held universally in high regard by faculty, staff, and students and is undoubtedly one of the best men in our entire student body. He reflects fine preparation, an excellent mind, and a thorough grasp of material."[63] It is significant that Batten did not say King was one of the best "Negro" men in the student body, but one of the best men. Professor of church history Raymond J. Bean wrote similarly about King's intellectual prowess, contending that he was not only "the outstanding student in his class," but that he "would be outstanding in any institution."[64] Chosen valedictorian of his class, King graduated in June 1951.

Having discussed with Davis some of the first-rate graduate schools from which he might obtain a Ph.D. degree in the philosophy of religion or systematic theology, King applied to Yale University, Boston University, and the Divinity School at Edinburgh University in Scotland. In his letters recommending King to graduate schools, Enslin (revealing his racial and cultural bias) expressed his "surprise that a colored man from the South had done so well at Crozer."[65] In a parenthetical comment in a letter to Sankey Lee Blanton for a postgraduate fellowship from Crozer, King said that Yale was his preference.[66] However, despite his impeccable academic credentials, selection as valedictorian, and strong references, Yale turned him down.[67] This rejection stemmed from King's failure to take and submit the results of the graduate records examination, which he acknowledged as "a prerequisite for acceptance."[68] The other two schools accepted him.

King was very close to his mother, and therefore discussed the matter of doctoral studies with her before speaking with Daddy King, who, by the summer of 1951, was not as enthusiastic about his decision to pursue doctoral studies as he had been regarding his desire to obtain formal theological training three years earlier.[69] Remember, in Daddy King's judgment his son had acquired some questionable habits (smoking, drinking, and playing pool), which he linked to Crozer's liberalism. In any event, King decided to go to Boston University. In his application he expressed a desire to study there because Brightman, the noted personalist, was on the faculty.[70] The case for going to Boston was made even stronger because of the influence and encouragement of George Washington Davis, and the fact that King was seeking a deeper metaphysical and ethical grounding in personalism.[71]

Before proceeding to a discussion of the Boston University years, more attention should be devoted to the influence of the social gospel movement, specifically the work of Walter Rauschenbusch. The next chapter discusses the contributions of the black social gospel as well as the significance of Rauschenbusch in King's efforts to find a theological basis on which to ground his social conscience.

Social Gospel and Walter Rauschenbusch

We saw in the previous chapter that King had two chief aims when he went to seminary: to find both a reasonable theological rationale to ground his strong social conscience and a method that could effectively address the racism and economic exploitation that plagued his people. The first goal was achieved early in his studies under Davis, who formally introduced him to the liberal theological tradition, including Walter Rauschenbusch's *Christianity and the Social Crisis*. King himself acknowledged that in Rauschenbusch he found the theological foundation he sought. This does not mean that he uncritically accepted everything espoused by Rauschenbusch and other white leaders of the social gospel movement. In fact, he could not. In King's estimation one of the most serious social ills that threatened the well-being of his people and the country was racism. From the time he was a little boy, he wanted to contribute toward its eradication. Although King did not expressly criticize Rauschenbusch's "benign" racism, he clearly rejected that aspect of white social gospelism. King must have known that the social gospel project was flawed in this regard. Precisely because of this, we dare not say that he was the uncritical successor of Rauschenbusch, Washington Gladden, Lymann Abbott, and other white social gospelers. King's idealism and activism were far different from that of white social gospelers of Rauschenbusch's era. Not only did King's vision of the community of love—that is, the Kingdom of God—exclude racism, but he invoked nonviolent resistance as the method to eradicate its most obvious institutional forms and manifestations.

King's version of the social gospel had a much stronger element of the equality of the races than that of white social gospelers. In this regard, he was much closer to the social gospelism of late nineteenth- and early twentieth-century Afrikan Americans such as Reverdy Ransom, Ida B. Wells-Barnett, Francis J. Grimké (nephew of

Sarah and Angelina Grimké), Henry McNeal Turner, the venerable and all but forgotten socialist preacher George Washington Woodbey, and his eager disciple Reverend George W. Slater, Jr., who converted to socialism when he heard Woodbey lecture on how only socialism could help eradicate poverty.[1] Darryl Trimiew rightly contends that King's social gospel project was a continuation of his black foreparents' "Christian struggles for freedom and equality for blacks and for the creation of a multi-ethnic, multiclassed society."[2]

Before turning explicitly to King and Rauschenbusch, it will be helpful to summarize basic social gospel ideas. This will be followed by an examination of racism in the social gospel movement and Rauschenbusch. These discussions provide the foundation for the ensuing one on King and Rauschenbusch.

The Early Social Gospel Movement

Early rudiments of the white social gospel may be dated, roughly, to the 1830s, during the antislavery movement under the leadership of William Lloyd Garrison, Theodore Dwight Weld, Angelina and Sarah Grimké, and others. Both before and contemporaneous with these, Denmark Vesey, Gabriel Prosser, David Walker, and Maria W. Stewart, all "free" blacks, engaged in their own version of abolitionist activity and social gospel Christianity. The white social gospel picked up steam by the 1870s and 1880s, although its major breakthrough in the churches began to occur in the 1890s.[3] Prior to the common introduction and use of the term "social gospel" after 1900, the general tendency was to use the term "social Christianity."[4] The influence of the social gospel movement peaked in the first two decades of the twentieth century until, roughly, the beginning of the Great Depression and World War II. These major events undermined a number of its more utopian beliefs, including the establishment of the Kingdom of God on earth.

Prior to the social gospel movement, there had not been an attempt at a systematic study of the social teachings of Jesus and their significance for addressing dehumanizing social problems. The social gospel sought to show the relevance of Christian principles to the affairs of persons in the world, both interpersonally and collectively. Walter Rauschenbusch described it thusly: "The social gospel seeks to bring men under repentance for their collective sins and to create a more sensitive and more modern conscience. It calls on us for the faith of the old prophets who believed in the salvation of nations."[5] This was not a completely new idea; Christians from the time of the early church sought to apply the ethical teachings of Jesus to the social problems of the world.[6] Indeed, Rauschenbusch himself said that the social gospel was "the old message of salvation"[7] needing a theology. Shailer Mathews, a leader in the social gospel movement who taught at the University of Chicago, wrote: "Churches and sects have repeatedly undertaken to abolish some social evil or to develop a social order. In a few cases like that of the Anabaptists of Munster these attempts have become revolutionary. Only the historically illiterate can think of Christianity as being concerned solely with *post mortem* salvation."[8]

What came to be called the social gospel movement was a more consistent and systematic attempt to apply Christian principles to individual and social problems. Social gospel scholar Robert T. Handy has written: "The social gospel was particularly important in that it helped individuals and institutions to make the transition from a rural and small-town America to an industrialized and urban society with its inescapable social problems and regulations." The chief concern of the movement was "the human problems arising from industrial strife, from the unequal distribution of wealth, and from the worsening of urban conditions for the poor."[9]

As American Protestantism's response to the challenges of the industrial revolution, the early social gospel movement that was initiated by whites "took root and grew most vigorously among Unitarians, Congregationalists, and Episcopalians— three American religious bodies inheriting the state-church tradition of responsibility for public morals." These groups were later joined by Baptists, Methodists, and other denominations "whose heritage was pietistic and separatist." Charles Howard Hopkins has written that "the social gospel of this group was marked by an evangelical fervor and an ideology looking toward a Kingdom of God raised on earth by consecrated groups of individuals, whereas the former tradition inclined to apply the 'Christian law' of love to the transactions of society."[10]

SOME DOMINANT THEMES AND LIMITATIONS

The social gospel movement was characterized by several key themes:

1. The centrality of the doctrine of the immanence of God. God was thought to be everywhere present in the world, participating with persons in working out God's plan and purpose. Science, especially Darwinian evolution, contributed to this emphasis on divine immanence.

2. The focus on divine immanence led rather naturally to a communal view of society, with an emphasis on the interdependence and interrelatedness of persons in the world. This in turn implied the equality of all people under God. Such equality before a common Creator-Parent opened the door to the possibility of the achievement of the Kingdom of God on earth, or the beloved community (a term that was known to Rauschenbusch).

3. There was a focus on the higher criticism of the Bible, and on solid biblical grounding of the social teachings of Jesus Christ.

4. There was a strong emphasis on the ethical—on the greater good for human-kind—especially the achievement of the Kingdom of God on earth. "Considered as a corrective and a reaction against an extreme otherworldly individualism, the ethicizing strain must be regarded as a healthful influence even though it afforded an opening for the entrance of humanism and moralism."[11]

5. Increased significance of the role of the social sciences, particularly sociology. The focus was on the empirical, the *what is*, or the actual state of a social reality, rather than the *what ought to be* (i.e., the moral imperative or ought). This put pressure on Christianity to seek a more realistic appraisal of its tasks in the world. In addition, this attention to the social sciences "gave the practical working program of the movement a new appreciation" for social and environmental causes of social problems.[12] Strategies for social change were now based more on the empirical findings and conclusions of social scientists. This is an important point, for in later years when theologians began trying to define Christian social ethics the social gospel focus on the role of the social sciences was not forgotten. Nor was its importance lost on King, who stressed the significance of early fact gathering in every nonviolent resistance campaign. Therefore, any adequate definition of theological social ethics must not neglect awareness of both normative principles and the importance of social science methodology. For example, it is common to hear the theological social ethicist characterize her discipline as the critical study of the difference between *what is* (which points to the importance of the social science emphasis on the empirical) and *what ought to be* (which stresses the importance of normative principles).[13]

The social gospel movement also stressed an optimistic conception of human nature; Jesus Christ as moral exemplar; an evolutionary view of human progress in history, and the need to show the relevance of the Gospel to human and social problems created or exacerbated by industrialism. There was also a tendency to identify the social gospel with specific social institutions and procedures (e.g., democracy and pacifism), and to substitute religious experience as the criterion of authority in religion.[14] King agreed with many of these emphases in the social gospel, but we will see subsequently that he found several of them to be problematic.

Because King was deeply influenced by both the social gospel and the philosophy of personalism, it is important to observe that there are strong affinities between the two. Several of the similarities appear among the social gospel themes just listed, including the centrality of the doctrine of divine immanence, the communal nature of reality, and the interdependence of persons. In addition, the logic of the person-alism that influenced him points to the expectation and possibility of the achieve-ment of what King (following Brightman, Paul Johnson, and other personalists who were influenced by Josiah Royce) called the "beloved community." According to Royce, the beloved community is synonymous with the Kingdom of God ideal.[15] An additional personalistic theme is reverence for persons as such; for persons are created, loved, and sustained by God. This principle is implicit in the idea of divine immanence and the communal view of reality and persons, and it is explicit in the thought of most social gospelers (e.g., Rauschenbusch, Washington Gladden, and Henry Churchill King). For why would God even want to be everywhere present in the world were it not for the preciousness of persons? The sacredness of persons, then, is fundamental to both the social gospel and personalism. It is therefore possible to say that when King studied Rauschenbusch and the social gospel in seminary, he was indirectly studying per-sonalism. Likewise, when he studied the rudiments of personalism under Davis, he was indirectly reinforcing his study and understanding of the social gospel. This sce-nario would continue at Boston University. Moreover, Rauschenbusch and other so-cial gospelers were most assuredly in the personalist camp, although only (the lesser-known) Henry Churchill King, whose work was known to Brightman,[16] was an avowed or methodological personalist.[17] It is also true that a number of the early personal-ists, (Bowne, Brightman, Francis J. McConnell, George A. Coe, and Albert C. Knud-son) were much influenced by social gospel ideas. Therefore, when King studied per-sonalism under Brightman and DeWolf, a number of the chief social gospel themes were reiterated and reinforced.

Like every movement in history, the social gospel had its limitations. Critics charged that social gospelers neglected the individual and focused solely or primarily on the social, attempting "to convert the world *en masse.*" Shailer Mathews held that while understandable, the charge was unjustifiable. There was, he believed, a more basic problem: "The older evangelical orthodoxy regarded the gospel as the message of forgiveness of sins by virtue of belief in Jesus as the atoning sacrifice. Faith in him was of course to be followed by moral life but the good news of salvation was not pri-marily mortal. It was the work of God in which men had no real part. The social gos-pel was aggressively ethical. It naturally produced moral discontent rather than spiritual complacency."[18]

Another criticism of the social gospel was that some proponents seemed to iden-tify the Kingdom of God with a particular social or economic order, or with the re-forming of society, as if there was an absolute one-to-one correspondence between the two. King made this critique in his "Pilgrimage to Nonviolence."[19] A third criti-cism, and one also alluded to by King,[20] was that many advocates of the social gospel believed in inevitable progress, a belief that was spawned, in part, by the influence of evolutionary thought and social Darwinism. The problem with the idea of inevitable progress is that it can cause persons to stagnate rather than do what they can to address social ills. That is, there may be a tendency among many to feel that if things will inevitably get better in the world, why not just do nothing and instead depend solely on God or even some impersonal evolutionary force to do it? King had in mind this particular criticism of the social gospel when he frequently said that progress in the social order never rolls in on the wheels of inevitability.[21] Although he lived by the conviction that God is everywhere and always active in history, King was just as convinced that because persons are autonomous moral agents, God will not do what persons and God can do cooperatively. In this sense, there is no such thing as inevitable progress in the social order. Progress occurs because individuals cooperate with each other and with God, and strive relentlessly to bring it about.

A fourth criticism of the social gospel, also espoused by King,[22] was the tendency of many adherents to underestimate the prevalence and the depth of sin on both the personal and collective levels. This was a tendency among many, but not all, of the social gospelers. Walter Rauschenbusch is an important exception, as was King's teacher at Crozer, Kenneth Smith (although King did not seem to know this about Rauschenbusch). Smith was influenced by Reinhold Niebuhr's Christian realism, which was a combination of an emphasis on the seriousness of human sin in its interpersonal and collective forms, on every level of human achievement, as well as an awareness of the human capacity to do good. Let us explore this further by considering Rauschenbusch's last book.

In *A Theology for the Social Gospel* (1917), Rauschenbusch included chapters entitled, "The Nature of Sin" and "The Salvation of the Super-Personal Forces." In the former, he defined sin as essentially selfishness, arguing that this is more consistent with social rather than individualistic religion. Sin is less concerned with personal habits such as swearing and drinking, and more concerned with social misconduct that causes social oppression. "To find the climax of sin we must not linger over a man who swears, or sneers at religion, or denies the mystery of the trinity," writes Rauschenbusch, "but put our hands on social groups who have turned the patrimony of a nation into the private property of a small class, or have left the peasant labourers cowed, degraded, demoralized, and without rights in the land."[23] What the social gospel did for the older doctrine of sin was to revive the ideal of the Kingdom of God. Rauschenbusch argued that when persons see the actual world in relation to the Kingdom ideal, they immediately become aware that there is something fundamentally wrong in the world. Collective sin is more real than they previously imagined.

> Those who do their thinking in the light of the Kingdom of God make less of heresy and private sins. They reserve their shudders for men who keep the liquor

and vice trade alive against public intelligence and law; for interests that organize powerful lobbies to defeat tenement or factory legislation, or turn factory in-
spection into sham; for nations that are willing to set the world at war in order
to win or protect colonial areas of trade or usurious profit from loans to weaker
peoples; and for private interests which are willing to push a peaceful nation
into war because the stock exchange has a panic at the rumour of peace. These
seem the unforgivable sins, the great demonstrations of rebellious selfishness,
wherever the social gospel has revived the faith of the Kingdom of God.[24]

However, the social gospelers did not assume that because persons were made aware
of institutional sins, they would automatically take steps to eradicate them. Rather,
they knew that people had then to be pushed to do so by pastoral, lay, and other leaders, a role that King so often stressed from Montgomery to Memphis.

In the chapter entitled, "The Salvation of the Super-Personal Forces," Rauschenbusch shows that it is not merely individuals who need salvation, but the powers and
principalities, or what he called "the super-personal social forces" (societal institutions). Here he was reminded of the Hebrew prophets who essentially addressed
nations and powerful political leaders rather than individual citizens. The prophet
Jeremiah, for example, was called and commissioned to be prophet to the nations
(Jeremiah 1:10). Aware of the increasing complexity and difficulty of addressing the
super-personal forces of evil, Rauschenbusch naïvely maintained that the salvation
of these, like that of individuals, "consists in coming under the law of Christ."[25] Part
of the difficulty and naïveté behind this claim is the assumption that it would be as
simple for an unjust institution to be converted as it would be for an individual. The
truth is that it is not even easy for the powerful, privileged individual to be brought
in line with the law of Christ, a point that would frequently be made by King.

In part, Rauschenbusch's naïveté was a result of his definition of sin as selfishness. While there will always be an element of truth in this, Reinhold Niebuhr's later
definition of sin as pride helps us to understand why it was so difficult for the super-
personal forces of evil to bring themselves under the law of Christ. Rauschenbusch
was being more realistic when he said that "evils become bold and permanent when
there is money in them."[26] Whenever sin pays or can be seen to be profitable in terms
of money and property, it is considerably more difficult to remove. If the individual
does not easily relinquish or share money, power, and privilege, it most assuredly is
not an easy feat for groups and institutions to accomplish. As would be the case
with King, Rauschenbusch also had a good sense of this. Unfortunately, he did not
always apply the principle consistently, as when he implied that the group could
bring itself under the rule of Christ as easily as the individual. And yet at other times
Rauschenbusch expressed a more realistic stance, anticipating the Christian realism

of Reinhold Niebuhr: "Ordinarily sin is an act of weakness and side-stepping, followed by shame the next day. But when it is the source of prolific income, it is no longer a shame-faced vagabond slinking through the dark, but an army with banners, entrenched and defiant. The bigger the dividends, the stiffer the resistance against anything that would cut them down. *When fed with money, sin grows wings and claws.*"[27]

This is precisely what Rauschenbusch should have remembered when he wrote of the need for the group to come under the rule of Christ. In any event, add the element of deep-rooted human pride to this love of money, property, and power, and one begins to see just how difficult it is to bring super-personal forces of evil under the law of Christ. To Rauschenbusch's credit, he acknowledged that this redeeming of powers and principalities is the most difficult of all.[28] He seemed to have a better awareness than other white social gospelers of the depth of individual and corporate sin. Rauschenbusch's problem was that he failed to see sin in terms of individual and collective pride, the ultimate form of which is the desire of humans to usurp God from the throne of divinity and take up occupancy.[29] In addition, and crucial for this discussion, is the fact that for much of his career, Rauschenbusch failed to identify racism as a sin, an oversight that King avoided. Indeed, for most of Rauschenbusch's career he was silent on the race question. This, in effect, leads us to the fifth criticism of the social gospel.

Although the social gospelers devoted some attention to most of the pressing social problems of their day, they did not, by and large, commit persistent energy and attention to the problems of "war, imperialism, race, democracy, or the use of force."[30] In this respect, they were clearly unlike King. At this juncture, it will be helpful to diverge for a moment to examine the race question in relation to the Social Gospel movement.

The Social Gospel and Racism

In 1954, Paul Carter wrote of "how grievously far behind" denominations and national church councils (e.g., the Federal Council of Churches [FCC]) were on the question of race.[31] These were organizations presumably committed to the social gospel. The most that the FCC was able to manage was the introduction of the practice of "Negro-white pulpit exchange on 'Race Relations Sunday,' a date in the ecclesiastical year whose very observance is a sardonic and tragic mockery of human dignity,"[32] said Carter. Carter's critique anticipated concerns that King would raise regarding the church in general.

Robert T. Handy provides a helpful summary of the stance of that earlier generation of church historians who argued that the social gospelers were either silent on the issue of race or at best exhibited a benign neglect.

The proponents of the social gospel did tend to center their attention on the labor-capital problem and to touch upon other causes, including race and woman suffrage, only in passing. They tended to accept the views of race held by progressives generally. Josiah Strong was closer to being obsessed with the idea of Anglo-Saxon superiority than most other advocates of the social gospel, though there was some reflection of his sentiments in what they had to say. As the early social gospel leaders saw it, a major step had been taken for the Negro with the abolition of slavery; now it was the turn of wage-slaves to be freed.[33]

The social gospelers therefore tended to focus more on class and wage issues, and were nearly oblivious to the issue of race. In his biography of Washington Gladden, Jacob Dorn wrote that proponents of the social gospel "were for the most part strikingly silent on the problem of race in the United States."[34]

In *King Came Preaching* (2001), Mervin Warren uncritically cites William E. Hordern's claim that race relations was among the issues "close to the hearts of the Social Gospel thinkers." Warren contends, still following Hordern, that peace and race "were perhaps the two most discussed issues among social gospelers."[35] This contention is contrary to the belief of most early social gospel scholars that the leaders of the social gospel movement focused little on racism.[36] Nonetheless, there appears to be a growing sentiment among recent scholars that one should not draw easy conclusions in this regard. The work of recent social gospel revisionist scholars such as Ronald C. White and Ralph E. Luker makes a strong case for the view that race was a more significant issue for leading white social gospel leaders, but only at particular periods of their work.[37] This conclusion is based on extensive archival research which postdates by several decades the Hordern text. White and Luker each try to establish the argument that the issue of racism itself, as well as responses to it, was much more complex than previously acknowledged. In addition, they maintain that research supports their independently held thesis that the social gospel movement was not just a white story, but a black story as well.

White and Luker each devote considerable attention to the black social gospel and the contributions of lay and clergy proponents to resolving the race problem. It has long been established that from the time of American slavery, black religionists and non-religionists consistently attacked racism on religious, moral, and philosophical grounds. White and Luker do an admirable job of advancing scholarship on the social gospel movement by explicitly situating Afrikan American involvement within it. Neither man implies that blacks had to depend on whites for their involvement. Instead, both assert that blacks have always been committed to a social gospel. Here one need only recall the life and work of such nineteenth- and twentieth-century notables as David Walker, Maria Stewart, Frederick Douglass, Harriet Jacobs,

Henry Highland Garnett, Reverdy Ransom, Henry McNeal Turner, Anna Julia Cooper, Francis Grimké, and Ida B. Wells-Barnett.

An important criticism of Luker and White is their failure to name and address the social gospel tradition in King's family and at Ebenezer Baptist Church. Luker does go well beyond White, however, by explicitly linking King's development to the struggle of his people in the South. Thus, King "was bound to proclaim his message in its cadences." Luker also points to the importance of Morehouse College, particularly the influence of Mays, Kelsey, Samuel Williams, and other "models of the black intellectual as Christian social critics."[38] Furthermore, in his discussion on Baptist congregations in the twentieth century as "centers of religious life," as well as "social service agencies and bases of political power,"[39] Luker at least implies a social gospel connection between A. D. Williams, Daddy King, and Martin. In addition, he names many black pastors and churches in this mold, including Williams and Daddy King. One wishes, however, that Luker had more explicitly connected these men with the social gospel movement. At best he only scratches the ice. In any case, once one reads White's and Luker's books, it becomes clear that the social gospel movement in American Protestantism must never again be discussed and taught without revealing the integral contributions of Afrikan Americans.

We also learn from the revisionist work of Luker and White that the key personalities in the social gospel movement were frequently a study in contrasts. This was true not only from person to person, but a number of these individuals underwent various degrees of transformation regarding their stance on the race issue. Awareness of this fact should remind us of the complexity of issues involving race and the extent of the involvement of proponents of the social gospel movement. Let us consider briefly Josiah Strong and Lyman Abbott.

Josiah Strong

"A 'forgotten' leader of the social gospel,"[40] Josiah Strong is often reputed to have been racist and imperialist in his thinking. He was an adherent of what Luker calls "Anglo Saxon triumphalism." We get a sense of this from Strong's statement: "It seems to me that God, with infinite wisdom and skill, is training the Anglo-Saxon race for an hour sure to come in the world's future."[41] There is more than a little evidence to support the claim that Strong was a racist and a radical assimilationist, especially during the early part of his career as a pastor and as the author of *Our Country* in 1885. During this period he preached and taught the Anglo-Saxonization of the entire human race, i.e., the total reshaping of every race in the image of Anglo Saxons.[42] A number of Afrikan American scholars—including I. D. Barnett, the Personalist John Wesley Edward Bowen, Alexander Crummell, and Theophilus Gould Steward (an A. M. E. pastor)—both praised and criticized *Our Country*. They rejected Strong's radical assimilationism and Anglo-Saxon triumphalism. Bowen argued, for example, that Christians are to Christianize, not Anglo-Saxonize.[43]

Within a decade there appeared evidence that Strong's perspective on race was changing for the better. For example, during this period he proclaimed that there were not three races—blacks, Native peoples, and whites—but one race. For, "The blood of Jesus Christ," he said, "has made them brothers."[44] Slowly Strong began to see "persistent differences of culture and race as part of a divine economy."[45] White chronicles Strong's changing attitude and thinking on race from 1909 to 1916.[46] He concludes that Strong's stance changed between the publication of *Our Country* in 1885 and the publication of *Our World* in 1913, in which he included the chapter "The New Race Problem." However, that Strong's thinking on race changed near the end of his life is not to say that the race question became for him a top priority among social reform issues. It did not. Nor is it to say that Strong was by this time free of all racial bias. White has probably said all that can reasonably be said about the matter: "It is to suggest that he was changing his mind in the last years of his life."[47] Even so, his brand of the social gospel differed substantially from what was later promoted by King, especially on the race question. Moreover, it is most unfortunate, and indeed tragic, that for the greater part of Strong's life he was against equality of the races. By the time his views on race began to moderate he was already in the autumn of life and had not the energy and stamina needed to fight for real change.

Lyman Abbott

During Lyman Abbott's tenure as pastor of the Plymouth Congregational Church in Brooklyn, he was editor of the *Christian Union,* later named the *Outlook.* His leadership represented the shift that was occurring in race matters—from sending "free" blacks to Liberia (the practice of the American Colonization Society, 1816–1910) to the more accommodationist stance of conceding that blacks are in the United States to stay. This latter stance focused on the education and economic uplift of blacks. Abbott took this as his own position, although he favored gradualism rather than the immediate emancipation of blacks. He was thus against slavery, but not an abolitionist. Proponents of abolitionism generally rejected gradualism in favor of immediate emancipation. With Booker T. Washington and Edgar Gardner Murphy, Abbott rejected Strong's Anglo-Saxon triumphalism. "The missionary makes a mistake who tries to convert the Negro into an Anglo-Saxon," said Abbott. "Let us not be guilty of thinking that the white man and the Anglo-Saxon are the mold to which men must conform themselves."[48]

A younger Abbott believed that it would take the North and the intervention of the federal government to solve the southern race problem (as if there was not also a northern race problem!). By 1890, however, he began to retreat from this stance. Abbott conceded that he and others who shared his stance had been over enthusiastic, and that the solution to the southern race problem lay not with the North and the federal government, but with southern whites and blacks. He believed that since the Civil War and Reconstruction the white southerner had shown himself to be the friend of the formerly enslaved Afrikans (a view clearly open to critique). In his judgment, then, there was no need for continued northern intervention or the involvement of the federal government. Abbott was therefore optimistic that whites of the New South would do the right thing regarding blacks. This in part is why he even opposed the Federal Elections Bill.[49] Much of this was due to Abbott's naïveté, but he was also affected by what at best might be deemed racial and cultural insensitivity.

This bias is borne out by his 1912 interpretation of the parable of the Good Samaritan, which drew a scathing critique from W. E. B. DuBois. Applying the parable to whether blacks, Jews, or Roman Catholics should be allowed to attend white or Protestant schools, Abbott concluded that an affirmative response would be tantamount to having misread or misunderstood the parable. Luker has written about Abbott's interpretation of the parable, one that sharply contrasts with King's interpretation of it to mean that the faithful were required to come to the aid of the least (e.g., the striking sanitation workers in Memphis in 1968). Abbott's interpretation of the parable was narrow and exclusive and appealed primarily to the privileged and powerful: "A person has little, if any, right to bring a guest into the home who is unwanted by others in the family, he said. It was a 'moral blunder' to admit a Negro, a Jew, or a Roman Catholic to a white or a Christian or a Protestant school because the school was merely a larger home. 'This is not the way to promote the spirit of human brotherhood,' Abbott argued. 'It is not recorded that the Good Samaritan took the wounded traveler into his own home. He took him to an inn.' By extension, he concluded with a defense of immigration restrictions and of racial segregation in Southern schools."[50] This was not an anti-racist stance, nor was it identical to that of an earlier period of Abbott's professional life. In any case, DuBois was not pleased with Abbott's interpretation, and responded: "A friend of the freedman in Reconstruction, Abbott slowly 'transferred allegiance and became the most subtle and dangerous enemy of the Negro in America.'" DuBois went on to say that Abbott did this with "so straight a face and such an assumption of high motives and impeccable respectability that thousands of well-meaning Americans followed his lead."[51] Of course, Abbott, editor of the *Outlook,* had some years earlier permitted the inclusion of a scathing and, by many accounts, unfair review of DuBois's *Souls of Black Folk* (1903).

Washington Gladden and Jenkin Lloyd Jones were among the white social gospelers who defended *Souls* and criticized the unfairness of the review.[52]

It is important for us to remember that the shift in Abbott's stance, as well as in Strong's, is but further evidence of the complexity involved in the matter of race relative to some leaders in the social gospel movement. Many white social gospelers continued to possess perverted views on race and denied the moral agency of blacks. At least *some* of them, however, possessed, at one time or another during their careers, more benign views of race than previously believed.

Excursus

Christian ethicist Darryl Trimiew presents an instructive argument against some of the revisionist views of the racism of early social gospel leaders. Trimiew contends that the racism of early social gospelers has already been thoroughly and irrefutably documented.[53] He claims that a clear limitation of these men was their inability (or unwillingness) to see and be critical not only of their own racism but of the institutional racism from which they benefited as well. They also failed, according to Trimiew, to see that the Christian mission requires that believers of all races work together, rather than separately, to achieve the Kingdom of God on earth. White social gospelers intentionally excluded their black contemporaries from efforts to apply Christianity to the social problems of the day. Therefore, whites labored on their own and among their own, and the work of blacks paralleled in some ways that of their white counterparts. The social gospel work of blacks differed considerably, however, precisely because they intentionally rejected white supremacy in all its forms and sought to establish a society that was thoroughly egalitarian and democratic. Moreover, Trimiew rightly suggests that white social gospelers viewed blacks merely as moral subjects, as beings to whom moral duties and responsibilities were owed, but who may or may not be able to reciprocate. The implication, of course, is that blacks were the inferiors of whites. White social gospelers declined to treat blacks as moral agents who owe duties and responsibilities to themselves as well as others, in addition to being as capable as any group of making their own decisions and working toward the establishment of the community of love, in which every person is respected and honored just because they are beings imbued with the image of God. The logic of this stance is that since blacks cannot do for themselves, they must be objects of mission for the only true possessors of moral agency, namely, the whites.

Trimiew's is a significant contribution to ongoing discussions on the social gospel today. However, it is not as clear to me that he succeeds in his disagreement with Ralph Luker. Rather than examine Luker's *Social Gospel in Black and White*, he looks at an earlier article Luker published in 1977, "Social Gospel and the Failure of Racial Reform, 1877–1898." This article was but a foreshadowing of Luker's book, where he makes a more impressive case that while the social gospelers were indeed racists, a number of them were compelled by various circumstances to begin criticizing racism. Such was the case, for example, with Washington Gladden. Unfortunately, Trimiew did not cite either Luker's book or Ronald White's *Liberty and Justice for All: Racial Reform and the Social Gospel.* Luker and White argue convincingly that while racism was prominent in and among the social gospelers, a number of them were in fact transformed to work toward racial reform.

Where Trimiew really shines is his awareness that the white social gospelers were frequently blind to their own as well as structural racism in American institutions. In addition, he sees that they did not engage in the self-critique of their own racism. What Trimiew seems to be implying is that racism is part and parcel of the very fabric of the United States of America. That is, racism is embedded in all American institutions, as well as in the Constitution of the United States and the Declaration of Independence. This is a thesis espoused by a number of scholars on racism, including Manning Marable, Joe R. Feagin, Andrew Hacker, Paula Rothenberg, C. Eric Lincoln, and Derrick Bell.[54] This stance is the opposite of that put forth by Dinesh D'Souza, and by Paul M. Sniderman and Thomas Piazza,[55] who argue, respectively, that racism is no longer a significant social issue and that it is not endemic to major U.S. political documents. Trimiew supports the thesis purported by Feagin that "the central problem is that, from the beginning, European American institutions were racially hierarchical, white supremacist, and undemocratic."[56] Feagin argues further that this particular paradigm shift in the analysis of racist relations actually began in the work of Frederick Douglass and DuBois.

Institutional or systemic racism has been destructive to white-black relations at least since the Constitutional Convention held at Philadelphia in 1787. From day one, the very foundation of the nation was flawed in being built on the systemic exclusion of people of Afrikan descent. Reflecting on the Constitution, Feagin put it this way: "While most Americans have thought of this document and the sociopolitical structure it created as keeping the nation together, in fact this structure was created to maintain separation and oppression at the time and for the foreseeable future. The framers reinforced and legitimated a system of racist oppression that they thought would ensure that whites, especially white men of means, would rule for centuries to come."[57]

Trimiew is right to charge the leading white social gospelers with racism. But for the sake of a broader, more inclusive understanding, we should take seriously the carefully documented position of Luker and White that some white social gospelers— especially Rauschenbusch and Gladden—neglected racism during various periods of their work but, because of societal, personal, and other influences and experiences, were compelled to speak and write against racism. This is not to say that either man engaged in sustained self-criticism of his own racism, or that of the structures of church and society. Moreover, even after the experiences that compelled them to speak and write against racism, neither man did so systematically and forcefully. It should be pointed out, however, that at least one white social gospeler did in fact write and speak consistently and passionately against racism. This was Henry Churchill King, one-time theology professor and president of Oberlin College. He was a contemporary of both Gladden and Rauschenbusch.

In any event, I think the point of some of the recent revisionist writings on the social gospel movement is that while it cannot be denied that racism was prevalent in the movement and among the chief progenitors, there was less silence on and neglect of the issue than previously known. Furthermore, even their silence was not as simple a matter as once thought, but rather tended to be a much more complex matter.

RAUSCHENBUSCH AND RACE

Acknowledging that most Christians take seriously the obligation to love, Rauschenbusch was both aware and critical of the fact that many white Christians tended to place a limit on *who* was to be loved. They seemed to be of the view that it is all right to love persons in general, but when one gets down to particulars—for example, the loving of one's fellow human beings of color—well, that is another matter altogether. Rauschenbusch reflected on this matter in his first book-length manuscript in 1893, *The Righteousness of the Kingdom*.[58] There we find him saying, "The history of the Negro, the Indian, and the Chinese can tell how difference of color and race can warp the sense of justice and dull the fine perception of love."[59] Unfortunately, this is all that Rauschenbusch said then, and it would be a very long time before he again spoke or wrote about racism and Christian responsibility. More than twenty years later, Rauschenbusch declared: "Christianity stands for the doctrine that we must love one another—all men, without distinction of 'religion, race, color or previous condition of servitude.'" He went on to say that Christianity "does not advise eliminating the unfit, but seeks to make them fit. It stands for the solidarity of the race in its weakness and strength, its defeats and conquests, its sin and salvation."[60]

One reason for his silence may have been that he was not familiar enough with the problem given the little contact he had with blacks. His secretary, friend, and first biographer, Dores Sharpe, offered yet another possible contributing factor to Rauschenbusch's early pessimism regarding the matter: "Remember the great migration of Negro life from the South to the industrial centers of the North had scarcely taken place during his lifetime and had definitely not taken place at the time of the writing of his first great book. He was not, therefore, brought face to face with the problem as we in the North are today [in 1942]."[61] For the last twenty years of his life Rauschenbusch lived in Rochester, New York, a city with a population of nearly 163,000 in 1900. During this period, 90 percent of blacks still resided in the South. Barely 600 blacks then lived in Rochester. Yet surely Rauschenbusch was not completely oblivious to the race problem in this country. Even if he had little contact with blacks in Rochester, New York, he must have heard things about racism in conversations and through news reports.

In addition, there is absolutely no question that Rauschenbusch was aware of blacks' struggle for full equality and civil rights even during his years as pastor in the Hell's Kitchen section of New York City (1886–97). During that period he wrote of the wrongness of American slavery, and "how difference of color and race can warp the sense of justice and dull the fine perception of love."[62] This does not sound like one who knew only little about the plight of blacks, or who had not either been around or heard about large numbers of them. In addition, during the latter part of the nineteenth century (and during Rauschenbusch's pastorate), there were increasingly large numbers of blacks in New York City, so many, in fact, that race riots initiated by whites were not an uncommon occurrence.[63]

It is important to consider why Rauschenbusch, "the foremost theologian of the social gospel,"[64] finally broke silence on the race problem in 1913. During the winter of 1910–11, he traveled to Nashville, Tennessee, for speaking engagements that included a lecture to students at the historically black Fisk University.[65] He wanted to know more about sharecropping and education in the South. As was his custom, he did some personal investigating while in Nashville, only to find himself in a place called "black bottom." Here he witnessed conditions that rocked him. He saw black "life at its worst." Dores Sharpe speculates that this was the impetus that led him to break silence on the race question in the 1913 speech.[66]

In time, in his own way, Rauschenbusch would come to reject the stance of southern whites and others who believed blacks to be less than human and were not of one blood with whites. In 1914 he espoused what he considered the Christian way toward solution: "However great the practical difficulties may be, the Christian way out is to take our belated black brother by the hand and urge him along the road of steady and intelligent labor, of property rights, of family fidelity, of hope and self-confidence, and of pride and joy in his race achievements. . . ."[67] His tone here is paternalistic, and he fails to acknowledge that blacks were autonomous moral agents. Despite good intentions, Rauschenbusch did not proceed to say why there was concern about blacks' attitude toward labor, property rights, fidelity toward family, hope and self-confidence, and pride of achievements of the race. From his omission of the role of the enslavement of the Afrikans by whites, one could conclude that the Afrikans themselves were to blame for their condition.

In principle, however, it can be said that Rauschenbusch's doctrine of the sacredness of persons was intended to include everyone. We get this sense from his lesson, "The Solidarity of the Human Family," where he argued that people belong together. "Every man has worth and sacredness as a man."[68] This, he proclaimed, is the basic social principle of Jesus Christ, a point that King would routinely make in his sermons and speeches more than two generations later. Reflecting on the importance of world mission, Rauschenbusch wrote: "The man who intelligently realizes the Chinese and the Zulu as his brothers with whom he must share the earth is an ampler mind— other things being equal—than the man who can think of humanity only in terms of pale-faces."[69] Although he clearly did not here refer to the race question in the United States, what Rauschenbusch wrote is suggestive of what he thought about it at the time. When he wrote about the sacredness of persons during this period (1916), he was not referring to a specific group, but to all human beings, regardless of race and gender. He also had this in mind when he approvingly quoted the words of Henry Churchill King: "The principle of reverence for personality is the ruling principle in ethics, and in religion; it constitutes, therefore, the truest and highest test of either an individual or a civilization; it has been, even unconsciously, the guiding and determining principle in all human progress; and in its religious interpretation, it is, indeed, the one faith that keeps meaning and value for life."[70] Unlike most of his social gospel contemporaries, Henry Churchill King not only espoused the doctrine of reverence for persons as such, but was consistent and relentless in applying it to the race problem,[71] thus foreshadowing Martin Luther King in profound ways. It is also significant that Rauschenbusch was acquainted with Henry King's writings on the subject. One wonders, for example, whether his statements on race would have been even more forthright and frequent had he lived longer and continued in association with King.

He had been virtually silent on the issue before making his first substantial comment in an address before the annual meeting of the American Missionary Society in 1913. At that time, he said: "For years the problem of the races in the South has seemed to me so tragic, so insoluble, that I have never yet ventured to discuss it in public."[72] One can even see Rauschenbusch's naïveté in this statement, as he implies that only the South had to contend with racism, which in turn implies that the problem did not exist in the North. Rauschenbusch gave no further reason in that speech for his silence on the issue of race. In addition, there is the implication that he did think about it, albeit in private.

Gary Dorrien makes the instructive observation that Rauschenbusch's early silence on the race question had something to do with his early statements on immigration, especially as they pertained to the Germans. Dorrien notes that sometimes in statements made in support of German immigrants, Rauschenbusch made racially insensitive comments:

Rauschenbusch's optimism on the culture-transforming character of American democracy caused him to underestimate the depth of American racism. Under the pressure of his concern to strengthen America's democratic culture and open its doors to German immigrants, he was not above making appeals to racial prejudice. He opposed all racially based arguments for closed immigration, but at the same time he strongly implied that German immigrants were more equal than others. In one of his fund-raising appeals for the German department at Rochester Seminary, he asked in 1905, 'Are the whites of this continent so sure of their possession against the blacks of the South and the seething yellow flocks beyond the Pacific that they need no reinforcement of men of their own blood while yet it is time?' In his 1902 Rochester commencement address, he warned that Anglo-Saxons needed to join with the 'princely Teutonic stock' to protect American democracy from the demands of 'alien strains' arriving from other parts of the world.[73]

In yet another statement that reflected his racial and cultural blindness and insensitivity at the time, Rauschenbusch said in 1897: "The Germans . . . are of the same stock as the English, readily assimilated, and a splendid source of strength for America, physically, intellectually, and morally."[74] On the one hand, Rauschenbusch argued vigorously for an America where all would be treated fairly and where democracy and the rule of equality would be applicable to all. On the other hand, in his defense of German immigration, he sometimes implied that some groups (i.e., the Germans) were superior to blacks and Orientals because of their racial similarities to white Americans, a position that Martin Luther King, Jr. would have rejected on moral and other grounds. Paul Minus comes to this conclusion in *Walter Rauschenbusch: American Reformer*. "Here was a moral blind spot that Rauschenbusch appears not to have recognized. His rhetoric was good—America is intended for all. But under the pressure of having to make an effective case for acceptance of the German immigrants, he concluded that it is intended for some more than for others."[75] Minus stops short of saying that the "moral blind spot" that Rauschenbusch failed to recognize was his own racism, or at best, his racial insensitivity.

Dorrien claims that Rauschenbusch's sense was that his early statements on immigration (which contained racist remarks) were made not primarily because of racial prejudice, but because of the overriding concern he had for the American democratic principle and "his fear that American democracy was fragile."[76] Rauschenbusch was especially concerned about the negative impact of the power of capitalism on the democratic principle,[77] an issue that would register profoundly with King as well. And yet Dorrien rightly points out that Rauschenbusch's early statements on immigration "contained unmistakably racist appeals using language that, even in its time, must be considered racially offensive."[78]

It is understandable and laudable that Rauschenbusch was concerned about the possible decay of democracy. We may concede with Dorrien that Rauschenbusch aimed to strengthen the otherwise fragile democratic principle by arguing that many more immigrants be admitted who came from European nations that had some experience with democracy. We may even concede that like Shailer Mathews and other social gospelers, Rauschenbusch seldom mentioned the race problem in his work, and that like his contemporaries he strangely believed that racism, gender inequality, and other social evils would be eradicated through the continued growth of democracy and other forms of progress—a philosophy of inevitable progress that King would find problematic. And yet this seems a contradiction to Rauschenbusch's claim in *Christianity and the Social Crisis,* that progress on issues such as the rights of women require the attention and vigilance of even a very small number of advocates, no matter what else is happening in church and society. Such changes do not occur inevitably— no matter how much the democratic principle expands—and without the conscious decision to work toward them. Reflecting on this point in 1907, Rauschenbusch, calling to mind Martin King's and Henry David Thoreau's stress on the creative minority, declared that it is generally not the Church that spearheads reform movements, but a minority of its members, and that their efforts are frequently against the Church's will: "For instance, the position of woman has doubtless been elevated through the influence of Christianity, but by its indirect and diffused influences rather than by any direct championship of the organized Church. . . . It is this diffused spirit of Christianity rather than the conscious purpose of organized Christianity which has been the chief moral force in social changes. It has often taken its finest form in heretics and free-thinkers, and in non-Christian movements."[79] The point to be kept in mind is Rauschenbusch's awareness that the Church itself does not tend to be the leader in such reform efforts. In addition, he seemed to be aware, as was always the case with King, that reform does not generally happen automatically and inevitably because of the advance of the democratic principle. Areas where reform is needed must be addressed specifically.

Ronald C. White contends that Rauschenbusch's silence on the race question was "falsely generalized to include other social gospel leaders,"[80] although it surely included some, e.g., Shailer Mathews. And what of Washington Gladden and Henry Churchill King's persistent outspokenness against racism? Why some, and not others?

A persistent concern is the extent to which early social gospelers were consistent and forceful in their efforts to address the race problem, an issue King never raised in seminary and graduate school. In any case, the time came when this was less a question in the case of Washington Gladden, who in 1903 met DuBois during a speaking engagement in Atlanta. While there, Gladden witnessed firsthand the living conditions of some blacks that he considered worse than those in northern slums. On the return train trip to Columbus, Ohio, he read DuBois's *Souls of Black Folk* (1903). Gladden was indelibly impressed and went on to devote much energy and attention to the race question when he returned home.[81] DuBois's writings would also figure prominently in King's challenge to this country's racist structures, as well as its desire for vengeance and war. King admired DuBois's "priceless dedication to his people,"[82] as well as his radical views and actions.[83] Indeed, King believed that few thought more deeply and wrote more poignantly on the destructive anatomy of the ghetto than DuBois.[84]

As previously observed, none was more determined to forthrightly address the race problem than the social gospeler and personalist, Henry Churchill King of Oberlin College. Luker maintains that many of the social gospelers were influenced by what he calls "theological personalism," a point that Martin Luther King, Jr. may not have been aware of during his time at Crozer and Boston University.[85] In fact, Luker claims that theological personalism was "ubiquitous among social gospel prophets who rejected both radical cultural imperialism and radical social separatism."[86] This should not be taken to mean that they were methodological personalists such as those that Martin Luther King studied under at Boston University. As far as I can tell, the only social gospeler in this category was Henry Churchill King. More than any of his white social gospel and personalist contemporaries, Henry King—in his writings— consistently and relentlessly applied the principle of *reverence for persons as such* to the race problem. Part of the reason for this likely had something to do with Oberlin College's long history of antislavery activity and inclusion of blacks in its student body (although Oberlin students did sometimes experience racism on campus).[87]

Martin Luther King did not explicitly criticize the social gospelers, including Rauschenbusch, for either their complicity of silence or failure to address the race question as persistently and forcefully as other social issues. As Trimiew points out, however, King completely rejected white supremacy in all its forms and sought to develop a multiracial, multiethnic, multicultural coalition to work toward the eradication of racism and injustice, and to work to establish the beloved community. This in itself is evidence enough that King was critical of the social gospelers' failure to do the same.

Nevertheless, Rauschenbusch did make specific references to the race question and sometimes criticized racism. He also commented on slavery. In each case, it was clear that to Rauschenbusch it was important to speak out. Regardless of the Apostle Paul's teaching on the subject of slavery during his day, Rauschenbusch declared in 1893: "But, Paul notwithstanding, we have abolished slavery and hold it to be wrong."[88] Unfortunately, this did not necessarily mean that white proponents of this view were also antiracists. Rauschenbusch did not applaud violence, but said elsewhere that although slavery had been overcome by violence, "It had to be overcome somehow, and all honor is due to those who poured out life, happiness, property to overcome it."[89]

In all things, he said he preferred "gentleness and meekness," and he went on to declare: "I have no faith in force methods, and even believe in non-resistance, but not in a non-resistance based on cowardice and silence. There was nothing cringing in Jesus. He did not strike back, but neither did he flinch. He was 'the terrible meek.' I am thinking of the Negro race in saying this."[90] Here Rauschenbusch clearly would have advised blacks to adhere to pacifist or nonviolent means to address racial oppression. The fact that King seemed unaware of Rauschenbusch's ideas on this matter, while taking seriously similar thoughts penned by Reinhold Niebuhr in 1932,[91] is indeed interesting and intriguing.

Notwithstanding the arguments of White and Luker, there remains much room for skepticism regarding the contributions of most early white social gospelers to solving the race problem, North and South. The sense remains that most of the social gospelers who addressed the race question did so gently and in ways that rocked few if any boats. Dorrien correctly maintains that neither Rauschenbusch nor Mathews "was willing to alienate his white liberal audience with anything more than a parenthetical aside regarding racism in America."[92] Moreover, most failed to acknowledge and criticize their own racism as well as structural or institutional racism. At any rate, where the issue of race was concerned, the vast majority of the white social gospelers were not prophets in the tradition of Hebrew prophecy in the eighth century b.c.e. The same cannot be said of Martin Luther King, Jr., and the tradition of black social gospelism.

KING, BLACK SOCIAL GOSPELISM, AND RAUSCHENBUSCH

Martin Luther King, Jr. was less concerned about what happens to the soul and body after life on earth than what happens to them in this world. In this belief, he was very much aligned with both Jewish and Afrikan American traditions, which contend that God is concerned primarily about what goes on in the world and how people relate and behave. What happens in and beyond the grave should be no concern of ours, considering that we can do nothing about it. But we *can* do something about life on earth. That, not the nature and content of heaven and hell, should be our concern. Writing about some of their many premarital discussions on religion, Coretta Scott King recalled a conversation she and her husband had about life after death. She reports that he said, "I'm not concerned with the temperature of hell or the furnishings of heaven, but with the things men do here on earth."[93] Statements such as this placed King squarely in the tradition of the best of social gospelism, which was also consistent with his black church background.

A. D. Williams and Daddy King were unquestionably part of the black social gospel tradition, and this had no small effect on Martin's understanding of the relevance of the gospel to social problems that adversely affected his people. Williams stressed the need for pastors to focus on both the social and spiritual well-being of persons.[94] Even more so, and unlike white social gospelers, Williams insisted on the need to take the fight to the oppressor by way of organized nonviolent protest or noncooperation. Like most blacks of his day, Williams was tried and tested in the harsh school of racial hard knocks. He learned firsthand the importance of stubborn self-determination and acting to recover one's lost sense of dignity. He therefore understood the need for the black pastor to provide leadership in both traditional spiritual matters and in the more practical areas of the people's lives. This is why Williams did not hesitate to challenge the racist Atlanta newspaper, the *Georgian,* for its daily insults against blacks. He also took the Atlanta school board to task because there was no high school for black students. The *Georgian* soon went out of business while the school system went on to build Booker T. Washington High School, the first for black students in Atlanta, and the school that Martin King attended.[95]

These things happened because of Reverand Williams' social gospelism and the fact that he was adamant about the need for persons to be self-determined and to believe that God requires that they be treated with dignity. In light of this stance, even the battered and oppressed are not permitted to passively receive insults and affronts to their personhood. If individuals truly possess intrinsic dignity and worth because they are children of God, they are morally obligated to be proactive and self-determined in efforts to defend and enhance their dignity. For Williams, and later for Daddy King, people are obligated to relentlessly contend against all acts of dehumanization as they aim for complete personhood.

Daddy King was simply adamant about the need for ministers in particular and Christians in general to be intentional about linking faith and politics, or thinking theologically about politics. Addressing the Atlanta Missionary Baptist Association on October 17, 1940, Daddy King reminded his colleagues that the church's ministry ought to touch every facet of the black community, not just the spiritual needs. Daddy King said further:

> Quite often we say the church has no place in politics, forgetting the words of the Lord, 'The spirit of the Lord is upon me, because he hath anointed me to preach the Gospel to the poor; he hath sent me to heal the broken-hearted, to preach deliverance to the captives, and the recovering of sight to the blind, to set at liberty them that are bruised.' . . .
>
> In this we find we are to do something about the broken-hearted, poor, unemployed, the captive, the blind, and the bruised. How can people be happy without jobs, food, shelter and clothes?[96]

Daddy King went on to urge all ministers to become registered voters and to partici-pate in every movement to better the lives of all blacks. The ministers themselves must set the standard and model it for the people.

When Daddy King was not able to get the members of Ebenezer Baptist Church to unite to take proactive measures for social change and against injustice, he used his influence as a member of many important civic and financial boards to press for such change. He never tired of criticizing white pastors' lack of courage and of reminding them that "it is time we followed the teachings of Jesus and all be treated as God's children."[97] As A. D. Williams believed before him, Daddy King maintained the view that blacks could not, indeed must not, depend on even the most well-intentioned white people to take up their cause. "No initiative to end segregation and the bigotry it helped maintain would emerge from the white community. Any actions that pro-duced change would have to come from the Negro community. . . . White support, if it ever came, would be welcome, but depending on it made for a fool's errand."[98] The experience of Daddy King and of numerous southern blacks was that generally no such championing of black personhood and rights was forthcoming from either white religious leaders or their institutions. Daddy King recalled that the most hu-mane support came from a white political leader, Mayor William Hartsfield,[99] not from the white churches in Atlanta. Blacks had to look to themselves, he insisted. "We would have to change things. Whites were not interested in change."[100]

This discussion of Daddy King's social gospelism is a corrective of the tendency of some scholars to claim that while Martin's early theological development was most assuredly influenced by the fundamentalism of the black church in general and Daddy King's preaching in particular, he was not influenced by the social gospel tra-dition until he entered Morehouse College and came under the influence of Ben-jamin E. Mays, George Kelsey, Samuel Williams, and others. Unfortunately, scholar Michael G. Long makes this mistake in *Martin Luther King, Jr., on Creative Living.*[101] Al-most from the inception of the black church in this country black preachers generally tended to be theologically conservative, but politically liberal and progressive. Only in exceptional cases have black preachers not seen and acted on the social and political implications of the Christian faith. In the preceding discussion we see with clarity that no matter how fundamentalist Daddy King's theology was, he persistently acted on a clear sense that his faith required that social ills that adversely affected his people be addressed forthrightly in both word and action.

Martin Luther King, Jr., was clearly influenced by his father and grandfather. Although there were times when he thought that decent white people of good will—especially Christians—could be counted on, King came to see that this was often an il-lusion. For example, he expressed disappointment in the stance of the white moderate and "the appalling silence of the good people" in Birmingham in 1963.[102] In 1965, he spoke of his disappointment with the white church and its leadership. "As the Negro struggles against grave injustices, most white churchmen offer pious irrelevancies and sanctimonious trivialities."[103] In this regard, he was disappointed in the performance of both white moderates and white liberals.

Blacks had to depend on themselves and their God to address their oppressive socio-economic condition. Looking back, King recalled that even in his pastorate at Dexter Avenue Baptist Church he took "an active part in current social problems" and strongly urged the involvement of his congregation.[104] At one of the early boycott rallies, King spoke passionately about being told by a detractor that the Christian gospel required only that souls be saved. He told of an experience with a white man who tried to convince him that Christianity and politics do not mix. What King said in response was nothing short of a social gospel manifesto about the Christian requirement to be concerned about the well-being of the whole person.

> This good white citizen I was talking to said that I should devote more time to preaching the gospel and leave other things alone. I told him that it's not enough to stand in the pulpit on Sundays and preach about honesty, to tell the people to be honest and don't think about their economic conditions which might make them dishonest. It's not enough to tell them to be trustful and forget about the social environment which may necessitate their telling untruths. All of these are a minister's job. You see God didn't make us with just souls alone so we could float about in space without care or worry. He made a body to put around a soul. When the body was made in flesh, there became a material connection between man and his environment and this connection means a material well being of the body as well as the spiritual well being of the soul is to be sought. And it is my job as a minister to aid in both of these.[105]

King was also influenced by both the preaching and the Christian social activism of William Holmes Borders, pastor of the Wheat Street Baptist Church in Atlanta. Borders was called to Wheat Street Baptist Church in 1937, about three years after Daddy King was named pastor of Ebenezer Baptist Church. Taylor Branch has painted a portrait of the two pastors being rivals for forty years. He maintains that in part the rivalry developed as a result of socioeducational class differences. Although Daddy King was a graduate of Morehouse, he was not theologically trained. Borders, on the other hand, obtained theological degrees from Garrett Theological Seminary in Evanston, Illinois. Another aspect of the alleged rivalry had to do with young Martin's propensity during his junior year of college to make his way to Wheat Street along with two of his friends, Larry Williams and Walter McCall, to observe Borders' pulpit manner and preaching style.[106] The three were eager and determined students in this regard. Branch states that during this period the three could be frequently found in the pews at Wheat Street as many as three Sundays a month, a practice that did not make Daddy King happy.[107] In any event, what is important here is that although King was not impressed enough with Borders' preaching style to want to emulate it,[108] the fact that he heard so many of his sermons suggests that he had good exposure to Borders' social gospelism.

Borders was mentored by Harris Franklin Rall, a personalist and leading proponent of the social gospel.[109] We might say that Rall was to Borders what Davis was to King. And yet it would be going too far to say that Borders first became conscious of the social gospel under Rall. As was true for King, the social gospel was already deeply ingrained in Borders' being and experience by the time he arrived at seminary. Indeed, during one of the many conversational walks he had with his teacher-mentor, Borders explained to Rall the dual function of the black preacher, namely "to preach the gospel and to be his brother's keeper."[110] The concern was not merely the salvation of the souls of black folk, but that of addressing the socioeconomic conditions that threaten to destroy body and soul. Just like Daddy King and A. D. Williams,[111] Borders did not hesitate to speak out against segregation and other forms of human degradation and injustice in Atlanta and throughout the South. When in late 1945 a black man, boy, and two girls were lynched near Monroe, Georgia, Borders led a large contingent of black Baptist ministers to the scene. It happened that there were nearly 5,000 delegates of the National Baptist Convention meeting in Atlanta. Although most of the delegates refused to go, "a caravan of nearly two hundred automobiles, each filled with Negro Baptist ministers, pulled away from Wheat Street Baptist Church on a warm September morning."[112] When the caravan arrived in Monroe, Borders, clearly influenced by the prophetic tradition of the church, told the sheriff and white onlookers:

> These ministers have come to see this Georgia town where four innocent people were lynched. They've come to see the house where the man lives who double-crossed the victims. They would like to see the double-crosser himself, if he has the nerve. They are going to visit that lonely spot on the back road where the mob lynched these poor souls. They are going to visit the graves of the victims. And they want to see the sheriff who has failed the victims and their families and the promises of justice for all which is the heritage of this country.
>
> They are here to protest what happened here. They want the people of Monroe to know that they, as Christians, think the crimes committed here will be judged before both God and man. They want the people of this great country to know that the Negro ministers of America protest the absolute breakdown of law and order as represented here by the failure of justice in Monroe, Georgia.[113]

This was in the deep South in the mid-1940s. It was a time when blacks were tortured and lynched for having done much less than directing such prophetic and plainspoken speech to white men. King was college age by this time and would surely have known about this incident, as well as about Borders' efforts to desegregate the city buses in Atlanta. It was how Borders understood the Christian faith and ministry. "The pastor's first obligation is to God. His next obligation is to the community and the people where he serves."[114] Borders was always involved in civic affairs, declaring that *one simply cannot be Christian and not be political.* The preacher who leads the people "should help demonstrate how the Negro has been wronged; and the preacher should be in the forefront to demonstrate how his people are ready and willing to shoulder additional responsibilities."[115]

We need to remember that King also had regular exposure to social gospel preaching while a student at Morehouse. Coretta King verifies this when she maintains that Benjamin Mays's tendency to preach "a great deal about social justice" in chapel services at Morehouse influenced King. She maintains further that, "You might say he [Mays] preached a social gospel. This conformed exactly with Martin's ideas, and it helped to form them."[116] There is no question that George Kelsey challenged King on the relevance of the Christian faith for social problems of the day. Exhibiting the influence of neo-orthodox theology as well, Kelsey also taught "that the Kingdom of God could 'never be realized fully within history' because the sinful nature of man 'distorts and imposes confusion even on his highest ideas.'"[117] The influence of Daddy King, A. D. Williams, Borders, Mays, and Kelsey prepared the young Martin for what would be an easy reception of the formal writings of Rauschenbusch and the white social gospel tradition.

It was through reading and study of Rauschenbusch during his first year at Crozer that King discovered the formal theological basis for his still developing social conscience.[118] Rauschenbusch made a lasting impression on him, but King did not agree with all that he had written. For example, he believed that Rauschenbusch and many social gospelers had fallen victim to the nineteenth-century doctrine of "inevitable progress." King believed in the principle of cooperative endeavor between persons and God. In a related sense, and unlike white social gospelers, he believed in the moral autonomy and self-determination of individuals. King rejected the idea of "inevitable progress" in favor of the view that progress in the social order comes only when persons intentionally and actively work together and with God to bring it about. King was convinced that the God of his faith was always active and working in the world to achieve the divine purpose with respect to humanity and the world. The question that has always to be addressed is whether people, individually and collectively, will cooperate with God to this end.

Neither God, nor persons alone, can solve the problem of social evil. People can choose (or not) to work toward the elimination of social problems, and then make the choice to establish and maintain the beloved community. In addition, King did not believe that social advancement or progress would automatically occur as a result of education or individual advancement. One must intentionally apply the fruits of these attainments to the social progress of the broader community and the establishment of the beloved community.

Since many of the social gospelers were exponents of liberal theology,[119] many had a too optimistic and sentimental view of human nature and destiny, and they paid little attention to the dynamic of sin in its individual and corporate forms. We have seen that in *A Theology for the Social Gospel*, however, Rauschenbusch took sin in its individual and corporate forms quite seriously. If King was exposed to this text, we find no reference to it in his writings and speeches, notwithstanding the claim of Kenneth Smith that King revealed to him during his student days that Rauschenbusch was one of his favorite thinkers and that he was familiar with all his major writings.[120] King criticized Rauschenbusch for coming perilously close to identifying the Kingdom of God with a specific social movement or system in the United States, (i.e., socialism).[121] However, we need to pause here and ask whether this is a valid criticism. For had King read and pondered *all* of Rauschenbusch's major works, we must wonder why he did not seem aware of Rauschenbusch's claim in 1916 that the kingdom idea is not to be identified with any particular social movement or ideology.[122] In addition, King essentially agreed with criticisms that early social gospel historians made of the social gospel movement, and therefore took them as his own.[123]

There is no question that King found in Rauschenbusch some of the answers he so desperately sought about Christianity's relevance to social justice issues and the obligation of Christians to be intentional about applying basic principles of Christianity to social maladies that undermine the humanity and dignity of persons. In other words, in Rauschenbusch, King found the *formal* theological rationale he sought for his long held conviction that Christianity is relevant to social problems such as racism. King also found in Rauschenbusch a clear preference for siding with the weak and the poor, a point that was consistent with his upbringing in the black church, his understanding of Hebrew prophecy, and his knowledge of the life and teachings of Jesus. Like Daddy King, A. D. Williams, and William Holmes Borders, Rauschenbusch emphasized the need to act in behalf of the kingdom, a point that seems to undercut the criticism that he believed in inevitable progress. Standing with the least, taking seriously the Hebrew prophets, the ethical principles of Jesus, and the need to engage in action to achieve the kingdom ideal, were important points for King's leadership in the civil and human rights movements, and served as theological grounding for his own involvement.

King was also influenced by Rauschenbusch's doctrine of the centrality of the Kingdom of God in Jesus' teachings, and thus in the social gospel itself. Rauschenbusch even maintained that the doctrine of the Kingdom of God is the social gospel.[124] Accordingly, the kingdom is a social rather than an individualistic ideal—despite the fact that Rauschenbusch himself sometimes implied that at bottom the kingdom ideal was individualistic. In this regard, Dores Sharpe quotes him as saying: "Remember the Kingdom of God can never come perfectly in the world until it comes perfectly in your own life."[125] On the surface, this implies an individualistic emphasis, and much of the evidence suggests that for Rauschenbusch, Jesus frequently addressed individuals and worked through them. However, and this is a critical point, Rauschenbusch was adamant that Jesus' "real end was not individualistic, but social." That is, Jesus aimed more at the creation of the new society, rather than the new individual. The kingdom was "not a matter of getting individuals into heaven, but of transforming the life on earth into the harmony of heaven."[126] It was based on the hope of the radical transformation of the world into the likeness of heaven, a place where reverence for persons as such is of paramount significance and where love, justice, equality, and righteousness will reign supreme.[127] Rauschenbusch argued that since persons are gregarious and social by nature, their morality consists in striving to be good citizens in their communities. It follows, then, that love is the chief imperative of the Christian ethic, "because love is the society-making quality,"[128] the magnetic glue that draws and binds persons together in community.

King must have also been influenced by Rauschenbusch's emphasis on both the dignity of the person and the need for Christianity to be proactive in addressing social evil in the world. Rauschenbusch clearly believed persons to be the highest intrinsic values, and thus expressed appreciation for the Kantian imperative that people ought always to be treated, in their own, and the humanity of others, as ends, and never as a means only.[129] In his commentary on Kant's imperative, Rauschenbusch anticipated some of the views of King concerning that philosopher: "So far as our civilization treats men merely as labor force, fit to produce wealth for the few, it is not yet Christian. Any man who treats his fellows in that way, blunts his higher nature; as Fichte says, whoever treats another as a slave, becomes a slave. We might add, whoever treats him as a child of God, becomes a child of God and learns to know God."[130]

Although he nowhere declared himself a personalist, Rauschenbusch was clearly an exponent of ethical personalism, which stresses the absolute, inviolable dignity of persons as such. He seemed to ground this conviction in his Christology. Jesus, according to Rauschenbusch, went well beyond ordinary conceptions of human worth. What is needed, especially among Christians, he maintained, is an attitude of the highest conceivable estimate of the sacredness of persons.

As to the need for Christians to be proactive in seeking to eradicate social evil, Rauschenbusch did not espouse a method for doing so. Like Reinhold Niebuhr after him,[131] however, he did advise that blacks be nonviolent in their efforts to address racism.[132] King was the better in this regard, inasmuch as he actually sought and produced a method to address social injustice.

King was critical even of black Christians who subscribed to an otherworldly Christianity that did little or nothing to address harsh social ills in this world. He must have beamed with joy when he read about Rauschenbusch's call for a "thorough and far-seeing determination or effort to transform and Christianize the social life of humanity."[133] Rauschenbusch rejected the notion that Christianity will surely affect society, but that it must not intentionally seek to do so, since to implant divine principles into the souls of individuals will somehow radiate outward and lead to the transformation of social practices and institutions. He argued that it would be much more effective if such individuals added "conscious purpose" to the task of transforming the world. Writing in *Christianity and the Social Crisis,* he asked: "Why should the instinctive and unpurposed action of Christian men be more effective than a deeply rooted and intelligent purpose? Since when is a curved and circuitous line the shortest distance between two points? Will the liquor traffic disappear if we say nothing about it? Will the atrocities on the Congo cease if we merely radiate goodness from our regenerate souls?"[134] Rauschenbusch saw clearly the need to address social evils, but he apparently knew not the means. As we know, discovering the best method for addressing the social evils that hounded his people would be one of King's aims in going to seminary.

The Kingdom of God ideal was the organizing principle of Rauschenbusch's theological ethic. He characterized this ideal as an all-controlling "master fact" which, when believed in, prompts in believers a sense of the need for a revaluation of all values: "When the Kingdom becomes a reality to us, we cannot live on in the old way. We must repent, begin over, overhaul the values of life and put them down at their true price, and so readjust our fundamental directions. The conduct of the individual must rise in response to higher conceptions of the meaning and possibilities of the life of humanity."[135] Acceptance of the kingdom ideal effectively causes one's whole life to be radically transformed in the face of things as they presently are in the world. Rauschenbusch's point seemed to be that by truly accepting the kingdom ideal, a person will immediately feel compelled to work toward the establishment of a society and world that reflects its principles. It is not enough to understand the kingdom ideal merely in intellectual terms. One must do, in the world, what it requires:

A collective moral ideal is a necessity for the individual and the race. Every man must have a conscious determination to help in his own place to work out a righteous social order for and with God. The race must increasingly turn its own evolution into a conscious process. It owes that duty to itself and to God who seeks an habitation in it. It must seek to realize its divine destiny. "Thy kingdom come! Thy will be done on earth as it is done in heaven!" This is the conscious evolutionary program of Jesus. It combines religion, social science, and ethical action in a perfect synthesis.[136]

Not only are individuals obligated to intentionally contribute toward the actualization of the Kingdom of God on earth, but so too is this the obligation of religious establishments. "In our own country, if the Church directed its full available force against any social wrong," Rauschenbusch proclaimed, "there is probably nothing that could stand up against it."[137]

Rauschenbusch saw the Kingdom of God on earth as a real possibility. Stressing the self-determinative capacity of persons and their ability to effect the realization of the kingdom on earth, Rauschenbusch said: "We are standing at the turning of the ways. We are actors in a great historical drama. It rests upon us to decide if a new era is to dawn in the transformation of the world into the kingdom of God, or if Western civilization is to descend to the graveyard of dead civilizations and God will have to try once more."[138]

For King, Rauschenbusch's work, especially *Christianity and the Social Crisis,* only enhanced what he witnessed as a product of the black church and as the son and grandson of southern Baptist preachers. Persons have to *work* for the attainment of the kingdom, or what King preferred to call the beloved community. King knew the potential of the church as a prophetic force for change in the world. Reflecting on the early days of the Birmingham campaign and the resistance of black pastors to get involved, King was adamant that the minister—especially the black minister—cannot preach about the glories of heaven, while ignoring the hellish conditions of people on earth. Like his father and maternal grandfather, King reminded the ministers that they possessed a level of "freedom and independence to provide strong, firm leadership,"[139] something many of their people did not.

RAUSCHENBUSCH AND *CHRISTIANITY AND THE SOCIAL CRISIS*

Rauschenbusch, "the seventh in an unbroken line of ministers,"[140] began his career as a pastor in an abjectly poor section on the edge of Manhattan known as "Hell's Kitchen." Sherwood Eddy said that Rauschenbusch was aroused from his more individualistic and conservative tendencies by reading Henry George, Edward Bellamy,

Leo Tolstoi, Karl Marx, Sidney Webb, and the English Fabians.[141] In addition, so horrendous was the condition of the working people in Hell's Kitchen that he was compelled to begin reformulating his understanding of the Christian faith. It was there that he began understanding the connection between the faith and social problems, for by his own admission his social consciousness before this time was underdeveloped. In addition, at the beginning of his ministry he found early that his previous individualistic way of thinking about the faith made no sense in Hell's Kitchen. Although he was advised by friends to attend to the real "Christian" work and not concern himself with "social" work, he decided to return to a critical reading and study of the Bible to determine whether he or his critics were right about the matter. In 1913, Rauschenbusch looked back on his experience as pastor in Hell's Kitchen and said: "I had to revise my whole study of the Bible. . . . All my scientific studying of the Bible was undertaken to find a basis for the Christian teaching of a social gospel. I kept on that way for eleven years in New York. I lived among the common people all the time. . . ."[142] This approach anticipates aspects of the one taken by King himself and by Latin American liberation theologians in the late 1960s. It should be remembered that King moved to the impoverished Lawndale section in Chicago in 1965 to be with those in the ghetto. This ghetto was filled with exorbitantly high-priced housing in the worst dilapidated condition.[143]

By the time his tenure as pastor in Hell's Kitchen ended, Rauschenbusch had begun placing the Kingdom of God ideal at the center of his theology. Remember, he had written a draft of *The Righteousness of the Kingdom* during his pastorate, although he did not submit it for publication. He had initially thought it "a dangerous book" and yet "a religious book." The book was never actually completed, for each time he returned to work on it he found that he "had out-grown" it.[144] The realization of the Kingdom of God on earth was for Rauschenbusch the equivalent of the Christian transformation of the whole of society.

With the publication of *Christianity and the Social Crisis* in 1907, Rauschenbusch was unexpectedly catapulted into the leadership of the social gospel movement, and he became known as "its greatest theologian."[145] When he sent the manuscript to several large publishers, he was surprised to find that all were interested. On reflection, Rauschenbusch said: "I expected there would be a good deal of anger and resentment [apparently among faculty colleagues at Colgate Rochester Seminary where he taught, as well as among more conservative pastors and laypersons]. I left for a year's study in Germany right after it appeared and I heard only the echoes of its reception. I eagerly watched the first newspaper comments on it and, to my great astonishment, everybody was kind to it. Only a few 'damned' it."[146] Upon his return to the United States, Rauschenbusch found that the book's reception had made him a celebrity.

For the first time in his career, he was a hotly pursued lecturer. Before the book appeared, the evidence suggested that people did not want to hear his message about the relevance of Christianity to the social crisis.[147]

Christianity and the Social Crisis was truly a book whose time had come, and whose basic ideas had been tracked down by the spirit of the times. Dores Sharpe wrote of the events and changes in American society that paved the way for the fantastic reception the book received:

> Seldom has a great book ever appeared at so precisely the right moment. Like a confluence of rivers, separate streams of historical development converged. The author himself was just arriving at the high point of his intellectual maturity and the fullest command of his powers. In the religious world the results of the "historical method," as applied to the Scripture and the development of Christian theology and the Christian Church, had become generally known and accepted by Christian thinkers. In American economic life, the changes caused by the closing of the frontier, by the rapid industrial expansion after the Civil War, and by the unexampled agglomeration of human beings in great cities, were beginning to be manifest even to the unthinking. A cyclic business depression was taking place, and there was widespread suffering and exceptional unemployment. The so-called "muck-raking" revelations of Lincoln Steffens, Ida Tarbell and others, had awakened the public mind to the fact that all was not well either in business or in politics. Yet the churches were numerous and influential and many of their people very earnest: religion was a dominant force. The public mind was patriotic and hopeful, even if shocked. Labor restlessness was evident, and socialism, though regarded as a radical and alien doctrine imported from Europe, was growing rapidly among the working classes. The great coal strike of 1905 was still in people's minds.[148]

Like the eighth-century prophets, Rauschenbusch focused on the affairs of this world, not the afterlife, and on the ethical demands of the faith, not ritualism, creedalism, or ceremonialism. Notwithstanding his early failure to address the race problem, Rauschenbusch was concerned to express the relevance of the Christian faith to the major social issues of his day, proclaiming that the gospel was concerned about justice here and now, not in the hereafter. There was nothing otherworldly in his ethics of the Kingdom of God. Furthermore, he was convinced that the chief duty of the religious ethicist was "to stand for the rights of the helpless,"[149] a point that surely got King's attention when he read *Christianity and the Social Crisis*. Rauschenbusch was convinced—much like A. D. Williams, Daddy King, and both Afrikan and Afrikan American religious traditions—that the entire world belonged to God, and therefore "all the affairs of the nation were the affairs of religion."[150] He argued that although throughout its history Christianity had an impact on social issues, it was often not a result of intentionality and conviction on the part of the larger Church. Instead, it frequently occurred only as a result of a small minority of protest voices within its ranks. Rauschenbusch illustrated this in an instructive passage:

> For instance, the position of woman has doubtless been elevated through the influence of Christianity, but by its indirect and diffused influences rather than by any direct championship of the organized Church. It is probably fair to say that most of the great Churches through their teaching and organization have exerted a conservative and retarding influence on the rise of woman to equality with man. . . . It is this diffused spirit of Christianity rather than the conscious purpose of organized Christianity which has been the chief moral force in social changes. It has often taken its finest form in heretics and free-thinkers, and in non-Christian movements. The Church has often been indifferent or hostile to the effects which it had itself produced. The mother has refused to acknowledge her own children. It is only when social movements have receded into past history so that they can be viewed in the larger perspective and without the irritation created by all contemporary disturbance of established conditions, that the Church with pride turns around to claim that it was she who abolished slavery, aroused the people to liberty, and emancipated woman.[151]

In *Christianity and the Social Crisis* and elsewhere, Rauschenbusch's perspective on Christianity was much more direct about such matters. He was convinced that no one who claimed to be a Christian could be taken seriously if he or she was at peace with the status quo, a conviction that would also stand at the core of King's social activism. Rauschenbusch said: "If a man wants to be a Christian he must stand over against things as they are and condemn them in the name of that higher conception of life which Jesus revealed. If a man is satisfied with things as they are, he belongs to the other side."[152] Influenced as he was by the Hebrew prophets and by Jesus' practice of rubbing shoulders with those forced to the boundaries of society, it is understandable why Rauschenbusch came to this conclusion. The very logic of Hebrew prophecy and the ethical teachings of Jesus is such that faithful proponents are *compelled* to stand against injustice and oppression, for the One they serve requires it. King would come to a similar conclusion prior to entering seminary. Through his reading and study of Rauschenbusch, however, he discovered the formal theological foundation he sought.

Rauschenbusch called for a bold, proactive Christian faith in light of most existing major social problems in the United States. In addition, he was critical of earlier ascetic tendencies in Christianity. "Ascetic Christianity called the world evil and left it," he said. "Humanity is waiting for a revolutionary Christianity which will call the world evil and change it."[153] Rauschenbusch did not by any means call for the violent overthrow of existing institutions in this country. Rather, he called for both a radical critique and transformation of the nation and the world. Under no circumstances, however, were Christians to merely criticize the world and then seek ways of removing themselves from it. They were to point out the evils and then take steps to eradicate them. For this reason King was determined to find a method that would effectively address and eventually eradicate such sins against God and humanity. As noted previously, King held that progress in the social order is guaranteed only through the intentional and relentless cooperative endeavor between persons and God. We can see from the discussion in this section that Rauschenbusch believed similarly, although he did not, like King, introduce a method to actually eliminate the social evils he decried.

The doctrine of the Kingdom of God, or the idea of a radically transformed and regenerated society based on this principle and the agapé love ethic—spontaneous, unconditional, redeeming, and redemptive good will for all persons—provided the theological basis for Rauschenbusch's social conscience. He therefore became obsessed with the idea of christianizing the entire social order, and wrote a book by that title.[154] Right or wrong, he argued that all of the basic institutions in the United States had been christianized and were being brought into line with the democratic principle, except the economic order.[155] The concept of christianizing the entire social order is important as we seek to understand King's later thought. As King developed the ethics of the beloved community, he brought together four important principles in a coherent mosaic: The Kingdom of God ideal; aspects of Josiah Royce's thinking on the beloved community (to be addressed in chapter 6); basic elements of the philosophy of personalism; and the principles and values he learned from the black church, his parents and grandparents, about the role of religion in the world.

Rauschenbusch's ideas appealed to King because they were similar to ideas that he carried to seminary. He declared, "Rauschenbusch had done great service for the Christian Church by insisting that the gospel deals with the whole man, not only his soul but his body; not only his spiritual well-being but his material well-being." This message left a deep and lasting impression on King's understanding of religion. Thus he could write: "It has been my conviction ever since reading Rauschenbusch that any religion which professes to be concerned about the souls of men and is not concerned about the social and economic conditions that scar the soul, is a spiritually moribund religion only waiting for the day to be buried. It well has been said: 'A religion that ends with the individual, ends.'"[156]

Because Rauschenbusch took seriously Jesus' attempt to work through individuals toward the social end of the kingdom, it is reasonable to say that the kingdom ideal was for him both personal *and* social. He frequently acknowledged the autonomy and value of the individual person, and as noted above, he also stressed the social character of persons, who, by nature, are communal beings. He emphasized the value and claims of both the individual and the community, just as Jesus did. Remember, Rauschenbusch himself maintained that Jesus essentially worked through the individual person, but his aim was for the social ends of the kingdom.

From Social Gospel to Personalist Influence

The influence of the social gospel movement in the United States began dissipating during and after the era of the Great Depression. Robert T. Handy summarized its declining influence, as well as its major lesson and message. "By the 1940s the social gospel as a distinct, self-conscious movement with a clear sense of direction had largely disappeared. Its major contention, however—that Christian churches must recognize and deal responsibly with social and economic questions—has not been forgotten."[157] In this regard, the social gospel movement has left a lasting impression for ministry and church life in the United States. There is no question as to its influence on Martin Luther King, Jr., although we have seen that he went well beyond the major social gospelers in primarily two ways. From the beginning of his ministry, King explicitly named and sought to eradicate racism in both individuals and structures of American society. By taking this stance, King was clearly rejecting the racism and "benign neglect" that characterized most of the leading personalities in the social gospel movement. Second, King introduced and applied a method (nonviolent resistance) to the leading social evils of his day, inasmuch as his aim was to eradicate such evils.

Having been first introduced in a formal way to Rauschenbusch and the social gospel in seminary in the late 1940s and early 1950s King was clearly not completely satisfied with the end result of his studies in seminary. He therefore sought the counsel of his academic advisor about the possibility of pursuing doctoral studies. Obviously, he was eager to gain further philosophical and theological grounding for what continued to be his two basic convictions: that God is personal and that persons have inestimable and inviolable worth, because they are summoned into existence and loved by God. King's interest in deepening his understanding of personalism and his desire to study it under Edgar S. Brightman, led him to Boston University, which was known as one of the two major centers of personalistic studies in the United States.

CHAPTER 3

King and Personalism

One of the reasons that King was attracted to the personalism of Edgar S. Bright-man from seminary through graduate school was its acknowledgment of the impor-tance of both nonintellectual sources—one's own experiences—and the experiences of one's group. In this regard personalism was much influenced by the Hegelian dic-tum: "The true is the whole." Therefore, family, church, and black cultural contribu-tions are important in any serious study on King as a person of ideas. Unfortunately, King himself did not always place enough emphasis on the nonintellectual sources of his thought when he wrote autobiographical accounts of his life, nor did most early King biographers. As a thoroughgoing personalist who was invested in personalistic methodology, however, King knew that informal and nonintellectual sources and ex-periences were important in the quest for knowledge and truth.

To gain the fullest understanding of King's theological social ethics, which in-cludes his ethics of the beloved community, one will need to understand the philoso-phy of personalism and its significance for him. As influential as personalism was for King as both a conceptual framework and a way of living and relating in God's world, this does not mean that it was a philosophy that was impressed onto a blank, passive, mind. The philosophy of personalism gave much to King (contrary to the claim of some King scholars).[1] However, we will see that King also contributed much to personalism's deeper meaning and significance. For example, he gave personal-ism a texture and concreteness that it lacked during his formal academic study of it. King's relentless efforts to apply the basic principles of personalism to solving de-humanizing social problems was his greatest contribution to that school of thought. For King philosophical study meant nothing if it could not be applied to eradicate the conditions that demeaned the worth of his people. The real questions for him were:

What does the dignity or sacredness of persons mean in the most concrete sense of day-to-day living for those with their backs pressed against the wall (to use a phrase coined by Howard Thurman), that is, those among the disinherited? What does the conviction that God is personal mean concretely for those victimized by racism as well as for those who benefit from it? What will such personalistic convictions look like once they have been applied to the struggle for freedom and justice?

Long before King was formally introduced to philosophical personalism, he was the heir to a homespun personalism that reflected major black religious convictions about a Creator God who is personal and loving, who demands that justice and righteousness be done, and that compassion be exhibited toward the least fortunate. In this conviction is also the idea that each person, regardless of gender and race, is inherently precious to God, and therefore should be treated as such under actual living conditions. These two convictions are traceable to the Bible, as well as to Afrikan traditional thought and among Afrikans during and after American slavery. Consequently, these convictions are rooted deep in King's family history and were espoused by his parents and grandparents in their respective ways. When Daddy King's mother fought the white man who beat him when he was a boy, she did so not merely because he was her son, but also because of her sense of his and her people's inherent worth and sacredness before God. She did so because her son was precious not only to her, but to her God. Daddy King was at that time unable to defend himself, but Delia King understood instinctively, and through her faith, that an assault upon one of her biological children was an assault upon her as well as on God. By the time Martin Luther King, Jr., was first introduced to academic personalism, then, such convictions about God and the dignity of persons were already deeply etched into his being, having been an integral part of his family history and teachings. This made him more than receptive to the thoroughgoing personalism of Brightman, DeWolf, Muelder, and others at Boston University.

In a nutshell, minimal personalism is any philosophy that stresses God as personal and human beings as innately precious because they are summoned into existence, sustained, and loved by God. In *The Negro's God*, Benjamin E. Mays showed that these two ideas are deeply rooted in Afrikan American religious faith and history.[2] Personalism also stresses the moral autonomy and freedom of persons, as well as the fundamental communal nature of persons. I have shown elsewhere that these basic ideas are traceable to Afrikan traditional thought, as well as the religious experience of enslaved Afrikans in the United States.[3]

King was much more than a minimal personalist, however. He went to Boston University to study personalism systematically under its chief proponents and interpreters. He therefore developed into a thoroughgoing or methodological personalist in two senses. First, he consistently adhered to personalistic methodology (criteria for determining the truth) and basic principles of personalism. King also engaged the moral law system developed by Brightman to aid in the process of moral deliberation. Second, more than all of his academic personalist forebears, King applied the principles of personalism in his efforts to achieve a world community of love in which every person will be treated justly, with dignity and respect. Because his personalism was forged in the heat of the struggle against racism, economic exploitation, and militarism, it invariably developed a texture and look that was noticeably different from that of his teachers and the vast majority of others who wrote and lectured on it. In this sense we can say that personalism was not only a conceptual framework for King, but a faith and life that he *lived* in a way and to a degree that others did not. His teachers expounded the basic principles of personalism through course lectures, debates, articles, and books. Most of this was done in the serenity and peacefulness of an academic setting. King knew instinctively that if personalism was all that his teachers said it was, it had to be battle tested, that is, it had to be both lived and implemented in the face of tough social problems. While in graduate school, King wrote many papers and examinations on personalism, for which he earned very good grades. However, he knew that the true test of personalism would come in another arena; that his most important examination on personalism would have to be written with his life's commitment to eradicating the social problems that hounded his people. The most significant test would be in the struggle to defend and enhance the dignity of oppressed people.

Although King himself said that his study of Walter Rauschenbusch and other social gospelers in seminary gave him the sound theological foundation he needed to ground his social conscience, the metaphysics and ethics of personalism helped him to ground it even more effectively. Most of the social gospelers were not systematic philosophical personalists—and probably did not even know the term—but they were at least minimal personalists in the sense that they were consistent advocates of a personal God and the dignity of persons. Because of the affinities between social gospel thought and personalism, whenever King studied either, it was invariably a reinforcement of the other, even when he was not aware of it. In any event, an understanding of the meaning and basic principles of personalism is prerequisite to an understanding of, and appreciation for, King's thought and work that goes beyond mere surface level. Of course, this means that I reject the stance of those King scholars who contend that the significance of personalism in his thought pales in significance in light of his early family and black church influences. Rather, I maintain that his family and his black church upbringing provided a framework that only enhanced his understanding of basic personalistic ideas that were conveyed to him throughout his childhood and adolescent years.

Although personalism has deep roots in Afrikan traditional thought, Oriental, classical Greek, and Roman thought, as well as the idealistic traditions from Plato to Kant and Hegel, there is an important sense in which it is a peculiarly American philosophy. For it was in the United States that personalism of the most systematic and thoroughgoing type was first made into a philosophical method. By the time Borden P. Bowne was called to chair the philosophy department at Boston University in 1876 he had already published *The Philosophy of Herbert Spencer* (1874) and numerous articles, which revealed him to be an original and creative thinker. Although it is true that a systematic study of Bowne's writings reveals the influence of many thinkers, it was he alone who organized and systematized the ideas that influenced him most and seemed to him closest to the truth.

Bowne made personalism "a going concern" in the United States. So thorough and systematic was his mature philosophy that one of his students, Albert C. Knudson, characterized it as *"systematic methodological personalism."*[4] Bowne made *person* the organizing principle of his entire philosophy. "It was he who first took the personalistic conception of reality, grounded it in the Kantian epistemology, developed its implications in a comprehensive way, and made it the center and constitutive principle of a complete metaphysical system," said Knudson. "This principle he formulated in the statement that "the categories of thought do not explain intelligence but are explained by it."[5]

A few years after he was called to Boston University, Bowne was appointed dean of the graduate school. His teaching and heavy administrative responsibilities made it almost impossible for him to spend much time making the rounds to professional philosophical societies. In addition, known to be an extraordinary but demanding teacher, Bowne had a reputation for making scathing criticisms of the work of other philosophers he read. For example, he used the work of Herbert Spencer as a kind of philosophical cadaver in his classes and writing.[6] For these (and perhaps other) reasons, Bowne's own work and contribution to the history of philosophy in much of the West was not always taken as seriously as should have been the case. One of his students argued that he was better known among German philosophers than those in the United States.[7] But in addition, Bowne was a professional philosopher who took God seriously in his writings on metaphysics, epistemology, ethics, etc. He was an avowed theist, which was not the case of most of his philosophical contemporaries. There seemed to be a tendency among many to feel that a philosopher who took God so seriously should not be taken very seriously. Since Bowne was bogged down with administrative responsibilities, he was not able to travel either the country or the world sufficiently to spread the principles of personalism.[8] However, personalism is the oldest extant American philosophy and is in its fifth generation. Martin Luther King, Jr., a fourth generation follower of Bowne's ideas, was enamored with personalism, especially its adamant theism and ethical bent (its emphasis on the inviolable sacredness of persons as such). Moreover, King is unquestionably personalism's most famous disciple. Why then have some King scholars been so energetic and passionate in efforts to downplay or minimize the significance of personalism for King?

Attempts to Undermine the Importance of Personalism

Scholars such as David Garrow and Keith D. Miller erroneously downplay the importance of personalism as a major philosophical influence on King.[9] Peter Paris makes the same mistake when he claims that we cannot easily place King in any particular school of thought: liberal theology, Christian realism, social gospelism, or personalism.[10] From our discussion to this point it is reasonable to say that Paris may be able to make his case regarding a number of schools of thought that influenced King, but he is very hard pressed to do so regarding the influence of personalism, the school of thought that King named as his fundamental philosophical point of departure.[11]

Garrow argues that King frequently used the phrase "the dignity and worth of all human personality" in sermons and speeches primarily because "it was the consonance between King's already-developed views and the principal theme of personalism that led King to adopt and give voice to that tenet so firmly and consistently."[12] In addition, Garrow complains that King's teachers and mentors at Boston University "have badly overstated the formative influence their instruction and personalism had on King."[13] Garrow contends that, "the two greatest religious and intellectual influences on King and the content of his thought were the text and teachings of the Bible, and the black church sermonic tradition. . . . These are both of greater significance in understanding King than the divinity and graduate school texts—whether of evangelical liberalism, of Walter Rauschenbusch's social gospel, or Reinhold Niebuhr's Christian realism, or Boston University personalism."[14] In order to support his claim regarding the personalistic influence, Garrow then invites the reader to examine writings by DeWolf ("Martin Luther King, Jr., as Theologian") and Muelder ("Communitarian Christian Ethics: A Personal Statement and a Response" and "Martin Luther King, Jr.'s Ethics of Nonviolent Action").[15]

Nevertheless, there is no question that King was, by his own admission, both a metaphysical and an ethical personalist. That is, he believed in a personal God who is the source of all things. In addition, he lived by the conviction that every person is sacred, because every person is created and loved by God. Therefore, when his house was bombed during the Montgomery bus boycott he counseled angry black residents not to retaliate but to love their enemies. King was at this time basically reacting on the basis of the influence of the teachings of the Sermon on the Mount and personalism, rather than principles of Gandhian nonviolence (which would come later).[16] But what is important is that even during this early period, King was already living the basic personalistic conviction that persons as such are sacred. He exhibited this in a more dramatic fashion when, at the close of a speech at the SCLC convention in the early part of the Birmingham, Alabama, campaign, he was attacked on the stage. King was hit solidly about the face by a racist white man. According to Taylor Branch, the blow spun him halfway around and caused him to stagger backward. King refused to retaliate. Nor would he allow the crowd to harm the man.[17] By this time, a transformation had taken place in King, and he was intentionally enacting the principles of Gandhian nonviolence. As in the previous instance, however, the doctrine of the sacredness of persons loomed very large indeed. King had a similar experience of being physically attacked in the lobby of a Selma, Alabama, hotel in 1965. Again he did not retaliate.[18] "Every man is somebody because he is a child of God," said King. "Man is a child of God, made in His image, and therefore must be respected as such."[19] For King, persons have infinite dignity and worth precisely because they are created and sustained by God, who is the source of human dignity.

An examination of King's writings indicates that there is no question of the significance of personalism for him and his work. And yet Garrow maintains that because a number of King's speeches and essays were ghostwritten, we should not give much weight to references in his speeches and writings to the key role of personalism. The problem with this stance, however, is that long before King was so popular and busy that he needed others to write out speeches, articles, and chapters of books, he had already spoken and written of the fundamental role of personalism in his intellectual development.[20] In addition, it is significant that King nowhere denounces or rejects personalism or any of its fundamental principles. Instead he persistently articulates those principles even when he does not explicitly name them as personalistic.[21]

Furthermore, one even gets a sense of the importance of personalism for King in papers that he wrote in seminary and graduate school. He grappled long and hard with the meaning and concrete application of basic principles of personalism. In addition, there is no question of the importance of personalism for King in his doctoral dissertation. For example, we find him rejecting the stance of Paul Tillich and Henry Nelson Wieman that God is "supra-personal." By "supra-personal" critics of personalism frequently mean to convey the idea that characterizing God as personal is too human or anthropomorphic, and thus too inadequate for describing the source of all life. Critics like to say, against theistic personalism, that God is *more* than personal. However, King maintained with chief proponents of personalism that one may characterize God in one of two ways: as *impersonal* or *personal*. In this regard he wrote: "The 'supra-personal' is a term without any concrete content; it is at best a label for the unknown, and not a definable hypothesis. If we are, therefore, to think of God, it must be either under the personal or some impersonal term. There is no third alternative."[22]

In addition, King argued, against Wieman and Tillich, that the term "personality" as applied to God is theomorphic, not anthropomorphic. That is, it is in God that we get our best idea of the essence of person, not in human beings. When applied to God, the category of person is not necessarily the limiting factor implied in the work of Tillich and Wieman, King argued. To be sure, created persons give us our best empirical clues to the meaning of person. However, King adhered to Bowne's view that the true essence of person is to be found only in God or the Absolute. "The idea of personality is so consistent with the notion of the Absolute that we must say with Bowne 'that complete and perfect personality can be found only in the Infinite and Absolute Being, as only in him can we find that complete and perfect selfhood and self-expression which is necessary to the fullness of personality.' The conception of God as personal, therefore, does not imply limitation of any kind."[23]

The claim that complete and perfect personality inheres only in God was the view of Bowne's teacher, Hermann Lotze, who maintained: "Perfect Personality is in God only, to all finite minds there is allotted but a pale copy thereof; the finiteness of the finite is not a producing condition of this Personality but a limit and a hindrance of its development."[24] In his second book, *Studies in Theism* (1879), Bowne wrote that, "we must say with Lotze that full personality is possible only to the infinite. It alone is in full possession and knowledge of itself. . . . Full personality exists only where the nature is transparent to itself, and where all the powers are under absolute control. Such personality is not ours; it can belong only to the infinite, while ours is but its faint and imperfect image."[25] God is perfect consciousness, selfhood, will, and wisdom. These traits as such are not limiting factors.

Following Bowne, King held that essential person is not commensurate with corporeality. Rather, in its most basic sense, to be a person "means simply self-consciousness and self-direction."[26] This classic stance of philosophical idealism may be traced back to Plato and through Descartes, Kant, Hegel, Lotze, Bowne, and third-generation personalists. Classical and neoclassical idealism knew not what to do with the body, and thus the tendency was to think of it as a prisoner of the spirit. In Brightman, we begin to see signs of taking the body more seriously in metaphysics, but it would be his students (Bertocci, DeWolf, Muelder, and John Lavely) who would give even more attention to the matter. Early personalists, following too closely the idealist influence, had argued that essential person has nothing to do with the body as such. In God, qualities such as self-consciousness, intellect, and will reach a perfection that far surpasses that of human persons, who are but faint images of essential personhood.

Early personalism was so thoroughly influenced by Platonic, Cartesian, Kantian, and Hegelian idealism regarding the mind-body relation and their emphasis on the mental, that little attention was given the significance of the body. Never a problem in personalistic ethics, it is nevertheless true that to this day personalism has not fully escaped this difficulty of the mind-body relation on the metaphysical level. It remains the quintessential Achilles heel in personalism. Indeed, even King uncritically accepted this metaphysical stance as his own. For example, in *The Measure of a Man* King said: "You look at me and you think you see Martin Luther King. You don't see Martin Luther King; you see my body, but, you must understand, my body can't think, my body can't reason. You don't see the me that makes me me. You can never see my personality."[27] The body is not one's real self. This was the classical idealistic view, which King found in his study of Bowne, and uncritically adopted.[28] So deeply influenced by personalism was King, that he also uncritically adopted some of its metaphysical limitations (the subordination of the body to the mind). And yet we know that from a religious and ethical standpoint King understood perfectly that the body is sacred and warrants respect and care. The purpose of his ministry was not the care of souls detached from bodies, after all, but of enfleshed or embodied souls. In a 1966 sermon preached on a Chicago radio station King declared: "The body is both sacred and significant in Christian thought. Christians then have legitimate interest in man's physical and material well-being. When Jesus said that man cannot live by bread alone he did not imply that man can live without bread."[29] From the standpoint of metaphysics, critics ask a legitimate question, as my colleague Brynolf Lyon asked in the spring of 2000 when he, Edgar Towne, and I discussed my *Personalism: A Critical Introduction* in a community forum: "With so much emphasis on the primacy of mind, intellect, will, and other things spiritual, what does metaphysical personalism do with the body?" The truth is, that until proponents of personalism can get beyond the current heavy emphasis on classical and modern idealism there is little that it can do. And yet there is a movement afoot by personalists such as John Lavely, Tom Buford, and Jack Padgett to resolve this problem.[30]

In any event, strongly influenced by the Bowne-Brightman strand of personalism, King held that God is the chief exemplification of what it means to be person. Not *a* person, but Person: the fundamental cause of all persons—human and non-human. In addition, King quoted approvingly Knudson's statement about Thomas Aquinas's reference to God and essential person. "As Thomas Aquinas says: 'The name *person* is fittingly applied to God; not, however, as it is applied to creatures, but in a more excellent way (*via eminentiae*).'"[31]

The purpose of all this is to show that both during his formal theological and graduate studies, as well as the writing of his dissertation, King was unquestionably and immeasurably influenced by personalism, which does not preclude the measureless influence of his upbringing in the black church and the values instilled in him by his parents and maternal grandmother. In addition, there is no evidence in any-

thing that King said or wrote after graduate school that lends itself to a sense of di-
minished influence of personalism on his life, thought, and work. The claim of Garrow and others who hold that personalism was not as significant a factor in King's
formal intellectual development is unfounded.

Those scholars, however, are most assuredly right in their efforts to direct much
more attention to the early familial, black church, and cultural influences on King's
intellectual development. Garrow was right to criticize early King scholars' failure to
name and examine the familial and black church influences on King's intellectual development. Intellectually or otherwise, no person develops in a vacuum. King was no
different. He was the recipient of a homespun personalism that was further developed and sharpened through formal study in seminary and graduate school.

No scholar has more cogently and convincingly made the argument that there
is need for closer attention to King's cultural roots than Lewis V. Baldwin in *There Is
a Balm in Gilead* and *To Make the Wounded Whole*. Whether one seeks to understand
King's doctrine of the beloved community, or even his doctrine of God, it is important
to remember and to know something about the social, familial, and church context in
which he grew up and was shaped. In this regard, Baldwin has been the major contributor among King scholars. Insofar as Garrow and others imply that the focus on
nonintellectual contributions (e.g., family and church sources), somehow precludes
the significance of the more formal ones such as the philosophy of personalism, we
should reject that part of their stance.

Since King also studied under both Brightman and DeWolf, there is no question
that he was familiar with all of the basic concepts of personalism. King acknowledged
personalism or personal idealism as his fundamental philosophical point of departure,[32] and he was without peer in applying personalism to the struggle for social
justice. Therefore, it is reasonable to say that he was indeed a personalist in the best
sense. Although John Wesley Edward Bowen (1855–1933) was the first Afrikan American to actually study personalism (then known as objective idealism) under Bowne, I
know of no place in Bowen's writings where he actually professed that personalism
was his fundamental philosophical standpoint, though he expressed a number of its
basic ideas in his writing.[33] We have seen that Martin Luther King, Jr., did in fact make
such a declaration. We need now to consider more explicitly family and church contributions to the emergence of personalisic ideas in King's thought and practice.

The Family and Black Church Influences

King's family background and his upbringing in the Ebenezer Baptist Church
in Atlanta were neglected as influences by most of the pre-1980 King scholars who

sought to uncover the roots of his formal theological and philosophical development. Most of these scholars focused almost exclusively on the work of white scholars in the United States and Europe. King himself may have unwittingly contributed to this tendency. In his post–graduate school, intellectual autobiographical statements, for example, he failed to comment on the role that family and church upbringing played in his intellectual development. Nor did he clarify the importance of black history and culture.[34] Moreover, often when King named world personalities who exemplified excellence in various fields, such as the arts and science, and philosophy, he generally named only Europeans and European Americans. A good example appears in a July 4, 1965, sermon, preached at Ebenezer Baptist Church, "The American Dream." On the way to defining the phrase "all men are created equal," King points out that this does not mean that every person has equal talent and intellectual ability. To further clarify his point he said: "It doesn't mean that every musician is equal to a Beethoven or Handel, a Verdi or a Mozart. It doesn't mean that every physicist is equal to an Einstein. It does not mean that every literary figure in history is equal to Aeschylus and Euripides, Shakespeare and Chaucer. It does not mean that every philosopher is equal to Plato, Aristotle, Immanuel Kant, and Friedrich Hegel."[35] Considering the audience he was preaching to, it seems reasonable that King would have named primarily Afrikan American "bright stars," or that he would have at least included several among the ones he named.

King seldom mentioned race, slavery, and related issues in papers written in seminary and graduate school. There were, however, exceptions. In a paper written during the second term of George W. Davis's course, Christian Theology for Today, King observed that his sometime leaning toward a neo-orthodox conception of human nature was connected to the "vicious race problem" he encountered growing up in the South.[36] In another paper written for the same course, King tried to show how the concept of the Fatherhood of God gave even to his enslaved foreparents an immediate sense of belonging to the human-divine family. He wrote of how they would secretly gather for religious meetings after a long hot day in the fields where they had been abused verbally and physically. Here they would be comforted by an old, untrained, illiterate, enslaved preacher who had a deep sense of their inherent worth and membership in God's family. Reporting a story familiar to many black preachers,[37] King wrote: "But as they gathered in these meetings they gained a renewed faith as the old unlettered minister would come to his triumphant climax saying: 'You—you are not niggers. You—you are not slaves. You are God's children.' This established for them a true ground of personal dignity."[38] This is important, because it goes to the issue of King's deeply ingrained sense of the preciousness of persons—a basic tenet of personalism—long before he entered seminary.

On at least one occasion, King wrote a paper that focused on the influence of his family and church on his development. "An Autobiography of Religious Development" was written for Davis. King related the ways that his family upbringing contributed to his thinking about God and human beings. Although we should acknowledge the caution that Clayborne Carson raises about "An Autobiography of Religious Development"—namely that, "The dependability of the paper is limited by the fact that King self-consciously fits his life experiences into the framework of then-popular theories of personality and attitudinal development during childhood"[39]—the comments that King made about God as personal and loving and his own sense of self-worth are not contradicted by subsequent writings either in seminary or graduate school. Rather, they are supported and developed by statements during his ministerial career. We learn from the paper, for example, that his parents were loving, caring, and affectionate toward each other and their three children, and that it was to this that he attributed his conviction that God is personal and loving. Love, he concluded, was central in his family and was easily expressed in all relationships.

King's sense of a personal and loving God and his recognition of the need to love and respect self as well as others actually arose and were nurtured in the context of his family and church upbringing. The strong emphasis that his parents placed on family, both immediate and extended, is also important, since we see in this the beginnings of his sense of the importance of community. The community ideal has a central place in personalistic ethics, and it became a crucial part of King's theological ethics and his formulation of the beloved community ideal.

From the same paper on his religious autobiography, we get other glimpses of the rudiments of King's homespun personalism. He wrote, for example, of his admiration for his father as a "great moving factor" in his decision to enter ministry.[40] King admired his father's love, leadership, and determination to provide for his family, as well as his sense of the Christian gospel's commitment to addressing social evils in the world. He wrote of his admiration for the spirit of social protest exhibited in his father's ministry, as well as in his maternal grandfather's. This was social gospelism at its best. King was proud to write of his father's long interest in fighting for the freedom and rights of his people. "He has been president of the NAACP in Atlanta, and he always stood out in social reform. From before I was born, he had refused to ride the city buses after witnessing a brutal attack on a load of Negro passengers. He led the fight in Atlanta to equalize teachers' salaries and was instrumental in the elimination of Jim Crow elevators in the courthouse."[41] King acknowledged that his father's sense of outrage and social protest against injustices against blacks did much to shape his own conscience about such matters.[42] From this, we can see that whatever philosophical framework King adopted, he would have added the all-important element of social activism. As it turned out, his was social activist personalism at its best, and it is in this sense that we may characterize him as the most distinctive disciple of Boston personalism.

In both the paper on the foundations of his religious development and his later autobiographical statements, then, we get a sense of the four fundamental themes of King's personalism: God as personal and loving; the inherent dignity of persons as such; the importance of the personal-communal spirit; and the need to protest injustice and social evil in order to create the conditions for the establishment of a community consistent with the ideals of the Kingdom of God or what King referred to early in his civil rights ministry as the beloved community. It is important to remember that the rudiments of these four personalistic themes take deep root in King's early life, and that we see the influence of each in almost all that he preached and wrote, from Montgomery to Memphis. King tested these elements of personalism in the struggle for civil and human rights, and by doing so he enriched them and gave them a more concrete texture than the personalism he read about and was taught by his personalist teachers. In a word, King made personalism live, because *he* lived it. He was witness to the idea that philosophy or theology as such means little in the face of human oppression and degradation in the world, especially if they are concerned merely with the abstract and not with the realities of human existence. Indeed, what Jean-Paul Sartre said about what it means to be an existentialist is applicable to what King believed about being a personalist—especially a Christian personalist. "Existentialism must be lived to be really sincere. To live as an existentialist means to be ready to pay for this view and not merely to lay it down in books."[43] This is precisely the way King thought about personalism. It was the way life was to be lived, which meant that he had always to be relentlessly committed to making the effort to live this way, even when he experienced momentary failures. In other words, he must be faithful in the attempt to live the personalistic faith.

All in all, King's was a positive, uplifting childhood, the type that is conducive to development of a healthy sense of self, as well as reverence for others.[44] The fact that his parents loved and cared for him enough to explain both why the parents of his best childhood friend would no longer allow the two to play together, and why he must not hate white people, left an indelible impression on him. When King's mother placed him on her lap, gave him a brief history of race relations in the United States, and told him that he was as good as anybody, it was an important occasion for an Afrikan American mother to affirm her son's humanity and dignity. By reminding him that the Christian ethic did not permit the hatred of whites, regardless of their racist behavior toward blacks, Alberta King was giving her son instruction on the need to acknowledge the fundamental sacredness of all persons, regardless of their race or behavior. King acknowledged that it was his mother who instilled in him and his siblings a sense of self-respect and "somebodiness." She impressed on him the words that numerous black mothers in those days uttered to their children: "You are as good as anyone."[45] This message was reinforced by Daddy King.

Daddy King modeled for his son the importance of acknowledging one's own humanity and sense of worth. For example, when he took young Martin to buy new shoes, the salesman refused to wait on them because they did not seat themselves in the racially prescribed section of the store. Daddy King angrily said that either the man will wait on them where they were seated or they would buy no shoes. He was in touch with his own humanity and was essentially demanding that the white salesman behave in a way consistent with the idea of the inherent worth of self and of others. Young Martin didn't know it at the time, but he was witnessing personalism in action. One who recognizes that as a person he is an end in himself and is sacred by virtue of being imbued with God's image is morally obligated to defend and enhance his dignity. King witnessed this attitude in his father, who refused to passively receive words and treatment that were intended to undermine his humanity and dignity.

King's father exhibited no fear for his own life in such instances, even though it was a time when blacks, regardless of socioeconomic status, were expected to defer to whites and "to remember their place." It was not their place to express indignation toward whites or to behave like full-fledged persons in their presence. In neither speech nor behavior were blacks to imply that they commanded the respect of whites. Nonetheless, Daddy King effectively modeled for his son just what it meant to be a person, even in the face of racist and discriminatory behavior. On one occasion when he and little Martin were out for a drive, Daddy King failed to stop at a stop sign. A policeman pulled alongside his car and said:

"All right, boy, pull over and let me see your license."
My father replied indignantly, "I am no boy." Then, pointing to me, "This is a boy. I'm a man, and until you call me one, I will not listen to you."
The policeman was so shocked that he wrote the ticket up nervously, and left the scene as quickly as possible.[46]

The witness of his parents left King with a profound sense that he was somebody, precious in the eyes of God, and thus he should not only respect self and others, but should be respected by others as well.

Lewis Baldwin writes of Daddy King's contribution to Martin's growing sense of self and dignity. "Declaring on one occasion that 'I have never believed that anybody was better than I,' Daddy King's entire life of service to his family, church, and community was developed around this concept of respect for personality. He never wanted Martin, Christine, and A. D. to work for white people, fearing that such exposure would inevitably damage their young personalities."[47] Alberta King was more subdued, while Daddy King, because of his personality and his public leadership, was much more vocal and passionate. But each of them were excellent role models for their children in terms of what it meant to be a human being and the expectation that they be respected. The result for Martin was the development of a strong sense of his own dignity, and the sense of the need to respect others.

The growing sense of his own humanity and dignity was put to the test a number of times during his teenage years. One of these occurred during his return trip from Simsbury, Connecticut, the summer before beginning college. He had gone there to work on a tobacco farm to earn money for school. While there he was awed by the fact of being able to eat in one of Hartford's finest restaurants. The return trip to the South meant having once again to deal with segregation. King recalled the experience and what it did to his sense of humanity and dignity. "It was hard to understand why I could ride wherever I pleased on the train from New York to Washington and then had to change to a Jim Crow car at the nation's capital in order to continue the trip to Atlanta. The first time I was seated behind a curtain in a dining car, I felt as if the curtain had been dropped on my selfhood. I could never adjust to the separate waiting room, separate eating places, separate rest rooms, partly because the separate was always unequal, and partly because the very idea of separation did something to my sense of dignity and self-respect."[48]

The strong sense of self and of his own sacredness that was instilled in him by his parents, maternal grandmother, and the teachings of Ebenezer Baptist Church made it impossible—even at age fifteen—for King to accept the injustice of racial segregation. He refused to passively adjust to dehumanizing treatment. This point of view was only reinforced during his student days at Morehouse College. What Mays wrote in *The Negro's God* in 1938 was surely expressed in his many Tuesday morning chapel sermons and talks with his students. Mays recalled that King listened intently during these talks.[49] Indeed, in later years King characterized Mays as "one of the great influences in my life."[50] Blacks' belief that they were imbued with God's image and that they derive from the same source as other races make it easier for them to accept themselves as "somebody." Mays expressed this basic personalistic idea as follows: "It is common knowledge that the idea has been and is constantly used by Negro parents, teachers, and preachers in their effort to teach Negro boys and girls that they are as good as members of other races. The phrase 'you are as good as he is, God made you all alike' is commonly heard in Negro circles, especially where the color line is tightly drawn and where Negro children are called derogatory names by members of the dominant group."[51]

Baldwin adds an instructive comment about the role of King's parents in this regard. He said that King "knew who he was and what he was because of his parents. The King family's emphasis on self-worth, pride, and dignity provided a foundation for the abiding faith, optimism, and self-confidence that young Martin would later display in his efforts to transform and redeem human society."[52] In seminary and graduate school, he would be introduced to the formal theological and philosophical foundations for the values and convictions that he had literally grown up with.

King linked his later, mature views about God and the nature of the universe to his family upbringing. In the aforementioned religious autobiography written during the first year of seminary, he said: "It is quite easy for me to think of the universe as basically friendly mainly because of my uplifting hereditary and environmental circumstances. It is quite easy for me to lean more toward optimism than pessimism about human nature mainly because of my childhood experiences."[53] The idea that the universe is fundamentally friendly to persons and value is also a basic personalistic principle that is traceable to King's family upbriging.

Even though the Kings did not know the term personalism, they knew instinctively that every person is sacred because each is a child of God and a bearer of the divine image. Such beliefs were supported by the Bible, which the King family took very seriously. In addition, King's parents knew that every person is created in freedom, for freedom, and that the universe itself is created in such a way that there are certain moral laws (e.g., the law of love) that ought to be obeyed, and that when they are not, there is serious trouble in the land. They also knew that God is personal and loving. These ideas were instilled in King and his siblings when they were children. King took these deep-rooted convictions to seminary and graduate school, a point that Coretta Scott King makes in *My Life with Martin Luther King, Jr.*[54] The importance of black family, religious, and cultural contributions to King's intellectual development should never again be undermined or ignored in King scholarship. If one desires to really get at the roots of his intellectual ideas, it will be crucial to examine both the pre-academic and academic training from Morehouse to Boston University. Only then will one be in position to make sense of why King found some of the formal influences to be so meaningful for his life and work. Whether one begins by examining the formal influences or by considering the more informal ones is not as important in the end as looking at both sets of influences.

BOSTON UNIVERSITY AND PERSONALISM

Having already studied personalism in courses on the philosophy of religion under Davis at Crozer, King was well equipped to continue the study of it when he began doctoral work in systematic theology at Boston University in the fall of 1951. At this time, there were two powerhouses in personalistic studies in the United States:

Boston University and the University of Southern California under the leadership of Ralph Tyler Flewelling (1871–1960).[55] Flewelling earned his doctorate under Bowne and was the founder and long time editor of the *Personalist.* Of the two, Boston University was the stronger center for the systematic study of philosophical and theological personalism. Nevertheless, it is important to remember that there was a strong West Coast center for personalistic studies that also flourished during King's days as a doctoral student at Boston University.[56]

At Boston University, King primarily studied personalism under Brightman and DeWolf. He also studied various subjects in philosophy and theology under other representative personalists, such as Peter A. Bertocci, Jannette E. Newhall, and Richard M. Millard.[57] In addition, although he took no courses under Dean Walter G. Muelder,[58] the personalist social ethicist, they had many private conversations in which Muelder was able to help clarify for King Reinhold Niebuhr's interpretation of pacifism.[59] But it was through the teaching of Brightman and DeWolf that King was able to hone his understanding of personalism, and to see its relevance for addressing and solving social problems. Of a total of twelve courses taken at Boston University, and three at Harvard, King took eight with DeWolf and two with Brightman. He likely would have taken more courses under Brightman had his teacher not died suddenly during King's second year of course work. King wrote passionately of Brightman's influence on his formal intellectual development, and in a sermon preached in 1966 he characterized DeWolf as "one of my beloved professors."[60] DeWolf considered King to be one of the top five or six graduate students he had taught over a period of thirty years.[61]

King also studied Hegel under his personalist teachers, having first been introduced to his work while in seminary. After his first year of courses at Boston University he enrolled in Brightman's year-long seminar on Hegel. The textbooks for the course included Hegel's *Phenomenology of Mind, Philosophy of History,* and *Philosophy of Right.* King was absolutely fascinated by Hegel's argument "that a master could become so dependent upon a slave that a slave could assume the dominant role in the relationship. This was apparently the incident that ignited King's interest in Hegel's dialectical method of thinking."[62] Kenneth Smith and Ira Zepp provide a description of Hegel's method in the search for truth. "According to Hegel, the self ascertains truth through the introduction of opposites (i.e., a thesis and an antithesis) and the combination of them into a synthesis. Every truth is the synthesis of two seemingly contradictory elements. Every affirmation implies a negation; every 'yes' implies a 'no.' Truth is the product of a synthesis of an affirmation and the negation. The historical process is also characterized by the constant emergence of theses, antitheses, and syntheses."[63] According to the Hegelian dialectic, then, the movement is always from thesis to antithesis to synthesis; from abstract to more concrete. The aim is always the same: higher truth. This dynamic process continues, according to Hegel, culminating only in the Absolute.[64]

One sees the influence of Hegel and his method in many of King's writings, sermons, and speeches. For example, in his book of sermons, *Strength to Love* (1963), King explicitly cites the influence of Hegel when he writes that "life at its best is a creative synthesis of opposites in fruitful harmony. The philosopher Hegel said that truth is found neither in the thesis nor the antithesis, but in an emergent synthesis which reconciles the two."[65] King's language is not always this specific, but one sees in many places his use of Hegel's method. In 1966 he preached the sermon, "What Is Man?" on a Chicago radio station. In true Hegelian fashion, he said: "A synthesis between the extremes of pessimistic materialism and optimistic humanism represents a more realistic idea of the nature of man. Man is neither villain nor hero. He is a bit of both. The realist agrees with Carlisle that there are depths in man which go down to the lowest hell and heights which reach the highest heaven, for are not both heaven and hell made out of him, everlasting miracle and mystery he is."[66] King used this same method in his doctoral dissertation, where his discussion of Paul Tillich's and Henry Nelson Wieman's doctrines of God culminated in the higher personalistic synthesis of a God who is both immanent and transcendent, personal, and matchlessly powerful. After graduate school, the Hegelian dialectic proved helpful to King on numerous occasions, frequently making it possible for him to be open to the truth of the most radical and the most conservative viewpoints, even as he sought to combine what was usable into a higher synthesis. This approach made it possible for King to manage opposites well. It also made it possible for him to at least tolerate the most vicious racist, as well as the most liberal white person who did not seem aware of her own racism.

When Brightman became severely ill during the first month of the Hegel seminar, his protegée, Peter A. Bertocci, took over. Bertocci was appointed the Borden Parker Bowne Professor of Philosophy upon Brightman's death. He became the premier interpreter of the Bowne-Brightman type of personalism. In an interview with John Ansbro on June 13, 1973, "Professor Peter Bertocci recalled how King in the seminar on Hegel 'almost took over the class' in his enthusiasm for Hegel's insight that the master is dependent on the slave for his consciousness of himself as master. Hegel had perceived that just when the master achieves his lordship, he achieves a dependent consciousness and finds his truth to be 'the universal consciousness.'"[67] King could see that the freedom of master and enslaved was integrally interconnected, and that the person who enslaves another is, on a deeper level, as enslaved as the other. Clearly the two are not enslaved in the same sense existentially, for one is bound physically, psychologically, and emotionally, while the other is not bound physically. For example, white enslavers in the United States were not bound by chains and force. However, because of his fundamental relatedness to the enslaved by virtue of their common Creator, the enslaver could be free only when he set at liberty the ones he enslaved. In fact, King surmised that because the slave master was spiritually enslaved, he was more enslaved than the Afrikans he sought to keep bound in physical chains.[68]

King was also influenced by Hegel's doctrine that progress and growth comes through struggle,[69] an idea that might not have been novel to him by the time he was formally introduced to Hegel's work. King's maternal grandfather also espoused the idea that social progress in the world comes through self-determination and struggle. Williams conveyed this idea to his son-in-law, Daddy King, who was also influenced by it, and modeled its meaning for his children.[70]

PERSONALISM AND KING INFLUENCE EACH OTHER

By now it should be clear that there are a number of personalistic ideas at the center of King's theology and ethics. At least five of these have already been discussed briefly and will subsequently be examined in greater detail: reality is personal; persons are the highest intrinsic values; reality is social; the existence of an objective moral order at the foundation of the universe; and the need to protest social injustice and to work for the establishment of the community of love. Each of these principles plays a key role in King's theological social ethics in general, and in specific aspects of his ethic of the beloved community and his doctrine of nonviolence. That King so easily and readily resonated to personalism as the philosophical framework which helped him to further clarify and ground his most important faith claims is a testimony to the importance of the family and religious values that were instilled in him during his childhood and adolescent years. Each of these principles also has deep roots in Afrikan traditional and Afrikan American history and culture.[71]

King's most original and creative contribution to the personalist tradition was his persistence in translating it into social action by applying it to the trilogy of social problems—racism, poverty/economic exploitation, and militarism[72]—that he believed plagued this country and the world. By focusing on socioethical personalism, King was only following the precedent already set by Afrikan American John Wesley Edward Bowen. More than any other personalist, King worked out the concept of the dignity of the person in the most concrete of terms through his persistent efforts to apply its meaning in the struggle for social justice. Indeed, his most mature idea of human dignity was forged in the heat of struggle during the momentous period of the civil and human rights movements of the late 1950s and 1960s. This is why he could write in the late 1960s not merely of the need for blacks to strive to regain their sense of dignity, but that they struggle long and hard in that direction. Once regained theirs would be nothing less than a "rugged" sense of dignity.[73] They will have gone through the fires of hell to regain their sense of what God imbued them with when they were summoned into the world. King did as much for personalism, as it did for him.

Before considering at length the principle of the dignity of persons, it is important to examine King's doctrine of God, since he believed God to be the more basic idea, and therefore the source of human dignity and the beloved community. For King, belief in a personal God as the ground of morality and human dignity is fundamental to any adequate theological social ethic. The next chapter is devoted to an examination of his conception of God—from seminary to the end of his ministry.

CHAPTER 4

King's Conception of God

Throughout his seminary and graduate school experiences, King worked relent-lessly to develop a doctrine of God that made sense to him. From his father and other black preachers, he learned that the God of the Hebrew prophets and Jesus worked cooperatively with humans to achieve the divine expectation that justice be done in the world. What King needed was an intellectual conception of God that was consis-tent with this stance. We get a sense of how important this was to him from the many papers he wrote in seminary and graduate school which addressed various aspects of the divine nature and God's relation to human beings and the world. King's doctoral degree was in systematic theology. His struggle to develop a reasonable conception of God culminated in his doctoral dissertation which examined the conceptions of God developed by Paul Tillich and Henry Nelson Wieman.

King wrote his dissertation under L. Harold DeWolf, a third-generation person-alist. My reading of the dissertation suggests that King actually used the thought of Tillich and Wieman as foils to look even more critically at the (more traditional) per-sonalist conception of God to determine whether it might be the more reasonable framework for thinking about God. Essentially, he sided with Bowne's and DeWolf's conceptions of God rather than Tillich's or Wieman's. Bowne's and DeWolf's doc-trine of God was closer to the traditional orthodox view, and consequently to that of King's Afrikan American religious heritage. Although King did not address Afri-kan American ways of thinking about God, there is no question that the doctrine of God learned while growing up in the black church was not forgotten as he wrote the dissertation. Historically the vast majority of Afrikan Americans have adhered to the more orthodox doctrine of the omnipotent-omnibenevolent God. James Cone is adamant that "Black Theology finds itself in company with all of the classic theologies of the Christian tradition."[1] In doing so, he rejects William R. Jones's suggestion that God is a white racist and therefore is not perfectly good, as well as Brightman's theory that God is perfectly good but has limited power. Cone and other black theologians contend that King was sympathetic *only* to this tradition. I agree that King was sympathetic, but am not convinced that subsequent to graduate school he was consistently sympathetic with the classical view of the omnipotent-omnibenevolent God. Nor am I convinced that such consistency existed in seminary and graduate school. We will examine the ideas of Cone and other black liberation theologians relative to King's view of God later in this chapter.

There is no such thing as *the* personalist conception of God, even among those with whom King studied at Boston University. Personalists share a number of basic tenets, including but not limited to: reality is personal, persons have inviolable dignity, to be is to be free, reality is social, and the universe is friendly to value. Beyond agreement on these and a few other fundamental principles personalists diverge along a number of lines. For example, the majority of personalists in the Bowne-Brightman tradition espouse a doctrine of God that is very similar to the orthodox view of the omnipotent-omnibenevolent God.[2] The most significant difference with the more orthodox position is that these personalists, following Bowne, tend to soften the term omnipotence to mean that God is only able to do the *doable*, although they also maintain that apart from human freedom God's power is limited by no factor either within or outside the divine nature. On the other hand, a minority of personalists in this school of thought reject this view, claiming that there is an internal uncreated factor that limits the power of God's will to achieve God's purposes in the world. Brightman developed this strand of personalism and had a number of outstanding disciples, including Peter A. Bertocci and Walter G. Muelder, who taught and mentored King. S. Paul Schilling had a strong affinity for Brightman's doctrine of God as well. Schilling was not as close to King, but he was the second reader and examiner of his dissertation. King, of course, had occasion to examine both Bowne's and Brightman's doctrine of God and ultimately found the latter's to be wanting, although we will see that he actually vacillated on the matter. And yet there is no question that at the conclusion of King's dissertation his own doctrine of God was closer to that of Bowne and DeWolf, and thus the more orthodox view of the black church. The question that this chapter asks and tries to answer, however, is whether this remained the case in King's postdoctoral years, during his leadership in the civil and human rights movements. In other words, just how amenable was the postdoctoral King to Brightman's doctrine of the finite-infinite God?

THE FINITE-INFINITE GOD

During his formal academic training a vacillating Martin Luther King, Jr. came to reject Brightman's doctrine of the finite-infinite God, the theory that God's power is limited not only by the incidence of human freedom, but also by an uncreated, internal factor that Brightman called "the Given."[3] In addition, Brightman maintained that God is infinite in love, compassion, righteousness, and justice. Brightman retained this much of the more orthodox view of God in his own largely unorthodox conception as it developed.

Until the mid-1920s Brightman was a proponent of theistic absolutism. While a student at Brown University, he came under the strong influence of the absolute idealism of Josiah Royce, which he "accepted as a whole for two or three years." When introduced to William James's *Pragmatism* in graduate school, however, he could no longer accept the entirety of Royce's absolutism. Brightman declared that *Pragmatism* "swept" him off his feet. It was through his study of personalism under Bowne, however, that he was able to synthesize the truth in Royce and James.[4]

Brightman's continued reading and reflection began revealing to him signs of a God who was struggling to achieve God's purposes in the world—something that must not be the case with the God of theistic absolutism, since such a God presumably does not have to struggle. In addition, there were some painful empirical occurrences which, coupled with Brightman's reflections, suggested the need to modify his earlier adherence to an infinite, absolute, and omnipotent God. For example, he had witnessed the slow, painful death of his young wife, who succumbed to facial cancer. He witnessed the terrible deeds of a close acquaintance, a very good man, who was stricken with insanity. Another close acquaintance was paralyzed as a result of a freak swimming accident. These and other experiences, in addition to his reading of works on emergent evolution, forced Brightman to rethink his conception of God and evil.

The first evidence that Brightman sensed the need to alter his more traditional conception of God appeared in a 1925 publication.[5] He probably had been mulling over the idea long before this time. Brightman's first systematic exposition of the theory of the finite-infinite God appeared in *The Problem of God* (1930). He explicated the doctrine further in a number of other books: *The Finding of God* (1931), *Personality and Religion* (1934), arguably the best brief exposition of the theory, and *A Philosophy of Religion* (1940).[6] (The reader is also encouraged to read Brightman's presidential address to the eastern division of the American Philosophical Association at Cambridge, December 29, 1936, "An Empirical Approach to God.")[7]

Even in his unorthodox doctrine, Brightman, unlike other theistic finitists such as Plato and Herbert G. Wells, argues that God remains infinite in many ways.

Consequently, Brightman does not speak only of the finite God. Rather, he characterizes God as finite-infinite. God is infinite in love, goodness, and justice, for example.
God's power of will is finite, however, in the sense of being limited by eternal, uncreated, unwilled conditions within the divine nature. "The limiting conditions must be
within God, if we are to avoid an unintelligible dualism; but they must be limits to his
will, not products of it, if his will is good. . . . The evidence points to a finite-infinite
God whose will is in control of the whole range of experience."[8] Brightman maintained that God's will retains such control without being perfectly powerful. It is powerful enough, however, to accomplish what God needs to accomplish in the world,
although God cannot do so alone. Brightman was aware that to many persons the
idea of a finite-infinite God is incompatible with traditional religious faith and the demands of reason, which maintain that all power has its source in God. But this claim is
not incompatible with Brightman's doctrine of the finite-infinite God, for he remained
adamant that this God is the most powerful being in the universe and the fundamental source of all that is good and perfectible. Therefore, to claim that all power has its
source in God is not in itself an argument against the theory of the finite-infinite God,
for this God's power is surpassed by no other entity in the universe. This God, Brightman maintains, "is the source of all being,"[9] who eternally wills and strives toward
nothing but the best possible good. To speak of God as the infinite or absolute, means
only that all being has its origin in God.

In the doctrine of the finite-infinite God we have, finally, the most powerful will
in the universe that eternally strives to achieve the highest good. It confronts obstacles that sometimes lead to disappointments and temporary setbacks, but never
to defeat in any final sense. The will of the finite-infinite God is eternally loyal to reason and righteousness. This God suffers, but always conquers; faces obstacles, but frequently overcomes them in cooperation with created persons. This means that God
and persons are fellow sufferers and overcomers. An extended passage from *The Problem of God* summarizes Brightman's doctrine of the finite-infinite God.

> This conception of God means that we think of him as the one who can
> bring good out of evil. If he is supreme value, he cannot allow any evil that will
> permanently frustrate his purpose. He may delay, but he cannot fail. Whatever
> the origin of evil may be, and however awful it may be, God is the one who is
> never baffled by any evil. It may be that many goods are possible only through
> a co-operation of God's will and man's will, and it may be that man may fail to
> co-operate. Yet, in any given situation, we may suppose, God can achieve cer-
> tain goods through man's co-operation; if man does not co-operate, then differ-
> ent goods will have to be achieved by God in a different way. But no situation is

finally evil. Beyond every obstacle there lies a possible achievement, out of every evil a possible good may grow. This is the meaning of faith in God.

. . . God is not simply a happy, loving Father; he is the struggle and the mysterious path at the heart of life. He is indeed love; but a suffering love that redeems through a Cross. . . . On our view, God is perfect in will, but not in achievement; perfect in power to derive good from all situations, but not in power to determine in detail what those situations will be. *It is not a question of the kind of God we should like to have. It is a question of the kind of God required by the facts.*[10]

As we can see, Brightman did not consider the finite-infinite God to be a weak deity, but one who possesses unsurpassable power (to use Charles Hartshorne's term) and infinite love. He believed his conception of God to be more consistent with the facts of experience than the traditional hypothesis of the omnipotent-omnibenevolent God.

In any event, while in graduate school King wrote numerous papers that compared and contrasted the Bowne-Brightman type of personalism with others, such as the atheistic personalism of John M. E. McTaggart.[11] He also compared it to the systems of other thinkers like the absolute idealism of William Ernest Hocking.[12] This practice culminated in King's dissertation: "A Comparison of the Conceptions of God in the Thinking of Paul Tillich and Henry Nelson Wieman." His comparison of these theologians was essentially done through the lens of personalism, for he cites approvingly Bowne's conception of God a number of times.

DIVINE OMNIPOTENCE: SEMINARY AND GRADUATE SCHOOL

King's most systematic discussion on the doctrine of God appears in his doctoral dissertation. His ministry after graduate school made it impossible for him to return to systematic scholarly writings on God, although nearly everything he wrote and spoke, from Montgomery to Memphis, had something to do with how he understood God. Peter J. Paris is correct in his contention that God is the most pervasive theme in King's writings and speeches.[13] King was seeking a way of thinking about God that was consistent with his growing passion to help his people, which meant getting into the fray. Whatever doctrine of God he came to in the academy would only be precursor to the God who would lead him into and sustain him in the struggle for justice and righteousness in the civil rights movement. The view of God arrived at in his formal studies would have to be battle-tested. Out of this would emerge a conception of God that would make sense to him.

In the dissertation, King examined the theistic finitist view of Wieman's and Tillich's claim that God is *being-itself*. King concluded that both men essentially espoused impersonal views of a God whose power to accomplish the divine will was questionable at best. Against both men, King argued for the conception of a God who was in direct communion and fellowship with created persons. Such a God, he concluded, could only be personal and loving, the type of God one can pray to and expect answers. Furthermore, King rejected Wieman's and Tillich's claim that because "personality" is essentially anthropomorphic and limiting it should not be applied to God. For King, God, by definition, is not limited. Agreeing with Bowne, King argued that "human personality" is limited, but that "personality as such" has nothing at all to do with limitation. Instead, no other term is as consistent with and applicable to "the Absolute" than "personality." King did not clarify his own reasoning for this claim, but we know that from a formal academic standpoint he was so influenced by Bowne's conception of God that his own view differed but little. Bowne made the claim that no term is as applicable to God as personality, for he was describing "personality" as a metaphysical category. Bowne sought what he considered the deeper meaning or essence of personality. In *Theism* (1902), Bowne discussed essential personality, claiming that it must be distinguished from all human limitations.

> The very objections urged against the personality of the Absolute show the incompleteness of human personality. Thus it is said, truly enough, that we are conditioned by something not ourselves. The outer world is an important factor in our mental life. It controls us far more than we do it. But this is a limitation of our personality rather than its source. Our personality would be heightened rather than diminished, if we were self-determinant in this respect. Again, in our inner life we find similar limitations. We cannot always control our ideas. They often seem to be occurrences in us rather than our own doing. The past vanishes beyond recall; and often in the present we are more passive than active. But these, also, are limitations of our personality. We should be much more truly persons if we were absolutely determinant of all our states.[14]

Human persons and all finite being have their source in God, and thus "owe their peculiar nature to their mutual relations and to the plan of the whole."[15] The human person is always dependent on something not itself. Causally the finite person is a dependent being, unlike God. We will see later that God depends on human persons, but not in the causal sense. For now suffice it to say that King was much influenced by Bowne's description of essential person, with all of its idealistic baggage. For from a metaphysical standpoint the view made it difficult to know what to do with the body. Basically Bowne sought to show that the tendency of critics to see personality as a limiting factor when applied to God was due to their mistaken tendency to con-fuse or equate it with corporeality.[16] The essence of the personal, according to Bowne, meant only: selfhood, self-knowledge, and self-direction. These traits "have no impli-cation of corporeality or dependent limitation."[17] King argued that it is in this sense that person as such is not limited, and, therefore, the category of personality is more applicable to God than Tillich and Wieman seemed to know.[18]

According to King, then, person is indeed a large enough category for God. King would have been in fundamental agreement with Personalist Francis J. McConnell's critique of critics on this point. According to McConnell, "If the 'more' means more personality than we can conceive of, who can protest? If it means that there is some other principle greater than self-consciousness and self-direction we do protest that personal life is the highest form of existence conceivable by us. To say 'more' beyond personal existence is to say what to us has no meaning."[19] The most perfect example of person, accordingly, is the Supreme Person, not isolated human persons. There might well be a principle greater than person, but we humans have shown no capability of knowing what it is.

King himself had some very explicit things to say about the power and goodness of God in his dissertation. King scholars maintain that the stance articulated there changed relatively little after graduate school. In what follows, I am less concerned about King's view of divine goodness, for Afrikan Americans have seldom called into question this particular attribute of God, although the philosopher William R. Jones is an important exception.[20] In addition to affirming God's goodness, Afrikan Ameri-cans have generally affirmed the omnipotence of God. Historically, this meant that God possesses *all* power. What was King's view of divine power?

If we trace King's view of divine power from seminary through the mature pe-riod of his ministry, it will not be difficult to understand why I contend that he was, and was not, a proponent of divine omnipotence. That is, at times he talked, wrote, and acted as if he believed God possesses absolute power, while at other times he seemed more comfortable proclaiming the "matchless power of God," which did not at all mean for him that God possesses perfect, absolute power. Nor did it mean that God was in any way a weak God.

Indeed, James Cone may have inadvertently created an opening for making sense of this seeming vacillation, despite his claim that King was in no way a theistic fini-tist. In *Martin & Malcolm & America* (1991), Cone wrote that King essentially had two audiences: one white and one black, and that he adapted his speech for each.[21] King's wife made a similar observation.[22] One might surmise from this that before black church audiences King was more inclined to use more orthodox or traditional lan-guage about God. However, when addressing predominantly white audiences, he was not as apprehensive about using language that sounded more like theistic finitism.

King knew that the predominantly Afrikan American audience could not manage this as well. For their historical experience was such that the more traditional doctrine of the omnipotent-omnibenevolent God gave them more reason to be optimistic in a racist society.

In his last year in seminary, King wrote a paper on Brightman's and William P. Montague's doctrine of theistic finitism. He concluded that theistic finitism was unacceptable. He wrote: "To suggest a finite God as a solution to the problem [of evil] is to fall in the pit of humanizing God."[23] It seemed to King that while both Brightman and Montague escaped cosmic dualism, they both "fall right back into the dualistic trap by setting forth a dualism in the nature of God. But dualism affords no real answer to the problem of evil. With such a view faith in a supreme God is endangered and the triumph of good left uncertain."[24] King concluded that the "ultimate solution" to the problem of evil is not intellectual, but spiritual. For him, "the ultimate solution" is a matter of faith. Once we go as far as reason can take us in the attempt to solve the problem of evil, "we must leap out into the darkness of faith."[25] One takes such a leap, however, not in a spirit of pessimism or fatalism. Rather, one does so with the confidence that he has done his best in utilizing his God-given intellect, knowing that over the course of time more divine truths will be revealed as persons apply reason and remain open-minded to what is being discovered. Not all of the mysteries will be solved, but one presses on in the faith that God does not deliberately hide God's self from created persons.

King first began studying Brightman's doctrine of the finite-infinite God in seminary and continued his study in graduate school. When King began doctoral studies at Boston University he enrolled in Brightman's course on the philosophy of religion. In a major paper for the course King praised Brightman's theory of the finite-infinite God: "There is much that can be said to commend Dr. Brightman's view at this point. It has the advantage of accounting for the evil in the world without involving the character of God. Moreover, it has the advantage of establishing the Christian ideal of sacrificial love on metaphysical grounds."[26] In an earlier essay, written for the same course, King cited what he considered to be limitations or "difficulties" in Brightman's doctrine of God.

> First, Dr. Brightman does not completely escape dualism. It is true that he escapes cosmic dualism, *but only to leave a dualism in the nature of God*. Does not such dualism leave faith in a supreme God endangered and triumph over the non-rational Given uncertain? What evidence is there that God is winning a gradual mastery over the limitations in His nature? Then, too, this theory seems to establish too sharp a dichotomy between God's nature and his will. We use these terms to denote different aspects of the divine life, but at bottom they involve each other.

God's nature gives content to His will and His will gives meaning to His nature. It is the union of the two which constitutes the divine Personality.[27]

At first glance, it appears that King was exhibiting some independence of thought, rather than merely accepting uncritically all that Brightman taught. However, his critique was one that Knudson, Harris Franklin Rall, and other scholars had already made of Brightman's doctrine of the finite-infinite God.[28] King uncritically accepted these criticisms as his own.[29] Brightman's reply to those who offered this criticism was that if one understands that persons—human and divine—are complex, indivisible unities, it should not be difficult to understand why placing the limiting factor within God's nature does not set up an internal dualism. For as perfect Person, God is a perfectly unified being through and through.

Interestingly, in his final examination in Brightman's class on the philosophy of religion King addressed the statement: "Define the 'finite God' as treated in this course." In his concluding paragraph King wrote:

At present I am quite sympathetic with this idea. After a somewhat extensive study of the idea *I am all but convinced that it is the only adaquate [sic] explanation for the existence of evil.* Moreover, it is significant and adequate from a religious point of view because it establishes the Christian idea of sacrificial love on metaphysical grounds. *It is the most empirical explanation that we can set forth in relation to the God idea.* It makes a thorough distinction between good and evil, given an explanation for the existence of both. This theistic absolutetism [sic] fails to do.[30]

How does one account for King's vacillation regarding Brightman's doctrine of the finite-infinite God? While in seminary, King studied Brightman's philosophy of religion under Davis. King undoubtedly felt the freedom to express himself, and he rejected the doctrine. On the other hand, when he finally began graduate studies under Brightman, he commended the doctrine (albeit with qualification). One can imagine the sense of awe that he must have felt to be studying with the chief interpreter of personalism, who, by all accounts was bigger than life. The difficulty of disagreeing with Brightman was compounded by the fact that a major component of personalistic method is that one readily subject to critical reason *all* viewpoints, evidence, and facts. Brightman insisted on this critical method (as did his students, e.g., Bertocci and Muelder, who were my teachers in graduate school in the mid-1970s). No doubt it was easier for King to be critical of Brightman *before* he became his student. More than this, I find it interesting that King agrees with Brightman's theory in a qualified sense in a major paper that he wrote for him, while in the final examination for the same course he wrote of his unqualified agreement with Brightman's concept of the finite-infinite God. What we really need in order to establish King's sympathy with Brightman's concept of God is a statement to this effect *after* the completion of course work done under Brightman. Short of this, we are left with indirect evidence of King's appreciation for a God whose power is sufficient but not perfect in every sense.

King chose to write his dissertation on God because of the central place of God in religion and his own life, as well as the ongoing need for reexamination and reinterpretation of the concept of God. He chose to write on Tillich and Wieman because they were two giants in the academy, and because they represented two different philosophical theologies that were gaining in popularity.[31] King rejected both what he perceived as Wieman's minimization of God's power and Tillich's minimization of God's goodness.[32] Both men, according to King, overemphasized one of these divine attributes to the detriment of the other. King believed that a balance was needed between divine goodness and divine power. "God is not *either* powerful *or* good; he is *both* powerful *and* good," said King. In this regard he quoted Matthew Arnold approvingly. "God is a power, not ourselves, making for righteousness. Not power alone, nor righteousness alone, but a combination of the two constitutes the meaning of God."[33] King liked this idea. It is significant that Arnold's reference was not to the absolute, perfect, or infinite power of God. The reference is to "power alone." Not an absolutely perfect power, but a power not our own that makes for righteousness. The need is for a power that is adequate or sufficient to God's purpose of achieving justice, righteousness, and the beloved community in the world. Because King's was the God of the Hebrew prophets, it may be said that he thought of God as relentlessly compassionate and faithful in every moment. Such a God does not want evil to destroy persons and communities. King's God was defined more by goodness and compassion than by sheer power. What was King really getting at?

Wieman's and Tillich's conceptions of God would have been more acceptable to King had each of them viewed God as both a power not ourselves and one making for goodness. Moreover, each man needed to affirm God as Person—not *a* person. As Person, God is the ground of all things. Tillich's notion of God as the ground of being would not do because it was not a personal being. Not only did the idea of God as the ground of being contradict King's religious heritage and experience, but it did not make sense to him how an impersonal ground of being could be the cause of the personal. This was a basic criticism shared by personalists.

King said that Wieman boasted the goodness of God at the expense of God's power, while Tillich stressed the power of God while minimizing God's goodness.[34] King rejected outright the idea that God was either a power (Tillich) *or* a good (Wieman), rather than both at once. In fact, when he finally discussed divine omnipotence in the dissertation, King made it clear that he did not accept the traditional idea that the term meant that God could do absolutely anything, even that which is not doable.

Hence a God devoid of power is ultimately inacapable [*sic*] of actualizing the good. But if God is truly God and warrants man's ultimate devotion, he must have not only an infinite concern for the good but an infinite power to actualize the good. This is the truth expressed in *the somewhat misleading doctrine of the divine omnipotence.* It does not mean that God can do the nondoable; neither does it mean that God has the power to act contrary to his own nature. It means, rather, that *God has the power to actualize the good and realize his purpose.* Moral perfection would be an empty possession apart from a corresponding and sustaining power. It is power that gives reality to the divine being.[35]

By "infinite power" King did not mean all, absolute, or perfect power in the traditional sense. Nor does infinite power mean that God does not also share power throughout creation. What King meant is that God is the source or ground of all being and possesses sufficient power to achieve the good in concrete terms. Accordingly, God, by definition, must possess not only infinite concern for the good but power sufficient to actualize it. It is worth reiterating that (in the above quote) King himself explicitly refers to "the somewhat misleading doctrine of the divine omnipotence." This is a clue, if ever there was one that King was aware of the problematic meaning of omnipotence in the traditional sense, and thus was mindful of the need to redefine it so that it was more intelligible. Therefore, to consider God to be omnipotent did not mean, for King, that God can do the impossible or the ridiculous (e.g., act out of character).[36] This was also the stance of Bowne, who held that God is the infinite or the absolute only in the sense that God alone is the self-sufficient source or cause of all finite being.[37] God is the independent foundation of all existence, and in God, all things live and move and have their being.[38] This is the only reasonable sense in which it can be said that God is absolute. Similarly, King's reinterpretation of omnipotence is in line with Tillich's rejection of traditional meanings of the term. Interpreting Tillich, King said: "The omnipotence of God does not mean that God has the power to do anything he wishes. Nor does it mean omni-activity in terms of physical causality. Such conceptions of omnipotence, asserts Tillich, are absurd and irreligious."[39] King was in basic agreement with this and similar claims, which should be borne in mind whenever we see references to terms like omnipotence in King's postgraduate school sermons, speeches, and writings.

But it is also the case that Brightman, even after the formulation of his doctrine of the finite-infinite God, characterized divine omnipotence in a way that King would approve. Brightman said that in the strictest sense his view is not that of a finite God, but of a God whose will is finite. He said that it remains the case that the finite-infinite God is "absolute in the sense of being the ultimate source of all creation." As we just saw, this was also Bowne's description of God. God as infinite or absolute means only that God is the independent ground of all being. What is important to remember, however, is that Bowne, unlike Brightman, considered himself to be an absolutist, notwithstanding his redefinition of omnipotence.[40] Brightman maintains that while the power of God's will is limited by the non-rational Given, God is unlimited in many significant ways. In this regard he wrote: ". . . arguments for the objectivity of ideals give ground for the postulate that his will for goodness and love is unlimited; likewise he is infinite in time and space, by his unbegun and unending duration and by his inclusion of all nature within his experience; such a God must also be unlimited in his knowledge of all that is, although human freedom and the nature of The Given probably limit his knowledge of the precise details of the future."[41]

For King, divine omnipotence did not mean that God could do the impossible or the ridiculous. "It means, rather, that God has the power to actualize the good and realize his purpose," said King. Not sheer, raw power as such, which is worthy of worship, but the power to achieve moral purpose, for God is fundamentally love. King grappled with this issue in a paper written during the second semester of Davis's course on the philosophy of religion.

> We are never to think of God's power in terms of what he could conceivably do by the exercise of what we may call sheer omnipotence which crushes all obstacles in its path. We are always to think of God's power in terms of his purpose. If what he did by sheer omnipotence defeated his purpose, then, however startling and impressive, it would be an expression of weakness, not of power. . . .
>
> We must realize that *God's power is not put forward to get certain things done, but to get them done in a certain way,* and with certain results in the lives of those who do them.[42]

King struggled with the relation between divine power and divine purpose. However, the response he gave is similar to Brightman's treatment of the subject. In a chapter on "The Power of God," Brightman wrote:

> *Not through power alone, but through the goal of power and the adequacy of power to attain the goal, is God to be defined.* "Not by might, nor by power, but by my spirit." In its deepest moments, religion has always scorned mere power. Any power which our theories ascribe to God beyond the power to achieve his purposes is a superfluous theological luxury; and any power for good which theory ascribes to him and experience shows he does not exercise is a moral embarrassment. . . . *the goal of divine power is a universe in which all persons through freedom and pain may achieve ever nobler forms of goodness and beauty, joy and love.*[43]

Power, in this sense, is not simply the ability to get things done. It is the ability to get things done in a particular way, one that is consistent with the highest and noblest ideals or purpose. Power as such is not the most defining trait of God. Rather the idea of sufficient power to accomplish the most noble ends or purposes in cooperation with created persons is the view closest to King's.

Nowhere does King repudiate or contradict either Brightman's statement or what he himself wrote in the paper for Davis. From seminary onward, King seemed to recognize the unavoidable problem that arises for traditional theism when divine power is exalted out of all proportion and relation to divine moral perfection. Different from this tendency, Brightman's conception of God "exalts God's moral perfection, denies his omnipotence (as traditionally understood), but ascribes to him sufficient power to solve all problems and to bring good out of all evil; this gives both his character and his power a basis in experience and supplies a more intelligible faith than does the older view."[44]

During his formal academic training, King aimed for a reconceptualization of omnipotence and its relation to divine purpose. And yet, when he preached during his postdoctoral period, he had no real interest in actually redefining divine omnipotence before audiences of (especially) black Christians. King knew how tenaciously many black Christians tended to cling to the idea of God as perfectly powerful and able to do anything whatever. This notwithstanding, King learned from firsthand experience in the civil and human rights movements that if meaningful progress is to be made it would take the cooperative efforts of persons of good will of all races and God. After all, God creates persons in freedom, for freedom, to be free in their relations with each other, with God, and the rest of creation. Minimally this means that persons have the capacity to choose to cooperate with each other and God, or not. Implicit in this idea is the assumption that God cannot do it all and that God in fact needs persons—not causally but morally—to help in the accomplishment of God's purpose in the world.[45] It is virtually impossible to make sense of why a perfectly powerful God who ostensibly possesses all power would *need* you and me for anything at all. This is one of the reasons I try to show later that while King never explicitly contended for a version of theistic finitism, his frequent references to the need for cooperative endeavor between persons and God implies an openness to the concept.

It is true that as a student, King did not think of himself as a theistic finitist. He rejected what he perceived to be the theistic finitism of Wieman as well as Tillich's absolutism devoid of goodness. In addition, in papers he wrote in seminary and graduate school, King rejected the theistic finitism of McTaggart, Montague, and at times Brightman.

King was an acute and careful thinker in his own right, and therefore did not just uncritically accept all that his own religious heritage said about divine omnipotence. King was able to come to the conclusion, as Brightman did, that if God were truly omnipotent beyond humans' ability to conceive, then God could do even the unintelligible. Brightman said that such a God

> could have created a race of free beings who would always choose righteously (as he himself, being also free, always chooses righteously), even though in theory they were free to sin (as he also is). There must be something in "the nature of things" to render impossible the creation of a race of free beings who would never sin, even though they were free to. The impossibility must lie in the very nature of God, for if it lay merely in the created world, we should have to ask why God created such a world. There would have to be something in him which rendered such a creation the best possible.[46]

Brightman argued that the facts of experience reveal the existence of a God who is "powerful" and "unconquerable," but not perfectly and absolutely powerful according to traditional theism.[47] King was in essential agreement with this aspect of Brightman's doctrine of God and the idea of God as relentlessly faithful and compassionate.

King's Doctrine of God

The type of personalism that appealed most to King stressed the sacredness of persons and was thoroughly theistic. King's deepest faith was in a personal God of love and reason who is the creator and sustainer of all life. In theistic personalism we find a metaphysical grounding for the biblical claim that in God we live and move and have our being, a theme that frequently appears in Bowne's writings. King perceived such a God to be infinitely loving, caring, responsive, active, righteous, just, and on occasion, wrathful. Because many will cringe at the idea of the wrath of God, it should be understood that this was unquestionably the stance of King, who was, after all, influenced by ancient ethical prophets, most especially Amos, Isaiah, Jeremiah, and Micah. King considered the Hebrew prophets to be the greatest prophets on justice and righteousness. Divine wrath is an important element in understanding their sense of divine justice. In addition, King was the descendant of three generations of preachers who preached God's hatred of injustice as passionately as did the eighth-century prophets. They also preached God's promise to punish evildoers. King himself was deeply influenced by this tradition. In his first speech as the newly elected president of the Montgomery Improvement Association (MIA) on December 5,

1955, he made it clear that God is not merely the God of love and justice. King said: "He's also the God that standeth before the nations and says, 'Be still and know that I am God—and if you don't obey me I'm gonna break the backbone of your power— and cast you out of the arms of your international and national relationships.'"[48] This would not be the only time King would use such language to characterize God's dis- taste for and actions against the unjust. He also used the language of the wrath of God in his "Drum Major Instinct" sermon, in which he essentially preached his own eu- logy two months before he was assassinated.[49] No study on King's theological ethics would be complete without consideration of the place of divine wrath.

We get a sense of the thoroughgoing nature of theistic personalism in Bowne's contention that God is the foundation of truth, knowledge, and morals. The study of any of these, Bowne maintained, ultimately results in questions about the existence and nature of God. Although he argued that it is impossible to demonstrate the exis- tence of God, Bowne was, nevertheless, eager to show that the problems of the world and life cannot be solved without God as the fundamental assumption.[50] This was King's basic stance as well. God is the ultimate source of, and key to, the solution to human problems, including sin. Human problems and sin exist because of autono- mous moral agents who are called into existence by God, and who choose to behave contrary to God's expectations.

The conviction that the universe is grounded in morality says something quite significant regarding the way King thought about God. The most obvious implica- tion of the claim is that the Creator God must be nothing short of perfectly personal, loving, good, and reasonable. To have infused reality with value implies not only God's infinite love for created existence and the expectation that persons behave in ways that exhibit their respect and appreciation for all life, but it also says something about God's intention to accomplish the divine purposes in ways that are respectful of life, especially human life. Moreover, since King also believed God to be a God of infinite reason, the conclusion must be drawn that God has a plan for the world and works toward its fulfillment in logical rather than illogical ways. This means, for ex- ample, that since God has created persons in freedom to make choices (within lim- its), God does not then try to force persons to do what is good and just in the world. The reasonable thing for God to do is to seek persuasive means to urge them to choose alternatives that may be pleasing to God. Because God is love, God respects persons' right to choose, even when they make choices that frustrate the accomplishment of God's purposes. But this also means that when people see the devastating effects of moral evil in the world, they should not accuse God of either being absent or as the perpetrator in some way. Because God creates persons with the capacity to be self- determining, and because God loves and respects them, reason suggests that God can- not then force them to behave in ways that are pleasing to God.

Without question, King believed the universe to be under the guidance of a personal and loving God, who is its creator and sustainer. Nowhere did he express this more poignantly and movingly than when he reflected on some of the hardships and threats made against him and his family during the civil rights movement. "I am convinced that the universe is under the control of a loving purpose, and that in the struggle for righteousness man has cosmic companionship. Behind the harsh appearances of the world there is a benign power. To say that this God is personal is not to make him a finite object besides other objects or attribute to him the limitations of human personality; it is to take what is finest and noblest in our consciousness and affirm its perfect existence in him."[51]

King agreed with his personalist forebears that the metaphysical attributes of person—including self-consciousness, self-determining, intelligence, and worth—are not in themselves limiting factors. The limiting factors, we have seen, are the corporeal elements characteristic of human beings. In any case, King also was in agreement with the personalist thesis that people are but imperfect images of what it truly means to be persons. After all, people depend on the Supreme Person for their very being.

From the time he was a boy, King believed God to be personal, although as an adult, especially during the Montgomery struggle, he did not know from a personal, existential standpoint what this really meant. He knew as well as anybody what it meant intellectually or academically. But he recalled a time when he had not been as conscious of the personal character of the God of his faith and of his ancestors. At times, he thought of God in a more abstract and academic sense. But his struggle alongside his people for freedom and dignity helped to reestablish and anchor his belief and trust in a personal God who hears, is affected by, and responds to prayer and other human endeavor. Reflecting on his own personal sufferings and persecutions reminded King of his earlier dependence on the personal and loving God of Jesus Christ, the God of his parents and grandparents. This was the same God who had so often been present with him during the most difficult, frightening, and uncertain moments of the struggle for freedom and dignity. In 1963 King said:

The agonizing moments through which I have passed during the last few years have also drawn me closer to God. More than ever before I am convinced of the reality of a personal God. True, I have always believed in the personality of God. But in the past the idea of a personal God was little more than a metaphysical category that I found theologically and philosophically satisfying. Now it is a reality that has been validated in the experiences of everyday life. God has been profoundly real to me in recent years. In the midst of outward dangers I have felt an inner calm. In the midst of lonely days and dreary nights I have heard an inner voice saying, "Lo I will be with you." When the chains of fear and the manacles of frustration have all but stymied my efforts, I have felt the power of God transforming the fatigue of despair into the buoyancy of hope.[52]

The use of such language can only be attributed to a personal God, a being capable of hearing, understanding, feeling compassion, and responding to human beings.

Indeed, by the time the Montgomery bus boycott was half over, King had discovered firsthand that the metaphysical conceptions of God he studied and mastered in seminary and graduate school could not in themselves provide for him the comfort, strength, and companionship he needed to sustain him and the movement. At no point was this more evident than the night—early in the Montgomery struggle when—he received one of numerous similar calls from an angry white voice that threatened to kill him and blow up his house. Things were not going well in the boycott, and that particular night King was affected by the threatening phone call in a way he had not experienced before. He could not sleep, and therefore went to the kitchen to brew a pot of coffee. It was there that he had what he referred to years later as "a vision in the kitchen."[53] At his kitchen table he bowed down before the God of his parents and ancestors and sought divine guidance, comfort, and assurance. For the first time, he acknowledged that he needed to experience for himself the God that his parents and maternal grandmother taught him about. The problem was not that King was not religious, for he had more than demonstrated that in his studies and his acceptance of the "call" to preach. Although the church and religion had long been important to him, King said that before that night in the kitchen he "had never felt an experience with God in the way that you must have it if you're going to walk the lonely paths of this life."[54] Prior to bowing in prayer he tried to find comfort in the theologies and philosophies he had not long ago studied in school, "trying to give philosophical and theological reasons for the existence and the reality of sin and evil, but the answer didn't quite come there." King wrote about the kitchen experience in *Stride Toward Freedom.*

> I was ready to give up. With my cup of coffee sitting untouched before me I tried to think of a way to move out of the picture without appearing a coward. In this state of exhaustion, when my courage had all but gone, I decided to take my problem to God. With my head in my hands, I bowed over the kitchen table and prayed aloud. The words I spoke to God that midnight are still vivid in my memory. "I am here taking a stand for what I believe is right. But now I am afraid. The people are looking to me for leadership, and if I stand before them without strength and courage, they too will falter. I am at the end of my powers. I have nothing left. I've come to the point where I can't face it alone."

At that moment I experienced the presence of the Divine as I had never experienced Him before. It seemed as though I could hear the quiet assurance of an inner voice saying: "Stand up for righteousness, stand up for truth; and God will be at your side forever." Almost at once my fears began to go. My uncertainty disappeared. I was ready to face anything.[55]

King was convinced that the answer that he received came from the very same God that his parents had taught him about when he was a boy. But that night in his kitchen he discovered that to merely know that this was the God of his parents was not enough. Nor was it enough to know this God simply as an intellectual concept. He had to know and experience God for himself. As generations of old black Christians have been known to say: "Honey, you got to know Him for yourself." There is not a little truth in David Garrow's contention that the vision in the kitchen experience "was the most important night of [King's] life, the one he always would think back to in future years when the pressures again seemed to be too great." That experience was for King "a source of inner strength."[56]

After uttering that prayer at the kitchen table, King was convinced that the essence of religion is not some impersonal, abstract, metaphysical conception of God's relationship with human beings. It was not a "process" or "event," "being-itself," or "the power of being." Rather, the kitchen experience and many other experiences thereafter confirmed for King that the essence, the soul of religion is a personal, omnibenevolent, omniscient God of "matchless power." After the kitchen experience it was clear that God was "that power that can make a way out of no way,"[57] and God would do so precisely because God is personal, loving, and reasonable. This is the God of the Hebrew prophets. This is the God of Jesus Christ. This, King concluded, is the God of his parents, grandparents, and great-grandparents. This was the same God who would see black people to a successful conclusion in the Montgomery bus boycott and in subsequent civil rights campaigns. King put all of his trust and faith in this God. It is what sustained him subsequently when he was faced with particularly difficult times. Even when he became discouraged in the struggle, he now had the assurance of God's great faithfulness and promise to be with him to the end of his days. This faith sustained him.

In addition, King was periodically encouraged by some elderly black Christian who had been tested in the faith and knew from personal experience that God is always faithful and never reneges on a promise. One of these was old Mother Pollard. Early in the Montgomery bus boycott, when it seemed to her that King was discouraged and not his energetic, passionate self during a speech at a mass meeting, she inquired of him whether he was all right. Not deceived by his claim that all was well, she asked: "Is it that we ain't doing things to please you? Or is it that the white folks is bothering you?" She then looked him squarely in the eyes and spoke with the authority of a saint: "I done *told* you we is with you all the way. But even if we ain't with you, God's gonna take care of you."[58] In addition, King must have been much encouraged during the bus boycott when he heard the story of Mother Pollard walking to work. Although she was having a difficult time walking, she refused the offer to ride in a car. She was clearly tired, but waved off the driver. When asked if she was tired, she reportedly said: "I'm not walking for myself. I'm walking for my children and my grandchildren."[59] She went on to say: "Yes, my feets is tired, but my soul is rested."[60]

Therefore, we can see why for King, God was neither Wieman's "interaction" or "process" nor Tillich's "being-itself" or "power of being," for neither of these can account adequately for what he believed to be the two fundamental religious values for religious persons: fellowship with God, and trust in God's goodness. Both of these implied for King a being who is perfectly conscious, self-aware, intelligent, free, just, and loving. Only such a God—not one who is only symbolically personal as we see in Tillich's theology—is capable of fellowship, love, and goodness. King wrote about this in his dissertation:

> No fellowship is possible without freedom and intelligence. There may be interactions between impersonal being, but not fellowship. True fellowship and communion can exist only between beings who know each other and take a volitional attitude toward each other. . . . Fellowship requires an outgoing of will and feeling. This is what the Scripture means when it refers to God as the "living" God. Life as applied to God means that in God there is feeling and will, responsive to the deepest yearnings of the human heart; this God both evokes and answers prayer.[61]

This is what King meant by a personal God. Such is a God with whom persons can fellowship and commune; a God who cares and is always working on their behalf; a God who knows created persons in the most intimate way, because every person— indeed all life—belongs to God. This is a God who works most effectively when persons open themselves to God's energy and persuasive love; when persons decide to work cooperatively with God and with each other. This is not a God who simply does everything but rather one who works *with* persons as they choose to surrender themselves as co-workers in the quest for the beloved community.[62]

Similarly, King reasoned, following Knudson and Bowne, that "personality" is a necessary presupposition of divine goodness. In his dissertation King wrote: "Only a personal being can be good. . . . Goodness in the true sense of the word is an attribute of personality."[63] King wrote similarly about love, claiming that person is a necessary presupposition of love. The personal God is the God of love. The best in the Bible and the Jewish and Christian traditions attest to the living God who is both good and loving. But as we will see momentarily, this is not the God of Paul Tillich, who was quite adamant that God is, instead, being-itself. King concluded that between Wieman and Tillich, the latter provided the most potentially devastating argument against the idea of God as Person. In light of Samuel K. Robinson's recent study on Afrikan American Christian ethics, which he grounds on Tillich's doctrine of God as being-itself,[64] rather than as personal, it may be instructive to devote more attention to the doctrine of God as Person and King's response to Tillich's argument. It will be seen in this regard that King's stance is diametrically opposed to any that views God as an impersonal ground of being. King bases this not solely on Afrikan American religious tradition, but on biblical, philosophical, and theological grounds.

GOD AS PERSONAL

When reading Tillich, King, of course, was reading through the lens of his Afrikan American religio-cultural heritage and his understanding of personalism.[65] Unquestionably, by the time he embarked on a systematic reading of Tillich's views on God he was firmly committed to the philosophy of personalism. One who is steeped in this tradition, and that of Afrikan American Christian faith, easily detects what appears in Tillich to be impersonal views on God.

According to Tillich, all statements about God are symbolic, except the statement that God is being-itself, the ground of being, or the power of being. To speak of God as personal means that God "carries within himself the ontological power of personality."[66] King took this to mean that Tillich denied literal personality to God, since he maintained that personality limits God. He writes that in this regard, Tillich would agree with Wieman's claim: "God towers in unique majesty infinitely above the little hills which we call minds and personalities."[67] And yet, Tillich (like Wieman) concludes that God cannot be impersonal. God is not subpersonal but suprapersonal. If anything, then, God is more, not less, than personal. Tillich writes, "The depth of being cannot be symbolized by objects taken from a realm which is lower than the personal, from the realm of things or sub-personal living beings. The supra-personal is not an 'It,' or more exactly, it is a 'He' as much as it is an 'It,' and it is above both of them. But if the 'He' element is left out, the 'It' element transforms the alleged supra-personal into a sub-personal, as usually happens in monism and pantheism."[68]

Tillich rightly maintains that persons can only speak of and approach God through the categories of finitude. This means, necessarily, that the language does not exist that can fully and adequately characterize God. To refer to God as personal, then, is not to say that God is *a* person, nor that God is less than person, for God is the source of the personal, and therefore "carries within himself the ontological power of personality."

One is almost at a loss to know whether in Tillich's thought God is person or not. In the James W. Richard Lectures given at the University of Virginia in 1951, Tillich said: "*Against* Pascal I say: The God of Abraham, Isaac, and Jacob and the God of the philosophers is the same God. He is a person and the negation of himself as a person."[69] Alexander J. McKelway contends that statements such as this give lie to the criticism that Tillich was an impersonalist.[70] This makes some sense, considering Tillich's belief that a true symbol is more than a sign. That is, it does more than point beyond itself. The symbol participates in some way in the reality to which it points.[71] But it should be pointed out here that the God of the Bible is most assuredly a personal God who is immanent enough to care about what happens to persons in the world, unlike the god of Epicurus, Cicero, and Aristotle, who seemed to be so distant, impassive, and uncaring regarding human beings in the world.[72]

Persons are limited to the categories of finitude, but Tillich observes, "the finite reality they use is not an arbitrary means for an end, something strange to it; it participates in the power of the ultimate for which it stands."[73] Therefore he maintains that the religious symbol expresses both what it symbolizes and that through which it is symbolized. It symbolizes and is directed toward both the infinite and the finite. The religious symbol "is double-edged." Tillich clarifies the meaning of the double-edged nature of religious symbols this way: "They force the infinite down to finitude and the finite up to infinity. They open the divine for the human and the human for the divine. For instance, if God is symbolized as 'Father,' he is brought down to the human relationship of father and child. But at the same time this human relationship is consecrated into a pattern of the divine-human relationship. If 'Father' is employed as a symbol for God, fatherhood is seen in its theonomous, sacramental depth."[74] Statements such as this led King to conclude: "So when Tillich speaks of personality as a symbolic expression of God's nature, he is sure that here is an implicit indication of the nature of God."[75]

King concluded, finally, that no matter how much Tillich denied it, his God is impersonal. Tillich's certainly is not the living, personal God of the Bible, for he himself characterized this God differently from being-itself. He described the biblical God thusly: "Most of the so-called anthropomorphisms of the biblical picture of God are expressions of his character as living. His actions, his passions, his remembrances and anticipations, his suffering and joy, his personal relations and his plans—all these make him a living God and distinguish him from the pure absolute, from being-itself."[76] Tillich's God, then, is not the living, personal God of the Scriptures, nor the God of Martin Luther King, Jr. Rather, Tillich's God is being-itself.

In any event, we must allow King to have the last word. In the dissertation he concluded that Tillich's God is not the God of the Bible or of black religious experience:

[A]ll of Tillich's conclusions tend to point to an impersonal God. Despite his warning that God is not less than personal, we see traits throughout Tillich's thinking that point to a God that is less than personal. Even those things which Tillich says about God with personalistic implications are finally given impersonal explanations. For instance, Tillich speaks of God as love. But on closer scrutiny we discover that love, for Tillich, is just the dialectical principle of the union of opposites. . . .

So Tillich ends with a God who is a sub-personal reservoir of power, somewhat akin to the impersonalism of Hindu Vedantism. He chooses the less than personal to explain personality, purpose, and meaning.[77]

King believed in a thoroughly personal God, a God who is at once immanent enough to assure created persons they are cared about and yet transcendent enough to warrant their worship. Like many Afrikan Americans, King often described God as being able to help blacks to make a way out of no way. When King spoke of God in such language, especially well into the civil rights struggle, it was not always clear that he uncritically adhered to the traditional idea of an omnipotent God or that he accepted the view that God possesses perfect and absolute power. Indeed, there are statements in his writings and speeches that suggest that he did not. Therefore, the contention of James Cone that King rejected Brightman's doctrine of the finite-infinite God because his "commitment to the faith of the Negro church was too strong to allow him to embrace a limited God" is not compelling.[78] There is a sense among most King scholars that because he was steeped in the theistic tradition of the black church, and thus assumed God's existence, power, goodness, love, and justice, this alone proved evidence enough for his rejection of the theistic finitism of Tillich, Wieman, and Brightman. Lewis Baldwin is one such scholar. He contends that "King opposed Tillich's efforts to limit God's goodness and Wieman's and Brightman's insistence on God's limited power."[79] It seems to me a big leap from the traditional Afrikan American religious assumption of God's power, even infinite power, to an outright rejection of all views that see God's power as limited in some way(s). What I shall argue is that King's postgraduate school thinking about divine power was more complex. Furthermore, even as a theistic finitist, Brightman still maintained that God is the most powerful being in the universe. This conviction is quite compatible with King's thinking about divine power during the civil rights movement. Moreover, King was a very good thinker who could see the contradiction in claiming on the one hand that God possesses all power, while claiming on the other hand that God shares power throughout creation.

If reality is fundamentally communal in nature and God shares power, what sense does it make to insist that God possesses all power? And, in light of King's reinterpretation of divine omnipotence, how did he come to characterize God's power, especially during his ministry?

THE MATCHLESS POWER OF GOD

The phrase "matchless power" of God is of utmost importance in serious discussions on King's doctrine of God. King wrote frequently on God in seminary and graduate school, and then chose to write his doctoral dissertation on the subject. This is the best indicator we have of his interest in developing a rational conception of God that would somehow provide a foundation for his participation in the struggle of his people to regain their lost sense of dignity and worth. In addition, beyond graduate school King frequently talked about a personal and loving God in sermons, speeches, lectures, articles, and books.

One of King's earliest uses of the phrase "matchless power of God" appears in his article "An Experiment in Love" (1958). In the course of naming and discussing six characteristics of the philosophy of nonviolent resistance to evil (which took shape during the later stages of the Montgomery bus boycott), King referred to God as an eternal force in the universe which sides with justice. He observed that this force had been named many things, including "a Personal Being of matchless power and infinite love."[80]

To characterize God's as "matchless power" was a masterstroke of the pen on King's part. It is not clear from his writings, sermons, and speeches how he happened upon this phrase. What is clear, is that through his use of it he seemed to want to steer clear of the more problematic traditional conception of divine omnipotence. Especially in sermons to predominantly black congregations, King did not expressly take up the classical issue of divine omnipotence, for this would have caused alienation among many of those present. Instead, in the aforementioned article King slipped in the term "matchless power," making clear that a God who possesses such power is able to accomplish the divine purposes in the world and thus possesses power sufficient to God's purposes and to human needs. What more do we humans need? God, declared King, is God of "infinite love and boundless power," and thus is "the creator, sustainer, and conserver of values."[81]

Elsewhere King writes of the "need to know that in this universe is a God whose *matchless strength* is a fit contrast to the sordid weakness of man."[82] This is different from the way King has generally been interpreted by King scholars and black liberation theologians. The idea of "matchless" power or strength seems to be a subtle but quite significant qualification or softening of the traditional view of divine omnipotence. Even Brightman, whose doctrine of God King both appreciated and criticized, would appreciate the idea of the "matchless" power or strength of God, as opposed to the classical view of divine omnipotence. For the former does not mean that God possesses either absolute or even all power, in the traditional sense of the term's meaning. King's introduction of the term therefore has some affinity, at least, with Brightman's doctrine of the finite-infinite God.

It is not the case, however, that King stopped using the term "omnipotent" in his writings, speeches, and sermons to characterize God. But as one reads his work, it seems evident that he used the term selectively, depending on the audience he was addressing. He knew full well that most black Christians believed that God possesses absolute perfect power, and King would not have used language in their presence that implied anything different. A term like the "matchless power" of God, however, could be easily inserted into a speech or sermon without arousing concern among those who adhere to the more traditional view. It would not have mattered that King intended only to convey the idea that God is the most powerful being in the universe. King's reference was to a mighty power, not our own, that is able, and cooperates with persons toward the realization of justice, righteousness, and the beloved community. The point here is that even when King did use the term "divine omnipotence," the context, tone, and emphasis did not appear to point to the traditional idea of perfect, absolute power. Remember, in his dissertation King concluded once and for all that omnipotence did not mean that God could do either the impossible or the ridiculous, for God is also the God of reason.

In the sermon "Our God Is Able," King explained his sense that God has sufficient or matchless power to accomplish God's purposes in the world.

> At the center of the Christian faith is the conviction that in the universe there is a God of power who is able to do exceedingly abundant things in nature and in history. This conviction is stressed over and over in the Old and the New Testaments. Theologically, this affirmation is expressed in the doctrine of the omnipotence of God. The God whom we worship is not a weak and incompetent God. He is able to beat back gigantic waves of opposition and to bring low prodigious mountains of evil. The ringing testimony of the Christian faith is that God is able.[83]

Notice that King did not say that the ringing testimony is that God possesses absolute and perfect power. His faith was in "that power that can make a way out of no way."[84] And yet this did not mean that the God of matchless strength would do for blacks and other oppressed people what they, in cooperation with each other and with God, could accomplish together. There were few things King was more certain of than his conviction that progress in the social struggle would come only as a result of the relentless cooperative endeavor between persons and God. Persons cannot resolve the problem alone. On the other hand, God respects humans' moral autonomy so much that God will not intervene to solve the problem without their decided cooperation with each other and God.

COOPERATIVE ENDEAVOR BETWEEN GOD AND PERSONS

There is a second emphasis in King's thought that points to my hypothesis that he rejected the traditional way of thinking about divine omnipotence: his firm belief in the need for cooperative human-divine endeavor as blacks struggled to regain their sense of dignity and their freedom. From Montgomery to Memphis, King insisted on the need for his people to cooperate with each other in the struggle. Looking back in 1967, he said of the Montgomery struggle: "It was one of the most amazing things I've ever seen in my life. . . . We stuck together."[85] When the call went out to not ride the buses, the black community of Montgomery cooperated fully, knowing that only through such cooperation would they help to usher in the new day, as well as gain a renewed sense of their own dignity. King also was aware and thankful that they did not struggle alone, but that many people of goodwill all over the country struggled with them, if only through the sending of money and-or moral support.[86]

This conviction about the need for cooperative endeavor between persons and God was instilled in King when he was a boy, and he witnessed it frequently in his father's ministry and that of other black ministers. He grew up in the tradition of black Christian faith and the spirit of black protest, dating back to before the time of his great-grandparents. Even in his youth, King must have had a clear sense that his people had to be self-determined and dependent on each other in the struggle for freedom, even as they looked to divine cooperation and guidance. King saw his father involved in social protest. Surely this must have led him to believe that it was important that persons work cooperatively and in conjunction with God to rid society of social evils. An infinitely loving God of "matchless power" (not absolute or perfect power) would *want* and *need* the cooperation of free self-determining beings in the struggle to overcome injustice and to achieve (as nearly as possible) the beloved community. In an important passage King wrote:

Even though all progress is precarious, within limits real social progress may be made. Although man's moral pilgrimage may never reach a destination point on earth, his never-ceasing strivings may bring him closer to the city of righteousness.

. . . God is at work in his universe. He is not outside the world looking on with a sort of cold indifference. Here on all roads of life, he is striving in our striving. Like an ever-loving Father, he is working through history for the salvation of his children.[87]

No one expressed more powerfully and persistently than King the idea of the importance of cooperative endeavor between God and persons. In this, he was influenced not only by the protest tradition of the black church but also the ideas of Bowne, Brightman, and Heschel. Bowne argued that the world could be "vastly better than it is," and consequently persons are obligated to make it so, "and so we seek to work together with God to bring in the better day." God has not made the world perfect, but perfectible. "The human world is nothing ready-made by God apart from our activity. We must work together with him."[88] God will not do for human beings what they can do cooperatively together, and with God. Brightman argued that inasmuch as love is a social category and God is love, this implies God's need for "comradeship."[89] Brightman also held that when persons work cooperatively their "will is freed from bondage to selfishness and is able to gain the joy and strength that come from shared work— as man works with and for his fellow man with and for his God."[90] God always needs persons to achieve God's purposes in the world.[91] Although this was not the stance of classical Greek philosophy,[92] it has always been the dominant view of most of black religious tradition. Historically, black Christians believed that God does not expect that they sit back, do nothing, and wait for God to deliver them from white oppression.[93] Moreover, they believed that God does for the oppressed what they cannot do for themselves.[94]

As self-determining moral agents, King believed blacks to have a major role in the struggle for human dignity and freedom. This is why he was so adamant about stressing black self-determination and the need for blacks and other oppressed people to take the initiative in their own liberation struggle. It is also why he thought it so important after 1966 that more and more blacks be selected, not by whites or the establishment to occupy positions of leadership in the civil rights struggle, but by the black community.[95] In light of his belief that racism was embedded in the structures of the United States,[96] however, King believed it necessary for both blacks and whites to make ways to form alliances. This would be the surest means to meaningful political progress, the eradication of racism, disparities in employment and unemployment, as well as to ensure movement toward the establishment of the beloved community.[97]

Cooperative endeavor was not just an abstract philosophical or theological principle for King. Instead, it meant an actual coming together and conscious collaborating together by human beings in efforts to solve common problems and to establish a community that more nearly approximates one based on the ethical principles and practices of the Hebrew prophets and Jesus Christ. "There must be a grand alliance of Negro and white. This alliance must consist of the vast majorities of each group. It must have the objective of eradicating social evils which oppress both white and Negro. The unemployment which afflicts one third of Negro youth also affects over twelve and one-half percent of white youth. It is not only more moral for both races to work together but more logical."[98] From Montgomery to Memphis he brought together vast numbers of people to work in concert toward the eradication of injustice and the establishment of the beloved community. This was yet another concrete difference between his brand of Personalism and that of his teachers.

This type of cooperative working together for the attainment of the beloved community cannot happen merely by fiat, King maintained. It will take sustained determination, courage, effort, and sacrifice, all of which requires choice and power of will. Blacks and whites will have to want to come together "on the basis of a real harmony of interest and understanding," said King. In addition, it will need to be a cooperation based on mutual respect. Of course, none of this can happen overnight. It will require faith in both the moment and the future.[99]

King characterized the beloved community to come as one "in which men will live together as brothers; as [a] world in which men will beat their swords into ploughshares and their spears into pruning hooks; a world in which men will no longer take necessities from the masses to give luxuries to the classes; a world in which all men will respect the dignity and worth of all human personality."[100] Just as King believed that such a community could be attained through human and divine cooperative endeavor, he believed that injustice could be overcome through the same means. That, after all, was confirmed through his own efforts in the civil and human rights struggle over a period of thirteen years.

The concrete struggle to provide leadership in blacks' struggle for freedom and to regain their lost sense of dignity did not allow King the luxury of engaging in either written or oral debates on whether God possessed absolute perfect power. Periodically, King expressed a desire to engage in the niceties of philosophizing and theologizing that would be made possible through a university or seminary faculty appointment.[101] However, his call to be a Christian minister and to provide civil rights leadership left no time for such an intellectual engagement. King's understanding of the eighth-century prophets, the life and ministry of Jesus Christ, and the long protest tradition of his people convinced him of the need for a conception of God that would give his people the confidence that through cooperative endeavor with each other and with God they could go a long way toward accomplishing their purpose. What was needed was faith in a God who possessed both matchless power and infinite love for persons and the world, and who worked cooperatively with them to overcome evil.

It should be pointed out that in the majority of King's writings and speeches we find him talking more about the love of God than the absolute power of God. Moreover, often when he has divine power in mind, he does not even use the term "power." Rather, he frequently uses a term or phrase that implies power. For example, in "Antidotes for Fear," we find him saying: "Above the manyness of time stands one eternal God, with wisdom to guide us, *strength* to protect us, and *love* to keep us. His *boundless love* supports and contains us as a mighty ocean contains and supports the tiny drops of every wave. With a surging fullness he is forever moving toward us, seeking to fill the little creeks and bays of our lives with unlimited resources."[102]

God's agapé love—the overflowing love of God operating in the human heart—the idea of cooperative human-divine endeavor against evil and injustice, and the ethic of the beloved community are more important for King's doctrine of God than is the traditional concept of omnipotence. This suggests that in King's conception of God goodness, love, justice, and righteousness are more fundamental than power as such, that is, that the ethical attributes of God may be more fundamental than the metaphysical attributes. In this view, King was in agreement with Bowne who said: "If God is to be of any religious value to us and an object of real and adoring worship, he must be supremely good."[103]

Bowne saw the law of love as being applicable to divine power, which again implies the superiority of love to power as such. Whatever power God has must be ethical or for the purpose of ethical achievements. As the greatest power in the universe, then, God is the most heavily morally obligated being in the universe as well—a point consistent with the principle that from one who has much, much is required. For Bowne this meant that "the greatest of all must be the servant of all, and the chief of burden bearers."[104] What Bowne argued for most consistently was the idea of a God who is supreme reason, supreme righteousness, and supreme goodness.[105] King defended this concept of God in his doctoral dissertation. For King (as for Bowne), God is worthy of worship not simply because of God's matchless power, but because of the integral relation and balance between that power and God's unsurpassable goodness and love. God need not possess absolute power, but God must possess matchless ethical power. This distinction might not have been as important to King the preacher and speaker to Afrikan American church audiences, but one cannot minimize the fact that in studying for his Ph.D. degree in systematic theology he grappled long and hard with the doctrine of God.

Bowne argued that since it is actually persons who cause most of the evil and suffering in the world through the misuse of human freedom, it is they who must contribute much to working out their own salvation. He did not mean by this that persons could work out their salvation without divine assistance but rather that persons have a major part to play. Ultimately persons are in "partnership" with God. In the final analysis, Bowne argued, it is God who works within persons as they do their best to eradicate unnecessary suffering and pain. As autonomous moral agents people must accept responsibility for much of what happens in the world and "learn that Heaven helps only those who help themselves," said Bowne. Rejecting the "obsolete notion" of works righteousness, Bowne wrote: "In the great field where he [God] has taken us into partnership, what he does will depend on what we do. He will do nothing in this field without our cooperation."[106] Bowne was adamant that persons should not ask or expect of God what they themselves could do if they both will and strive in earnest to achieve in the world.[107] As shown throughout this discussion, this was also King's stance.

Black liberation theologians, as well as others who have written most systematically on King, have frequently claimed that he could never have espoused a doctrine of God that did not include the elements of perfect power and perfect goodness. The reason generally given is that King was too committed to the tradition of black religious faith. On this matter, it is important to consider the perspective of a significant minority in Afrikan American literature, especially between 1914 and 1920. This was during the period and aftermath of World War I, the war to end all wars and to make the world safe for democracy. Of course, things did not get better for Afrikan Americans, even though large numbers of them fought in the war. There was essentially a return to business as usual. This led black literary artists and others to argue that God was impotent, white, and thus did not care about blacks, or simply did not exist. An important reason we need to focus on this minority perspective about God among Afrikan Americans is that it suggests the need for what King himself sought to do in graduate school: to develop a conception of God that was broader than the more traditional views that did not seem to permit divine involvement in social struggles for freedom. King sought a conception of God that was supportive of his social conscience. Although black literary artists of the period cited did not go on to explicitly suggest the characteristics of the God they believed necessary to be supportive of black uplift, they made it clear that blacks either needed to reject God altogether or alter their conception of God so that it was more empirically adequate and consistent with their experience of oppression in the United States.

GOD IN AFRIKAN AMERICAN LITERATURE

In *The Negro's God as Reflected in His Literature,* Benjamin E. Mays tells us that black literary artists such as Countee Cullen doubted God's usefulness to blacks in their struggle for freedom.[108] Cullen actually rejected the white God who seemed not to understand or even care about the plight of blacks. He thought it more likely that a black God would be more sympathetic and would work with blacks to overcome their oppression, although he seemed also to believe that whether God was black or white, blacks probably could expect little divine help in their struggle. Cullen expressed this view in his poem, "Heritage." Significantly, he was not the only black literary artist of his day to doubt God's usefulness to blacks and their struggle.

At various periods of his long, illustrious career, W. E. B. DuBois expressed a similar view. He desired that God care about blacks and their struggle, but did not see sufficient evidence, nor had he sufficient experience, of divine assistance. He therefore wondered whether God was a "white," "pale," "bloodless, Heartless thing."[109] Neither DuBois nor Cullen denied the existence of God, but each clearly thought differently about God than most blacks. They were only skeptical as to God's usefulness in the black struggle for freedom and uplift of the race (whether God was white or black). Others, like Nella Larsen, went beyond this stance and completely renounced the existence of God.[110] When Larsen considered the plight of her people she concluded that there was no evidence to support the claim that God, even if God existed, loved all people equally.

Mays names and discusses the views of other black literary artists who doubted God's existence, lacked faith that God would help blacks, questioned God's usefulness, believed God to be too transcendent to help or to hear the pleas of blacks, or doubted that God will help.[111] A number of these writers, e.g., DuBois, wanted to believe that God can help blacks in their struggle against racism and economic exploitation, and yet doubted whether such assistance was forthcoming. In addition, some of these, most notably DuBois, did not consider God to be personal, a point that DuBois himself expressed in 1948.[112] Since he did not believe God would intervene in the black struggle, DuBois held that the moral onus was on blacks to be responsible for how they responded to their condition.

James Weldon Johnson was at best an agnostic regarding the question of whether God is personal and whether there is purpose in the universe. However, he sincerely believed that people needed God, or to believe in God, although they must first and foremost depend on themselves. This pointed to Johnson's humanistic tendencies.[113] George S. Schuyler—an atheist who declared with Voltaire that even if God did not exist, human beings would find it necessary to create God—held a similar view. Those who have such deep need for God, he maintained, have a right to believe that God exists and cares for them.

Langston Hughes was perhaps bluntest of all. An atheist and communist, he denied the existence of both God and Jesus Christ. In any case, neither God or Jesus had any usefulness for blacks and their struggle, he maintained. Hughes admonished that any hope for meaningful social reconstruction should be placed in communism.[114]

Although James Baldwin clearly had a strong humanistic outlook, no use for the institutional church (after he had been a boy preacher from age 14–17), and was as critical of the more traditional conceptions of God as any theologian or philosopher, he nevertheless exhibited a strong appreciation for God throughout his career. What he said in his essay, "In Search of a Majority," is quite instructive in terms of his thinking about God:

> I suggest that the role of the Negro in American life has something to do with our concept of what God is, and from my point of view, this concept is not big enough. It has got to be made much bigger than it is because God is, after all, not anybody's toy. To be with God is really to be involved with some enormous, overwhelming desire, and joy, and power which you cannot control, which controls you. I conceive of my own life as a journey toward something I do not understand, which in the going toward, makes me better. I conceive of God, in fact, as a means of liberation and not a means to control others.[115]

For Baldwin, then, God's "control" is God's love, care, and compassion. If God is truly love, then God does not control persons. Instead, Love's task is to love, and by so doing to work cooperatively with persons to be better than they are, individually, interpersonally, and collectively.

When Major J. Jones wrote *The Color of God* (1987), he claimed to present an authentic "Afro-Americanized God-concept." Jones cited part of the above passage from Baldwin in support of his view that there was need among black religious thinkers to develop a much deeper, broader conception of God grounded in black religious and cultural tradition. Here, Jones hit the target dead center. Where he went wide of the mark was his actual formulation of the Afro-Americanized God-concept. For what he essentially ended up with is little more than a blackened conception of the traditional doctrine of God espoused by white Western thinkers. His alleged Afro-Americanized God-concept is flawed in precisely the same ways as that of its white counterpart when it comes to addressing the problem of evil, including moral evil. We are left with the concept of a perfectly powerful and loving God who cannot seem to eradicate evil from the world, even if God wanted to. Whether one agrees with this assessment of Jones's view, it is clear that according to black liberation theologians, Afrikan Americans have historically adhered to the traditional doctrine of the omnipotent-omni-benevolent God. Although I have tried to show that King significantly nuanced this view, black liberation theologians did not.

Black Theology, King, and Divine Omnipotence

When James Cone talks or writes about King's doctrine of God, he quickly concludes that King was a proponent of "the classical view" of divine omnipotence. Cone maintains that King was too committed to the black faith tradition to take seriously finitistic theories of God,[116] such as that espoused by Brightman. Cone and other black liberation theologians essentially argue for an uncritical acceptance of divine omnipotence and goodness.[117] They do not consider seriously enough the inconsistencies that arise when these two divine attributes come face to face with nonmoral evil. Nor has much been done in the way of critically considering the question of how such evil (e.g., incurable disease) can exist in the world if God is perfectly powerful and perfectly good. If God is perfect love and goodness, God would most assuredly want to eradicate such evil, because a good and loving God does not want persons to suffer for reasons not their own. Non-moral evil is generally not a result of the misuse of human freedom. If this is so, and if God in fact possesses perfect, absolute power, then reason should tell us that God is the source of non-moral evil. But if this conclusion is correct, how can such a God be deemed a worthy object of worship?

In any case, these are only *some* of the types of embarrassing questions that arise for proponents of the traditional conception of an omnipotent God. But they are questions that black liberation theologians generally have not critically entertained and examined. Instead, they have been quick to appeal to the black faith tradition. Cone makes the point. "It is a violation of black faith to weaken either divine love or divine power. In this respect Black Theology finds itself in company with all of the classic theologies of the Christian tradition."[118]

Cone contends that William R. Jones, an Afrikan American philosopher who argues that God is a white racist, limits God's goodness, since the character of such a God is highly questionable. On the other hand, Cone observes that Brightman limits God's power. Black faith, he maintains, is in both divine goodness *and* divine power. What Cone does not seem aware of is that even in his doctrine of the finite-infinite God, Brightman's faith remained in both divine goodness and divine power. For Brightman, the God of the Hebrew prophets and Jesus Christ continued to be the most powerful being in the universe. Brightman essentially did two things that are absolutely crucial to any reasonable conception of God in the light of nonmoral evils. First, he took very seriously the traditional idea that God possesses absolute, perfect power. By doing this Brightman could see that such a God should, by definition, be able to do literally anything, and consequently should be able to eradicate nonmoral evils in a heartbeat. Brightman refused to pretend that absolute and perfect power means that there are some things that God simply cannot do, if God wants to do them. If God possesses absolutely perfect power, then God should be able to do absolutely anything.

In the second place, Brightman had the courage to redefine omnipotence, which, as we have seen, King also did. The point, Brightman maintained, was not to have the conception of God that one wants, but to have one based on reason and the most coherent orchestration of the available evidence and facts. Brightman essentially did what Charles Hartshorne did. He redefined omnipotence to mean that God possesses the highest conceivable power that is actually shared throughout the creation.[119] In a word, God possesses unsurpassable power, power that is sufficient to achieve God's purpose in the world.

It is of interest to note that J. DeOtis Roberts, the black liberation theologian who has quite possibly read and understood more of the literature on personalism than any of his colleagues in black theology, uses the nomenclature God's "sufficient power." Unfortunately, Roberts clearly means by this nothing different from the traditional meaning of omnipotence as possession of absolute, perfect power that, he assures us, "is consistent with [God's] character." He contends that an all-powerful God "is indispensable to a worthy doctrine of providence to be assured that God has sufficient power to back up his love, justice, and mercy."[120] Roberts was making the point that because of Afrikan Americans' grave predicament in the United States, they have a deep need to believe that God is all-powerful and is able to deliver them from oppression. Roberts writes that Brightman's finite-infinite God is presumably "near and related in that he has an impediment or a disability in his own nature [which Brightman calls the non-rational Given] over which his will has no control. He moves from an 'eternal crucifixion to an eternal Easter,' but this God is not adequate for the faith we need to confront the black experience. A God infinite in goodness, but finite in power does not satisfy an oppressed people." And Roberts once again appeals to the doctrine of sufficient power. "Black men need the assurance that God has sufficient power to sustain his love and justice."[121] But remember, by "sufficient power" Roberts means absolute, perfect power.

Three comments about Roberts' stance will have to suffice. First, Roberts is quite right to point to Brightman's problematic usage of the term "impediment" when characterizing the non-rational Given. Examining the work of Brightman's student (and reader of King's dissertation), Sylvester Paul Schilling, I have addressed this concern in my *Personalism: A Critical Introduction.*[122] Schilling rightly maintains that Brightman's description of the Given as an uncreated internal impediment implies a deity who literally fights against itself. This would not be an encouraging sign to would-be worshippers.

Second, Roberts misrepresents Brightman's concept of the non-rational Given. Nowhere does Brightman say that God has *no* control over the Given, as Roberts maintains. Analogously this would be equivalent to claiming that the human will and reason have no control over emotions, appetites, and desires of the moment. Experientially we know that this is not the case. How much more so must this be the case with the divine Person? That is, it is not that the divine will and reason have no control whatever over the non-rational Given. Rather, God's will and reason do not always have complete control over the non-rational Given in every imaginable moment, just as, analogously, the human will and reason do not always have absolute control over human appetites and emotions. And yet, we know that it is generally within our power to control and shape them through our reason and will. Likewise, and in a deeper sense, God is "Controller of the Given." Brightman explains:

> God's will is eternally seeking new forms of embodiment of the good. God may be compared to a creative artist eternally painting new pictures, composing new dramas and new symphonies. In this process, God, finding The Given as an inevitable ingredient, seeks to impose ever new combinations of given rational form on the given nonrational content. Thus The Given is, on the one hand, God's instrument for the expression of his aesthetic and moral purposes, and, on the other, an obstacle to their complete and perfect expression. God's control of The Given means that he never allows The Given to run wild, that he always subjects it to law and uses it, as far as possible, as an instrument for realizing the ideal good. Yet the divine control does not mean complete determination; for in some situations The Given, with its purposeless processes, constitutes so great an obstacle to divine willing that the utmost endeavors of God lead to a blind alley and temporary defeat. At this point, God's control means that no defeat or frustration is final; that the will of God, partially thwarted by obstacles in the chaotic Given, finds new avenues of advance, and forever moves on in the cosmic creation of new values.[123]

Third, Roberts wants a doctrine of God in which Afrikan Americans can be assured that God possesses sufficient power to achieve and sustain God's love and justice in the world. In the realm of religious experience I do not see how one can ever expect to have such "assurance," whether he be absolutist or finitist. What a person can have is his own faith and his trust and confidence in the witness and testimony of others who believe similarly. I submit that this is the most that Afrikan Americans can expect as well, whether they are theistic absolutists such as Roberts, Cone, and most other black liberation theologians, or whether they are, like the author, and as I have tried to show in this chapter, like Martin Luther King, Jr., reinterpreters of traditional omnipotence as applied to God. As a student of personalism, King understood that in the end it is not a question of the kind of God we should like to have, but the kind of God warranted by the evidence and the facts.[124]

My reading of King convinces me that his is a God who is the most powerful being in the universe and is supremely compassionate and loving; a power not ourselves, making for goodness and love in the world. Although God's power is unsurpassable, God works best in the world not through domination, but through sharing and cooperative endeavor with persons. King was less concerned about God's power than God's faithfulness, compassion, and love.

King's doctrine of God grounds everything else that King took to be important in his work. It provides the foundation for his doctrine of dignity, the beloved community, the objective moral order and moral laws, as well as the application of the latter. The next four chapters elaborate on the significance of these additional personalistic principles in King's work.

CHAPTER 5

The Dignity of Being and Sexism

From the time Bowne systematically developed personalism, it has included a deep respect and reverence for human and nonhuman life forms. He discusses this aspect in *Metaphysics* (1882, rev. 1898) and especially in *The Principles of Ethics* (1892). In the latter text we read of Bowne's developmental ethic that argued for the need to expand the moral field. This had two important, related implications for ethics. First, it meant that the ethicist should strive to bring an increased number of human acts under the heading of morality and duty. Bowne considered (white) women's suffrage to be one of these. Second, the expansion of the moral field meant that persons owe duties to beings who in times past were not included within one's moral sphere. Bowne did not push this form of expanding the moral sphere as he should have regarding issues such as racism and racial discrimination. Much like most early white social gospelers, he was more silent than vocal about the issue.[1] For now, suffice it to say that he at least provided the theoretical framework and created the opening for such expansion to occur. In his speech at Riverside Church on April 4, 1967, King himself spoke of the need to expand the moral sphere even further to include those social issues heretofore excluded—in this case, the war in Vietnam.[2] And, as we shall see, the moral sphere can, and indeed should be, expanded to include sexism and sexual discrimination.

The personalists' respect for human as well as nonhuman life forms is manifested most plainly in their writings on ethics. Their more philosophical and metaphysical writings leave us without clarity on the worth of nonhuman life forms and on whether they believe in reverence for all life forms. This may be attributed, in part, to the uncritical appropriation and application of some aspects of the idealism of Plato, Descartes, and Kant. For example, this is the sense one may get from Bowne's claim that mind is the only ontological reality.[3] The strong idealistic emphasis left the first three generations of personalists open to the criticism that their metaphysics undermined the significance of the body, for the tendency was to say that the truly valuable is the unseen or invisible. King himself was much influenced by this aspect of metaphysical Personalism. As we saw in chapter 3, he frequently characterized the real person in spiritual terms, stressing the invisible qualities of the person (e.g., mind and will). For example, King sometimes spoke of the need to look "beyond the external accidents" or the physical characteristics of human persons and focus on "those inner qualities that make all men human and, therefore, brothers."[4] On many occasions, King wrote and spoke of the real person as that which one cannot see with the human eye. One cannot see reason or will, for example, the traits that most characterize what it means to be a person.[5] These are presumably references to essential person, or person on the metaphysical plane.

Metaphysics notwithstanding, King, like his personalist forebears, exhibited reverence for life as such. He did not place the worth of nonhuman life forms on the same level with created persons, nor did he assume the personhood of nonhuman earthly creatures (e.g., foxes, coyotes, and horses). King's reflections on the causes of his people's predicament in the United States and the reason for the low sense of self-esteem and self-respect exhibited by so many of them, made it utterly important for him to focus on the sacredness of human life, and most particularly that of his people. Such an emphasis does not necessarily preclude an awareness of and respect for the dignity of nonhuman life forms. In King's case it may simply mean that circumstances were such that it was necessary to focus on people. Personalism's emphasis on reverence for persons requires an acknowledgement of the dignity of every human being just because she is imbued with the image of God. Beyond such acknowledgment, however, personalism requires that one behave toward every person in concrete ways that exhibit honor and reverence.

King traced the cause of much of blacks' predicament back to American slavery and, in the late 1960s, frequently called attention to its gruesome consequences. When one considers King's frequent attention to this topic, it should not be difficult to understand why he spent most of his time focusing on the absolute dignity of persons. This focus did not mean he had total disregard for the dignity and rights of nonhuman life forms, or that he would have supported any action that would indiscriminately abuse either the environment or the animal kingdom.[6] It would be accurate to say that King possessed a sincere reverence and respect for nonhuman life forms. However, King would have had little time for the view so popular among some animal rights activists today, that all animals are equal or that animals are as much persons as blacks or any other human beings and thus are as much deserving of respect.[7]

To the claim of environmental ethicists that the term "dignity" needs to be expanded to include nonhuman life forms, Garth Baker-Fletcher also raises an important caution flag, one which King would have applauded:

It is disturbing that so much academic attention is given to the nonhuman world when human beings are still allowed to exist in undignified living conditions. Strong theological censure of human injustice as well as concern for the nonhuman world is needed. Without such censure one suspects that ecological concern could become an abstract exercise of those detached from and unconcerned about genuine human oppression. Expressing moral concern for the nonhuman world without an explicit call for human dignity leads to an inadequate view of dignity. Embracing King's understanding of human dignity could be a helpful supplement to the scholarship of ecological consciousness by including the suffering of human beings with the suffering of the world.[8]

In any event, it is important that we understand that King knew well the moral, spiritual, psychological, emotional, and physical consequences American slavery had on his people. "All too few people realize how slavery and racial segregation have scarred the soul and wounded the spirit of the black man,"[9] King wrote. Slavery itself was based on the assumption, not that the Afrikans were beings created in God's image and therefore ought to be respected. Rather, slavery was based on the premise that black Afrikans were objects or things to be used for creating lives of leisure, ease, comfort, and wealth for white people. Slavery meant total denial of the humanity, and therefore the dignity, of the Afrikans. King was also aware of the systematic attempts of whites to completely exterminate Native peoples, a practice that was reported in American history books as "an example of bravery and progress."[10]

The year before he was murdered, King lamented the fact that so many otherwise good white people, moderates and liberals, could not bring themselves to support the full freedom of blacks. He concluded that the frequently misstated reason was that they carried on the long tradition of whites in this country who believe those of black Afrikan descent are less than human—and most assuredly not as human as they are! They rather believed blacks to be "innately inferior, impure, depraved and degenerate."[11]

King maintained that the greatest of all tragedies of American slavery and the long history of racial discrimination is that it instilled in far too many blacks a sense of worthlessness—or the sense that they are nobody. Unfortunately, many of those who were strong enough not to be destroyed by this practice were still adversely affected by the dehumanizing practices in that they internalized the values of white oppressors, which has caused many to actually blame blacks for their predicament in American society. Present-day scholars on racism refer to such Afrikan Americans as pro-racist.[12] Such persons have lost sight of the fundamental causes of blacks' situation and have latched on to the symptoms and consequences. What this amounts to is but one more thing Afrikan Americans have to expend time and energy trying to make sense of that whites do not. King saw that, historically, all that was done in this country was done to support and enhance whites' sense of worth, rather than destroy it. In 1967 King summarized what it meant to be an Afrikan American:

> [Being] a Negro in America is not a comfortable existence. It means being a part of the company of the bruised, the battered, the scarred and the defeated. Being a Negro in America means trying to smile when you want to cry. It means trying to hold on to physical life amid psychological death. It means the pain of watching your children grow up with clouds of inferiority in their mental skies. It means having your legs cut off, and then being condemned for being a cripple. It means seeing your mother and father spiritually murdered by the slings and arrows of daily exploitation, and then being hated for being an orphan. Being a Negro in America means listening to suburban politicians talk eloquently against open housing, while arguing in the same breath that they are not racists. It means being harried by day and haunted by night by a nagging sense of nobodyness and constantly fighting to be saved from the poison of bitterness. It means the ache and anguish of living in so many situations where hopes unborn have died.[13]

Is it no wonder that King could be so focused in his emphasis on the dignity of his people, while devoting little attention to the dignity of nonhuman life forms? In this regard, he was only being consistent with his personalist teachers and his upbringing in the black church.

Unlike most of his personalist forebears, however, King saw clearly the importance of the body when characterizing the human person. This was due, in part, to the long history of black suffering in this country, and to the fact that King too was Afrikan American and knew firsthand that inevitably every black person experiences the dehumanizing and depersonalizing effects of racism. Racism adversely affects not merely the rational and spiritual side of black personhood, but the entire person— mind and body. When Daddy King was insulted by the white policeman and by the white shoe salesman, his entire being—spiritual and physical—was assaulted. It is the embodied black person who is disrespected, not simply a black soul or a black will. King wrote and spoke about the dignity of the body, and he was supported in this stance by his upbringing in the black church and his understanding of the Bible, as well as his daily experience of being black in the South. King knew that chapter one of the Book of Genesis reminds us more than half a dozen times that God looked out on all that had been created and saw that it was good. This included both human and non-human life forms. He also knew that God declared through the mouth of the prophet Ezekiel: "All life is mine" (Ezekiel 18:4). Therefore, the question for us is: Did King apply his doctrine of dignity consistently to all persons, male and female, or were there contradictions? The remainder of this chapter explores this question.

KING AND THE DIGNITY OF WOMEN

We may as well acknowledge at the outset that King's doctrine of dignity was not flawless. In this, he was different from most of his personalist forebears in that his personalism broke down at the point of applying it to women. The problem with most of his personalist predecessors is that their personalism broke down in their failure to apply it to the issue of race, or to apply it in ways that landed them in contradiction.

The "presupposition of male dominance" in King's thought and his failure to acknowledge it is the most obvious place we encounter a serious flaw in his doctrine of human dignity, and thus in his personalism.[14] Although there is no question that in general King fought for the dignity of all his people, he was also traditionalist in his thinking about the public and private roles of women in the black community. We know, for example, that even in the organization of which he was president, the Southern Christian Leadership Conference, there were numerous significant contributions made by black women. However, these women were not allowed to be in leadership positions, nor were their contributions always fully acknowledged. James Cone has addressed this issue in *Martin & Malcolm & America* (1991). Reporting on what King included in "jailhouse diary" from Albany, Georgia (July 27–August 10, 1962),[15] Cone wrote:

Identities, with names and titles, were given to the men, but the women were rendered invisible even though their number was larger. "One can find scant indication that Dr. King recognized the indispensable work of black women within the Civil Rights Movement," June Jordan has correctly written. "There is no record of his gratitude for Ella Baker's intellectual leadership. There is no record of his seeking to shake the hand of Mrs. Fannie Lou Hamer." King also failed to acknowledge properly the major role that Jo Ann Robinson, Mary Fair Burks, and other women of the Women's Political Council played in the success of the Montgomery bus boycott.[16]

King did acknowledge that the idea of the Montgomery bus boycott was first conceived by Jo Ann Robinson and the Women's Political Council (WPC).[17] In addition, he expressed appreciation for Robinson's courage to challenge Montgomery city officials.[18] However, he did not publicly acknowledge the many leadership and other contributions of black women in the civil rights movement from Montgomery to Memphis. More than black men in Montgomery, it was black women who initiated the bus boycott, agreed to be plaintiffs in the federal case against the city segregation ordinance, and consistently turned out in the greatest numbers at the numerous mass church rallies that kept things going. And yet the women were conspicuously absent from the planning and strategy sessions held by black male leadership.[19]

Robinson and other members of the WPC were irritated by the older established black male leaderships' apprehensiveness about challenging the white power structure and their contentment with compromising for what amounted to mere crumbs. Considering that some of the black leaders were more financially well off and secure than most blacks in the city, Robinson was outraged at their willingness to play along with the white authorities. In her account of the Montgomery story she said: "Despite the fact that the [Rufus] Lewises and some of the other members of the group were self-employed and financially secure, nobody had called for the boycott! Black Americans were still riding those buses, and still being insulted as they rode. Black leaders were still trying to compromise with officials for better treatment, and still enduring embarrassing experiences each day."[20] Robinson and other women of the WPC had a strong sense that the time had come for Montgomery blacks to stand up. Mary Fair Burks described Robinson as "the Joan of Arc of the Montgomery Bus Boycott" and Rosa Parks as "its patron saint.[21]

Interestingly, Robinson, although critical of the old guard black male leadership in Montgomery (e.g., E. D. Nixon and Rufus Lewis), records in her memoir no criticism of either King's leadership in Montgomery or of his attitude toward the public and private roles of women. In part this may have been because Robinson was a member of the church King pastored. This does not explain why Burks, also a member, was not hesitant to point out that the black women of Montgomery, not King, were the trailblazers. King, she said, was the torchbearer.[22] Burks' criticism of King was fairly tame. But there were more outspoken black women who, though they appreciated what King sought to do for his race and the many sacrifices he made, were critics of King's stance regarding the role of women.

The late Pauli Murray, "passionately devoted" to King's cause, wrote in her autobiography that she "had not been a passionate admirer of Dr. King . . . because I felt he had not recognized the role of women in the civil rights movement (Rosa Parks was not even invited to join Dr. King's party when he went abroad to receive the Nobel Peace Prize)."[23] E. D. Nixon accused King and his supporters of using Mrs. Parks for their own ends (envy or jealousy may have been behind his criticisms), and then refused to hire her for a paid position at the Montgomery Improvement Association when she desperately needed a job. Virginia Durr, a close (white) friend, said that Parks was "very disgruntled with MLK."[24] In addition, at the first mass rally that was held at the Holt Street Baptist Church in Montgomery, Rosa Parks was introduced after King spoke. When she asked black ministers if they wanted her to speak, they said: "You have had enough and you have said enough and you don't have to speak."[25] Parks accepted that, and apparently thought little of it at the time. In later years she said: "The other people spoke. I didn't feel any particular need to speak. I enjoyed listening to the others and seeing the enthusiasm of the audience."[26] And yet, one must find it interesting that the person whose arrest ultimately sparked the boycott was not encouraged to speak at that first rally. Lynn Olson, a white scholar, puts it more bluntly when she writes that the black community of Montgomery had made it clear at the Holt Street Baptist Church rally that they had had enough, "but the woman who had shown them the way was denied a voice of her own."[27] Although we may grant that it was not King who denied voice to Rosa Parks that night, he was nearby when she asked whether the ministers wanted her to speak. Furthermore, Parks was not invited to ride the desegregated buses with King and Abernathy the day after the Supreme Court ruling against Montgomery's segregation ordinance. Their failure to include her in this powerfully symbolic gesture spoke volumes about their attitudes toward key women in the boycott.

Honest and courageous black women did not hesitate to point to the contradictions in King's liberation project relative to the place of women in general, and black women in particular. One of these was Ella Baker. What was her role, and how did she perceive King's leadership and attitude toward the public role of women?

Ella Josephine Baker

Ella Baker (1903–86) was the second of three children born to Georgianna and Blake Baker in Norfolk, Virginia.[28] Georgianna Baker did not like the hot humid weather in Norfolk, and thus the family moved to Littleton, North Carolina, when Ella was eight years old. Like Norfolk, however, Littleton had Jim Crow laws, which meant that racism and discriminatory practices were harsh realities. In fact, by 1900 every southern state had Jim Crow laws that quite effectively kept blacks and whites apart in neighborhoods, churches, schools, restaurants, and other public accommodations, and on transportation.

In those days, as during slavery and after Reconstruction, blacks were expected to defer to whites in every way. Failure to do so could mean severe punishment or even the lynching of children as well as women and men. This makes it all the more interesting when we read of Ella's response as a six-year-old when a white boy called her a "nigger" as she and her father walked through downtown Norfolk during the Christmas season. Knowing even at that age that this was the worst thing a white person could call blacks, she instinctively began punching the boy. In yet another racial encounter that occurred when the family moved to Littleton, a white sheriff's son "made the mistake of hurling a racial epithet her way [and] was also made to regret the error. Ella threw rocks at the boy and chased him off her street."[29] These were very dangerous responses that could have had severe consequences for Ella and her parents. Self-confident, not one for holding her tongue, and possessing what womanist thinkers today call "sass" and strength of determination, this was the personality that would in later years do many battles with racial discrimination through her work with the NAACP, an organization called In Friendship (which provided financial assistance to southern blacks who suffered reprisals because of political activity), the Southern Christian Leadership Conference (SCLC), and the Student Nonviolent Coordinating Committee (SNCC). Baker in fact helped give birth to the latter two organizations and temporarily served as acting director of the SCLC.

Baker played a key role in the formation of In Friendship and served as executive secretary.[30] This was a New York–based organization devoted to raising funds to support the Montgomery bus boycott and other southern civil rights efforts. Even the MIA was a recipient of monetary support from In Friendship, which counted Stanley Levison and Bayard Rustin among its members. Baker became very concerned that any potential progress in the social struggle might come to a halt after the boycott. She and her colleagues at In Friendship had hoped that an organization in the South would be developed that could provide the type of leadership the NAACP essentially provided in the North. The bus boycott had proven that the elements for a mass movement were all present in the South during that time: a community sensitized and politicized by a common social issue, active clergy and civic leaders, and an involved black church which provided a strong base.[31]

Much to Baker's disappointment, the movement came to a screeching halt after the boycott. She met and talked with King about this, inquiring as to why he allowed this to happen. Paula Giddings records Baker's account of the conversation. "'I irritated [him] with the question,' she recalled. 'His rationale was that after a big demonstration, there was natural letdown and a need for people to sort of catch their breath. I didn't quite agree,' Baker said in understatement. 'I don't think that the leadership in Montgomery was prepared to capitalize . . . on [what] . . . had come out of the Montgomery situation. Certainly they had reached the point of developing an organizational format for the expansion of it.'"[32]

Baker and her cohorts at In Friendship were ready to capitalize on the momentum generated by the boycott. In fact, Baker, Levison, and Rustin had already discussed Rustin's idea of the possibility of using the momentum of the boycott to establish a broad-based southern organization to continue the fight for civil rights throughout the South.[33] They were northerners, which suggests that the idea for what came to be known as the SCLC might well have had northern roots.[34] "Baker recalled that she and her two New York colleagues spent many hours discussing ways that movement leaders might 'enlarge upon the gains of the Montgomery bus boycott.' Rustin and Levison relayed the content of those discussions to King and other ministers involved in the southern civil rights movement, urging them to call a regional meeting to discuss the idea further."[35] That meeting occurred on January 10, 1957, at the Ebenezer Baptist Church in Atlanta. Initially named the Southern Leadership Conference on Transportation and Nonviolent Integration, the group changed the name to the Southern Christian Leadership Conference in August of that year. The seeds, however, had been planted by northerners, more specifically, a black woman, Ella Baker.[36] When the SCLC was founded in 1957, Levison and Rustin tried to convince King that Baker was the best person to get it off the ground. "King was initially reluctant to hire Baker, because he had a different profile of the type of person who should share the leadership role with him at the helm of the coalition. King indicated that he did not personally believe that the director had to be a minister, but he recognized that many of his clerical colleagues strongly held that conviction."[37] Since most black ministers in those days were males, hiring a minister essentially meant hiring a male. But it also meant that since the SCLC's board was composed primarily of black male ministers, the organization was an extension of the black church. Since the latter was a patriarchal organization this meant that the ethos of patriarchalism—so pervasive in church and society—would be transferred to SCLC, a point that came home to Baker very early in her tenure.[38] Not all of the pastors viewed Baker as little more than "a glorified secretary," but Barbara Ransby is right to point out that the few who did not should have had the courage to be more vocal in their support of her.[39]

Baker was asked to set up the office and essentially lay the foundation for the organization. With no office space and very limited supplies and finances, she agreed to take on the task for six weeks, although in the end she served in that capacity for more than two years. An important thing to remember is that by this time, Baker was already in her fifties and had experienced and learned a great deal in civil rights organizations. Historians have referred to Baker as "one of the most dynamic organizers in black America" and "one of the great leaders of the modern Civil Rights movement."[40] Howard Zinn thought so much of Baker and her part in the birth of "the new abolitionists" (i.e., the young activists who organized the SNCC) that he dedicated his book about the organization to her. Referring to Baker, he wrote in the last paragraph of his acknowledgments: "And finally, there is the lady to whom this book is dedicated, who is more responsible than any other single individual for the birth of the new abolitionists as an organized group, and who remains the most tireless, the most modest, and the wisest activist I know in the struggle for human rights today."[41] Zinn's book was published in 1965, three years before King was assassinated.

In addition, James Forman described Baker as "one of those many strong black women who have devoted their lives to the liberation of their people." John Lewis said she had "all the qualities of a successful leader—she was intelligent, savvy, charismatic, an organizer."[42] She was a hands-on communal or participatory type of leader who did not shy away from doing the undesirable tasks that keep an organization going. Baker was "one who is willing to work behind the mimeograph machine and to do the work that others are not willing to do, the nitty-gritty, the sweeping of floors, the detailed and tiresome work of administration,"[43] wrote Forman. In this sense, she was both a true and a realistic revolutionary. The point was not to seek glamour and popularity through media publicity. The point, according to Baker, was to do the work of liberation *with* the people. This is a significant point that womanist literary artist Alice Walker stressed in "Duties of the Black Revolutionary Artist." "*The real revolution is always concerned with the least glamorous stuff.* With raising a reading level from second grade to third. With simplifying history and writing it down (or reciting it) for the old folks. With helping illiterates fill out food-stamp forms—for they must eat, revolution or not. The dull, frustrating work with our people is the work of the black revolutionary artist. It means, most of all, staying close enough to them to be there whenever they need you."[44]

Ella Baker was not so proud, high and mighty that she preferred to delegate the menial, dirty work to others. Unlike many leaders she valued and respected each person, regardless of class, race, and gender. To Baker the drunk who gets arrested and is abused by the police and the college-educated, highly respected socialite in the community should have equal access to the resources and assistance of civil rights organizations. Everything she did in relation to the "little people" revealed her respect and appreciation for the personhood and dignity of all. Barbara Ransby characterizes Baker best in this regard, which is also an acknowledgment of her affinity with the personalist tradition.

At the same time that she sought to recruit large numbers of people to join the NAACP, she still tried to recognize and affirm the value of each individual. This type of *personalism* or humanism became Ella Baker's trademark as an organizer. In her travels throughout the South on behalf of the NAACP, she met hundreds of ordinary black people and established enduring relationships with many of them.

She slept in these people's homes, ate at their tables, spoke in their churches, and earned their trust. And she was never too busy, despite her intense schedule, to send off a batch of personal thank-you notes, sending regards to those she did not contact directly and expressing gratitude for the support and hospitality she had received.[45]

Indeed, Baker believed this should be the approach of every leader among the people.

Having agreed to give six weeks to the newly founded SCLC in Atlanta, Baker's efforts were frustrated at the outset. There was no office, phone, or staff support. Baker recalled that she initially had to function out of a telephone booth and her purse.[46] That King was frequently unavailable and inaccessible only exacerbated the problems. It did not take her long to discover that neither King nor Abernathy, nor any of the other board members (all black male preachers) had organizing experience. Baker also found that her ideas and suggestions were not given serious attention by King and most of the men. In addition, she found that they wanted a "leader-centered" national organization rather than her preference for a "group-centered" or participatory leadership. In the leader or person-centered organization the tendency is for a few select persons to make decisions *for* the masses. The group or communal-centered organization focuses on the need for many well-prepared leaders, any one of which could step up to the plate and perform as well as any other. (One can easily see that Baker's preference for participatory leadership, had it been implemented, would not have left the movement in a leadership vacuum when King was assassinated.)

Baker's faith was in the people, not in a single leader, whether politician or civil rights worker. She had learned from many years of organizing experience that "strong people don't need strong leaders."[47] Baker urged that the emphasis be placed on building enclaves of strong local communities. Hers was "an endless faith in people and their power to change their status in life."[48] What mattered most to Ella Baker was the "organized will of the people" to decide and effect their own destiny. If the people were shown the light, she believed, they would find their way. The people do not need to be led, but rather to be provided information, skills, and opportunity to lead themselves.[49]

One of Baker's major problems with the SCLC from the beginning was its heavy dependence on the press and the promotion of one individual leader, King, rather than finding ways to develop indigenous leadership among the oppressed people. This was a major reason she refused to support the attempt of King, Abernathy, and (newly appointed executive director) Wyatt Tee Walker to make the newly formed SNCC the student wing of the SCLC. This would have meant the students would be subject to the dictates of the individual-centered leadership. In attendance at the SCLC's leadership's secret meeting to discuss a strategy that might cause this to happen, Baker rejected the idea and was passionately critical of the secrecy itself. James Forman maintains that

King, Abernathy, and Walker never forgave Baker for what they considered an act of defiance. "Throughout the years that followed they consistently made unkind remarks about Miss Baker and her influence in SNCC. What they did not understand, perhaps, is that her position simply reflected the students' attitudes,"[50] said Forman. The students were by this time already disillusioned with the older established or "official" leadership.

Baker had the same criticisms of and frustrations with her early efforts to organize the SCLC that she had when she was employed with the NAACP. Both organizations failed to democratize their decision making. Women formed the backbone of both organizations and were thus what Barbara Ransby characterizes as "indispensable but underappreciated."[51] Baker and other women were close to the center of power in the organizations, but were not allowed to enter the inner circle where decisions were made. In addition, Baker was critical of each organization's failure to see that the people needed to be their own leaders. They did not, in her view, need leaders from outside their community. They needed leadership from the grassroots—from the bottom up.[52] This view was heartily shared by Septima Poinsette Clark, initiator of the civil rights Citizenship Education Program that sought to teach blacks in the deep South how to read and write in order to vote.[53] Baker wanted the SCLC to develop into a thoroughly democratic organization, not the single charismatic leader type that the board of directors wanted. From the very beginning her involvement with these black ministers was marked and "shaped by pervasive tensions and fundamental contradictions."[54]

Remember, even as a child Baker exhibited sass, and did not run from a fight. She was not in awe of King, like most who surrounded him, nor would she kowtow to him. She considered neither King's nor the male board's word to be gospel. Baker therefore did not hesitate to raise questions of her own, make her own suggestions, talk back, and think for herself. These are traits of present-day *womanism*. Baker was self-determined, in charge of herself, and did not hesitate to take charge of her surroundings. But in any case, *she*, not men (of any race), would make that decision. She knew that this type of attitude in a black woman of that period did not go over well with most black men in leadership, and especially ministerial types. In a 1970 interview, she told historian Gerda Lerner: "I knew from the beginning that as a woman, an older woman, in a group of ministers who are accustomed to having women largely as supporters there was no place for me to have come into a leadership role."[55] Baker believed the SCLC ministers were not in the least interested in her or other women's political contributions, but were more comfortable "talking to women about 'how well they cooked, and how beautiful they looked.'"[56] Her type of personality was not appreciated and respected by most men of the period (and quite possibly would not be today). Barbara Ransby observes that whether during her stint with the NAACP as director of branches or as acting director of the SCLC, Baker "did not ingratiate herself with those in high positions, and she did not hesitate to speak her mind even when her ideas were controversial."[57] She was not a team player in the traditional sense of uncritically going along with everything for the sake of the team. Although she knew the consequences for "difficult" women[58]—i.e., women who were self-determinative and insistent on speaking their own mind—Baker was still a human being. She was therefore rightly, and quite naturally, angered and disappointed when she was not appointed executive director of SCLC, a point that Coretta Scott King confirms. Sympathetically, Mrs. King writes: "Ella eventually separated herself from Martin, and that was a breach that even he could not heal. . . . Later on she was upset that she did not get the job as executive director of SCLC—Wyatt Walker was chosen instead in 1960. *She always felt persecuted as a woman and I cannot say that she was not justified. I am sure there were a lot of slights to her.* She was a very intelligent woman. Often she was the only woman in the councils of men."[59] Although Baker did not develop a close personal relationship with Mrs. King as she did Juanita Abernathy (wife of Ralph Abernathy),[60] there appears to have been an unspoken mutual respect and admiration between the two women.

Baker did not hesitate to disagree with King and the SCLC board, especially since she knew that none of them had organizing experience that could match hers. Throughout her career in civil rights she constantly fought for the need to organize. A. Philip Randolph made the point that "Ella has the unique quality of having the necessary sense of struggle for an oppressed people to achieve the alleviation of oppression, and at the same time she is capable of understanding . . . certain principles of organizing that [are] necessary to achieve an objective. Many militants don't understand that. They think that a part of militancy is to disregard organized procedure."[61] It was this lack of ability to organize, and the unwillingness to grasp its significance, as well as the refusal to see the superiority of a group leadership approach over the individual type, that frustrated Baker most and kept her at odds with the leadership in SCLC. As the organization grew and was able to hire more female staffers, Baker complained that the women's abilities and contributions were being undervalued.[62] "A rhetoric of racial equality marked the public pronouncements of SCLC leaders, while old hierarchies based on gender inequities endured within their ranks. Baker refused to accept the situation in silence."[63]

John Lewis recalled that something went dreadfully wrong between Baker and SCLC. Although he could not say exactly what caused it, Lewis knew that "something poisoned her with the men there. . . . Long before people began using the term 'male chauvinism,' Ella Baker was describing it and denouncing it in the civil rights movement."[64] She was positioned to know what was going on in the organization, but she was neither a fully accepted member, nor did she have real power to effect changes.

This is not to say that Baker had no power at all, but what power she had was not given her. She was basically what Barbara Ransby refers to as an "outsider within." Ransby, following feminist sociologist Patricia Hill Collins' concept of the "conditional insider," characterizes this as "a person who functions in close proximity [to] those in power but who is never given official recognition as a member of the club. . . . The 'outsider within' has the benefit of observation up close, but she is still not an authentic member of the inner circle in terms of actual power, access to resources, or social status within the group."[65] Baker knew and to some degree had access to some of the most powerful figures in the civil rights movement, but she was never "one of the boys." Rather, she "consistently described herself as operating on the periphery of respected black leadership circles."[66]

Ella Baker never pretended that male chauvinism or sexism was either a nonissue in the organizations in which she worked or that it would somehow just go away. Instead, she was always proactive in addressing it, and seldom let pass an opportunity to protest against it or to create opportunities for the women in the NAACP, the SCLC, and other organizations with which she was affiliated. "She pushed for broader inclusion and fairer treatment of other women and took opportunities to make women feel valued within the organization, including women whose main roles in life were those of wife and mother."[67] In addition, Baker opposed any idea or practice that might "marginalize women and circumscribe their participation, excluding them from the mainstream of the organization." In particular she rejected the suggestion made by a male member to establish a separate women's auxiliary at one of the local NAACP affiliates.[68]

Considering King's clearly developed ethic of the dignity of persons as such, and his desire to forge SCLC into a powerful and influential southern organization, it is worth examining why he did not press the board of directors to call Baker as the permanent executive director. There is no easy answer.

The claim has been made that Baker had such difficulty with King and the SCLC board because she was not a minister (a cloaked way of saying she was not a man) and therefore did not possess the ministerial skills needed to work efficiently with black preachers.[69] There is surely some truth in this, but it is nowhere near the whole truth, nor the most significant part of it, for what Baker and the ministers always shared in common was their humanity and capacity to reason together. Ministers, whatever the race or gender, can relate to or work cooperatively with the non-minister. Any such qualities they might possess are a result of socialization. That is, they are learned, and therefore can be unlearned.

It was also charged that Baker was not a media figure. Of course this meant nothing to Baker, for she preferred that the SCLC have many outstanding and committed leaders, rather than one leader on whom all the media attention would be focused. Besides, in Baker's view there were vastly more important issues that demanded her attention than those of makeup and hair styling for the media. She had little patience for such matters.[70] The charge was also made that Baker's strong personality as a woman threatened King, who, according to James Lawson, "had real problems with having a woman in a high position."[71] Similarly, Andrew Young said, "we had a hard job with domineering women in SCLC because Martin's mother, quiet as she was, was really a strong, domineering force in that family. She was never publicly saying anything, but she ran Daddy King and she ran the church and she ran Martin, and so Martin's problems with Ella Baker, for instance, in the early days of the movement were directly related to his need to be free of that strong matriarchal influence."[72] Each of these claims, individually and collectively, factor into why Ella Baker was not selected to be executive director of SCLC.

However, because of King's stature and his commitment to personalist philosophy, we must still wonder whether something else might have been involved. By the end of the Montgomery campaign he was, in principle, totally committed to the doctrine of the absolute dignity of persons as such. Why then was he not willing to step in and give his own support to Ella Baker, the person most qualified among women *and* men to be executive director of the SCLC. The evidence clearly suggests that, in the matter of women in the public sphere, King's personalism, and most particularly his doctrine of dignity, was not as consistent as it could have been. His behavior regarding Baker and his failure to adequately credit other black women for their many contributions to the struggle was sexist. By definition, the type of personalism to which King adhered admits no place to sexism, racism, heterosexism, ableism, classism, or any other practice that alienates persons from each other.

The idea of having a woman, especially one like Baker, in a position of leadership was a problem for King and his male run organization. Wyatt Tee Walker said that Baker was incompatible with an organization whose leadership was comprised of black ministers. "It just went against the grain of the kind of person she is and was,"[73] Walker said. It would seem, however, that this statement says more about Walker and many of the SCLC board members than about Baker. In any case, this raises the issue of sexism and the personalist doctrine of the absolute dignity of persons as such.

PERSONALISM AND SEXISM

Sexism is male prejudice against women *plus* the power and resources to keep women in a subordinate position to men in interpersonal and collective relations. It chiefly harms women, but it affects men as well, since both genders are stereotyped and made to believe that by virtue of gender alone one is the superior or inferior of the other and that this is the natural order of things. Gender stereotyping is intended to keep women and men in a place appointed by males—women in the private sphere of the home and men in public leadership and decision-making positions. Women who aspire to the latter are often seen to be "unfeminine"; men who display sensitivity and artistic ability, for example, are thought to be effeminate.[74]

In principle, the thoroughgoing personalist rejects sexism in all of its forms, just as she or he rejects racism, classism, and heterosexism. However, we find that King's behavior toward Ella Baker (and undoubtedly other women) during the civil rights movement meets the definition of sexism, i.e., the prejudicial behavior against women plus the power to effect that behavior and to know that the perpetrator(s) will be insulated or protected from prosecution, or at least will be coddled if prosecution occurs. How is it that Martin Luther King, Jr., the personalist, is open to the charge of sexism? The point here is not that King was misogynistic. He was not. Nor is there evidence that he was intentionally abusive, verbally or physically, toward women.[75] The type of family and religious values instilled in him as a child, as well as his adoption of personalism as his fundamental philosophical standpoint, required that he respect, in theory *and* behavior, the dignity of all women. And yet there is unmistakable evidence that King did have difficulty with the so-called strong, sassy, confident woman in the public sphere. Ella Baker was one such woman.

King grew up in a household in which his father was seen as head of the family. Considering the systematic attempts of white enslavers to break up black families during the period of American slavery, it is understandable that black heterosexual couples in many instances agreed among themselves that as long as the family could be kept intact, it was important that the husband be the head of the household. At least in the context of the black family, then, the idea of male headship is not in itself entirely problematic. What came to be problematic, however, was the way headship often got interpreted and lived out by some of the men. Many came to think of it as their inherent right to rule over women and children, who had no right to question male decisions or actions. Additionally, many black men expected and even demanded the services of their wives and children, but frequently did not carry out their own responsibilities. Consequently, the practice of male headship went much further than was initially intended in the quarters of the enslaved.

Martin and Coretta had long discussions about the type of family arrangement they might have. Coretta knew of her husband's more traditional views about husband-wife relations and parenting. She essentially conceded this to him, although she herself had always been a very strong, independent woman. It would seem that this is precisely the type of thing that a would-be married couple would want to work through prior to marriage. King and Coretta did this. The problem with King's sexism, then, has less to do with the private sphere of the home and more to do with his stance regarding the public arena where women may be in positions of leadership. From a philosophical perspective, is there anything in personalism that supports sexist attitudes and behaviors toward women in any sphere? One way to get at an answer is to examine the response of key personalists to racism.

It has been shown that in principle personalism does not permit racism, for it implies that one group of people is necessarily superior to another on the basis of race alone. Racism also implies that one group is sacred and the other is not. Instead, personalism acknowledges the absolute and inherent dignity of all persons because each is created, loved, and sustained by the one God of the universe. In this regard, personalism may be considered the quintessential Christian philosophy. Every person has infinite, inviolable worth because each is infinitely valued by the Creator God. And yet we know that some early personalists were in fact racists.[76] Some were at best racially and culturally biased. Bowne himself, the father of American personalism, exhibited racial-cultural insensitivity. He did so, for example, when he implied that one with a strong aesthetic sense would surely know that the Venus of Milo is necessarily a fairer work of art than the Hottentot Venus (the former being white and the latter black).[77] In addition, Bowne failed to address the problem of racism forthrightly in any of his published writings, a point that completely baffles me.[78] The point is not that Bowne was a blatant racist who openly exhibited hatred toward blacks and people native to this country. He was not, and he did not. Although Francis J. McConnell, Bowne's student and biographer, maintained that he championed the rights of oppressed races,[79] we see nowhere in Bowne's published writings where this is explicitly supported. The most we can say is that in principle Bowne favored the rights and humane treatment of blacks, but like most early social gospelers he was guilty of benign neglect in this regard. We are therefore left with trying to explain this tendency toward racism and sexism on the part of some leading personalists, since they advocate the fundamental dignity of persons as such.

According to personalism, persons are both autonomous and communal beings. Each person is created in and made for community. One is never just a person, but a person-in-community. Persons invariably affect and are affected by their community, including its stance on other groups. One tends to take as his or her own the values and practices—good and bad—of the group. Martin Luther King, Jr., was certainly no different. He grew up in a society and culture that were not only racist but also sexist. The prevailing thinking and practice was that the place of women was in the private arena of the home, not in the public sphere. Therefore, unless one has experienced a radical conversion which liberates him from racism or sexism it is quite possible to be an adherent of personalistic principles and still be racist or sexist. That is, one can be a proponent of theoretical personalism while failing to live the personalistic faith. This is not different from what we frequently see in Christianity. There are proponents of the Christian faith who speak and write eloquently about the Christian ideal of love-justice, and yet they behave quite the opposite. What Étienne Gilson said about ethical theorists such as Plato and Aristotle applies here: that the trouble with these men was not their ethical theories, for in this regard they stood above their contemporaries. The problem, Gilson maintains, is that despite their careful theorizing and espousal of the high principle of justice, both Plato and Aristotle possessed a low estimate of the worth of persons.[80] Bowne argued similarly.[81] Furthermore, I know of no better way to explain the benign neglect of Bowne regarding blacks than to say that his estimate of the worth of Afrikan Americans was not the same as that he held for whites.

Something equivalent to this was involved regarding King's stance on women in the public sphere. As implied earlier, it would have been to personalists' advantage (including Bowne himself) had they taken more seriously, the idea of explicitly expanding the moral sphere to include those groups and issues that have been historically invisible. Those who are deemed invisible, and therefore left out, are frequently not regarded as beings to whom moral duty or responsibility is owed. One does not feel compelled to acknowledge the humanity and dignity of either groups or issues that are not even within the range of one's moral sphere. Since it is not acknowledged that they even exist, the tendency is to behave as if such persons are not owed common moral decency. It is sometimes the case that otherwise well-meaning persons simply do not know the issues that adversely affect a group. From the moral standpoint, one cannot be held responsible if one does not know. Clearly we can see that part of what needs to happen is the broadening and deepening of persons' moral awareness. Through this effort, their moral field can be expanded. King did this amazingly well throughout his twelve-year ministry. He did not live long enough, however, to expand his moral sphere sufficiently to include women's demand for equal treatment.

It is of interest to point out that Howard Thurman, who served as dean of Marsh Chapel at Boston University (1953–65), also understood the necessity of expanding the moral field to include persons and groups previously left out. He wrote of believing in the Kingdom of God, being active in the church, and having a reasonable intelligence when he was a youngster. And yet he realized that any sense of social morality he possessed had to do with his own people, not white people. Thurman attributed this to "the immorality of segregation." Looking back on growing up in Daytona, Florida, Thurman wrote: "it did not ever cross even the periphery of my awareness that I should recognize any moral responsibility to any of the white people in Daytona, Florida. They were not within the area of my ethical awareness. They were ethically out of bounds. What was true for me was true for any young white boy who may have belonged to the First Baptist Church, uptown."[82] He would complete college before the boundaries of what the love imperative required expanded beyond his sense of moral obligation to the black community.[83] Thurman found that one had to be both intentional and vigilant about finding ways to broaden and deepen the moral sphere, and thus the area of ethical concern and obligation.[84]

In *The Principles of Ethics*, Bowne argued for the need to expand the moral field to include those things, acts, and groups that have historically been left out. Accordingly, he argued, the expansion of the moral field ought to at least include all persons in their moral relations.[85] King was familiar with this concept. For example, when he finally broke silence on the war in Vietnam in 1967, King gave "seven reasons for bringing Vietnam into the field of my moral vision."[86] In other words, he had expanded his moral vision to include protesting against the war. And yet he did not expand his moral sphere to include women's rights in the public sphere. The argument is frequently made that King was a man of his time in this regard. It was simply that the culture permitted the relegating of women to specific places, and King grew up in that culture. But in light of King's personalism and doctrine of human dignity we must wonder whether this is an acceptable rationale for his practice.

Personalistic ethics seeks to make the whole of life an expression of good will and right reason. Bowne was certain that there was much in both private and social life that was in contradiction to this aim. There is therefore much room for moral development. The tragedy, Bowne maintained, is that far too few persons take this seriously. Whether it is a matter of overeating or overconsumption of alcohol ("indifference to one's own health, thus entailing often great loss and cost upon others") or sheer idleness, too many persons seem to possess little awareness of the need to bring such things under the rule of good will and right reason.[87] Bowne concluded that there is unlimited room for development in the life of individuals and society. But this is not all. The moral field can be, indeed must be, expanded, in yet another way.

Bowne saw the need to include more and more persons in the area of moral relations. He was aware that since much work needed to be done in order to extend good will and right reason to the lives of individuals, the inclusion of more persons was a great, if not greater challenge. Bowne implied in this, but did not say expressly, that various groups of persons had been left out, and that they had been left out because of differences of sociocultural background, race, class, and employment. Bowne put it this way. "The most arbitrary distinctions still limit our sympathy and affect our sense of obligation. Differences of clothing, diet, color, features, occupation, language, sect, nation serve to found prejudices and dislikes which influence our moral attitude, and from which the best of us are far from free."[88] Bowne might also have included gender difference in the list, but did not, although he elsewhere wrote persuasively and supportively about (white) women's rights.[89]

Two things will enhance the expansion of the moral sphere along the line of the inclusion of traditionally excluded groups: peaceful means of relating and the acknowledgment that all persons are "children of a common Father."[90] Bowne did not specifically name Afrikan Americans in general, or Afrikan American women in particular, as groups that had been historically left out. He should have. This was a matter that needed to be taken up by his students (and theirs) throughout the generations since his time. Some disciples of personalism did so (e.g., Brightman, Georgia Harkness, George A. Coe, Bertocci, Muelder, Schilling, and DeWolf). Others (e.g., Albert C. Knudson) did not.

Socialized in a patriarchal family, church, and society, King unfortunately was truly "a man of his time," by which I mean he was as sexist (and in the context of the Afrikan American community, privileged by his gender) as most men of his day and since. By putting it this way, I do not intend to excuse sexist behavior of any kind. There is no legitimate excuse, even though we are, each of us, products of our culture. For the truth is, we are also makers of our culture. Furthermore, King had Afrikan American forefathers such as Frederick Douglass and W. E. B. DuBois,[91] who relentlessly fought sexism in the public sphere. There is, therefore, no "protection" in the statement that King was a man of his time regarding male-female politics. He knew the work of both Douglass and DuBois, and surely must have known of their stance on women in the public sphere. He was much influenced by both men in a number of areas. Why was he not influenced by their stance on women in the public arena? Perhaps part of the answer to this question goes to the issue of King's close relationship and involvement in the politics and daily practices of the black church. This was not the case of Douglass and DuBois, however.

Clearly a personalist and Christian in the best sense, King had not begun the conversion process regarding the place and role of women by the time he assumed leadership in the civil and human rights movements. It must be said that he had a rather low estimate of the role of women in the public arena, and most particularly of strong-willed women like Ella Baker, who did not hesitate to talk back and to disagree with him. Indeed, had Bowne himself not reminded his contemporaries that one's estimate of the worth and significance of persons as such will have much to do with how one treats them? He argued that one who claims to be a proponent of the highest ethical ideals will likely mistreat persons, animals, and the environment if he has a low conception of their worth. In other words, "a low conception of the sacredness of personality or of the meaning of human life," Bowne said, "will result in corresponding action. If it does not produce inhumanity, it will certainly tend to indifference."[92] As for the treatment of animals, Bowne said: "We may not inflict needless pain upon the animals, but, except in this respect, we regard them as having no rights."[93] (It is arguable that animals have rights as such. The more important point is Bowne's recognition of their intrinsic dignity, which implies that people as moral agents have duties toward them.) In light of Bowne's claim, we may say that King's socialized view of the public and private roles of women, at least, had the effect of diluting his doctrine of the dignity of persons as such.

Now, in principle, King respected and revered persons, making no distinction between race, class, or gender. The problem, in King's case, was similar to that of those white personalist forebears who were also racist. King was socialized to think and behave in a particular way about women. Because of the thoroughness and subtleness of the socialization process, it just did not occur to him that, as a woman, Baker could be an effective leader of men. In a general, abstract way, King did in fact respect women and acknowledged their essential dignity as children of God. But his concrete, everyday practice was different. Lawrence D. Reddick interpreted King's stance this way: "Biologically and aesthetically women are more suitable than men for keeping house. And for the children, there is no substitute for an attentive mother."[94] Coretta King confirmed her husband's ambivalence:

> Martin had, all through his life, an ambivalent attitude toward the role of women. On the one hand, he believed that women are just as intelligent and capable as men and that they should hold positions of authority and influence. But when it came to his own situation, he thought in terms of his wife being a homemaker and a mother for his children. He was very definite that he would expect whomever he married to be home waiting for him.
>
> . . . From the beginning, he would encourage me to be active outside the home, and would be very pleased when I had ideas of my own or even when I could fill in for him. Yet it was the female role he was most anxious for me to play.[95]

By "female role," Mrs. King meant the traditional role of the woman as homemaker, primary parent, and caregiver to her husband and children.

King's own sense of headship in his family was much influenced by his parents' relationship. He had been socialized into this way of seeing and behaving and had not seen reason to criticize it, although he was not always comfortable with it. Coretta King gives an early example of his tendency to vacillate in this regard. "After we were married he said, 'I want my wife to respect me as the head of the family. I *am* the head of the family.' We laughed together at that slightly pompous speech, and he backed down. 'Of course, I don't really mean that,' he said. 'I think marriage should be a shared relationship.'"[96] Mrs. King was quite certain, however, that her husband meant it when he said he was the head of the family. She said that he did not want her working outside the home, since he believed it was his responsibility as head of the family to earn enough money to provide for his wife and children. She conceded to her husband, and *chose* to learn to live with this traditional headship model. "That was an adjustment I had to make," she said, "and I believe I made it very well."[97]

One cannot help but see the correlation between this stance and King's attitude and behavior toward Ella Baker. He clearly did not believe she should hold a high-level decision-making position of authority and influence in the public arena, most particularly as executive director of the SCLC. King agreed to hire Baker as the first full-time staff person, but he did so reluctantly. Although he claimed that his hesitancy had nothing to do with his view of women in public leadership, but rather with his awareness that this would be problematic for black ministers, King was clearly as much implicated in this regard as they. It is reasonable to say that in a theoretical or abstract sense, King really did believe women to be capable of providing significant leadership in the public sphere, much as some of them actually did during the Montgomery bus boycott and in subsequent campaigns. However, in the matter of placing women in positions of leadership in his own organization, King clearly did not act on this belief. He might have believed in women's leadership capability in *other* organizations, but apparently not within his own.

What we seem to be left with is the sense that King was a consistent and thoroughgoing personalist in every way but one. His doctrine of the dignity of persons as such did not fully accommodate women, especially in terms of public leadership and authority. This is strange indeed, considering that when he talked about dignity for his people in general, he did not have abstract dignity in mind, but dignity in the most concrete sense. He was concerned about how persons were actually perceived and treated in their daily lives. King would be the first to say that abstract dignity means nothing to the en-fleshed human being whose humanity and dignity are ignored. This must be the conclusion regarding women as well. Acknowledgment of some abstract notion of the dignity of women means nothing to women who have been historically (and presently) excluded from the moral realm of duty. Unless and until women have entered fully the moral sphere, it matters not that one claims to be a personalist and an advocate of the absolute dignity and preciousness of persons as such. Nor does it matter that a man advocates agapé love. Women must willingly be included on every level. If he does not do this he will likely, regardless of his philosophical, theological, or ethical stance, treat women as second-class citizens. Indeed, the literature on history and ethics reveals that whatever gains women have made in this regard have come as a result of mighty struggle and sacrifice on their part. This means that historically women, like other oppressed groups, have had to depend more on themselves to achieve their human rights than on males' high estimate of their value.

Nevertheless, many men, especially Afrikan American men, have found it very difficult to declare King a sexist. James Cone and Manning Marable,[98] were among the first to name the contradiction of sexism and to suggest what black males should be doing to address it. Only slowly have other Afrikan American males taken this stance as their own. Some continue to resist. Others publicly claim to be liberated, but resort to their old habitual ways when in an all-male audience. We will now examine select black male King scholars and their reaction to King's sexism.

KING SCHOLARS AND KING'S SEXISM

Two King scholars—Garth Baker-Fletcher[99] and Lewis V. Baldwin (one of the top five King scholars in the world)—have been reluctant to say outright that King was a sexist.[100] We will see later, however, that Baldwin has now fully and unequivocally acknowledged King's sexism. Baker-Fletcher and Baldwin acknowledged from the beginning that King's stance on women was a limitation, but their early tendency was to soften the criticism. For example, Baker-Fletcher writes: "Positively stated, there is no firm recording of King's philosophical, theological, and public view of women that would substantiate any claim that he had developed a sexist view of women's role. Instead it is better to say that King's practice toward women demonstrated his practical acceptance of women's inequality and his lack of critical reflection on the subject."[101]

The first part of this statement flies in the face of what we have previously learned about King's attitude toward Ella Baker. It also contradicts Coretta Scott King's statements about what King expected of his wife. Although he might have been comfortable intellectually or abstractly with the idea that women are as intelligent as men and just as capable of assuming high levels of leadership and authority, there is no evidence that King himself acted on this in any concrete way. In addition, just as white racists need not write or speak the language of white racism in order to be considered racists or beneficiaries of racism, it is not necessary for men (of any race) to write or speak the language of sexism to be considered sexists and beneficiaries of sexism or male privilege. As American society presently stands, every male, including the most liberal and progressive ones regarding gender issues, benefits from sexism. This, after all, is the point. Men benefit from sexism, even when we are also victimized by racism, classism, and heterosexism. We are privileged by virtue of our gender, if only in the context of our respective communities.[102]

Furthermore, just how important is it whether King's recordings and written record points to his sexism? What he did not say or write in this regard had the same effect, namely the exclusion of black women from leadership positions in the SCLC. Where black women did provide leadership they were not always given credit, and frequently their contributions were not valued as highly as those of men. In fairness, as Baldwin rightly maintains, King did sometimes praise women participants in the movement for their contributions, including Ella Baker, Diane Bevel, Rosa Parks, and Mahalia Jackson.[103] For example, in a letter to Mrs. Katie E. Whickam, president of the National Beauty Culturist League, King introduced Baker as "our associate director" at SCLC. He went on to say: "She is a very able person and a stimulating speaker."[104] Baldwin provides an instructive word, however, when he points out that it is quite possible to praise women for their many contributions to a movement while also doing nothing to open to them the door to leadership. This was the problem with King.

Baldwin has written on King's perspective on the public role of women in a number of his major writings. In *Toward the Beloved Community* (1995), for example, he discusses the institutional sexism in South Afrika in the context of King's ethic of the beloved community and points out that true liberation will not come in that country until it is eradicated.[105]

Baldwin and I have been engaged in ongoing conversation about King and black male sexism for a number of years. As noted previously, during an earlier period, he preferred a softer, more palatable description of King's stance on women. For example, responding to my review of *Toward the Beloved Community*, he wrote: "Your point concerning King and sexism is well-taken. My concern was not to negate that part of his character, but to note that his beloved community vision did include women (as evidenced by his frequent quoting of Galatians 3:28). *It is better to say that King was somewhat ambivalent in his attitude toward women, but his beloved community vision included all humans.*"[106]

Although Baldwin was reluctant to say without qualification that King was a sexist, it is quite significant that in *There Is a Balm in Gilead* (1991), Baldwin unequivocally names King as a male chauvinist who did nothing to encourage the involvement of women in leadership roles in the SCLC.[107] In the same text, Baldwin agrees with Ella Baker's criticism of the individual charismatic type leadership, which in male-dominated organizations led to women generally being excluded from leadership positions. This makes it possible for King, for example, to publicly acknowledge the contributions of black women to the movement, while excluding them from major decision-making roles. Women are therefore relegated to the shadows of male leaders. Baldwin is right to point to the complexity of this matter regarding King, even as he acknowledges that the problem itself continues to exist today. "Although King's leadership did much to free women and to give direction and momentum to the women's movement," writes Baldwin, "the problem of discrimination against women remained."[108] It is a problem that Afrikan Americans must face squarely and critically if they are to "effectively assume the messianic role King envisioned for them."[109] It is of interest to note that while Baldwin names sexism as one of the four great obstacles to the attainment of King's vision of world community,[110] not until the publication of *Between Cross and Crescent* (2002) did he expressly acknowledge that King failed to address his own sexism. Before then, Baldwin was only able or willing to say that "King never reached the point of addressing sexism as a global problem," but "his ideal of the beloved community still provides an inspiration and a model for millions who are struggling to resolve the problem."[111] To put it this way, however, implied that King was in touch with, and grappling with, his own sexism, although he did not live long enough to put sexism in a global context. With the publication of *Between Cross and Crescent*, however, Baldwin states unequivocally that King was a sexist.[112] There is no longer hedging or reluctance in this regard.

Baldwin is quite right to say that King's beloved community ideal includes all persons, regardless of gender, race, ethnicity, and class. However, what Afrikan Americans, Native Americans, Latinos/as, women, and others have learned in this country is that generally when the various groups are not named the consequence (intended or not) is that they are excluded and kept invisible. They are not within the sphere of moral duty, and so no moral duties are owed them. Or, the tendency may be to make them a part of some generic notion such as "human beings," when the truth is that the group in power means only to include itself as human beings, or to set itself up as the norm and to insist that all others meet its expectations of what it means to be a human being.

Andrew Billingsley, renowned scholar on the Afrikan American family, has not only found it difficult to name King a sexist, but at this writing refuses to do so, and is critical of those who do. Essentially, he argues that King was a man of his time and that Afrikan American males do not have the power to cause black women the amount of misery they suffer in this society. In this regard, Billingsley reacts to James Cone's flat-out assertion that both King and Malcolm X were sexists. Cone argued that the "most glaring and detrimental limitation of Martin's and Malcolm's leadership was not seeing sexism as a major problem connected with and as evil as racism."[113] Billingsley applauds Cone's own confession of the sin of sexism and acknowledges his challenge to other Afrikan American males, especially ministers and scholars, to renounce sexism in the black community and its religious institutions. Billingsley himself acknowledges the existence of black sexism, but he does not seem to think that it is a social evil of the same magnitude as racism. He seems to suggest that sexism is a problem to be sure, but it does not cause as much damage in black communities and families as racism.

Billingsley rejects Cone's charge that King and Malcolm were sexists, just as he rejects the claim that as a social evil sexism is on a par with racism in terms of the havoc and suffering it causes. Regarding the first charge, Billingsley writes:

While Cone is essentially correct, his criticism is a bit harsh, perhaps allowing a certain insensitivity to context to creep into his otherwise trenchant analysis.

The time, the place, the circumstance, and the experience of the leader help to shape the leader's perspectives. Just as Martin would not have been the same leader, for example, if he had lived 10 years earlier or 10 years later, if he had lived in Philadelphia or New York in 1956 instead of Montgomery, Alabama, so it is that his views on gender disparities and injustices might well have been more enlightened if he had lived in the enlightened era of the 1970s, which benefited from the revolution he helped to create in the 1950s and 1960s.[114]

Billingsley believes that because King and Malcolm were changing and developing so fast during the last months of their lives and both exhibited a profound ability and inclination to change, they might well have come home to the ideal of gender equality had they lived into the 1970s to witness the women's movement. There is much to be said for this. And yet the truth is that neither man was able to turn the corner cleanly and completely on this issue before he was assassinated. That is simply the reality that must be acknowledged, no matter how painful it may be to do so.

As for Cone's other charge—that the evil of sexism is of the same magnitude as racism—Billingsley prefers Cone's much earlier stance, in the early 1970s, that racism is the major social problem against which Afrikan Americans must contend. During this period, Cone was only peripherally aware of women's concerns in general and those of black women in particular.[115] By 1975 he was showing signs of the need to expand his black theological project to include gender analysis. In 1976 the die was cast. Cone was invited by Afrikan American women students at Garrett-Evangelical Seminary to address a black women's conference on the theme, "New Roles in Ministry: A Theological Appraisal." It was here that Cone strongly renounced sexism in the black churches and community.[116] He was the first of the black liberation theologians to do so in a public manner, and he has led the way since.

Billingsley's claim is not that sexism does not exist in the black community, or that it should not be addressed and eradicated. Few have written more passionately than he about the need to curb and eradicate domestic violence against Afrikan American women.[117] Nevertheless, his charge is that black sexism is not as serious as the racism that adversely affects all Afrikan Americans. Billingsley concedes that both racism and sexism are endemic and integral to the fabric of American society. He nevertheless concludes: "Black men simply do not have the power—even if they had the will—to inflict on black women the massive pain they suffer because of their race and their gender. At best or at worst, black men of whatever status are pawns in the game of life masterminded by others."[118] I hesitate to argue with Billingsley on this point, and yet I also know well the tendency of some thinkers to subsume a particular social issue under yet another, as if to imply that it is of lesser significance.

Historically, many socialists did this regarding race and gender; they subsumed them under classism, which in their judgment was the most significant social problem. Many white feminists tended to do this as well, presuming that (white) gender issues were the most basic. The problem with this approach, whether used by white male socialists, white feminists, or Afrikan American males is that they are frequently oblivious to the existence of other oppressions which might well be integrally connected to their own, and, which they themselves might be contributing to. They see only the immediate problem that affects them directly, while failing even to see their own contribution to and complicity in the oppression of groups within the context of one's own community. They fail to see that racism, sexism, and classism are each "an Individual Totality lockstitched into the ambiguities of contemporary history."[119] Each is a special issue, and although integrally related, is not reducible to any other.

Billingsley's reaction to Cone's critique of King is problematic. No matter what period of history a person lives in, he or she does not have to be a "person of one's time," if what we mean to convey is that because he or she lived in a particular era there was no way to avoid holding current views or engaging in certain practices, as if there were no choice in the matter. Furthermore, in virtually every historical period there is an internal irruption of dissenting voices. Even when these constitute the minority voice, the point is that there are frequently enough dissenting voices so that others know that they do not necessarily have to abide by the position that is common to the time. In the case of King, we have to be willing to acknowledge that he understood Hebrew prophecy as well as anybody. He knew full well that in every era of history God always has witnesses to God's truth and expectations of persons in the world. In addition, King was much influenced by both Douglass and DuBois, who lived during periods when women's equality was a critical issue. Although they too were also "men of their time," both *chose* to take the high road by standing up for women's rights in the public arena. Douglass and DuBois consciously refused to simply be carried along by traditions, beliefs, and practices of the day. Neither man was perfect when it came to the gender question, but both established a pattern of male feminist thinking and practice that far exceeded that of most males of any race during their day.[120] Neither man defended male superiority over women.[121] Douglass and DuBois were attentive to their time, place, circumstance, and the experiences of the disinherited, e.g., women. The point is it mattered little when and where they lived. There were choices to be made, and they each made the choice to go against the tide and insist on the rights of women. To have lived when and where he did, therefore, was not in itself an excuse or defense for King's chauvinism and sexism.

Finally, I do not find Baker-Fletcher's assessment of King and his theory of dignity relative to women to be compelling. For it can also be said that Bowne's (and all otherwise well meaning whites') attitude toward blacks was "somewhat ambivalent." While in principle Bowne's personalism affirmed the personhood and dignity of *all* persons, nowhere in his published writings did he specifically affirm the personhood and dignity of blacks and that of native peoples. Indeed, it must be added that historically Afrikan American scholars and activists have not been willing to let well-meaning whites off the hook so easily. But neither should Afrikan American women let black men off the sexism hook as easily as we would like. Instead, Afrikan American males should be willing to engage in self-critique regarding the issue of sexism, and especially black sexism.

Martin Luther King, Jr., was not a misogynist. However, reared and socialized in a thoroughly patriarchal home environment and society he generally adhered uncritically to the male-female politics of his day. Recent King biographer Stewart Burns maintains that King knew about the newly emerging National Organization for Women founded by Betty Friedan and her associates in 1966, but that he was not on record as having endorsed that organization's protests against sexual discrimination. According to Burns the rationale behind this was that King, like many black and white male reformers since the nineteenth century, placed race discrimination above that of gender discrimination in significance. Accordingly, Burns implies that King would not have taken feminists seriously in any case. In this regard, he writes: "If he was not noticeably concerned about women's plight in education and the work world, how much less would he have been sensitive to the major grievance of radical feminists— female subjugation in home and family. Given his background and his own patriarchal assumptions, he simply would not have understood where they were coming from."[122] The problem with Burns's contention is that by 1966–67 King had already developed a consistent pattern of exhibiting a profound capacity and willingness to broaden his moral field to include issues previously left out or not acknowledged. From Montgomery to Memphis we see a King who, in the face of new ideas, evidence, and current events exhibited both the courage and the willingness to change his ideas and practice. This was particularly the case when he was confronted with issues head-on.

Although receiving the Nobel Peace Prize in December 1964 contributed much to his breaking silence on the war in Vietnam in April 1967, the pattern of expanding his moral sphere and sense of duty had already been established. One need merely recall the narrow focus on race issues in Montgomery, followed by the inclusion of class and economic issues by the time of the Birmingham campaign in 1963, and the inclusion of issues of peace and militarism not long thereafter. I have argued elsewhere that this broadening of moral outlook had to do not only with the person King was, but with his adherence to personalistic method and objective moral laws. He was a man of ideas who exhibited an amazing ability to think his way to higher, more inclusive truths and then to change his behavior accordingly.[123] Echoing Andrew Billingsley, all of this leads me to the conclusion that had King lived into the 1970s and beyond when the women's movement gained energy and became more pronounced, and had he opportunities to have direct dialogues with feminists—especially Afrikan Americans—he would have broadened his liberation project to include women's rights in the public sphere and would have become a staunch advocate, and a recovering sexist, as he expanded the practice of his ethic of the beloved community, which we will discuss in the next chapter.

CHAPTER 6

Personal Communitarianism and the Beloved Community

What King thought, spoke, and wrote about persons and community ultimately comes together in his doctrine of the beloved community, which is grounded in the best of the Jewish and Christian faiths as well as his conviction that the universe is built on a moral foundation. The latter conviction will be examined more fully in the next chapter. Presently, our task is to determine a number of things related to the beloved community nomenclature: What is the origin of the term "beloved community?" When was King first introduced to it, and when did he show public signs of incorporating the term and its meaning into his own theological and ethical project? Does the term have any similarities to the Kingdom of God ideal that King learned about from his preacher father and other black preachers of his childhood? Was the beloved community *just* an abstract ideal for King? What is the role of freedom and moral agency in the actualization of the beloved community?

The term "personal communitarianism" is my own neologism. It is intended to hold in tension the value of two of the most important categories in King's philosophy of personalism—that of *the autonomous individual* and *the community*. Personalism maintains that reality is a society of interacting and communicating selves and persons united by the will of God. It therefore stresses not merely the individual *or* the communal, but *persons-in-community* (a term introduced by the third-generation personalist, Walter G. Muelder, who was one of King's mentors at Boston University).[1]

Although we see in personalism the dual emphasis on person and community, the personalism that influenced King tends to give the autonomous person the right of way, especially in matters of moral conduct. It is of interest to point out that Afrikan traditional thought also reveals a dual emphasis on community and person, although unlike personalism, it tends to give the community the right of way, even though the autonomous individual is also highly valued. An earlier generation of Afrikan scholars (e.g., John Mbiti) tended to stress a *hard communitarianism* which can tend toward the undervaluing of the person, intended or not.[2] The focus is intended to be on the community, not the individual; the we, not the I or me. However, more recent Afrikan scholars (e.g., Kwame Gyekye), have seen that even in early Afrikan traditional thought there is much evidence in Afrikan proverbs, folk tales, and myths which indicates that Afrikans have long valued and stressed not only the community but the autonomous individual as well.[3] Gyekye therefore argues for a *soft communitarianism* because it acknowledges the worth and autonomy of the person in community.

My term, "personal communitarianism," is intended not only to acknowledge the balance and creative tension between person and community, but to establish that because of the long practice in the United States of devaluing the worth and dignity of Afrikan Americans, the dignity of the autonomous individual must have the right-of-way in the person-community polarity. The basic aim, however, is to acknowledge the value of community and individual as well as person-in-community.

In King's personalism, we find an ongoing emphasis on the worth of the individual person, the community, and the ongoing interaction between the two. Each depends on the other for its fulfillment. It is not just a matter of the person needing the community in order to be fulfilled. For there to be a community at all, there must be individual autonomous persons who choose to abide by both civic and moral laws if a genuine beloved community is to be possible. Indeed, there must be autonomous persons who choose the beloved community, and commit their best efforts and resources toward its attainment.

From the time that King was a boy, he understood the meaning and value of both the individual and the community. His earliest ideas about love of self and neighbor came from the strong sense of family instilled in him by his loving parents and maternal grandmother. Their example made it easier for him later in life to accept the idea that the universe is friendly, one of his basic theological convictions—a conviction that also helped to ground his doctrine of the beloved community and his ethic of nonviolent resistance to evil. From this we may also surmise that King's later optimism about the actualization of the community of love is traceable to his having grown up in a loving family where he was taught to respect self, immediate family members, and others. This was not only a biblical mandate—that one love God and neighbor as one loves oneself. It was also part of Afrikan American cultural tradition, whereby one is expected to acknowledge the worth of self and of other persons, as well as the group or community. Benjamin E. Mays acknowledged this important point in a major publication in 1938. Mays found that Afrikan American literature (dating back to slavery) frequently emphasized the sacredness of persons as such, as well as love of self as Afrikan American.[4] These are ideas that Mays would have impressed upon Morehouse students throughout the 1940s, including King.

King preached and wrote about community, especially the beloved community, about as much as the dignity of the person, in whom are the seeds of community. He inherited individual as well as communal values, and he developed strong respect and appreciation for both. This is the reason it was so easy for him to embrace personalism; it provided him with the means to philosophically ground the personal-communal values.

King was neither an absolute communitarian, nor an absolute individualist. Rather, his theological ethics sought a mediating position. In this belief, the individual does not in every case necessarily have the right-of-way over the community, nor the community over the individual. Both have values that ought to be acknowledged, sought after, respected, preserved, and enhanced. Depending on the situation, it may be that the individual should have the right-of-way. Or, it might be the case that the individual should stand down, in favor of the community.

CREATED IN COMMUNITY, FOR COMMUNITY

King was much influenced by the personalistic principle that *reality is through and through social, relational, or communal.* According to personalism, the universe is a society of selves and persons who interact, communicate, and are united by the will of God.[5] The metaphysics of personalism maintains that the individual never experiences self in total isolation. Rather, the self always experiences something which it did not invent or create, but finds or receives from its "interaction and communication with other persons."[6] This idea is similar both to Bowne's early *objective idealism,* and to the Afrikan traditional worldview that emphasizes the importance of the communal. The focus in much of Afrikan traditional culture is on *we* rather than *I.*[7] This emphasis on the communal was carried over into Afrikan American culture. Having grown up in a traditional southern black Baptist church and family King must have been influenced by this focus on community. Is it any wonder that he was so easily drawn to the beloved community ideal implicit in personalism and explicit in the work of the absolute idealist Josiah Royce?

The focus on the communal nature of reality has been present in personalism since the time of Bowne, who maintained that reality is a system of interacting members that "cannot be construed by thought without the assumption of a unitary being, which is the fundamental reality of the system."[8] Bowne likened this unitary being to God. From this it may be reasoned that God alone is capable of creating and sustaining a community of persons in their interrelations. The many individual members of the community have neither their basic cause nor their chief characteristics in themselves, "but only in their relations or as members" of the community.[9] The ongoing mutual interaction means that each is essentially determined by the others. All are conditioned by the activities of the other members, and thus influence and are influenced by them. "If all its activities and properties are conditioned, it implies that the thing cannot exist at all out of its relations."[10]

Personalism's emphasis was never on individuals in a vacuum, on individuals as such, or on individualism. Instead, the reference has always been to "persons set in relations to one another, which relations are as much a fact as is the separate existence of the individuals."[11] This idea is expressed in Muelder's term *persons-in-community*. He writes that "man is a socius with a private center."[12] This description effectively holds in tension the primacy of both the person and the community, neither of which can be adequately fulfilled or understood apart from the other.

King's idea of the communal nature of reality and persons as well as his idea of the beloved community were grounded in his personalistic metaphysics and his doctrine of God. Although he followed more closely Bowne's, Knudson's, and DeWolf's conception of God, we have seen that King had deep affinity with Brightman's view that while God does not need us as we need God for our existence, God is love and love is a social category. In this sense God needs people. We cannot love to the fullest in isolation, but only in community, because we are created to live together. Brightman seemed to have this in mind when he said: "The maxim, 'Think for yourself', is basic; but the further maxim, 'Think socially,' must be added if philosophy is to do its whole duty."[13] This implies that the nature of persons is such that we need relationship with beings like us. We therefore possess *a natural urge toward community*. Moreover, persons are called into being in community. The very act leading to conception is a communal act between a woman and man. But more than this, God, the omnipresent One, is also present at every act of conception. This means that there is essentially a community present when each person is called into being.

King took as his own the Bible's and personalism's doctrine that community is what God requires of persons. He would have agreed with Knudson: "The real Christian world is a world of mutually dependent beings. It is a social world, a world of interacting moral beings; and in such a world love is necessarily the basic moral law."[14] For King, love is the essence of the Christian faith—the highest good. "I think I have discovered the highest good. It is love. This principle stands at the center of the cosmos. As John says, 'God is love.' He who loves is a participant in the being of God. He who hates does not know God."[15] Since love is at the center of the universe (and is also a social category), so, necessarily, is the idea of community. Indeed, this latter idea roots deep in the Afrikan American familial, religious, and cultural tradition.

The centrality of community for Afrikan Americans is implicit in May's *The Negro's God.* He said that during the period after 1914 one finds a number of themes about God that appear in the literature of Afrikan Americans. These include but are not limited to: the unity of all persons in God; God made no superior and inferior races; the rights of persons are divine; God made of one blood all nations; and all persons belong to God.[16] Personalism helped King to ground philosophically these ideas, as well as the conviction that persons are created in and for community.

King frequently expressed the idea of the interrelatedness of all life, and that persons are by nature social. This led him to reason that what affects one person directly affects all persons indirectly. "We are made to live together because of the interrelated structure of reality."[17] To treat even a single person unjustly, therefore, is an affront to *all* persons, including the Supreme Person.

For King, it was impossible for the individual to live a life of fulfillment without being in relationship with other persons. Although social psychologists affirmed the point empirically, King was convinced that philosophically and theologically "the self cannot be self without other selves."[18] The universe itself is so structured, King believed, that interaction among selves and persons is a necessity, lest they cease to exist. He maintained that: "All life is interrelated, and all men are interdependent."[19] What this effectively meant for King is that humanity is essentially one under God, a point that his black ancestors repeatedly stressed.[20]

King desired that persons be in community in a particular way, which requires directing one's energy and commitment in a particular direction. The achievement of the beloved community was not for King just an ideal or abstract philosophical notion. His understanding of the Gospel, his black church upbringing, and his awareness of the long tradition of black protest *against* racial injustice and *for* the right to be fully human with all the rights and privileges pertaining thereto, caused him to focus nearly all of his attention on what he called the beloved community. What is the origin of this term, and how did King define it?

KING AND THE ORIGIN OF "BELOVED COMMUNITY"

One of the earliest references to the term "beloved community," indeed possibly the first time it appeared in King's work occurred in his address to the fiftieth anniversary of Alpha Phi Alpha in Buffalo, New York, August 11, 1956. The Montgomery bus boycott was in high gear. In the address King said that the boycott was but a means to a noble end, "the creation of a beloved community,"[21] a society wherein persons will live together as sisters and brothers. Another early reference to the term appeared in King's address to the First Annual Institute on Non-Violence and Social Change in

Montgomery, Alabama, in December 1956. Here King cited a number of things that they had hoped to accomplish through and beyond the bus boycott. These included "reconciliation," "redemption," and "the creation of the beloved community."[22] King did not define what he meant by the beloved community in that address, but it was not long before he did. What is clear from these early usages of the term, however, is King's identification of it with the Christian imperative of agapé love. His aim was not just the development and enhancement of community in general. Rather, his focus was on developing a particular type of community, one based on the principle of agapé love. This community was to be modeled on the Kingdom of God ideal. "*Agape* is love seeking to preserve and create community," said King. "It is insistence on community even when one seeks to break it. *Agape* is a willingness to go to any length to restore community. . . . It is a willingness to forgive, not seven times, but seventy times seven to restore community."[23] Agapé is the glue that binds persons together in the beloved community. It is a social principle that points to the fundamental communality of reality and persons, one that grounded his conviction that all persons are sisters and brothers.[24]

King understood the beloved community to be a thoroughgoing integrated community in which persons are intentional about living in accordance with the meaning of agapé love. It is not enough to just bring diverse groups of persons together in a community (including an ecclesial community). The members and community must *intend* to be together and to live in those ways that acknowledge and respect the humanity and dignity of every person. What is more, persons must *want* to live in this type of community, and be willing to work cooperatively to achieve, sustain, and enhance it as far as possible. King would agree with Donald Chinula's description of the beloved community whose "citizens are transformed persons, imbued with a passion for peacemaking, justice, and love. The soul of such a society is healed by its love of justice and peace and kept healthy by its passion for love, justice and peace."[25] This was an idea that King was familiar with even before he enrolled at Morehouse College. Indeed, in their study on *The Negro Church* (1933), Mays and Nicholson included a sermon by a black preacher—which King must have known about at Morehouse—that provided a description of the Kingdom of God that sounded much like Chinula's characterization. The preacher said:

> If I understand what is meant by the Kingdom, it means the existence of that state of society in which human values are the supreme values. It means the creation of a world in which every individual born into it would be given an opportunity to grow physically, to develop mentally and progress spiritually without the imposition of artificial obstructions from without. Everything in the environment would be conducive to developing to the nth degree the individual's innate powers. At the center of our social, religious, political and economic life

would be not a selfish profit motive, not a prostituted conception of nationalism, not a distorted notion of race superiority; but at the center of our lives would be the sacredness of human personality; whatever we did, the chief aim would be to protect life and improve it.[26]

What we see here is a concrete rather than an abstract or purely philosophical description of the community of love, which was also consistent with King's conception. I cite Mays and Nicholson only as a reminder that although the beloved community nomenclature itself may not have been known to King prior to his studies at Boston University, he was familiar with its meaning as conveyed through the doctrine of the Kingdom of God. He would have heard much about this doctrine through listening to his father's and other black preachers' sermons when he was a boy. Since Mays served as one of his mentors at Morehouse and also preached frequently in chapel, it is likely that King heard much about the Kingdom of God as described in the above sermon selection.

The beloved community nomenclature, then, was not original to King. It is not even known with absolute certainty how, where, and when he came to know the term. Interestingly, not even Kenneth Smith and Ira Zepp try to track it down in their otherwise fine book, *Search for the Beloved Community* (1974), but neither do other King scholars who have written substantially on the beloved community (e.g., John J. Ansbro and Lewis V. Baldwin).[27] However, there are several important things we do know, and these have important bearing on how King came to know the beloved community nomenclature.

JOSIAH ROYCE

First, the term "beloved community," especially in its philosophical-theological usage, can be traced to the work of Josiah Royce (1855–1916), the American Absolutistic Personalist. Not all absolute idealists ascribed personality to the Absolute, but Royce did, as did his student, Mary W. Calkins (1863–1930),[28] a confessed personalist. As far as I can tell, Royce began expressing the idea behind the beloved community as far back as the publication of his first book, *The Religious Aspect of Philosophy* (1885). In his discussion on the highest good and whether or not humans could attain it, he wrote words that seemed to anticipate the later doctrine of the beloved community:

The moral insight, insisting upon the need of the harmony of all human wills, shows us that, *whatever the highest human good may be, we can only attain it together, for it involves harmony.* The highest good then is not to be got by any one of us or by any clique of us separately. Either the highest good is for humanity unattainable, or the humanity of the future must get it *in common*. Therefore the sense of community, the power to work together, with clear insight into our reasons for so working, is the *first* need of humanity. Not what good thing men may hereafter come to see, but how they shall attain the only sense whereby they can ever get to see the good, is the great present human concern.[29]

Any hope that persons may have of attaining the highest good is found not in individual effort alone, but in intentional cooperative communal endeavor. If the highest good is reachable at all, Royce argued, it will be through a community effort. What is important here is the emphasis Royce placed on community and cooperative intentional effort to work toward the achievement of the highest good.

By 1913, Royce was still fascinated with this idea of the necessity of cooperative community effort to achieve the highest good. By now, however, he was convinced that human salvation was possible only through membership in a certain type of community. In *The Problem of Christianity*, Royce considered the idea of community, as historically represented in the Church, to be one of three basic "Christian" ideas (the other two were sin and atonement). Writing on the relation between human salvation and community he observed: "The salvation of the individual man is determined by some sort of membership in a certain spiritual community,—a religious community and, in its inmost nature a divine community, in whose life the Christian virtues are to reach their highest expression and the spirit of the Master is to obtain its earthly fulfilment."[30] One may expect salvation only through membership in that particular community. Having first named this principle of community "the Universal Community," Royce finally settled on "the Beloved Community,"[31] which, he maintains, constitutes the "The Realm of Grace." Royce also equated the beloved community with the Kingdom of God ideal, as King would later do.[32]

For Royce, the beloved community ideal is "the principle of principles," the standard by which all morality ought to be judged.[33] Every act ought to be judged on the basis of Jesus' declaration of the centrality of the Kingdom of God, and persons should act and behave in ways that encourage the establishment and enhancement of the kingdom. "So act as to help, however you can, and whenever you can, towards making mankind one loving brotherhood, whose love is not a mere affection for morally detached individuals, but a love of the unity of its own life upon its own divine level, and a love of individuals in so far as they can be raised to communion with this spiritual community itself."[34] The beloved community is, then, the basic principle in Christian morality, according to Royce. Therefore, it may be argued that proponents of the Christian faith are obligated to do all they can to establish it in the world.

Royce's discussion of the beloved community has a more abstract quality about it than would King's. He did not give concrete descriptions of what such a community should actually look like in history, nor did he introduce and discuss a method for attaining it. Royce did not explicitly link the beloved community with the need to overcome specific injustices such as racism in the United States. King endeavored to do precisely this by seeking to know both what the beloved community could (or ought to) look like in everyday human existence and (also unlike Royce and white social gospelers and personalists) how to achieve it. He had an empirical and a historical sense about this type of community. In fact, King even believed that he witnessed the beloved community in microcosm at the Montgomery airport after the march from Selma to Montgomery in 1965. In addition, King fully expected that such a community would be realized in history. Who can forget the powerful words in the "Mountain Top" speech at Mason Temple in Memphis (the night before he was murdered) when he thundered: "I may not get there with you. But I want you to know tonight, that we, as a people will get to the promised land."[35] Implicit in his proclamation is the idea that the promised land, the beloved community, is ours if and only if we work cooperatively with each other and with God to establish and preserve it.

Ira Zepp provides an instructive word about Royce's and King's focus on the beloved community. "Due to his own idealistic, Hegelian orientation, Royce's beloved community is more of a rational construct than King's more historical and biblical conception. King was desperately concerned that it be realized and that it reflect certain specific ideals of justice and love."[36] The beloved community, then, was not just an ideal for King, eschatological or otherwise. Rather, King truly believed that as a Christian trying to abide by the teachings and ethical insights of the Hebrew prophets and Jesus Christ, he and others who believed similarly were required, indeed expected, to live and behave in ways that contribute to the actualization of the community of love. Such an achievement would require not only freedom and agency of will (to be discussed near the end of this chapter), but also the implementation of nonviolent direct action. Indeed, King's beloved community ethic requires that we live each day as if such a community already existed.

Before proceeding to a discussion on Brightman's contribution to King's awareness of the beloved community nomenclature, it is important to recall that King studied Rauschenbusch during his first year of seminary. In his intellectual autobiographies he refers to the influence of Rauschenbusch's *Christianity and the Social Crisis.* If we could only know whether King also read his *A Theology for the Social Gospel,* it would be possible to say with certainty that he saw in that text where Rauschenbusch linked Josiah Royce to the term beloved community.[37] We have seen, however, that some of King's criticisms of Rauschenbusch and the white social gospel suggests that he most likely did not read that book.

Brightman and the Beloved Community

The question of who introduced the beloved community terminology and when, has now been established. Royce did so in 1913 in his two-volume *Problem of Christianity*. Moreover, it is highly probable that this term was used frequently in the classrooms and hallways of Boston University, where King earned his doctoral degree. Brightman was at one time under the spell of Royce's absolute idealism: "My first real allegiance . . . was to Royce's absolutism, which I accepted as a whole for two or three years, until, in my graduate days, James's *Pragmatism* appeared and swept me off my feet."[38] When Brightman later studied personalism under Bowne, he concluded that this was the more reasonable philosophy, inasmuch as it provided a synthesis of the truth in both Royce and James, along with criticisms of the limitations in their thought.[39]

The Roycean influence remained even after Brightman became an avowed personalist. His first teaching appointment was at Nebraska Wesleyan University in 1912. About 1914, he taught a course on Royce.[40] Since *The Problem of Christianity* was published in 1913, it was most probably one of the required texts. Brightman maintained that worship, rightly understood and practiced, should point to the need to establish what he liked to refer to as a community of love. The "supreme consummation of worship," "the very goal and purpose of the universe," Brightman wrote, is "the Community of Love, or, as Royce called it, the Beloved Community."[41] Since for Brightman the "beloved community" was synonymous with his own phrase, "the Community of Love," whenever he cited this latter in his courses, his students, including King, would have understood him to mean essentially what Royce tried to convey in his doctrine of the beloved community.

In point of fact, John Cartwright maintains that "the beloved community" was "a part of the popular theological vocabulary of the Boston University School of Theology during the period when [King] was in attendance there as a doctoral student."[42] Cartwright, who arrived as a student when King was in his last year, concludes that King "would have been well acquainted with Royce." What is not clear from Cartwright's discussion, however, is whether King actually read Royce. Since King does not even mention Royce's name or the beloved community in either version of his intellectual autobiographies[43] nor in others of his writings, sermons, and speeches, it is reasonable to surmise that he did not read primary sources by Royce, but most likely heard of his beloved community ideal through lectures given by Brightman and De-Wolf. In addition, since King read many of Brightman's books, he might have seen Brightman's reference to both "beloved community" and to Royce in his *Religious Values* (1925). We know King was familiar with this book, for he quoted from it in Brightman's course in philosophy of religion in 1951.[44] Furthermore, King certainly would have been familiar with Royce's name, since Brightman frequently cited Royce's ideas in his own work. Moreover, in his theology and philosophy courses, DeWolf recommended that students read Royce.[45] Even if King did not take DeWolf's advice, from what has been said previously there is good reason to believe that he heard the beloved community terminology in conversations and class discussions with Brightman and DeWolf, as well as with other graduate students in religious and theological studies.

We know something else about King and the beloved community ideal. After graduate school he frequently spoke of it in terms of *a thoroughly integrated society.* Having first introduced the beloved community language in a speech in 1956, King went on to declare that the ultimate goal of the SCLC "is genuine inter-group and interpersonal living—*integration.*"[46] In the 1964 *Playboy* interview (published in 1965), King expressed his confidence that such a society would someday be a reality. Having declared that white supremacy is so endemic to American society and its structures that it will be many years before it ceases to be a judgmental factor, King proceeded to say: "Indeed, it is the keystone of my faith in the future that we will someday achieve a thoroughly integrated society."[47] The reference, of course, is to the beloved community. Confident that the civil rights movement was moving in the right direction at the time of the interview, King predicted that by the beginning of the twenty-first century the United States will have more nearly approximated a thoroughly integrated society.

We have determined that Royce first introduced the term "beloved community" into philosophical-theological literature in 1913, and we have discussed where King was most likely first introduced to the term in a formal way. However, since the discussion of King's personalism, theology, and ethics is also framed in this book around family and cultural influences, it is appropriate to consider whether specific Afrikan Americans used the term in any significant sense prior to King's usage.

HOWARD THURMAN AND THE BELOVED COMMUNITY

One of the earliest uses of the term beloved community among Afrikan Americans is traceable to John Malcus Ellison, homiletician and first Afrikan American president of Virginia Union University. Ellison cited the term in *They Who Preach* (1956). Unfortunately, he did not define the term, although the context in which he used it makes clear that he meant by it a special community quite in line with divine purposes.[48] There is presently no evidence that King was aware of Ellison's use of the term.

It was Lewis V. Baldwin who first informed me that Howard Thurman wrote an article on the beloved community. Thurman was an influential person in King's life. If the essay had been written during the 1940s or 1950s, King's first encounter with the term could have been through Thurman. This hope could not be sustained, however, at least not on the basis of the article in question. As it turned out the article, "Desegregation, Integration, and the Beloved Community," was unpublished and undated, although Thurman stated on the first page that he was writing the article for a series. In no fewer than five places, internal evidence reveals that the article was written post-1965,[49] most likely in 1966. At any rate, we learn several things about the beloved community; things that King would have known independently, especially after the Montgomery struggle. What do we learn from Thurman's essay?

First, Thurman maintains that the quality of the relations between persons in a community is what can lead theirs to being the beloved community. It is not just a matter of having a neighborhood or church full of diverse people. There must be a thoroughgoing commitment to qualitative interaction based on the principle of equality. Until this happens, until persons individually and collectively, consciously work toward establishing such a community, the beloved community is little more than an abstract concept. Implicit in this is Thurman's important point that the beloved community can neither be willed nor commanded into existence.[50] Although the beloved community ideal seems fleeting, it remains a continuous hope.

The next thing we learn from Thurman's essay is that as long as the hope exists, and there are persons here and there who embody and try to actualize it, the beloved community both is and becomes, despite the decadence of social conditions. "The presence of the beloved community is always manifesting itself in the lives of people in the very midst of the social decay by which they are surrounded," writes Thurman. The beloved community "begins in the human spirit," in the individual person, and then "moves out into the open independence of the society."[51] We may therefore think of the beloved community in teleological-historical as well as futuristic eschatological terms. The beloved community is, and is also that which is to come.

Thurman's essay enlightens us about the beloved community in a third way. Much of the initial onus for achieving the beloved community falls on individual persons. But because it is a special type of community to be achieved, it should be pointed out that as important as the role of the individual is, and the need for each to "feel personally responsible for bringing it to pass,"[52] it cannot happen without the sustained cooperative endeavor of like-minded persons in the community. Thurman maintains that the very reason for fighting to eradicate segregation and other social evils is that they deny persons and communities "the right to live in immediate candidacy for the beloved community," where there are no human made barriers that separate persons from persons, and groups from groups. Thurman described that community, as "a way of life that is worth living and a faith in one's self, in others, and in the society that can be honestly and intelligently sustained."[53] As we will see momentarily, there is nothing in this description that is not also in King's conception of the beloved community.

Thurman was convinced that persons are made to live in community and that the interrelationship between people is unmistakable. This is what Thurman meant when he said: "For this is why we were born: Men, all men belong to each other, and he who shuts himself away diminishes himself, and he who shuts another away from him destroys himself."[54] Persons enter into existence in community and may not hope to develop to maturity with a sense of moral responsibility for both self and the other if they are completely isolated.

THE KINGDOM OF GOD AND THE BELOVED COMMUNITY

There are two other things worth noting regarding King and the language of the beloved community. One has to do with his tendency, similar to Royce's, to think of the Kingdom of God—"humanity organized according to the will of God"[55]—and the beloved community as synonymous. The other pertains to King's claim that he caught a microcosmic glimpse of the beloved community at the airport in Montgomery in 1965.

In the second year of seminary, King wrote a paper for George Washington Davis, "A Christian View of the World." Reflecting on William Adams Brown's book, *Beliefs That Matter* (1928), King wrote:

Jesus took over the phrase "the Kingdom of God," but he changed its meaning. He refused entirely to be the kind of Messiah that his contemporaries expected. Jesus made love the work of sovereignty. Here we are left with no doubt as to Jesus' meaning. The Kingdom of God will be a society in which men and women live as children of God should live. It will be a kingdom controlled by the law of love. . . . Although the world seems to be in [a] bad shape today we must never lose faith in the power of God to achieve his purpose.[56]

According to this view, the Kingdom of God was something to be achieved in every era of history.

King thought of the world as a training ground for the establishment of the kingdom based on love. The kingdom was neither an abstraction nor an ideal to be worked out in the next world, said King. In this regard, he was reminded that in the Lord's Prayer Jesus said, "thy will be done in earth, as it is in heaven." Wherever else the kingdom was to be realized, earth was to be one of the places. The kingdom is God's supreme end. In this, King was in agreement with Rauschenbusch. Accordingly, the end to be sought is neither political nor economic power, but the beloved community or the Kingdom of God—a society based on the agapé love imperative. Political and economic power, however, are objectives on the way to the community of love. These are needed in this type of world in order for persons to be all they can be. The Kingdom of God on earth will be a society in which the chief ethical principles of Jesus—justice, righteousness, love, and mercy—reign supreme. The kingdom is the highest good, the ideal and most perfect social order, God's ultimate end for persons in the world. We are therefore obligated to work steadily toward its realization.[57] Every facet of this new society will be infused with, and governed by, these principles in the lives of persons.[58] This necessarily means that living in the beloved community will require a qualitative change in the soul, practice, and outlook of the members.

The other thing worth noting is that King believed that he had actually witnessed a small-scale model of the beloved community. He wrote about this in *Where Do We Go From Here: Chaos or Community?* (1967). Reflecting on the 1965 march from Selma to Montgomery, King recalled the experience of thousands of demonstrators waiting at the airport for return flights to their respective homes. Many flights were delayed, causing unusual crowding in the airport waiting areas. Demonstrators of all races and classes were crowded together on benches, chairs, floors, and other places that would hold human bodies. King described the experience. "As I stood with them and saw white and Negro, nuns and priests, ministers and rabbis, labor organizers, lawyers, doctors, housemaids and shopworkers brimming with vitality and enjoying a rare comradeship, I knew I was seeing a microcosm of the mankind of the future in this moment of luminous and genuine brotherhood."[59]

At the time, King no doubt believed that a situation like this would come to exist on a grander scale in the United States, if not in other parts of the world. (By this time King was what Lewis Baldwin described as an internationalist, or "an international symbol of community.")[60] But King was nonetheless aware that racism was endemic and deeply embedded in every American institution and that it would be many years before it would no longer be a factor in the life chances of blacks as well as whites. Although he did not use the language of today—"white privilege"—King knew that in the meantime whites would continue to be the chief beneficiaries of racism and racial discrimination.[61] In addition, King had not forgotten what he learned from studying Reinhold Niebuhr. There is no era in history that can boast of being free of sin. The nature of sin and human nature is such that sin appears on every level of human achievement.[62] This necessarily means that there can be no point at which persons should relax in the struggle against social evil. Instead, persons and communities must be ever vigilant in efforts to eradicate social sin and to establish the beloved community.

King's own experience tempered the sense of optimism he experienced at the Montgomery airport. For not long after the famous "I Have A Dream" speech that sweltering day in August 1963, he could say that the very dream he shared with the nation turned into a nightmare. Within three years he witnessed other tragedies that only confirmed and sustained the nightmare. In "A Christmas Sermon on Peace," he said:

I remember the first time I saw that dream turn into a nightmare, just a few weeks after I had talked about it. It was when four beautiful, unoffending, innocent Negro girls were murdered in a church in Birmingham, Alabama. I watched that dream turn into a nightmare as I moved through the ghettos of the nation and saw my black brothers and sisters perishing on a lonely island of poverty in the midst of a vast ocean of material prosperity, and saw the nation doing nothing to grapple with the Negroes' problem of poverty. I saw that dream turn into a nightmare as I watched my black brothers and sisters in the midst of anger and understandable outrage, in the midst of their hurt, in the midst of their dis-appointment, turn to misguided riots to try to solve that problem. I saw that dream turn into a nightmare as I watched the war in Vietnam escalating.[63]

In his thinking about the beloved community, and especially his conviction that it was achievable through human and divine cooperative efforts, and more specifically through nonviolent resistance to evil, King sought to avoid a naïve optimism on the one hand, and a paralyzing pessimism on the other. Remembering Niebuhr's claim that sin is present—individually and collectively—on every level of human moral-ethical achievement, King preached about what is achievable regarding the commu-nity of love. Although he clearly did not believe there would ever be a perfect mani-festation of this community in the world, he was also convinced that there could be greater approximations of it. The problem, as he saw it, had less to do with human re-sources and ability, and everything to do with human will. That is, persons and groups seemed to lack the will to do what is necessary to establish and sustain the beloved community. King preached about this in "The Death of Evil upon the Seashore":

Even though all progress is precarious, within limits real social progress may be made. Although man's moral pilgrimage may never reach a destination point on earth, his never-ceasing strivings may bring him ever closer to the city of righ-teousness. And though the Kingdom of God may remain *not yet* as a universal re-ality in history, in the present it may exist in such isolated forms as in judgment, in personal devotion, and in some group life. "The kingdom of God is in the midst of you."

Above all, we must be reminded anew that God is at work in his universe. He is not outside the world looking on with a sort of cold indifference. Here on all the roads of life, he is striving in our striving. Like an ever-loving Father, he is working through history for the salvation of his children. As we struggle to defeat the forces of evil, the God of the universe struggles with us. Evil dies on the seashore, not merely because of man's endless struggle against it, but because of God's power to defeat it.[64]

However, King's conviction that the universe hinges on a moral foundation led him to conclude that history itself would pose no social problems that were not resolvable,[65] especially if persons consciously choose to work cooperatively and relentlessly with each other and with God to eradicate them. Indeed, this must be the case if the universe is in fact friendly to persons' endeavors to achieve value in the world. We can be sure that this was King's firm conviction. Working toward the establishment of the beloved community is not the burden of persons alone. God eternally shares in the struggle toward this end.

SCHOLARS' VIEWS OF KING'S BELOVED COMMUNITY

King scholars such as Smith, Zepp, and Baldwin have written systematically on King's beloved community ideal. Each maintains, justifiably, that the keystone, indeed "the organizing principle" of King's entire philosophy, is his ideal of the beloved community. Smith and Zepp argue that King was almost totally preoccupied with the vision of the beloved community from the beginning to the end of his ministry.

The vision of the "Beloved Community" was the organizing principle of all of King's thought and activity. His writings and his involvement in the civil rights movement were illustrations of and footnotes to his fundamental preoccupation with the actualization of an inclusive human community.

All of King's intellectual concerns were directly related to the priority he assigned to the "Beloved Community." . . . The centrality of the "Beloved Community" in King's intellectual concerns is demonstrated by the fact that it can be traced from his earliest addresses and articles to his latest writings and public speeches.[66]

In his book on King's beloved community ideal and South Afrika, Baldwin points out that this ideal provoked as much discussion and debate among some South Afrikan leaders as King's unwavering commitment to nonviolence. The beloved community ideal is based on a radical transformation of values and emphasizes sharing and fraternity. Unlike Smith and Zepp, who pointed only to the influence of liberal theology, social gospel ideas of Walter Rauschenbusch, Boston personalism, and the Christian realism of Reinhold Niebuhr on King's ideal of the beloved community,

Baldwin is careful to point out that "the African American church, the extended family network, and the southern black experience, in which King was nurtured, constituted the most important formative influences in the shaping of his ideas about community."[67] These were the influences that laid the foundation for his acquired knowledge in seminary and graduate school. To be sure, Smith and Zepp concentrated on the formal intellectual influences, but this does not make as much sense if one is not also aware of the formative familial, black church, and cultural influences on King's understanding of community.

King's ideal of the beloved community had for him, as Baldwin observes, a place of "critical importance." It can be found in King's addresses, sermons, essays, books, and interviews from the beginning of his ministry in Montgomery to its tragic end in Memphis. King's emphasis throughout was on the unity and indivisibility of humanity. He lived by the conviction that persons are not created to live in a vacuum, but in community.

Although King's study of personalism and his understanding of the Christian faith convinced him that persons have in them an urge toward community, he also knew that living in community is not something that happens automatically or even inevitably. It is an ideal that persons must envision and toward which they must intentionally and cooperatively struggle. While on the one hand King believed that through cooperative and sustained human and divine effort persons can more nearly approximate the actualization of the beloved community, there was enough realism in his doctrine of human nature that he knew that it could not be achieved once and for all. King knew that as long as there are morally autonomous beings in the world, there will always be the occasion for sin. There will always be the possibility that people will misuse their freedom in ways that contradict the ethics of the beloved community. King was aware that the possession of human freedom is the occasion for both blessing and curse. Possessing freedom, persons may choose to commit their whole selves and resources and to work cooperatively with each other to establish the beloved community. Or, as is frequently the case, they can choose to delay its establishment. It was King's faith that because God is who God is, and because the universe itself is constructed to be friendly to God's creation, there will be present in every era of human existence persons who will commit their lives, resources, and creative energy to the achievement of the beloved community. In this sense, the seeds of the community of love are always present.

In Royce's language, we may say that individuals and communities are committed to establishing the beloved community only when their behavior and actions exhibit loyalty to that cause. In a minimal sense, loyalty is "the willing, the thoroughgoing, and practical devotion of a self to a cause."[68] The loyal person engages in courageous and sustained actions to achieve a particular cause and remains undeterred when confronted with what in the long view can only be temporary setbacks and defeats.[69] In the deepest sense, Royce defined loyalty as *"the Will to Believe in something eternal, and to express that belief in the practical life of a human being."*[70] King would have readily applied this doctrine of the need to be loyal to the attainment of the beloved community. One has faith or belief in the possibility of achieving the community of love despite momentary instances in which it seems an utterly impossible achievement. A person who remains faithful to this cause and demonstrates it in all that he or she does has a right to believe that its realization will some day be a reality. This must be the case for one like King who lived by the conviction that the universe is constructed on a moral foundation.

Baldwin rightly maintains that four principles "formed the core" of King's beloved community ideal.

> (1) The impartiality of God in creating and dealing with human beings; (2) a sacramentalistic idea of the cosmos as echoed by the psalmist, "the earth is the Lord's, and the fullness thereof—the world, and they that dwell therein"; (3) a belief in the dignity and worth of persons as such; and (4) a solidaristic view of society and the world, which holds that each person is a distinct ontological entity who finds growth, fulfillment, and purpose through personal and social relationships based on the agapé love ethic. This final principle is best characterized in King's use of the metaphor of the "great world house" or the "world-wide neighborhood," which suggests a totally integrated human family, unconcerned with human differences and devoted to the ethical norms of love, justice, and community.[71]

King believed that the beloved community ideal was relevant not only to the United States, but to South Afrika and other nations as well. Indeed, given the history of U.S. racial relations, it may be possible to more nearly approximate its actualization in these other countries,[72] which did not mean for King that it would be a perfect community which would no longer require that persons strive to maintain it. This is consistent with his acknowledgment of both human freedom and sin.

King believed in the basic goodness of human nature, but his sense of the depth and prevalence of human sin caused him to be adamant in his claim that there is no place in the world that the beloved community will roll in on the wheels of inevitability. Responsible persons, aware of their moral autonomy, will have to work relentlessly and cooperatively with each other and with God in order to attain it. From the end of the Montgomery struggle to that fateful evening in Memphis, King believed that it was possible to achieve, or at least to more nearly approximate the beloved community. In the struggle to actualize this ideal, freedom and moral agency are key elements. The next section of this chapter focuses more explicitly on their meaning and importance.

Freedom and Moral Agency

As a personalist, King stressed not only the absolute dignity of persons as such but also the primacy of freedom, an important cornerstone of personalism. Accordingly, King maintained that all being is characterized by freedom. At bottom, to be free is what it means to be a person. To be a person is what it means to be free. These metaphysical claims about freedom have important implications for the ethical and political freedom of people and what they ought to be willing to do in order to assert both their fundamental humanity and their freedom.

According to King, persons are called into existence by God as free beings with the capacity to be self-determining moral agents. At least he believed this to be God's intention. King was in essential agreement with Bowne, who argued that at birth every person is at least a "candidate" for freedom and morality,[73] which implies the need for conscious development and maturation. However, Bowne was not here referring to metaphysical freedom. He assumed the existence of metaphysical freedom because he believed that freedom characterizes all being. Instead, Bowne was referring to the need for one born in freedom to slowly mature to the point of being a responsible moral agent. At birth, persons lack moral agency—the capacity to act freely, responsibly, and intelligently and then respond appropriately to the consequences of their decisions and actions. This capacity develops or matures over time and through instruction, training, and socialization. However, this process may be severely curtailed should one happen to be mentally retarded or otherwise deprived, socially or economically. Such a case may (indeed does) raise the theodicy question, or it may prompt us to consider whether some persons are so deprived educationally, intellectually, sociopolitically, and economically that they simply cannot make responsible moral choices. However, it is because persons are created in freedom, for freedom, to be free—which is the divine intention—that *all* persons who are moral agents are morally obligated to resist fiercely anybody and anything that undermines or seeks to hamper or disregard that freedom, especially when the agent is acting responsibly. In addition, it means that the moral agent is obligated to act on behalf of the best interests of the moral subject who may or may not be a moral agent.

Just here, the distinction that Paul W. Taylor makes between *moral subject* and *moral agent* is a helpful one. Taylor's line of reasoning goes like this. Any conscious being—for example, the amoeba, ant, fly, dog, horse—is a moral subject. Obviously not all moral subjects are capable of making responsible moral choices. This is the case of some human beings as well. Furthermore, the moral subject is a being to whom the moral agent owes responsibilities. The moral agent is a special kind of moral subject. Her faculties are developed such that she is capable of making responsible moral choices and of anticipating the most foreseeable consequences[74] of those choices. Further, she is willing to take responsibility for her choices and actions, is able to assess the outcome of the choices made, and then to apply what is learned to new situations.[75]

Every conscious being, from an amoeba to a human person (and the Supreme Person) is at least a moral subject. However, not every moral subject is a moral agent. The moral subject who is not capable of making, abiding by, living with the consequences of choices, and applying what is learned to new situations, lacks moral agency. For the latter implies the ability to do each of the things noted, in addition to being able to critically examine the process of moral decision making itself, and applying what is learned to new and related situations as they arise. It is crucial to remember that the moral agent always owes responsibilities or duties to moral subjects.[76] In this sense, the moral agent is always more heavily burdened from a moral standpoint. From him who knows much, much is expected in the moral arena.

To be a person is to be an agent capable of acting, whether for good or evil. This capacity has important implications for the ethical and political freedom of people in the world and what they ought to be willing to do to assert, protect, and defend their fundamental freedom, individually and collectively.

IMPORTANCE OF SELF-DETERMINATION

Self-determination, coupled with the capacity to act, is important in the theological social ethics of King. Long before he was called to pastor Dexter Avenue Baptist Church in Montgomery, King believed that racial and economic justice would come to his people and to the poor only as they relentlessly struggle to achieve it. Although he was helped much by Karl Marx and Reinhold Niebuhr, King did not have to read their work in order to discover that privileged and powerful persons and groups—religious and nonreligious—do not willingly share privilege and power with the oppressed. King witnessed enough as a young boy and learned much as a college student, especially in sociology courses with Walter Chivers and during summer jobs he chose to work, to know that privilege and power are not willingly shared. They are seldom accessed without the determined struggle of the underprivileged and the disempowered. In addition, the young King witnessed his father's daily struggles against racism in the public sector, and developed the sense that it was necessary to staunchly contend against it, rather than passively endure and accept it, or to depend on otherwise well-meaning white people to fight the battle. It will be recalled that after the shoe store incident the boy King innocently told his father that he would help him to fight racism.[77]

As pastors, King's father and maternal grandfather insisted that the preacher is obligated to be an advocate for justice for those treated unjustly, and "in the South, this meant an active involvement in changing the social order all around us."[78] This was one of the things that Daddy King learned from A. D. Williams. Williams knew that his people had done nothing to deserve and warrant the systematic unearned suffering and pain inflicted on them by white supremacists and the structures they controlled and from which they benefited. Nevertheless, he insisted that blacks should not sit back and passively accept such treatment, as if waiting for whites to decide when enough is enough. As beings imbued with God's image, loved by God, and therefore in possession of infinite dignity, blacks were morally obligated to act against anything and everything that dehumanized and depersonalized them. Williams insisted that no matter how his people came to be in the predicament they were in, there would be no progress toward full personhood and all the rights and privileges pertaining thereto without conscious and sustained struggle on their part. King would later apply this idea to working toward the attainment of the beloved community. Persons would have to struggle relentlessly to actualize or more nearly approximate it.

In the judgment of Williams and Daddy King, there was no place in the black community for moral and social apathy, although much of this existed then, as now. There was no excuse for moral neutrality, especially among those blacks who, because of education and social status, had more privileges than the black masses. There was most assuredly no excuse for the black pastor.

Rather than support the view and practice of some in the black community that "the comfortable passenger is the last one who should think about rocking the boat," the legacy that King inherited from his father and grandfather was based on the opposite conviction. From those who have much, much is expected, especially in the area of championing the cause of the poor and oppressed for social justice. Looking back on the earlier days of his tenure as pastor of Ebenezer Baptist Church and his efforts to organize blacks for voter registration, Daddy King reflected on his reaction to those black pastors and other leaders who argued that the comfortable should not rock the boat, that "we've got to go slow," or that "'there's nothing you can do about the way things are until they [whites] decide the time has come.'"[79] Daddy King was not having it. Instead, he wrote: "Still, I felt that action was the only course for those of us whose relative financial security permitted a view of the overall situation that wasn't entirely available—or practical—for folks whose very livelihoods could depend on the sort of smiles I'd once learned to display in the Southern Railway yards. Any grinning I did now was on my own terms, and I'd come to feel that a certain responsibility went along with that very small freedom to be what I wanted to be."[80]

Daddy King persisted in this stance, even when black pastors railed against his suggestions that the black churches themselves should become the headquarters of a mass voter registration drive, and march to city hall to get blacks registered. In the final analysis, the destiny of black people was not in the hands of the whites, he insisted. Nor could blacks afford to take things slow and wait passively and patiently for whites to decide when it was most convenient for things to change.

Freedom, self-determination, and moral autonomy mean that one is morally obligated to own up to one's moral choices. If to be a person is to be free and to possess infinite, absolute dignity and worth, then persons are obligated to protest against all that undermines their humanity and dignity. Concretely, this means that persons are always and forever obligated to take steps toward removing any obstacles to the realization of complete personhood. It also means that by virtue of being a person, one chooses. In this regard none have written more profoundly than Jean-Paul Sartre, who said that persons are "condemned to freedom." Even when we pretend not to choose, that itself is a choice.[81] Accordingly, Sartre maintains that the claim that we sometimes do not choose is nothing more than "bad faith."[82] We may apathetically accept our oppressive situation, or we may protest against and fight it. Either way, we make a choice; we choose. By virtue of who we are as persons, we choose—whether we like it or admit it or not. We are, said Sartre, "condemned forever to be free."[83]

It should be remembered that metaphysical freedom does not necessarily translate into the sociopolitical freedoms that persons need in order to function fully as persons in the world. Here one need merely recall the experience of Native peoples in this country and *manifest destiny.* Or, one may recall Afrikan Americans and slavery. One might also remember the experience of the Jews during Hitler's reign of terror and the silence of countless people of goodwill. Although the members of each of these groups were fundamentally or metaphysically free, their actual experiences were characterized by anything but the concrete freedom they needed in order to be respected and treated like beings with infinite and inviolable worth. However, it is because of this essential freedom that *all* persons who are moral agents are morally obligated to resist anybody and anything that tries to crush their right to live as free beings in the world. Perhaps it will be instructive to say more about the meaning and importance of this fundamental freedom.

Metaphysical Freedom

Making choices is a basic fact of existence. It is not determined by circumstances external to it. Rather, one who chooses selects from available alternatives. Whichever alternative is chosen will have consequences for the future.[84] King said three things about metaphysical freedom. First, consistent with his personalist teachers, he maintained that freedom is the capacity to be self-determined and self-directed. It is "the capacity to deliberate or weigh alternatives," and to select one or the other. Second, King said that freedom "expresses itself in decision." That is, once one chooses a particular alternative, other choices are necessarily cut off. The third thing King said is that freedom implies responsibility. Once one makes a choice one is then responsible both for the choice made and for the most foreseeable consequences of that choice.[85]

So important was freedom to King that he concluded with Brightman that without it persons cannot exist. Freedom is "part of the essence of man."[86] Following Brightman and Bowne, King emphasized both the ethical and the speculative significance of freedom. The latter means that without freedom knowledge itself is not possible, for even though persons are made for truth, i.e., possess a rational faculty, they still must be able to choose to use it for the attainment of truth. The rational faculty must somehow be directed toward truth, or not. It is not capable of directing itself. This is where freedom comes into play.[87]

In a paper written in graduate school King wrote: "Not only is freedom necessary for moral choices, but it is also necessary for the act of reason. . . . Certainly without freedom, reason would go shipwreck. It was probably Bowne who, more than any other, stressed the significance of this point. For him freedom has both epistemological and metaphysical significance."[88] This was indeed Bowne's position—one that he developed in a number of his major writings, not least in his seminal essay, "The Speculative Significance of Freedom."[89]

Bowne maintained that although constructed for truth, reason alone has not the power to require that persons use it to acquire truth. It needs to be directed and urged to do so. In this regard he wrote:

. . . the question of freedom enters intimately into the structure of reason itself. It concerns not merely our executive activities in the outer world, but also our inner rational activity. The only escape from the overthrow of reason involved in the fact of error lies in the assumption of freedom. Our faculties are made for truth, but this alone does not secure truth. We must use those faculties carefully, critically, persistently, if any valuable knowledge is to be gained. Our faculties are made for truth, but they may be carelessly used, or wilfully misused, and thus error is born.[90]

Freedom is needed if there is to be any chance at all that reason will in fact be used for truth. Bowne's point is that without freedom neither morality nor knowledge is possible, since each depends on the capacity to deliberate and choose.

In DeWolf's class on personalism in 1951, King wrote a critical essay on the atheistic personalism of the British philosopher John M. E. McTaggart (1866–1925), in which he argued against his rejection of freedom. "In rejecting freedom," he said, "McTaggart was rejecting the most important characteristic of personality."[91] For King, freedom is an abiding expression of the higher spiritual nature of persons. "Man is man because he is free to operate within the framework of his destiny. . . . He is distinguished from animals by his freedom to do evil or to do good and to walk the high road of beauty or tread the low road of ugly degeneracy."[92]

If indeed to be is to be free, then without freedom there can be no persons. King was convinced that "a denial of freedom to an individual is a denial of life itself. The very character of the life of man demands freedom."[93] In addition, the denial of ethical and political freedom is a threat to one's personhood.

Like his personalist forebears, King had no interest in the freedom of a single, isolated aspect of the person, such as freedom of the will, for this is an abstraction. Therefore, his concern was for the freedom of the whole person in his everyday activities. In language not too different from Bowne's, he wrote: "The very phrase, freedom of the will, abstracts freedom from the person to make it an object; and an object almost by definition is not free. But freedom cannot thus be abstracted from the person who is always subject as well as object and who himself still does the abstracting."[94] If the realization of the beloved community is to be possible at all, it must be seen that freedom is the freedom of real human beings who are called by God to live together in a community of love. Although God requires that persons act to achieve the beloved community, persons themselves are created with the capacity to choose whether to do so. The first step toward the realization of the beloved community, then, is precisely the conscious decision to love it and to strive to actualize it.

It is precisely because of his belief in the essential freedom of persons that King, like Malcolm X, was so adamant about the importance of self-determination in his people's struggle for total liberation and the regaining of their self-respect and sense of dignity. For King, one is always morally obligated to fight for those things that ensure one's freedom in the world. King's emphasis, then, was on both metaphysical and social freedom.

Confident even near the end of his life that the beloved community could be more nearly approximated if persons applied their power of will, self-determination, and resources in that direction, King remained convinced that freedom and moral agency would play crucial roles, inasmuch as these inherent traits make it possible for persons to *decide* to work cooperatively with each other and with God. As we saw earlier, King was just as convinced that neither human persons nor God alone can make this happen. Although God is the most powerful, loving, compassionate being in the universe, the fact of human freedom is a limit on what God can accomplish in the world. God will not disregard or usurp human freedom. This means that persons always retain the inherent power to decide one way or the other.

Experience and the long sweep of history reveals a God who prefers to work persuasively and cooperatively with persons to achieve God's expectation that persons live together in a thoroughly inclusive and integrated society in ways that are respectful of each other. Accordingly, King contends with Bowne that persons and God together, "made one in a marvelous unity of purpose through an overflowing love as the free gift of himself on the part of God and by perfect obedience and receptivity on the part of man, can transform the old into the new and drive out the deadly cancer of sin."[95] King was adamant that God will not do for humans what we can choose to do cooperatively with each other and with God's assistance.

Because of human freedom and moral agency the attainment of the beloved community remains a real possibility, for these make possible compliance with God's will for the world. We have already seen that having rejected what appeared to be some early social gospelers' belief that social progress is inevitable, King was firm in his conviction that such is not the case. Rather, social progress "comes through the tireless efforts of men willing to be co-workers with God, and without this hard work, time itself becomes an ally of the forces of social stagnation."[96]

In addition to human freedom and moral autonomy, King believed that yet another fundamental principle gave credence to his conviction that the attainment of the beloved community remains a real possibility: the existence of an objective moral order and moral laws. This conviction led him to the further belief that the universe itself hinges on a moral foundation and is therefore friendly to the achievement of value. He could believe that the universe is friendly because of the loving tenderness expressed by his parents toward each other and toward their children, as well as the love experienced through the Ebenezer Baptist Church community.

Not enough attention has been given King's belief in an objective moral order and his faith that the universe itself sides with justice and all efforts to achieve the good, including the beloved community. We will see in the next chapter that this was a foundational belief for King and that failure to acknowledge and understand it will hamper the achievement of an adequate understanding of his theological social ethics, as well as his ministry and his confidence to the very end that the beloved community is achievable in history. We will need to consider the meaning and significance of the objectivity of value or the existence of an objective moral order relative to the dream of the achievement of the beloved community. One who lives by the conviction that the universe is situated on a moral foundation—as King did—has every reason to believe that the realization of the community of love is achievable, if persons do those things that are consistent with such a conviction.

CHAPTER 7

Objective Moral Order and Moral Laws

The belief that there is a fundamental moral order in the universe was already present in Bowne's writings before he studied under Rudolph Hermann Lotze in 1873.[1] He was undoubtedly pleased, however, to see this emphasis in the work of his teacher. Influenced by the ethical idealism of Johann Gottlieb Fichte (1762–1814),who replaced the Kantian *postulation* of freedom, immortality, and God with the *affirmation* of the existence of each, Lotze quotes him approvingly about the existence of a cosmic moral order: "To us too, it is not doubtful 'but most certain, and indeed the ground of all other certainty, that there is this Moral Order of the world; . . . that every good action will succeed and every evil action certainly fail, and that to those who do but truly love that which is good all things should work together for good.'"[2] In a number of his writings on the philosophy of religion and ethics, Bowne continued to develop the doctrine that the good that persons see in themselves and their experience of a moral nature implies that a more lofty goodness is at the center of the universe and that the universe itself is moral. All personalists in the tradition of Bowne maintain that persons possess an innate capacity for moral experience, that is, a moral nature.[3]

According to Bowne, moral evil could not even exist apart from a moral order. That persons speak of moral evil implies the existence of a moral order that is being violated in some way: "In its very notion it [moral evil] is a departure from moral order; and hence necessarily implies it in the system. Sin in the system, therefore, implies righteousness in the founder of the system; and the sin appears as a rebellion against the moral law which has been legislated into the very nature of things. If the system were not essentially founded in righteousness, there could be no proper sin."[4]

In any case, Bowne was confident that the universe possesses a moral character and believed that this could be grounded empirically. He named three sources of this empirical argument:

1. The individual's sense of possessing a moral nature. This in turn implies the existence of a moral author. Said Bowne: "He that formed the eye, shall not he see? He that giveth man knowledge, shall not he know? So also, He that implanted in man an unalterable reverence for righteousness, shall not he himself be righteous?"[5] Bowne essentially argued from moral effect (i.e., the fact of a moral nature and moral experience in persons) to moral cause. As it is inconceivable that intelligence can be derived from nonintelligence, he argued, so too is it inconceivable that the moral may be deduced from the nonmoral. Based on this method of argumentation, it is easy to see how Bowne concluded that the existence in persons of a moral nature and the fact that they have moral experience points to the moral character of the universe and of God.[6]

2. The structure of life and society. Here Bowne argued that life itself is so structured as to provide almost constant stimulus in moral directions. "Nature itself inculcates with the utmost strenuousness the virtues of industry, prudence, foresight, self-control, honesty, truth, and helpfulness."[7] In the long run, there seems to be something in the very structure or nature of things that supports self-control, rather than overindulgence; honesty, rather than dishonesty; justice rather than injustice. When all is said and done the indicators are that "the nature of things is on the side of righteousness."[8] Although it is true that persons, individually and collectively, frequently use their freedom of will to undermine the humanity and worth of others and to make the lives of massive numbers of persons miserable, it is also the case that persons cannot live without a society which is based on both civil and moral ideas. History has shown that the absence of such ideas frequently lead to injustice, oppression, and the rapid decay of the very foundations of society.[9] History has also revealed that there are particular values (e.g., love, truthfulness, righteousness, justice and honesty) in the absence of which persons and communities simply do not, in the long run, function well. Because the universe is friendly to value, in the end these and related values will have the last say. "No cunning, no power, can forever avail against the truth,"[10] writes Bowne. This is what Fichte meant when he said that "every good action will succeed and every evil action certainly fail." This is essentially a metaphysical claim. It does not mean that every good action I perform in this or the next moment will succeed right before my eyes in the sense of bringing about the intended good in the immediate context. What Fichte, Lotze,

Bowne, and King believed is that every good action is in harmony with the grain of the universe. To this extent it will in the end succeed, even if the one performing that action is not alive to witness it. This is why King could speak with such passion and confidence the night before he was assassinated, that even if he did not get to the promised land, the rightness and morality of the peoples' struggle for justice and liberation was such that they would ultimately get to the promised land.

3. The course of history. The long march of history reveals the existence of a power or force making for justice, righteousness, and love.[11] The drift of history points to the existence of such a force working toward this lofty end, even when persons and institutions work to the contrary. Students in my course on King's theological ethics have pointed out that this is what was happening in Montgomery, both before and after King's arrival. Vernon Johns clearly prepared the way for King's ministry and leadership, for example, and he did it against all manner of opposition from white racists as well as some of his own people. A greater force was at work than Vernon Johns, my students maintained. They also rightly insisted that this same force was at work in the witness of many black women of Montgomery who, long before Rosa Parks's refusal to give up her bus seat to a white passenger, had decided that enough is enough. Moreover, my students maintained that when black ministers did not want to assume leadership of the bus boycott, but considered King (still a newcomer) to be a safe choice, thereby protecting more established pastors from risk, they unwittingly and unknowingly fell into God's intention that King be the leader. What the ministers considered to be an action that would protect their own vested interests was in fact molded into a blessing by cosmic forces in the universe.

These three sources—persons' experience of a moral nature, the structure of life and society, and the course of history—essentially constitute the empirical argument for the existence of an objective moral order and moral laws. King possessed a strong sense of the existence of such an order and its laws even before he studied liberal theology under Davis and personalism under Brightman and DeWolf. Taylor Branch maintains that King expressed his awareness of the existence of an objective moral order and moral laws as early as his student days at Morehouse College. Addressing the student body and faculty in his senior sermon, King affirmed the existence of moral laws that one can no more violate with impunity than one can violate physical laws. There are consequences, sometimes severe, for violating either set of laws.

King's introduction to the concept of moral laws (if not the term itself) might well have occurred in private conversations he had with President Benjamin Mays or during the latter's Tuesday chapel sermons. While King was still a student at More-house in 1946, Mays wrote: "Christianity declares that the universe is essentially ethical and essentially moral. Just as there are scientific and physical laws by which the universe is governed and by which man must abide, there are ethical and moral laws by which man must regulate his life."[12] This is another way of saying that the universe is grounded on moral law, or that it hinges on a moral foundation, as King was so fond of saying. Mays held, and King would later declare, that the moral laws are what human beings find or discover. They do not create them. The world and human behavior must function in accordance with these moral laws (i.e., God's laws), or there will be serious consequences. "Man's task," Mays wrote, "is to discover God's laws and live by them."[13]

King's belief in an objective moral order is fundamental to understanding his theological social ethics. There is something about how the universe itself is constructed that mandates obedience to moral laws. The consequences for disobeying these may be devastating at times. It shall be the argument of this chapter that King's conviction that an objective moral order exists is the ground of his doctrine of the beloved community and his expectation of its attainment. In other words, it is possible to actualize the beloved community precisely because it is based on the principle that the universe itself is friendly and therefore supports the realization of such a community. A moral foundation undergirds the universe. This also says something about King's conception of God, the author and sustainer of the objective moral order, and indeed, of the beloved community. Such a God can only be the chief exemplification of love, justice, and righteousness in the world.

In an autobiographical paper on religious development written in seminary, King reflected on the idea that the structure of the universe itself is on the side of justice and righteousness. He wrote of how it was so easy for him to embrace the philosophical idea that the universe is friendly. King had not come to this primarily through study and reflection, but as a result of how he was brought up. "It is quite easy for me to think of the universe as basically friendly," said King, "mainly because of my uplifting hereditary and environmental circumstances."[14] His earliest inclination toward the conviction that there exists an objective moral order emerged as a result of a loving, caring, supportive home environment. The formal study of liberal theology and the philosophy of personalism later provided for him a framework through which to think further about this and the implications for actual living in the world.

King also early developed a sense that there exists a higher law than human law. His reference to objective moral laws in the aforementioned senior sermon at Morehouse College in 1948 sounded strikingly similar to Mays's claims about the ethical or moral laws, as well as Brightman's discussion on moral law. In that sermon, King said that to violate moral laws can have as devastating consequences as violating physical laws.[15] This lends credence to Stephen B. Oates's claim that King was first introduced to Brightman's work while in college;[16] that his first introduction to personalistic ideas was not in the predominantly white setting at Crozer Theological Seminary after all. Indeed, Lewis Baldwin has argued in a helpful way that King's earliest introduction to belief in the sacredness of persons, the existence of objective moral laws and moral order was in the context of his family and church upbringing.[17] This helps to explain why King so readily gravitated toward Brightman's doctrine of the existence of an *objective moral order* in the universe which persons ought to obey. Brightman wrote: "Idealists hold that moral experience points to an objective moral order in reality, as truly as sense experience points to an objective physical order, and most idealists believe that the objective existence of both orders can be understood rationally only if both are the activity of thought or experience of a supreme mind that generates the whole cosmic process and controls its ongoing."[18] Notice the similarity between Brightman's words and those spoken by King in the senior sermon. The very fact that persons have moral experience (i.e., have the experience of desiring, liking, or preferring this or that over something else), implies the existence of an objective moral order, just as much as the object that I see with my eyes implies the existence of an objective physical order. Just as sense experience implies the existence of something beyond itself, so too does moral experience imply something beyond itself, not least the existence of an objective moral order.

To speak of an objective moral order is to say something about reality or the universe itself. It makes a metaphysical claim. It says something fundamental about reality; something that applies to the whole of reality; something that will be acknowledged as true for all rational persons everywhere. Of course, if one believes that the universe is friendly, what more is needed to justify optimism and hope about what is possible in history, particularly if one wants to work with such friendly forces to overcome social evil?

We saw in chapter 3 that King and the personalists who influenced him most were thoroughly theistic in outlook. That is, they believed God to be the source of the objective moral order and law, of knowledge and truth. King's belief in the existence of an objective moral order and moral laws can be detected in a number of his sermons during the civil and human rights movements. In "Our God Is Able" he declares: "God walks with us. He has placed within the very structure of this universe certain absolute moral laws. For example, we can neither defy nor break them. If we disobey them, they will break us."[19] Elsewhere King could say: "There is a law in the moral world—a silent, invisible imperative, akin to the laws in the physical world—which reminds us that life will work only in a certain way."[20] For example, we may engage in acts of injustice and other behaviors that undermine the humanity and dignity of persons. However, the universe is founded on the principle of love, and, consequently, such practices in the long run will inevitably lead to the degeneration and ultimate destruction of societies.

What did King and other personalists mean by moral objectivity and the objective moral order?

PERSONALISM AND THE OBJECTIVE MORAL ORDER

Value objectivism means that there are certain values that are ingrained in the universe and will be acknowledged and accepted by any rational person. These values are thought to be woven into the very fabric of reality and consequently apply to everyone. It also means that life functions best when intelligent beings conform to these values. Because these values are ingrained in the universe, human beings have nothing to do with their existence. That is, they neither create nor destroy these values, rather they discover them. Objective values are those that the disciplined, responsible person finds or discovers and strives to live her life by. This line of thought suggests that there are certain values that exist whether you or I believe or want them to or not. Therefore, "objectivists hold that there are preferable qualities in objects, behavior, ideas, persons, and so on; this is a fact of existence independent of human preference."[21] The theist lives by the conviction that God instills certain values in the universe; to live contrary to them is a sure recipe for failure and destruction. Because God is their source, we may say that these values are of the highest quality and may be likened unto norms or standards by which all values should be measured. In addition, God creates persons in such a way that they can both detect and live by such values if they work to discover them. Unlike the nontheist and the agnostic, the theist insists that objective values do not simply exist, but that their source and sustainer is God.

We may trace the personalist emphasis on value objectivity and belief in the existence of an objective moral order and moral laws to Bowne, who believed that the universe is fundamentally rational and moral. The universe, accordingly, is not only knowable by potentially rational minds, but is essentially fused with value, and therefore is friendly to value or good. In a pregnant passage in *The Principles of Ethics* (1892), Bowne wrote: "There is a moral kingdom stretching over all worlds and ages. The moral law is not merely a psychological fact in us, but also an expression of a Holy Will which can be neither defied nor mocked. Hence, its triumph is secure. The universe, then, and God within and beyond the universe, are on the side of righteousness."[22] In other words, the world is essentially governed by moral law, i.e., a higher law than humanly contrived laws. The former is the criterion by which human law ought to be judged. Human laws must, therefore, be in harmony with moral law or they may be deemed unjust laws. King argued this point in his "Letter from Birmingham City Jail."[23]

Because moral low is objective, and not merely relevant for isolated individuals here and there, it will prevail in the end, for it is ultimately God's law. Moral law surely may be disregarded or even disobeyed, but because its source and sustainer is God, it will have the last word. It is in these ways that we may say that the universe and God are friendly, no matter how much injustice exists in the world. In the most fundamental sense, the universe and God are on the side of justice. This means that all that persons and nations do in the world will ultimately be judged by God and moral law.[24] It means that no matter how much and how long Afrikan Americans and other oppressed people suffer injustice, justice and righteousness will have the last say because the universe has a moral base.

Brightman kept alive Bowne's conviction that there exists an objective moral order which the rational, disciplined mind is capable of knowing and with which it can live in accord. Since King studied under Brightman, it is quite likely that Brightman helped to solidify his philosophical understanding of value objectivism. However, King's introduction to the concept most likely occurred during his studies under Davis. Davis himself had argued that in order for liberal theology to have depth one of the things it must be able to discern is that reality has a moral foundation and is under spiritual control.[25] Davis quoted approvingly the Federal Council of Churches' Commission on a Just and Durable Peace in 1951: "We believe that moral law, no less than physical law, undergirds our world. There is a moral order which is fundamental and eternal, and which is relevant to the corporate life of men and the ordering of human society. If mankind is to escape chaos and recurrent war, social and political institutions must be brought into conformity with this moral order."[26] Human relations, interpersonal and corporate, cannot function according to divine plans if they do not function according to moral law. Although Davis wrote about the moral foundation of the universe in 1951, the year King began doctoral studies at Boston University, this was undoubtedly an idea that he impressed upon King.

Brightman wrote about value objectivity, objective moral order, and moral law in a number of his books, including *An Introduction to Philosophy* (1925, 1951), *Religious Values* (1925), *Moral Laws* (1933), and *A Philosophy of Religion* (1940). King listed only *An Introduction to Philosophy* and *A Philosophy of Religion* in the bibliography of his dissertation,[27] but we know from a paper he wrote in Brightman's course on philosophy of religion that he was quite familiar with *Religious Values* as well.[28] He may or may not have been familiar with *A Philosophy of Ideals* (1928). This text, and *Religious Values* are important because one sees in them the express influence of William R. Sorley's argument for the dependence of all values on person, as well as the objective existence of values in the Supreme Person.[29]

Brightman was convinced that Sorley argued this thesis more convincingly than any thinker with whom he was familiar. This, despite his further contention that Sorley's stance had about it "what William James would call thinness, that is, a certain lack of sufficient contact with actual experience."[30] All philosophical thinking is characterized by some abstractness, Brightman said, "[b]ut philosophy, and particularly theory of value, has as sole function the interpretation and criticism of experience and cannot swing in the air."[31]

Persons find clues to the existence of an objective moral order both in their sense of an inherent moral nature and their own value experiences. Agreeing with Sorley, Brightman maintains that an objective moral order "can be real only in and for a personal God." The ground for persons' belief in the existence of such an order "is the fact that there is experience given which is capable of being organized into a coherent system, in some sense common to all and accessible to all. The appeal is to reason."[32] The warrant for belief in the objectivity of value is the fact that persons' "value judgments can be organized into a system that is most coherent when we interpret value-norms as objective claims that reality makes."[33] An ideal value such as justice, for example, is thought to have objective existence, and also to confer meaning on humans' desire to achieve justice in the world. Indeed, one must wonder how to account for the fact of value experience in persons if the universe itself is either valueless or indifferent to value. As his own thinking about the objectivity and subjectivity of value matured, Brightman came to the view that it is more reasonable to maintain that "values are subjective, but norms are objective." The former must be tested by the latter. Brightman provides the following example. "But A's love is objectively valid (true) if it conforms to the norm of what love ought to be—that is, if it is sincere, truly devoted, understanding, respectful of personality, co-operative, and emotionally satisfying. The subjective value of love for A and Miss B must be tested and criticized by this or some other coherent norm of love, if they care whether love be 'true' or not. If they desire 'true' love, then they acknowledge a norm which both ought to accept as reasonable."[34]

We may not know as much as we would like about the existence of such norms or standards, but the alternative—the nonexistence of such norms and the relativity of all value to desire—raises more questions than it answers. This caused Brightman to wonder whether reason itself would collapse if objective norms are thought not to exist. He maintained that the norms or standards exist in the mind of God. Human value judgments are to be tested by them. Value experience is not merely a psychological occurrence in a person's mind. One's perception is that such an experience actually occurs, just as if one perceives hearing a dog bark. As Brightman says, the perception may be wrong, but at the time I have it I at least believe that the barking dog is the object of my perception. "The presence of erroneous value judgments in experience no more destroys the objectivity of value than the presence of illusions destroys the objectivity of the world of nature."[35] Erroneous sense perceptions and value judgments may be corrected by critical reason. That there may be errors in these judgments does not preclude the existence of an objective moral order.

Crucial to Brightman's stance is his agreement with Sorley that the laws of value in the moral sphere are as objectively real as laws in physical nature. Interpreting Sorley, he writes: "For, he holds, *the laws of moral value point to a real objective order of value in the universe, just as truly as the laws of nature point to an objective natural order,* and for the same sort of reason, namely, the appeal to the logical ideal of reasonableness. In this he agrees with Spaulding's Platonic argument for the objectivity of value. Our valuations, our conceptions of justice and benevolence, love and veracity, point to and presuppose an ideal standard to which they ought to conform."[36] Notice the similarity between the italicized text and the earlier citation from George Washington Davis where he quoted approvingly the Federal Council of Churches' Commission on a Just and Durable Peace. At any rate, according to Brightman the ideal standards or norms—the objectivity of values—exist in the mind of God.

KING AND THE OBJECTIVE MORAL ORDER

There is at this time no evidence that King knew that one of his favorite statements is actually attributed to the nineteenth-century abolitionist preacher Theodore Parker (1810–60). Parker believed the facts of history revealed "a continual and progressive triumph of the right."[37] He based his claim on the conviction that "justice is the constitution or fundamental law of the moral universe, the law of right, a rule of conduct for man in all his moral relations."[38] Therefore, at the end of the day injustice and wrong will not and cannot succeed, for the universe itself is on the side of justice and right. Indeed, the universe has been constructed for justice and right. Parker put it quite eloquently in a sermon preached in 1852. "*I do not pretend to understand the moral universe; the arc is a long one,* my eye reaches but little ways; I cannot calculate the curve and complete the figure by the experience of sight; I can divine it by conscience. And from what I see *I am sure it bends towards justice.* Things refuse to be mismanaged long."[39]

The line that King frequently uttered and wrote is: "[T]he arc of the moral universe is long, [but] it bends toward justice."[40] This is clearly a reconfiguration of Parker's words. When one surfs the Internet in search of the author of these words, there are more than one hundred hits. However, none attribute the oft-quoted statement to Parker. Many link it to King. At any rate, in a footnote Taylor Branch writes that in an issue of *Liberation* in the mid-1950s an elderly Harry Emerson Fosdick praised the Montgomery bus boycott as a "godsend," and then "quoted one of King's favorite lines, from the abolitionist preacher Theodore Parker."[41] From this it appears that Fosdick may have been the one who reconfigured Parker's words into the statement that King so frequently quoted. Although Branch did not cite the source from Parker, he implies the possibility that King first became acquainted with the statement by way of alleged comments made by Fosdick.

One looks in vain for the authorship of the statement in King's writings. Indeed, I know of no place in King's writings and speeches where he refers to Parker. What is clear, however, is that Fosdick was not the one who cited the line that King frequently quoted, as Branch claimed. The person who actually did so was John Haynes Holmes who, along with Fosdick and others in the December 1956 issue of *Liberation* gave a salute to those who participated in the Montgomery bus boycott. Holmes declared that "the forces of righteousness" were on the side of those struggling for justice in Montgomery. And then this: "The victory may seem slow in coming. The waiting for it may seem interminable. We perhaps may not live to see the hour of triumph. But the great Theodore Parker, abolitionist preacher in the days before the Civil War, answered this doubt and fear when he challenged an impatient world. '*The arc of the moral universe is long, but it bends toward justice.*'"[42]

What King intended to convey by this last assertion was his own fundamental conviction that no matter how much injustice exists in the world; no matter how badly one group is treated by another, there is a benevolent power that is the beating heart of the universe, one which sides with good, justice, and righteousness. The basis of this faith was King's belief in the existence of an objective moral order which he believed to be created and sustained by God. King's many references to his belief that the freedom fighters have cosmic companionship, for example, was further evidence of his conviction that the very grain of the universe is on the side of right and justice. With such companionship, the poor and the oppressed need never be overcome by apathy and the temptation to cease struggling against the forces of evil and injustice. All that people have to do is choose to work cooperatively with each other and with the grain of the universe. As long as one lives by the conviction that reality is fused with value and that the universe is friendly to all efforts to achieve the good, this itself is ground for hope for freedom fighters. At least this was King's conviction.

In the early days of SNCC, King said to a crowd of Fisk University students, "a substantial minority" of which were white: "No lie can live forever. Let us not despair. *The universe is with us.*"[43] This is why he could then urge the students to work together and not get weary, and to press ever onward. In light of this conviction, then, there was every reason to be optimistic, despite temporary setbacks in the struggle for freedom and justice. This is what sustained King during the difficult periods of the movement. He was convinced that a mighty spiritual force was working in and guiding history.

This belief is not only a basic principle of personalism, but of Afrikan American Christian faith as well. Brightman had said: "Personalism interprets the universe as friendly. It justifies hope. It finds in the relation of human and divine wills an inexhaustible meaning and purpose in life."[44] Essentially, then, personalism maintains that "supreme goodness" is at the center of the universe. Some critics of personalism rejected this idea because it raised for them the question of whether the world was already perfect in a fundamental sense. If this is the case, critics wondered, does it then make sense to argue that persons should commit themselves to working to perfect what is already perfect? In other words, if the world is the handiwork of a perfect Creator God, what could persons possibly do to perfect it further? Brightman's response to this criticism was shared by King:

> This criticism arises from a failure to take personalism seriously enough. Personalism does not believe that now, or at any point in time, the universe is perfect. It finds in God a being of perfect goodness, but not of mechanical perfection. His perfection is perfection of purpose, a teleological perfection. In its practical bearing on human beings this means not that the universe is perfected, but that it is perfectible; not that nothing can be improved, but that real change, real improvement, is the purpose of life. The sufferings of man and the ideal obligation to attain the highest values are stern factors in life, rendered more stern by the personalistic interpretation of suffering and obligation as entailed by the divine purpose. Personalism, therefore, is not too delicate and beautiful to face the facts. It too sees life as a tragedy; there is the shadow of a cross on the face of the personalistic universe. Humanity suffers and dies. Many fail to see the suffering in the light of ideal values. The world is tragic enough still, although all that personalism teaches be true. *The secret of the practical significance of personalism is that it faces the tragedy and sees that it is not all. There is tragedy, but there is also meaning; and the meaning includes and transforms the tragedy.*[45]

King knew full well that neither the universe or the world is perfect. Racism and injustice could not exist in a perfect world. And yet he believed in the ongoing perfectibility of the world when persons choose to cooperate with each other and God to make the world better than it is at any given moment.

King's parents and ancestors also believed there was something at the center of the universe that sided with all who sought good and justice. In *The Negro's God* Benjamin Mays observed that according to black literary artists, "God is on the side of the righteous and the oppressed; and God will eventually bring to judgment those who continue to violate His laws."[46] Such ideas of God tend to be those of an oppressed people who seek justice and liberation. Indeed, enslaved Afrikans believed that those who held them in bondage would have to answer to this God. A former enslaved Afrikan, J. W. C. Pennington, who became pastor of the Colored Presbyterian Church of New York, told crowds in Glasgow and London: "There is no solitary case on record of a minority, with justice on its side, being crushed, while adhering to the law of forgiveness and endurance. It is not the nature of God's moral government to permit such a thing. . . . He that reproveth God by taking moral agents which he has made for himself, and reducing them to the perpetual drudgery of brutes, will surely have to answer for it."[47] At the center of the universe is a God who is just, and who will not allow injustice to prevail.

Some may interpret such a view as capable of having an anesthetizing effect on the oppressed and unjustly treated. That is, to be taught by black preachers, as many enslaved Afrikans were, that God is on the side of the suffering and oppressed and would ultimately bring about justice and righteousness could have the effect of making them patient in their condition of oppression. We can be sure, however, that this was not the intention of most black preachers during and after American slavery. The aim of such teaching was generally intended to lead to immediate change of the Afrikan Americans' sociopolitical and economic condition. It is true that in some instances it was white enslavers who were encouraged to take the initiative to liberate enslaved Afrikan Americans in order to avoid divine wrath. In other instances the Afrikan Americans themselves were encouraged to take the initiative to liberate themselves. We recall that this was the approach of Daddy King and A. D. Williams. Consistent with personalistic method Martin came to see value in both approaches, and thus challenged both white oppressors and blacks to initiate actions for black liberation. What King, his father, and grandfather added that was so significant is the idea that God needs persons to help toward the attainment of justice and liberation. King far surpassed the efforts of others in this regard. His method of nonviolent resistance to evil was intended from beginning to end to be the method by which human beings can best assist God in bringing about the liberation of the oppressed and the establishment of the beloved community. King had no doubt that the universe was on the side of justice, but he was convinced that human beings had to work cooperatively to bring it into existence.

After considering Christian faith and the Bible, King himself declared in 1965 that "the universe is friendly because God is love."[48] In "Discerning the Signs of History" King said, "There is a process in history. There are certain laws in the Universe not only certain natural laws but certain moral laws."[49] The source of natural and moral laws is the God of Jesus Christ. King marveled at "the stars as they bedecked the heavens like swinging lanterns of eternity." He went on to say that "behind those swinging lanterns of eternity there's a purpose that embraces all mankind, a God concerned about his children."[50] From here it is an easy move to the view that evil may ascend to the throne for a period of time, but one who lives by the conviction that the universe is friendly can only conclude that there is "at the end of the road of evil, a sign which says Dead End Street."[51] This faith in the morality of the universe led King to frequently quote a verse from the familiar words of James Russell Lowell's "Present Crisis":

Truth forever on the scaffold, Wrong forever on the throne,—
Yet that scaffold sways the future, and, behind the dim unknown,
Standeth God within the shadow, Keeping watch above his own.[52]

Although I know of no place that King quotes the following verse from "The Present Crisis," there is no question that he would have approved. It further substantiates the view not only that evil reigns only for a moment, but that truth is mightier indeed, and receives divine assurance that it will prevail over all that fights against it:

Though the cause of Evil prosper, yet 'tis
Truth alone is strong,
And, albeit she wander outcast now, I see around her throng
Troops of beautiful, tall angels, to enshield her from all wrong.[53]

Indeed, in the last months of his life a mature but tired Martin Luther King, Jr., concluded that any hope that "peace on earth and goodwill toward" all persons will ever be a reality hinges on the absolute faith "in *the ultimate morality of the universe, and [the belief] that all reality hinges on moral foundations.*"[54] Here lay King's deepest faith, thus rendering foolish the question raised by many as to whether his faith was in the goodwill of otherwise good white people, those whom King often referred to as "un-Christian Christians." Whatever faith King had in such persons was a result of his much deeper fundamental conviction that through cooperative efforts between persons and God the higher good of the beloved community could be achieved. *The critical point, then, is King's faith in God,* not his faith in a particular group of human beings. As his faith in God went, so went King's faith in created persons.

King did not just believe in the existence of an objective moral order, which is the most important underlying principle in his ethic of the beloved community. He believed that because persons are moral agents who are imbued with freedom of will and a moral nature, they are obligated to work toward the actualization of the community of love, rather than to sit back passively and behave as if some cosmic force will make it happen. This point is illustrated in King's reflections on the Montgomery struggle in July 1956:

We have the strange feeling down in Montgomery that in our struggle for justice we have cosmic companionship. And so we can walk and never get weary, because we believe and know that there is a great camp meeting in the promised land of freedom and justice. And this belief, and this feeling that God is on the side of truth and justice and love and that they will eventually reign supreme in this universe, this comes down to us from the long tradition of our Christian faith. There is something that stands at the center of our faith. There is a great epic. There is a great event that stands at the center of our faith which reveals to us that God is on the side of truth and love and justice. It says to us that Good Friday may occupy the throne for a day, but ultimately it must give way to the triumph and beat of the drums of Easter. It says that evil may so shape events that Caesar will occupy the palace and Christ the cross, but one day that same Christ will rise up and split history into A.D. and B.C. so that even the life of Caesar must be dated by his name. There is something in this universe that justifies Carlyle in saying, "No lie can live forever."[55]

King wanted his followers to know that no matter how much he talked about a new age and the progress made toward it, no matter how much he spoke of God working in history to bring about such an age, they were not to believe that they could relax or be patient and that the beloved community would automatically establish itself. Instead, King cautioned them that to adopt such a stance would mean that they "are the victims of a dangerous optimism." The beloved community *is* coming. Of that much King was certain. However, "We must speed up the coming of the inevitable."[56] The way to do this is for people of goodwill to organize and work together with each other and with God to make it happen. From Montgomery onward, King was confident that God is always working toward the establishment of the beloved community. In his first book, he wrote that "some extra-human force labors to create a harmony out of the discords of the universe. There is a creative power that works to pull down mountains of evil and level hilltops of injustice."[57]

Faith in the existence of an objective moral order at least implies that persons ought to live in ways that are consistent with the idea that the universe is friendly to value achievement. Luther D. Ivory provides an instructive word in this regard: "For King, the moral structure of reality placed unavoidable ethical demands upon the moral agent to work for the establishment of justice in the human community. Liberative acts and resistance efforts against injustice were in line with God's moral law. At the same time, the engagement of justice-oriented action meant that one had 'cosmic companionship.' The struggle for justice and community did not take place in cosmic isolation."[58]

It only makes sense to believe in the existence of objective moral laws *if* one also believes in the existence of an objective moral order, and that the universe is thoroughly fused with value. It is hard for human beings to know whether God established the objective moral order first, and then added immutable, eternal moral laws; whether the laws were first established, or whether the establishment of either was even possible without the other. Because King and his personalist teachers believed that the universe itself is grounded on value, it seems reasonable to believe that the objective moral order is the foundation on which the moral laws are established. In any case, personalism gives considerable attention to both. And it is necessary to understand the significance of both if one wishes the fullest understanding of King's theological social ethics in general, and of his beloved community ethic in particular.

Elsewhere I have shown that Bowne's ethics anticipates many of the moral laws in the moral law system that Brightman developed for responsible moral delibera-tion.[59] Because of the importance of the system of moral laws in personalism and its influence on King, it is important to give some attention to it.

BRIGHTMAN, "LAW," AND THE SIGNIFICANCE OF "SYSTEM"

Brightman used the term "law" rather than "principle" when he formulated the moral law system. However, there is clear evidence of his discomfort with "law," for it implies a sense of rigidity that troubled Brightman.[60] In addition, the term was not consistent with his conception that truth grows, and what is always needed is the most coherent rendering of the facts and evidence. Since created persons are not omnis-cient, and since the facts are always forthcoming, the term law implies the possibility of foreclosure on this. The term principle, on the other hand, is more plastic and dy-namic, and therefore is a better fit with Brightman's method and criterion of truth. For our purpose it should be observed that of the personalists who wrote on the moral law system only Bertocci and Millard and DeWolf chose to substitute the term "prin-ciple," primarily because they believed it to be more dynamic.[61] Troubled by the im-plications of "law," as was Brightman, they simply made the change. Although I think this an improvement, for the purpose of this discussion, and because King himself was clearly acquainted with Brightman's usage, I retain "law" in the discussion that follows. It is hoped, however, that the reader will keep in mind Brightman's uneasi-ness regarding its use.

In the literature on personalism a moral law is defined as one which is intended to be *universal in application*. It applies to all cases and is valid for all persons every-where. It was Brightman who first developed a *moral law system*, which was later simply enhanced through consideration of more empirical evidence and examples by some of his followers (e.g., Bertocci and Millard), who saw no reason to increase the number of laws. Others saw the need to increase the number of laws, as we shall see.[62] Brightman himself left the door open to this possibility. In addition, he intended that the moral law system be relevant and meaningful in every culture. As one who believed in the ex-istence of an objective moral order, he also believed the moral laws to be objective, and thus relevant and applicable to all persons. Consequently, Brightman maintained that the moral laws must be knowable and meaningful to every rational, disciplined person anywhere in the world. To his credit, however, Brightman recognized that cultural differences may require certain adaptations of the respective laws.

It is also important to observe that Brightman stressed "system" in his formulation of the moral laws. This means that one cannot simply pick and choose which law(s) to abide by during the process of moral deliberation. Instead, the moral laws must be taken as a set of interacting laws forming a coherent whole, if they are to be as effective as they can be in specific situations requiring moral judgment. The reason for the emphasis on system is that Brightman recognized that, taken in isolation, an individual moral law may be as much a law for evil as for good. By way of illustration Brightman writes: "If one wishes to be maliciously and successfully evil, one will have to obey the Logical Law; his will must be consistently evil. The Law of Consequences is observed by the prudent sinner as much as by the thoughtful saint. The Law of Individualism is very dear to egoist and lawless lover of 'personal liberty.'"[63] We can see the problem that arbitrarily abstracting a law here and there from the moral law system poses. It is therefore imperative that each law be seen in its relation to the one that comes before and after it, in addition to how it relates to the entire system of moral laws. Therefore, one who desires to be as moral as he can be in a moment requiring moral deliberation must appeal to the entire system of moral laws. Only in this way will there be possibility of moral gain. Brightman maintained that to uphold and develop one value while intentionally violating another leads to no gain. "Morality is rational; and reason demands that the moral ideal shall be taken as a whole."[64] To be truly moral, then, one should appeal to the entire system of moral laws.

Brightman distinguished moral law from civil, religious, natural, and logical law.[65] Moral law has two necessary conditions: It must be a universal law or norm, and it must apply to the obligation of the will in choosing.[66] The will to choose implies the need for intelligence or a mature rational faculty required in order to deliberate responsibly. According to the moral law system, no act is moral simply because it conforms to a social or civil code. One might well respond obediently to a legal code, for example, but only because of fear of legal or other consequences. An act is moral, on the other hand, only if it conforms to moral law,[67] which also implies responsible deliberation and choice. This means that every social code is subject to critique by moral law.

The moral law system is regulative, not prescriptive. Some of the laws do have strong implications for a social ethics, but Brightman was not seeking to develop a social ethics of personalism through the moral law system.[68] The system is intended to be a *rational guide* for persons as they strive to make responsible moral choices. It specifies what *all* persons *ought* to do in the course of moral deliberation—that is, how they ought to make responsible moral choices. Because the moral laws are rational, Muelder states, they are "not arbitrary or conventional."[69] Nor is it the aim of the moral law system to tell persons what to do (or not), as do the Ten Commandments and civil laws.

Muelder provides further commentary on the nature of the moral laws: "They are not principles of applied ethics like the principle of 'informed consent' in medical ethics. They are not like the traditional *natural law* of the Roman Catholic Church which mixed church law with universal rational principles. They are not heteronomous, that is, they are not handed down from an external authority either divine or human."[70] This means of making moral judgments makes it possible for the moral agent to determine the reasonableness of choices among available alternatives and values. Because the moral law system does not tell the agent what to decide, it is possible that no two agents who are faced with the same moral dilemma will make the same moral decision.

The moral law system is essentially a method for responsible moral deliberation *and* action. This latter point is crucial. According to personalism the process of moral deliberation, regardless of the system used, is not merely an intellectual exercise. Rather, it is intended to lead to actions consistent with the moral decision arrived at. In the best case scenario the action(s) will be coherent with the decision. The best possible moral decision should be accompanied by the best possible moral action(s). In other words, means and ends ought to cohere, a point that King frequently made during his ministry.[71] In the struggle for justice King constantly sought actions that were consistent with the moral choices at which he arrived.

The centrality of the person is presupposed throughout the moral law system as formulated by Brightman. Each of the moral laws, from the most abstract to the most concrete, features the significance of the person. Each law begins either with the phrase, "All persons ought," or "Each person ought." In the moral law system, then, both person and ought are *sui generis* or irreducible.[72]

Because it is a "system," its use requires intelligence, will, and intention. For in order to accomplish what Brightman intended, the moral law system should always be seen in its totality. One should be aware at all times of the name, meaning, place, and role of each law, as well as how it relates to others in the system, and with the system itself. Because it is a system of moral laws, it is necessary for one to be able to think holistically when choosing it as a means to responsible moral deliberation, choice, and action.

THE CATEGORIES OF MORAL LAWS

The basic outline of the Brightman system of moral laws follows. Beginning with the first law in the system the movement is from the most abstract to the most concrete. The moral law system is dynamic and processive, moving from most minimal to maximal, from least to most inclusive. In this regard, we see the influence of the Hegelian method. The method of the moral law system is dialectical in that the movement is always from thesis to antithesis to synthesis. The system moves from the most abstract set of laws (Formal Laws) to the more concrete (Axiological Laws), and finally to what for Brightman was the most concrete (Personalistic Laws). Beginning with the second law in the system (the Law of Autonomy) each subsequent law retains in itself the strength of the preceding one. In this way the content of each law is both deepened and enriched, even as it points to the next law in the system.

Postponing the defining of each law until the next chapter, I want now to present a chronological rendering of the system of moral laws from Brightman's initial eleven laws to the four added by Muelder and DeWolf and the two added by Deats. It should be kept in mind that the logical rendering would reverse the place of the Laws of Praxis and the Metaphysical Law. That is, the latter would be last in the system since it grounds the entire system, for this is the law that requires the agent to look to the source or ground of the moral law system:

I. The Formal Laws
    1. Logical Law
    2. Law of Autonomy

II. Axiological Laws
    3. Axiological Law
    4. Law of Consequences
    5. Law of the Best Possible
    6. Law of Specification
    7. Law of the Most Inclusive End
    8. Law of Ideal Control

III. Personalistic Laws
    9. Law of Individualism
    10. Law of Altruism
    11. Law of the Ideal of Personality

IV. Laws of the Ideal of Community (DeWolf and Muelder)
    12. Law of Cooperation
    13. Law of Social Devotion
    14. Law of the Ideal of Community

V. 15. Metaphysical Law

VI. Laws of Praxis (Deats)
    16. Laws of Conflict and Reconciliation
    17. Law of Fallibility and Corrigibility

King knew firsthand the eleven laws of the system composed by Brightman. He cites *Moral Laws* in several papers written in graduate school (e.g., in DeWolf's course on personalism).[73] He may not have been familiar with the specific laws introduced by DeWolf and Muelder into Brightman's system,[74] but he was very likely influenced by similar laws of community. (He was clearly not familiar with the fifth set—Laws of Praxis—since he was assassinated nearly twenty years before Paul Deats, Jr., introduced it.)[75] Nevertheless, it is unmistakably the case that "community" is an important term in King's theological social ethics and ministry.

It is important to remember that each set of moral laws, including the individual laws in each category, presuppose the one which came before, while simultaneously anticipating or pointing to the law which follows in the line of progression toward the most concrete or summary law in the system. What this effectively means is that each law beyond the Logical Law is more concrete and therefore includes more content than the one it precedes. Brightman sums up the contribution of each set of laws to the system. "The Formal Laws deal solely with the will as a subjective fact. The Axiological Laws deal with the values which the will ought to choose. The Personalistic Laws are more comprehensive; they deal with the personality as a concrete whole."[76] In the Personalistic Laws the emphasis is on both the person and—implicitly—persons-in-relationship as the subjects of the preceding laws. The Law of the Ideal of Personality is, for Brightman, the summary law of the entire system. It states: "All persons ought to judge and guide all of their acts by their ideal conception (in harmony with the other Laws) of what the whole personality ought to become both individually *and socially*."[77] One can see in this wording an anticipation of the Communitarian Laws. And yet, it is important to point out that in Brightman's version of the moral law system the centrality of the individual person is presupposed. Inasmuch as Muelder and DeWolf believed *person-in-community* to be an even more basic fact than the individual person—a point that was also stressed by Francis J. McConnell in 1914[78]—they introduced the Laws of Community.

Brightman did not claim that his version of the moral law system was the last word on the moral ideal. He wrote: "The laws which are presented in this book are principles of rational development, not rigid prescriptions of specific acts which are supposed to be eternally right. . . . Doubtless the laws here defined can and will be improved. It is only through confidence that reason is more than any insight which it has yet attained that a system of moral laws can be proposed."[79] Brightman was therefore open to the possibility that adjustments may need to be made to the original system of moral laws. It is not likely, then, that he would have rejected the addition of the Communitarian Laws and the Metaphysical Law.

Unlike in Brightman's system, the summary law for Muelder is the Law of the Ideal of Community. This law states: "All persons ought to form and choose all of their ideals and values in loyalty to their ideals (in harmony with the other Laws) of what the whole community ought to become; and to participate responsibly in groups to help them similarly choose and form all their ideals and choices."[80] We can see here an emphasis on the value of both the community and the individual, as well as a reminder that even as the summary law of the system it is necessary to acknowledge the contributions of every other law in the system if one is to choose and act responsibly. Muelder's commentary on the law is instructive: "This is the principle of inclusive responsibility, personal and communitarian, at once pluralistic and organic. It prescribes in advance no specific pattern of culture or society. In itself it is neither centralist nor decentralist, socialist nor capitalist, and it decides for neither world federalism nor any one political instrumentation. Yet it does confirm and emphasize the supremacy of personal worth and the idea of responsible society."[81] This law seeks a balance between the claims of the autonomous individual and the group or community.

Although Brightman would not be troubled by the addition of the Laws of Community, he would likely be puzzled by Deats's Laws of Praxis. The problem with these laws is that on the basis of how they are worded, one gets the sense that, important as they are, they are not integral to the moral law system itself. Instead, they seem merely to provide important commentary on the system. Deats characterizes these laws as follows:

Law of Conflict and Reconciliation: "All persons, in their own lives and in the lives of groups to which they belong, ought to accept conflict in the course of seeking to formulate and achieve the ideals of personality and of community, and to work through conflict—with others, 'friends' and 'enemies' alike—toward consensus, justice, and reconciliation."[82]

Law of Fallibility and Corrigibility: "All persons ought to expect to make—and suffer—mistakes, failures, and defeat, without being overcome by these experiences or losing hope. When mistakes are made, and repentance is acknowledged, and forgiveness asked, the way is opened for resources, human and divine, to be made available."[83]

Unlike Deats, Muelder and DeWolf merely took what was clearly the next logical step when they expressly named and introduced the Communitarian Laws into Brightman's system. Based on the wording of Brightman's Law of the Ideal of Personality it appears that the Communitarian Laws of DeWolf and Muelder easily follow. Deats's Laws of Praxis, on the other hand, seem to provide commentary on behavior—individual and collective—*after* the other laws have been engaged and one has come to decision. The Laws of Praxis do not, like the other laws in the system, serve as an actual guide in the moral deliberation process itself. This notwithstanding, what the Laws of Praxis propose is important for actual behavior, but do not seem to be necessary to the moral decision making process itself.

Little has been said to this point about how King actually used the moral law system and how he characterized the idea or principle behind each law. In addition, although a number of references have been made to his conviction that the universe is friendly to value, the connection was not made to the influence of George Washington Davis. This connection is important because Davis contributed much toward helping King to ground his already deeply embedded belief that there is an objective moral order and moral laws that persons ought to live by. Chapter 8 attends to Davis's influence, as well as King's use of the moral law system as the most reasonable way to make important moral decisions, e.g., his decision to break silence on the war in Vietnam. In fact, the process leading to this momentous decision will be used as a case study on King's use of and appreciation for the moral law system.

CHAPTER 8

Use of Moral Laws and the Vietnam War

I have elsewhere examined King's postgraduate school use of the moral law system, although I did so primarily through interpretations provided by Walter G. Muelder and John Ansbro.[1] Presently, I look specifically at some of King's sermons and speeches, in order to establish a sense of how he was influenced by the convictions that the universe is fundamentally moral and under spiritual guidance and that there exists an objective moral order. These important convictions ground King's belief in objective moral laws and the corresponding belief that there are moral absolutes.

The chapter also considers King's use of the moral law system as devised by Brightman. It should be understood at the outset that King did not engage these laws merely for the sake of philosophical exercise. Instead, he engaged the moral law system in the crucible of moral struggle against social injustices. In so doing, King contributed much to the philosophy of personalism, as well as the viability of the moral law system. Therefore, it is not merely a matter of how much personalism and the moral law system influenced King. There was clearly mutual influence. The significance of what King did is that it allows us to see in a concrete way just what may be the actual consequences for the moral agent who appeals to a system of moral laws as the means to making responsible moral judgments. We do not have to guess at or hypothesize about the consequences.

This chapter begins by further exploring the intellectual roots of King's faith in the existence of an objective moral order. There follows an examination of most of the moral laws that King appealed to as he made the important moral decision to break silence on Vietnam. However, one should not expect to see in King's writings and speeches explicit reference to individual moral laws, but only the ideas or principles they represent. Because he did not name the individual laws, one will need to have a sense of the name and meaning of each. Near the end of the previous chapter each of the laws was named and presented in the order they appear in the moral law system. Later in the present chapter each of the laws will be described.

THE UNIVERSE IS FRIENDLY

In 1951 King's mentor and professor at Crozer Theological Seminary, George W. Davis, published an article entitled "Liberalism and a Theology of Depth" in the *Crozer Quarterly*. Davis sought in this article to sum up some of his most mature theological views. King graduated from seminary the same year, but we can be sure that as a student he was exposed to many of the ideas expressed in that essay.

It is important to call attention to Davis's article because King expressed two of its chief ideas in a February 28, 1954 sermon he preached at Second Baptist Church in Detroit, Michigan. In "Recovering Lost Values," King declared the need to rediscover or reclaim two important values that his people once held dear, but then lost: the universe is based on a moral foundation, and it is under spiritual control. This sermon was preached about two and a half years after King graduated from seminary. It is not unusual for seminary graduates to express in their early sermons ideas gleaned from their seminary training.

Davis named and discussed four chief elements of what he called "depth theology":

1. Christianity points to moral foundations of the world and reality (a point we saw in the previous chapter that was also emphasized by Benjamin E. Mays in 1946 during King's student days at Morehouse).
2. The moral foundation of the universe implies that it is under spiritual control.
3. The need for specific, personal, divine action beyond the moral nature of reality and spiritual and cosmic control.
4. The acknowledgment of ongoing, unending divine presence and concern, as well as human beings' opportunity for fellowship with God.

Of these four, King explicitly named and discussed the meaning of the first two in "Recovering Lost Values." Throughout this discussion, we should remember that King was not first introduced to these ideas by Davis, but rather through the preaching tradition of the black church, including the sermons given by Mays and others at Morehouse College.

Reality as Value-Fused

Davis wrote that the genius of Hebrew prophecy was its depiction of Yahweh as "the God of moral grandeur." Individuals and nations abandon this God at tremendous cost—"only at the risk of substituting a state, a class, or a human institution to which men pledge their last full measure of devotion."[2] This conclusion was based on the deep conviction that inasmuch as God's moral nature is love, reality itself must be fused with value. Disvalue or moral evil enters the world through human choice. In the most fundamental sense, then, the world is good, and therefore just, despite dastardly choices and behavior of human beings and the consequences that follow. No matter what people do or fail to do, goodness and value remains secure throughout the structure of the universe.

This is nothing short of the handiwork of God, the friend behind, or the cause of, all phenomena.[3] God has so structured the universe that it works and responds best to goodness, justice, and love. This implies that in the area of morality there are some things that are absolutely right, and some things that are absolutely wrong, despite the fact that many people—even in the Christian community—reject this type of language as absolutist. Davis himself said as much when he wrote of the need to acknowledge "moral absolutes plus the conviction that action in harmony with them will not fail of saving results."[4] This point was not lost on King. "Some things are right and some things are wrong, no matter if everybody is doing the contrary," he said. "Some things in this universe are absolute. The God of the universe has made it so."[5] Love, for example, is absolutely right, and hatred is absolutely wrong for one who lives by the conviction that the universe has a moral foundation.

In "Rediscovering Lost Values," King said that black Christians have "left a lot of precious values behind," and that if they are to get on the right track in order to contribute toward making the world a better place, it will be necessary to recover these "precious" lost values. The wording of the two values that he chose to name and discuss is similar to that of Davis, as well as Mays. The first is that "all reality hinges on moral foundations, that there are moral laws of the universe just as abiding as the physical laws."[6] It is significant that King maintained that these lost values need to be *rediscovered*. Once they are rediscovered, persons should then live in accordance with them. An implication of this is that King was aware that these values were staples of Afrikan American religious faith. They were needed to insure continuing progress toward the achievement of a thoroughly inclusive, integrated, or beloved community. King would have gotten a sense of the importance of this first value from his study of the Bible dating back to his youth. For the creation stories in the Book of Genesis teach that God created human and nonhuman beings, looked out over all that was created, and said that it was good. How can that which was fundamentally built on goodness be anything but good?

King's conviction that the universe is built on a moral foundation led him to reject relativism in ethics. He reasoned that it was logical to conclude that if reality rests on moral foundations there must also be moral laws that are of abiding significance. This means one cannot base moral decisions and behavior on consensus or what the majority might do. Instead, one has to look to the moral law within (one of the two things that awed the philosopher Kant),[7] and then choose and behave in ways that are consistent with it. Morality has nothing to do with how many persons are doing or not doing a thing, according to King. One's decision or action is morally right only if it squares with the moral law. This must mean, "that some things are right and some things are wrong. Eternally so, absolutely so."[8] King argued that this is the case even when some persons are behaving to the contrary. There are some things that are absolutely right and absolutely wrong because the God of the universe made it so. To live as if this is not the case, King said, is to be in violation of God's laws.[9]

Because he believed that the universe hinges on a moral foundation and that there are objective moral laws, King also argued against a purely pragmatic test for what is right and wrong. In this, he revealed the influence of Brightman's discussion on criteria of truth and distinguishing truth from error.[10] Whenever persons appeal only to the pragmatic test they have strayed from the conviction that the structure of the universe is fused with value. King did a parody on the pragmatic test in one of his sermons:

If it works, it's alright. Nothing is wrong but that which does not work. If you don't get caught, it's right. That's the attitude, isn't it? It's all right to disobey the Ten Commandments, but just don't disobey the eleventh, 'Thou shall not get caught.' That's the attitude. That's the prevailing attitude in our culture. No matter what you do, just do it with a bit of finesse. You know, a sort of attitude of the survival of the slickest. Not the Darwinian survival of the fittest, but the survival of the slickest—whoever can be the slickest is the one who [is] right. It's all right to lie, but lie with dignity. It's all right to steal and to rob and extort, but do it with a bit of finesse. It's even all right to hate, but just dress your hate up in the garments of love and make it appear that you are loving when you are actually hating.[11]

One who believes that the universe is fundamentally moral sees the illogic in the purely pragmatic test of right and wrong, with its basic emphasis on workability. Both history and experience reveal that what works may or may not be either right or good. In addition, what may work for one group may not work for others, but may instead make the lives of one group unnecessarily miserable. King came to see, for example, that the United States' policy on Vietnam worked for the wealthy and powerful, but not for the powerless and voiceless.

King was convinced that what was needed in the United States and the world was a group of people—however small—who were committed to doing the right thing just because it is the right thing to do, and who will do it whether others agree or are watching them. This, King argued, is the stance of those who live by the conviction that the universe is erected on a moral foundation, because God has made it so. Such persons tend to believe that in the long view of history one cannot do wrong and get by. Accordingly, our wrongs eventually catch up with us, even if we remain undetected for many years. Byron De La Beckwith, accused of murdering civil rights leader Medgar Evers, was released after a number of mistrials and remained "free" for many years. After more than thirty years, however, he was finally brought to justice. In early 2003, Ernest Avants, a Mississippi Klansman, was found guilty of the murder of black farmhand, Ben Chester White in a forest in southwest Mississippi. Part of a trio of Klansmen, Avants was part of a plot to lure Martin Luther King, Jr., to the area and then assassinate him.[12] These are but reminders that we may slay justice in the moment, but by and by justice will be vindicated, because reality is value-fused, and thus is on the side of justice. "The arc of the moral universe is long, but it bends toward justice." Hatred of Afrikan Americans, Latinos, Native peoples, and homosexuals may prevail in the moment, but because the universe itself is friendly to value, and because God's law is infused in the nature of things, love will have the final word. King declared: "There is something in this universe that justifies Carlyle in saying 'No lie can live forever.' There is something in this universe that justifies William Cullen Bryant in saying 'Truth, crushed to earth, will rise again.' There is something in this universe that justifies James Russell Lowell in saying: 'Truth forever on the scaffold, Wrong forever on the throne. Yet that scaffold sways the future. Behind the dim unknown stands God within the shadow keeping watch above his own.'"[13]

According to this line of reasoning, the universe is so constructed that there will be no ultimate defeat of truth and justice. King would not have disagreed with Theodore Parker's view that, "though my private injustice be my foe, the justice of the universe is still my friend. God, acting in this universal mode of moral force, acts for me, and the prospect of future suffering has no terror."[14] There may be temporary setbacks and delays because of human selfishness, pride, and misuse of freedom, but God's justice and truth will have the last word, even if this or that generation does not live to witness it. Justice is at the foundation of the universe and will, in the end, prevail.

King's argument was that in the long drift of history things get better when persons persistently work together to establish the community of love. Not long after the Montgomery bus boycott King began talking about the emergence of "a new age" of race and human relations in the United States. The fact that such an age was evolving through human-divine cooperative endeavor led King to declare that this itself said something very basic about the nature of the universe. "It tells us something about the core and heartbeat of the cosmos," he said. "It reminds us that the universe is on the side of justice. It says to those who struggle for justice, 'You do not struggle alone, but God struggles with you.'"[15] King went on to ground this belief in the long tradition of the Jewish and Christian faiths.

And it is important to remember that King never speaks and writes only of what God can do or of what persons can do. Instead, he invariably conveys his conviction about what God and persons can, indeed must, do cooperatively.

THE UNIVERSE HAS SPIRITUAL CONTROL

The claim that the universe is thoroughly fused with value suggested to King, as it did to Davis, that it must also be under cosmic or spiritual control. Therefore, King proclaimed that the second value that his people lost touch with, but needed to rediscover and appropriate, is the idea that "all reality has spiritual control."[16] This, he maintained, is as fundamental as the conviction that the universe is based on a moral foundation. It means, if nothing else, that persons have assured help (i.e., cosmic companionship) in their struggle against social evil, and that the nature of this help is a power not ourselves, but makes for justice and righteousness in the world.

King rejected the deistic view that God simply set the creative process in motion and then removed God's self to some distant corner of the universe to contemplate God's own thoughts, while caring little for the well-being of persons and the rest of creation. God is ever at work in history, "not outside the world looking on with a sort of cold indifference,"[17] said King. The God of Christianity, King maintained, "is living and active. He is not the Aristotelian God who merely contemplates upon himself,"[18] but rather continually works with the people. Furthermore, King did not take it as a given that just because persons claimed to be Christian they actually believed in a living, active God in the world. They may verbalize and write about their belief in such a God. However, King knew that their day-to-day behavior frequently implied a denial of God's very existence. He saw this as a type of atheism, not "theoretical" but "practical." He argued that the latter is "the most dangerous type" of atheism, for one preaches and teaches the existence of God, but behaviorally he lives as if God does not exist.[19] This was a major problem in the churches and other religious institutions in King's day, as in our own. Once persons begin to proclaim the existence of God verbally, while behaving as if God does not exist, they effectively leave God behind.

God is no longer in the human drama for them. When this happens anything goes. Consequently, all that is done is done out of economic, political, or other expediency, not because of a sense of religious faith or moral responsibility. It is then easy to substitute other things for God, especially material things. King cautioned against putting our faith in "things" or "gadgets." Christians, he proclaimed, should put their faith and trust in "the God who has been our help in ages past, and our hope for years to come."[20] This is the God who has been characterized as "the great companion—the fellow-sufferer who understands."[21] This is the God of Martin Luther King, Jr. Because God works in history and cares about persons, King said: "Here on all the roads of life, he is striving in our striving. Like an ever-loving Father, he is working through history for the salvation of his children. As we struggle to defeat the forces of evil, the God of the universe struggles with us. Evil dies on the seashore, not merely because of man's endless struggle against it, but because of God's power to defeat it."[22]

These two convictions taken together—that the universe rests solidly on a moral foundation and that God is effectively guiding history—should be sufficient to provide encouragement for those who struggle against injustice and seek to establish the beloved community. For these two principles serve as a reminder that no matter how difficult the struggle, no matter how many setbacks, no matter how stubborn the forces of injustice and inhumanity, there is a benign and compassionate God in and behind the process who struggles with those who are committed to establishing justice and righteousness in the world. The idea that persons must willingly organize to work toward the attainment of justice is a major contribution made by King. His emphasis was not on one or the other, but was rather on the cooperative endeavor between persons and God.

King's strong faith in the fundamental morality of the universe convinced him that, God structured it to work in a certain way, and that persons, groups, and nations fare best when they strive to live in harmony with it. King said that the structure of the universe is such that "when you hate somebody, you can't work right, . . . you can't think right, you can't look right, . . . There's something about hate that distorts values and that distorts the personality."[23] The reason for this is that the universe is constructed out of and built on love. Love, King maintained, is the highest good, and is at the center of the universe.[24] He therefore declared love to be an integral part of his philosophico-theologico orientation.[25] King liked to quote historian Arnold Toynbee's emphasis on love as ultimate. "Love is the ultimate force that makes for the saving choice of life and good against the damning choice of death and evil. Therefore the first hope in our inventory must be the hope that love is going to have the last word."[26]

We also need to remember that one who believes as King did also believes that it is possible to do the right thing, but for the wrong reason. On the surface the deed itself may be good, but underneath, the reason behind it may in fact be selfish, or otherwise convoluted. This is what King meant when he said: "You may even give your body to be burned, and die the death of a martyr. Your spilt blood may be a symbol of honor for generations yet unborn, and thousands may praise you as history's supreme hero. But even so, if you have not love your blood was spilt in vain."[27]

MORAL ABSOLUTES

King believed that moral laws are always relevant to every person and group everywhere in the world. The existence of moral laws is confirmed both by the long history of the Jewish and Christian traditions, as well as theologically and philosophically. The source of the moral laws, in other words, is the God of the Hebrew prophets and Jesus Christ, who implanted in persons the sense of moral law. Personalist that he was, King understood moral laws to be discoverable through reason. For King, moral laws are part of the grain of the universe, and therefore are absolute. This means that the only way persons may hope to live life to the fullest and in ways that are pleasing to God, is to live in accordance with these laws. Since agapé love was for King the supreme moral law, he was adamant that persons—interpersonally and collectively—must live in accordance with the requirements of love, as well as other moral laws. Failure to do so would alienate persons from each other, from community, and from God. King believed that the violation of moral laws exacts a high price of persons and groups. In "Our God Is Able," he said: "We can neither defy nor break them. If we disobey them, they will break us."[28] Failure to conform to eternal moral laws makes us vulnerable to hateful behavior of all kinds. On the collective level this hatred unleashes the forces in nations which can lead to horrific tragedies such as the annihilation of thousands in the World Trade Towers in New York City on September 11, 2001, and the retaliatory counter-annihilation of many thousands more in Afghanistan and Iraq. There is no question that King believed that the only way to avoid the recurrence of such devastating tragedies is for persons and nations to be brought into conformity with the objective moral order and moral laws. King's faith in this regard was based on the further conviction that God is directing the course of history, even as we humans make death-inducing choices. Consequently, even though evil may reign for a day, it will not rule forevermore, for the universe is itself fundamentally moral, and is being guided by a righteous cosmic power that is making for good and for justice in the world.

King's conviction that the universe is moral led him to proclaim that means and ends ought to cohere in the struggle for justice, righteousness, and the beloved community. He argued that in the moral universe the end sought is preexistent in the means,[29] for "ultimately destructive means cannot bring about constructive ends."[30]

If the universe is indeed fused with moral fiber, then what we humans do in any given moment ought to cohere with the purpose we are striving to achieve. One who truly believes love is the fundamental moral law of the universe must also see that any behavior that is not consistent with love for self and for others can only eventuate in severely reduced chances for establishing the community of love. Indeed, King would be the first to argue that the Logical Law, i.e., that "all persons ought to will logically," or in such a way to avoid self-contradiction, while also seeking to be consistent with their own intentions,[31] requires that those who seek noble ends ought to do so by appealing to noble means. So too with the objective moral order. Individuals, groups, and nations may well ignore moral laws, but they do so at their own serious peril.

King's conviction that to live in harmony with the moral law makes it possible to avoid hatred, war, and other destructive social maladies suggests the appeal of the moral law system. In his own use of this system, King nowhere names the laws and then proceeds to the concrete application of them as academic personalists have done. However, an examination of some of his speeches, sermons, and writings reveals that he did in fact consider these laws whenever he was compelled to make important moral decisions. Walter Muelder illustrated this in "Martin Luther King, Jr., and the Moral Laws," a lecture given at Morehouse College in Atlanta on March 24, 1983. His discussion was based on a thorough examination of King's book, *Why We Can't Wait.*[32] Muelder's lecture inspires my own approach to this subject.[33]

Any serious discussion of King's use of the moral law system should be grounded on two of his basic personalistic convictions: persons as such are sacred, and the universe hinges on moral foundations. With these two underlying convictions in mind, I will examine King's appeal to many of the moral laws in order to arrive at the very controversial decision between late 1966 and early 1967 to take an unequivocal and public stance against the war in Vietnam. Indeed, inasmuch as these were self-imposed convictions or ideals for King, it was his sense that he was morally obligated to behave in accordance with them. We will see that by so doing, King was in strict compliance with both the Logical Law and the Law of Autonomy. His decision to break silence, however, was ultimately based on his appeal to the entire moral law system. In order to provide the context for his momentous decision, however, I first provide some of the sociopolitical background to his decision.

KING AND THE WAR IN VIETNAM

As a seminary student King was introduced to, but was not persuaded by the pacifism of A. J. Muste. Although he deplored war at the time, he nevertheless accepted the party line view of most of his seminary peers—that "while war could never be a positive or absolute good, it could serve as a negative good in the sense of preventing the spread and growth of an evil force."[34] During this period King believed there might be worse things than war itself, for example, the spread and proliferation of systems of totalitarianism such as nazism, fascism, and communism.[35] It was also during this period that King read Nietzsche and concluded that it was naïve to think that love could solve social problems, let alone be the answer to war.

King was rescued from this stance only after he heard Mordecai Johnson's lecture on Gandhi during his senior year in seminary. He would become a devoted Gandhist, however, only gradually during the Montgomery bus boycott. Only slowly did King come to the realization that if one truly believes persons are sacred and that life is worth living, war, even the so-called just war or limited war is not an option.[36] In fact, we know that as early as 1956 King declared that he could "see no moral justification for . . . war. I believe absolutely and positively that violence is self-defeating."[37] By 1959 King made it clear that he was finished with the whole sordid business of war, wherever it occurred in the world. Reacting to Robert F. Williams's charge that he was "cashing in on the spoils of war," and was among those black leaders who did not have the courage to advise retaliatory violence against white racists, or even to criticize the warmongers in Washington,[38] King said: "Merely to set the record straight, may I state that repeatedly, in public addresses and in my writings, I have unequivocally declared my hatred for this most colossal of all evils and I have condemned any organizer of war, regardless of his rank or nationality. I have signed numerous statements with other Americans condemning nuclear testing and have authorized publication of my name in advertisements appearing in the largest circulation newspapers in the country, without concern that it was then 'unpopular' to so speak out."[39] Clearly not referring specifically to the Vietnam War, this general condemnation of war in 1959 put King on record as unwilling to support any war campaign, let alone one that he considered unjust. In light of this, it is almost completely baffling that many of his detractors seemed both surprised and outraged at his criticism of the nation's escalating war in Vietnam in the mid-1960s.

Vincent Harding reports that as early as 1964 King felt morally compelled to preach sermons at Ebenezer Baptist Church against the war in Vietnam.[40] As president of the leading civil rights organization, King was politically astute enough to know what could happen to that organization's funding base if his statements against the war offended the wrong persons. King had the very tough challenge of trying to negotiate the tension caused by being a moral-spiritual leader, but one who also understood the political realities, limitations, and obstacles that invariably confront such a leader. What was he to do?

Regardless of historical and political forces that are emphasized by a number of King scholars, the position put forward here is that King simply could not have avoided arriving at the conclusion that he *had* to take a public stance against the war. I base this on the three basic, interrelated ideas that he inherited from the black church tradition and the philosophy of personalism: the conviction that every person is sacred; the belief in the existence of an objective moral order and moral laws; and the influence of the coherence criterion in personalistic method, which insists on the need to see not only the value and nature of the individual parts, but how they interrelate and function together as a whole. The social, political, and historical factors that first influenced King's decision not to speak out, and then led to his unwillingness to remain silent were clearly important factors as well. My argument, however, is that these factors were secondary to the more important influence of King's fundamental theological and ethical convictions.

Adam Fairclough, Stephen B. Oates, and David Garrow each do an admirable job of portraying the historical and political factors involved in King's decision first to remain silent, and then to finally speak out forcefully against the war in Vietnam.[41] Fairclough argues, for example, that although King first spoke publicly against the war in 1965 (i.e., outside the context of sermons preached at Ebenezer Baptist Church), something caused him to remain silent for nearly two years thereafter. The reason that Fairclough gives is that from the time of the Reconstruction period (roughly 1865–77), Afrikan American leaders had "viewed loyalty to the federal government as a *sine qua non* of progress toward racial equality. Such loyalty was particularly important in times of national crisis."[42] This is why Frederick Douglass, and later W. E. B. DuBois, could encourage officials to permit blacks' participation in the Civil War and World War I, respectively.[43] The thinking was that if blacks supported "their" country in times of crisis and war, the federal government and other institutions would in turn support their efforts to gain equality along racial lines. However, historically, blacks as a race did not receive much substantive support from the federal government for their patriotism and willingness to support war campaigns from the Civil War to the war in Vietnam.

King himself began to see this pattern by late 1966, although for a brief period he did not openly criticize the traditional party line view that by supporting the country's war campaign in Vietnam blacks could count on the Johnson administration's support for civil rights and the war on poverty. This is essentially what Johnson, other civil rights leaders, and even some of King's key advisors told him when he first made public statements against the war in 1965. This criticism caused King to resort to silence on Vietnam. By late 1966, however, King could see that even if he remained silent the war would continue to escalate, which also meant that money and other resources would be siphoned off that could otherwise be directed toward the war on poverty. King could also see that his silence regarding Vietnam was doing nothing to promote civil rights efforts, and that for all intents and purposes civil rights was, by this time, a dead issue for the Johnson administration.

What Fairclough and other King scholars have not considered seriously enough, and what I take to be paramount, are the fundamental theological and ethical reasons for King's decision to break silence. According to King's aide Bernard Lee, this decision was made when King picked up a copy of the January 1967 edition of *Ramparts* magazine at an airport. So stunned was King by the pictures of Vietnamese children who had been severely burned and killed by napalm that he was not able to eat the food set before him. Lee claims to have never seen King react this way before. Recalling the incident, Lee said: "When he came to *Ramparts* magazine he stopped. He froze as he looked at the pictures from Vietnam. He saw a picture of a Vietnamese mother holding her dead baby, a baby killed by our military. Then Martin just pushed the plate of food away from him. I looked up and said, 'Doesn't it taste any good?' and he answered, 'Nothing will ever taste any good for me until I do everything I can to end that war.'"[44] According to Lee, who might well have been overly dramatic and simplistic in his reporting, it was at that moment that King made the decision to break his silence.

Although there were clearly other factors that led to King's decision, unlike Fairclough, I hesitate to downplay the importance of Lee's statement,[45] for King himself recalled the incident of reading the article in *Ramparts* and the effect it had on his decision. Looking back, King said: "As I went through this period one night I picked up an article entitled 'The Children of Vietnam,' and I read it. And after reading that article, I said to myself, 'Never again will I be silent on an issue that is destroying the soul of our nation and destroying thousands and thousands of little children in Vietnam.' I came to the conclusion that there is an existential moment in your life when you must decide to speak for yourself; nobody else can speak for you."[46] The experience of reading that article and seeing those pictures made an indelible impression on him. And yet Fairclough is quite right when he contends that King's emotional reaction to the pictures of the burned children was not the *only* reason for his decision to break silence. For by the time he saw those pictures he was already convinced that the Johnson administration was going to continue the escalation of the war, which also meant reneging on the earlier promise to support civil rights and the war on poverty. Therefore, Fairclough rightly maintains that the earlier political arguments for King's silence were no longer relevant or compelling.[47] It might well be, however, that the photos he saw in *Ramparts* were the straw that broke the camel's back, thus compelling him to break silence.

As previously observed, King had spoken publicly against the war as early as March 2, 1965. This was the day that President Johnson authorized "a sustained aerial assault on North Vietnam." The exercise was called Operation Rolling Thunder. On the same day, King, in a speech at Howard University, urged a "negotiated settlement" of the escalation of the war. He also spoke against the war later in August and was roundly and severely criticized by many of his advisors, newspaper columnists, other civil rights leaders, as well as the White House. President Johnson's advisors essentially told King that he should stay focused on the one thing he knew something about— civil rights.[48] He was told that he knew too little about foreign policy in general and policies pertaining to Vietnam in particular to be publicly critical of the administration's position on the war. Consistent with the acceptable party line dating back to the time of American slavery, the National Urban League, the NAACP, as well as the SCLC Board considered the federal government to be a necessary ally in the fight for civil rights. Understandably, Whitney Young and Roy Wilkins were concerned that King's public stance against Vietnam would jeopardize what they considered strong support from President Johnson on civil rights. But, more and more, it seemed to King that his silence was little more than an indication of his complicity in what he believed was an unjust war.

When King first spoke publicly against the war in 1965, he received no support from his own organization. By the end of 1966, however, more and more SCLC board members were also becoming critical of the war. Nevertheless, for political reasons and a desire not to do anything to hurt the SCLC's already shrinking funding base, King decided to return to silence on the war issue. It is important to point out, however, that from a moral standpoint he was never comfortable with this purely pragmatic stance. King never believed that it was logically consistent and morally right for him to remain silent on Vietnam, while preaching nonviolence in the fight for civil and human rights in the United States. He came to see that his silence implied support of a complete, but false, separation between his sense of racial injustice on American soil, and the injustice being perpetrated on Vietnamese soil by Americans. This was ethical dualism at its worst. For King injustice anywhere in the world is a threat to justice everywhere else in the world. In turn, this meant that one cannot pretend to be concerned about achieving justice for Afrikan Americans and the poor in the United States, while simultaneously turning a deaf ear to injustices being perpetrated in Vietnam and elsewhere in the world.

Compelled to Speak Out

In a way, many things came to a head for King when he decided to go to Jamaica in January 1967 for some long overdue respite and an uninterrupted period of time to work on *Where Do We Go From Here: Chaos or Community?* It was during this period that he picked up that copy of *Ramparts* magazine. He was also convinced by this time that the administration was talking peace while clearly continuing the build up of troops and redirecting economic resources to support the proliferation of the war.

The point to be made here is that important as glancing at those pictures may have been, important as social and political factors were in prompting King's silence and then the breaking of his silence, he was literally being driven by theological and moral convictions, as well as the coherence criterion in personalisic method, to break his silence on Vietnam.

King's convictions left him no choice. As Dorothy Cotton (a member of the SCLC staff in 1960) said, "Dr. King could not be limited that way. He could not be limited because he was a larger thinker. He was a larger person. He was, in fact, a leader."[49] Perhaps because of his faith, educational training, and experiences in the civil rights movement King saw things—and saw them with a clarity—that many of his contemporaries did not. We have seen that in the area of social morality King was not a consensus person. It was not his habit to seek majority opinion or support for important ethical decisions. Although it hurt him that a Louis Harris poll done after his speeches against Vietnam in April and May 1967 showed that approximately 60 percent of Americans believed his antiwar stance was harmful to the civil rights movement,[50] it finally did not matter to him. King was now determined to follow his conscience and his faith. Deep down he knew that the person with a strong moral sensibility must at times be courageous enough to stand up and be counted. Thereafter the only remaining question was *when* to do it and what would be the best venue.

We need to remember that Martin Luther King, Jr., was, by his own admission, fundamentally a Baptist preacher who grounded his important stances morally and theologically. He was a religious person who therefore did not see the world primarily through the eyes of the historian, the economist, the political scientist, or the politician. King tried to see occurrences in the world through the eyes of the God of the Hebrew prophets and Jesus Christ. If we fail to understand this important point, any argument or reasons that scholars propose for King's decision to break silence on Vietnam (as well as his decision to go to Memphis) will fall well short of the mark.

Politicians and historians see things primarily through the eyes of human beings and human institutions. King was less concerned about what we finite and limited creatures think is possible in the world. What mattered to him, finally, was what God requires of persons in their interpersonal and corporate relations. King gleaned his sense of this from his understanding of the Bible, the black religious tradition, and his upbringing in the black church. With the Hebrew prophets he believed that God requires that persons do justice, love kindness, and walk humbly with God.

What Abraham J. Heschel said about the Hebrew prophets is applicable to the point being made about King. "The prophet does not see the world from the point of view of a political theory; he is a person who sees the world from the point of view of God; he sees the world through the eyes of God."[51] This is not easily accomplished, and because of human finitude the prophet may sometimes err. The point, however, is that the prophet is vigilant about trying to see things from the divine perspective as portrayed in the Bible and evidenced in the best of the Jewish and Christian traditions, which is quite different from the historical, political, or sociological perspective. Most King scholars who have written on his rationale for speaking against the war in Vietnam (e.g., Fairclough and Garrow) do not highlight this important point.

For moral and theological reasons, King was willing to risk everything, including severe reduction in financial contributions to the SCLC, mass exits from the ranks of supporters, friendships, as well as the loss of his own life. He came to the conclusion that the war was immoral and therefore wrong, which meant he was now obligated to choose and behave in accordance with this self-imposed ideal. This is precisely what is required by the Law of Autonomy (in the moral law system)—self-imposed ideals are obligatory. From a moral standpoint, then, King *had* to break silence. In addition, one who, like King, believes love to be the supreme moral law, and seeks to live in harmony with it, does all that is humanly possible to avoid hatred, war, and other practices that are destructive of life and human values.

Although King's decision to break silence represented a clear shift in his political stance, it was not a shift in his moral-theological position. The decision was actually consistent with the ongoing expansion of his moral-theological outlook that had been taking place since the Montgomery bus boycott. King's broadening of the moral sphere was most noticeable not long after he was awarded the Nobel Peace Prize in December 1964. Lewis Baldwin has rightly pointed out that King's decision was consistent with his conviction that nonviolence was not just a strategy for social change, but more significantly, a way of being in the world. "King was consistent in that he was simply advocating that nonviolence be lifted from the domestic context and applied to America's foreign policy."[52] He knew that it was inconsistent to advocate nonviolence in local campaigns for justice while ignoring or condoning violence as a means for working out the nation's problems with other countries.

IMPORTANCE OF PERSONALISTIC METHODOLOGY

Under Brightman and DeWolf, King became familiar with personalistic methodology, its criterion of truth (growing empirical coherence), and synoptic method. These loom large in any attempt to understand his decision to break silence on Vietnam. The argument here is that the very logic of personalistic methodology was driving King to his momentous decision.

The aim of synopsis is to see the object as a whole, but it is also crucial to see and analyze its parts and their interrelations. Critical analysis of the parts is important, but this alone does not tell the whole story. Synopsis and analysis must go hand in hand and be seen in dialectical tension if one is to get the most adequate picture of the whole. Brightman made a helpful comment in this regard. "Synopsis without prior analysis is superficial and inarticulate; analysis without synopsis is the dissection of a corpse; synopsis and analysis combined yield the richest and completest knowledge of which the human mind is capable."[53]

Personalists consider a number of criteria or tests of truth, but settle on *coherence* as the chief criterion.[54] Coherence literally means *a sticking together whole*. This means that the method of personalism is always driving one to a fuller, clearer, more coherent sense of the whole and of truth. Because we are finite, limited beings and do not possess the trait of omniscience, personalism maintains at the same time that the most we can hope for in any given moment are most reasonable and coherent hypotheses.

The aim of personalistic method is the attainment of more and more intelligibility. The method, therefore, moves from the most abstract, often least clear view to the most concrete, clearest view based on empirical and other types of evidence. This means that the searcher should be willing to consider all of the relevant evidence and facts that may be pertinent to a particular problem or issue under consideration. The moral agent is then required to retain an open mind as well as a sense of wonder in creatively orchestrating all of the available data into a symphonic whole. Since the searcher lacks omniscience and the facts of experience are always forthcoming, the process continues ad infinitum. Personalism recognizes, then, that in our present human state persons never attain truth once and for all, for truth grows or becomes. Nevertheless the goal is to always consider and examine new evidence, facts, and experiences and be willing to alter one's hypothesis about truth as required. At every step, however, one tries to grasp the comprehensive whole.

Brightman provides a good analogy of how this process works in the search for higher truth or the most reasonable hypothesis based on the most relevant evidence available. He described this process as "the flight of the arrow of intelligibility." He characterized the process as follows:

One may picture that arrow (1) as starting with the unintelligible given, but aiming at intelligibility; (2) as flying toward the mark of analysis, but discovering that a bull's eye hit is not completely intelligible; (3) then with new aim, as flying back toward the starting point, which then is enriched and transformed by the results of the analysis. This process goes on forever; but the essence of it is that fuller and truer intelligibility is found at the synoptic end than at the analytic end of the flight of the arrow. The arrow can never rest in a developing world, but its target is a synopsis enriched by analysis rather than an analysis that exhausts synopsis and renders it superfluous. For it is in synopsis that actual experience, the seat of verification and process and life, is found.[55]

Put in the context of King's ministry and ethical decision making, we may say that from the beginning of his ministry in 1954, King's primary intention was to work for the attainment of freedom and justice for his people. As his experience and travels increased, his moral vision expanded to include efforts to end poverty and to provide jobs and a guaranteed income for the unemployed and underemployed, regardless of race. By the time he received the Nobel Peace Prize, his theological and social action project had expanded and been enriched even more. There was already clear evidence (at least from 1959) that King abhorred violence of all kinds, including war. In his acceptance speech he said that he refused to believe that persons are condemned to "the starless midnight of racism and war" and "that the bright daybreak of peace and brotherhood can never become a reality." King concluded by saying that he accepted the award on behalf of all persons who love peace and brotherhood.[56]

King understood that it does no good to grow in truth if such development has no significant bearing on one's outlook and behavior. As one attains more truth there ought to be evidence of the will and courage to change in light of the newly acquired truth. Indeed, King revealed a number of times an uncommon willingness to change as his comprehension of truth expanded. Throughout his leadership in the civil rights movement he exhibited a pattern of a profound capacity to change.

With Brightman's analogy in mind we can see that within a decade (1955–65) King had moved from activism for the civil rights of his people to activism for the human rights of all people everywhere. He had been carried by events, as well as theological maturity, from the local to the national to the world stage and thus could never again focus solely on the oppression of a single group of persons (e.g., Afrikan Americans, or the people in but one hemisphere). His own intellectual development and current events had taken him to the point that he had to be concerned about the condition of all persons everywhere in the world, a point made by Charles E. Fager, who marched with King in Selma in 1965. Writing in the *Christian Century* magazine, Fager said: "When he accepted the Nobel peace prize he baptized all races into his congregation and confirmed the world as the battleground for his gospel of nonviolence and reconciliation. He is no longer—and probably never again can be—a spokesman for just an American Negro minority. . . . The war in Vietnam is perhaps the gravest challenge of Dr. King's career—and conceivably its culmination."[57]

Fager went on to say that, should King fail to act or to make the right decision regarding Vietnam, the question will be whether history can forgive him. In truth, King was not primarily concerned whether history would forgive him. He was much more concerned as to whether he would be forgiven by the God of his faith, since it was his faith in the morality of the universe, more than anything else, that compelled him to take a public stance against the war. King wanted more than anything to be faithful to his call to ministry, a point that was highlighted in a moment of extemporizing during a sermon in Chicago in early 1967. He was preaching at the church of his friend, Rev. John Thurston. Bernard Lee was also present. King said (in language anticipating "The Drum Major Instinct," a sermon delivered at Ebenezer on February 4, 1968):

> And John, if you and Bernard happen to be around when I come to the latter day and that moment to cross the Jordan, I want you to tell them that I made a request. I don't want a long funeral. In fact, I don't even need a eulogy of more than one or two minutes.
>
> I hope that I will live so well the rest of the days. I don't know how long I'll live, and I'm not concerned about that. But I hope I can live so well that the preacher can get up and say he was faithful. That's all, that's enough. That's the sermon I'd like to hear. 'Well done thy good and faithful servant. You've been faithful; you've been concerned about others.'
>
> That's where I want to go from this point on, the rest of my days. 'He who is greatest among you shall be your servant.' I want to be a servant. I want to be a witness for my Lord, do something for others.[58]

More than anything he wanted to be faithful to God; he wanted his heart to be right. He recognized that as a human being he made mistakes and sometimes missed the moral mark. But he was adamant about the need to be on the right road, to *want* to do the right thing, even if one periodically missed the mark.[59]

While still in college, King had developed the conviction that God is personal, loving, and compassionate, and that persons as such are inherently precious because created, loved, and sustained by God. While he had a general sense that this applied to all persons everywhere, King initially set out to awaken and reinvigorate in his own people the sense of their dignity and sacredness. There was evidence that this was in fact occurring by the end of the Montgomery bus boycott. Blacks were gaining a new sense of dignity, self-respect, as well as a sense that they are somebody.[60] As the movement began to take on national and then international implications, it became increasingly clear to King that his doctrine had much broader implications. He saw that what was occurring in the southern United States was also connected to what was happening in other parts of the country and the world. The serious religious person had to see that one cannot be solely concerned about the well-being of a particular group of persons in a particular place in the world. Rather, one has to be concerned about the well-being of all persons everywhere, for this is what God expects. Philosophically, King knew early in his ministry that the universe is so constructed that love and justice are indivisible. As his faith and experiences were broadened, and as he reflected on their meaning in light of what he believed God required the world to be—a beloved community—one can understand how he was compelled to break silence on the war in Vietnam, and why he became in the remaining months of his life its staunchest critic.

The politician and political scientist may argue that King was being naïve when he called for the halting of all bombing of Vietnam and a unilateral ceasefire. King himself acknowledged that in this regard he was "politically unwise but morally wise."[61] By making such a politically "unwise" proposal, he was only being faithful to and consistent with his deepest theological and philosophical convictions about God, the universe, and persons-in-community. The fundamental reason that King was compelled to speak out against the war was moral-theological. Such a reason is generally not in accord with prevailing political wisdom. King himself told New York Times correspondent John Herbert: "It is out of this moral commitment to dignity and the worth of human personality that I feel it is necessary to stand up against the war in Vietnam."[62] If this was considered naïve by politicians and others, so be it. King wanted no bifurcation of worlds such that the private and political worlds adhered to radically different ethical standards. There is one world, called into being and sustained by the one God of the universe. There is therefore no dual standard for moral behavior at the individual and political levels.

King was only trying to convince political, civil rights, and other leaders of the reasonableness of taking seriously the nonviolent approach to solving political and other conflicts on even the grandest scale. Maintaining that the world is fundamentally moral, he therefore concluded that it only makes sense to try to solve differences in ways that do not diminish and destroy beings of such high value as persons. If God loves persons and the world, King reasoned, how does one justify reacting violently toward them?

"A Time to Break Silence"

Unlike the more philosophical, formal, and academic examination of objective moral laws undertaken by King in graduate school, there are many examples of his application of these in the heat of the socio-moral struggle. Walter Muelder correctly observes that although King did not discuss the moral laws "in a bookish fashion," they are clearly "implicit in his arguments and practices."[63] We do not find King naming the individual moral laws in his speeches and writings. That he actually applied these in the social struggle, however, gives us a clue as to how he both made their meaning concrete and altered and even enhanced their meaning in actual experience. King was not just interested in the abstract meaning of the moral laws. Rather, he was interested in what they actually required of persons in their everyday lives, and the implications of their application to pressing social ills such as war.

A close reading of King's inspiring and provocative speech, "A Time to Break Silence," delivered at the Riverside Church in New York City on April 4, 1967 (exactly one year before he was assassinated), reveals that he appealed to a number of the moral laws during the course of his decision to speak out about the war and regarding the Johnson administration's foreign policy. As noted previously, two of King's basic assumptions were that persons as such are sacred, and the universe stands on a moral foundation. With these in mind he appealed to the moral law system as he grappled with his conscience regarding Vietnam.

We saw in chapter 7 that Brightman's three sets of moral laws include: Formal Laws, Axiological Laws, and the Personalistic Laws. The two Formal Laws depict the minimal formal requirements of moral behavior. The six Axiological Laws provide guidance in the movement from value claim to true value. The third and final set of laws was for Brightman the most concrete. These three Personalistic Laws focus on the choices and contributions of the individual, as well as the community.[64] DeWolf added a fourth and fifth set of laws: three Communitarian Laws and the Metaphysical Law. The former stresses the need to make decisions that have the best interests of the community in view, while the latter turns attention to the ground or source of the entire system of moral laws. We have seen that King may or may not have been formally familiar with these last two sets of laws, and yet there is no question that they are implicit in many of his moral decisions. What follows now is an illustration of King's use of the moral laws as he moved toward breaking silence on the war in Vietnam.

Logical Law

"All persons ought to will logically; i.e., each person
ought to will to be free from self-contradiction and to
be consistent in his intentions" (*Moral Laws*, 98).

The very first thing to notice is that each of the moral laws begins with the words "All persons ought" or "Each person ought." This wording highlights the universal element in the laws; they are objective and thus are applicable to everybody everywhere. The wording also points to the irreducibility of the experience of "ought." Moreover, and especially in the case of the laws as formulated by Brightman, the wording applies to the centrality and significance of the individual person. These ideas influenced King's ethical decision making, for he frequently spoke and wrote about the inherent dignity of the person, who needs to feel that he or she is somebody and is capable of freely making choices that are logically consistent and reasonably harmonious with his or her intentions.

For King, as for moral law theorists, the imperative to will logically and to be consistent with one's intentions applies not only to the individual person, but to groups as well. Already living by the conviction that persons as such are loved by God and therefore possess absolute, inviolable dignity, King knew that he could not continue to make this claim only in the context of the Civil Rights movement, as if it applied only to oppressed and other persons in the United States. By the end of 1966 he realized more and more that his conviction about the inviolable worth of persons literally applied to persons all over the world, including the Vietnamese. The Logical Law permits no other conclusion.

In "A Time to Break Silence" (hereafter "A Time"), King illustrated the principle of logical consistency as he discussed the seven reasons he felt compelled to speak publicly against the war.[65] The third reason he named emerged as a result of the time he spent in the ghettos of the North and West (e.g., Chicago, Cleveland, and Los Angeles). As he walked among and conversed with the angry young black males of these communities, especially after the eruption of the "riots," he realized that he could no longer insist that they adhere to nonviolence rather than firing guns, throwing Molotov cocktails, and destroying public property, while he remained silent about the Vietnam War. For whenever he would admonish those young men to put down their weapons and resort to nonviolence, they would invariably ask about the massive violence the United States was perpetrating against the Vietnamese, ostensibly as a means of solving its problems and procuring proposed changes. King saw the inconsistency of his earlier position of encouraging ghetto youth to appeal to nonviolence to address their grievances and solve their problems, while he resorted to silence on Vietnam. King reflected on this point: "Their questions hit home, and I knew that I could never again raise my voice against the violence of the oppressed in the ghettos without having first spoken clearly to the greatest purveyor of violence in the world today—my own government. For the sake of those boys, for the sake of this government, for the sake of the hundreds of thousands trembling under our violence, I cannot be silent."[66]

King was merely acknowledging that one who believes that every person is sacred because created and loved by God, cannot be in compliance with the Logical Law if he advises one group of people to be nonviolent when they have legitimate moral claims against their government, while remaining silent when that same government, with virtually no moral claims against the people of Vietnam, perpetrate mass violence against them. To assume, as King did, that life is worth living and that persons have a right to live meant that he had to speak out against violence not only locally and nationally, but also in Vietnam.[67] In this regard, King was adhering to the Logical Law.

Law of Autonomy

"All persons ought to recognize themselves as
obligated to choose in accordance with the ideals
which they acknowledge. Or: Self-imposed ideals
are imperative" (106).

According to this law, the ideals that one chooses and imposes upon self are morally obligatory. This applies not only to individuals but to groups and nations as well. These are not ideals that are imposed from without, either by another person, group, the state, or even God, and they might be in opposition to civil codes or laws. According to the Law of Autonomy, since King lived by the conviction that the universe is built on a moral foundation, and persons are sacred, he was morally obligated to choose in accordance with these self-imposed ideals. In addition, because of King's sense of divine call and what this meant for his ministerial vocation, he was adamant about the need to speak for the voiceless in this country, in Vietnam, and other places in the world. For his understanding of the biblical message was that God is fundamentally concerned about the plight of the least. Therefore, when King accepted the call to ministry he in effect entered into a covenant relationship with God that bound him to advocate for the poor and the oppressed both at home and abroad. King found corroboration in what he considered the commission of the Nobel Prize for Peace: "to work harder than I had ever worked before [for] 'the brotherhood of man.' This is a calling that takes me beyond national allegiances. . . ."[68] What is important here is that these are ideals that King imposed upon himself. In light of the Law of Autonomy then, he was morally obligated to live in accordance with them. Without actually naming this law, King clearly understood that by virtue of his calling, as well as the commission of the Nobel Prize for Peace, he was obligated to speak out, even if such action violated civil laws or social codes. King was convinced that the law and voice he obeyed regarding Vietnam must enhance or uplift every person. As a self-imposed ideal, he was obligated to do his best to conform to it.

Axiological Law (Law of Value)

"All persons ought to choose values which are
self-consistent, harmonious, and coherent, not
values which are contradictory or incoherent
with one another" (125).

This law requires that persons recognize that as important as logical consistency and autonomy are, these alone do not make one fully moral. They are but the formal requirements of moral decision making and behavior. The moral person not only must conform to law but must engage in the critical selection of available values. There is need for the formal laws to be supplemented by laws of value. In his commentary on the Axiological Law, Brightman contends that life is such that we cannot have all that we desire, and consequently it is necessary that we make the best, most rational selection of the available values in a specific situation. After all, a value is anything that is liked or desired, and we know that our likes and desires sometimes contradict each other. Therefore, we often have to choose among conflicting or competing values. The aim is to avoid choosing values that contradict each other.

Adhering to the best in the Jewish and Christian traditions, King chose life and the sacredness of persons as the highest values. He came to see that his silence about Vietnam was a contradiction, for the cost in terms of human life was utterly devastating. The fact that King appealed to the first two laws (i.e., Logic and Autonomy) is clear indication of his respect for civil law, even if conscience demands that he violate it as he did the unjust laws in Birmingham.[69] King believed he retained his moral integrity in that situation because even though he violated segregation laws, he was just as determined to submit to the legal consequences. By so doing, he felt that he closed the door to the criticism that he was being logically inconsistent since he was obeying some laws and disobeying others.

Law of Consequences

"All persons ought to consider and, on the whole,
approve the foreseeable consequences of each of
their choices. Stated otherwise: Choose with a view
to the long run, not merely to the present act" (142).

As he deliberated on whether to break silence, King not only knew that there would be consequences for his decision, but he noted some of the foreseeable ones. The Law of Consequences requires that one choose in a way that considers not merely the present, but with a view to the long run. Remember, when King earlier spoke against the Vietnam War it was clear to him that if he did not revert to silence there could be serious financial and other consequences for the SCLC, and thus for the civil rights movement. On an even broader scale, by the time he delivered his speech at Riverside Church, King was convinced that the consequence for any nation that annually spends more on military defense than for social uplift is spiritual destruction. Only arrogance, greed, and a grossly underdeveloped moral sense militated against reordering moral and social priorities so that the pursuit of peace takes priority over the pursuit of war and destruction.[70]

Law of the Best Possible

"All persons ought to will the best possible values
in every situation; hence, if possible, to improve
every situation" (156).

This law is a reminder that the moral agent is not merely to abide by self-imposed ideals as required by the Law of Autonomy. Rather, he or she has to abide by the best ideals in the hope of improving every situation. Because of its emphasis on finding the best in every situation, this Law implies both *meliorism* and *creativity*. Brightman in fact said that it may also be called the Melioristic Law and the Law of Creativity. The Law of the Best Possible further enhances the Law of Value (Axiology) inasmuch as it "now means not merely a consistent organization of the values actually given in individual and social life, but it means a critical selection, improvement, and creation of values" (156). At the same time, the law moderates the others, since it requires not that one does or attempt the impossible, but the possible. The parameters or limits of this will be different for different persons because of their respective gifts, intellectual ability, and sociocultural advantages or disadvantages. One's duty is to do one's best in a specific situation. Just as this law does not require the impossible, one should be realistic in judging the outcome of one's efforts. A person is not to be seen as morally culpable if he or she, unknowingly and unwillingly, commits an act that leads to his or her own or the deaths of innocent persons. So, not only is the law one of meliorism and creativity, but of "tolerance" and "mercy" (157).

Because of his earlier inability or (painful) unwillingness to allow his moral sense to lead, King publicly criticized the war in Vietnam and then reverted to silence for nearly two years. As it became clearer to him that even his silence made him morally culpable, he knew he had to take his stand on moral rather than sociopolitical grounds, and that as long as he was silent his name was on the bombs being dropped on Vietnam.[71] Consequently, in "Standing by the Best," a sermon preached at Ebenezer, King acknowledged that he was morally obligated to do what he considered the best, regardless of the consequences. He told the congregation:

> I've decided what I'm going to do. I ain't going to kill nobody in Mississippi . . . [and] in Vietnam. I ain't going to study war no more. And you know what? I don't care who doesn't like what I say about it. I don't care who criticizes me in an editorial. I don't care what white person or Negro criticizes me. I'm going to stick with the best. On some positions, cowardice asks the question, "is it safe?" Expediency asks the question, "is it politic?" Vanity asks the question, "is it popular?" But conscience asks the question, "is it right?" And there comes a time

when a true follower of Jesus Christ must take a stand that's neither safe nor politic nor popular but he must take that stand because it is right. Every now and then we sing about it, "if you are right, God will fight your battle." I'm going to stick by the best during these evil times.[72]

The Law of the Best Possible merely reinforced King's conviction that the best means to addressing all types of violence and war is nonviolent resistance. This was consistent with his view of the fundamental goodness of the universe and the inviolable sacredness of persons. If one is committed to choosing life rather than death, it follows that one will do all in his power to avoid the use of violence to address social ills. The aim must be to establish the beloved community. If nations resort to the use of weapons of mass destruction and destroy human life, this will end the possibility that such a community can be achieved.

Law of Specification

"All persons ought, in any given situation, to develop the value or values specifically relevant to that situation" (171).

This law makes the system of moral laws even more concrete. It focuses on the immediate situation. In King's case, not war in general, but the war in Vietnam was at issue. Specificity. What ought one to do in the specific situation?

As important as the Law of the Best Possible is, it should be remembered that it focuses more on the universal than the immediate or individual (171). The Law of Specification acts to balance it (172). The latter law points to ideal perfection toward which persons aim in the process of moral deliberation. The former forces the moral agent to keep one foot planted on the ground or in an actual moral situation requiring decision and action. "Thus the law of Specification gives body and substance to all the other Laws, as well as to the Law of the Best Possible" (172). The Best Possible can be determined only by examining each specific situation. Therefore, the Law of Specification is a reminder that there are values relevant to every specific situation.

In the 1965 *Playboy* interview, King was asked whether he had made any tactical and other mistakes in civil rights campaigns. He said that a number of errors were made in the Albany, Georgia, campaign of 1962. One of these goes to the issue of specificity. King said that rather than focusing their energies, resources, and attention on a specific aspect of the broader issue of racial segregation in the city, their "protest was so vague that we got nothing, and the people were left very depressed and in despair. It would have been much better to have concentrated upon integrating the buses or the lunch counters. One victory of this kind would have been symbolic, would have galvanized support and boosted morale."[73] This was a concrete illustration of the need to be aware not only of the general, but the immediate and specific context, its inherent values, as well as the potential for creating new values or further enhancing those already present in the situation.

This law also points to the urgency of addressing the immediate situation right now, rather than in some distant future. Brightman did not explicitly include the element of urgency in his discussion and commentary. This might well have had something to do with his status as a white male and his position of privilege. Philosophically he could see the need to attend to the immediate context. However, one who knows firsthand what it means to be dehumanized and excluded primarily on the basis of his race, also has a real sense of the need to address such a situation immediately. This is why in numerous speeches and sermons King reiterated the need for love and justice to be done now rather than later. In one of the most passionate passages in "A Time," he reminded the audience that so massive and serious was the destruction of human values in Vietnam, the United States, and other parts of the world that there was really no time in the future for well-meaning persons of faith to do the right thing regarding militarism, economic exploitation, and racism. The time to act in these specific situations was now. King put it this way.

> We are now faced with the fact that tomorrow is today. We are confronted with the fierce urgency of now. In this unfolding conundrum of life and history there is such a thing as being too late. Procrastination is still the thief of time. Life often leaves us standing bare, naked and dejected with a lost opportunity. The 'tide in the affairs of men' does not remain at the flood; it ebbs. We may cry out desperately for time to pause in her passage, but time is deaf to every plea and rushes on. Over the bleached bones and jumbled residue of numerous civilizations are written the pathetic words: 'Too late.' There is an invisible book of life that faithfully records our vigilance or our neglect. 'The moving finger writes, and having writ moves on.'[74]

This element of urgency adds something qualitative to the Law of Specification that we do not see in the original characterization of and commentary on it. It makes sense that he would add the element of urgency in addressing moral crises given King's deep sense of the degradation of oppressed people in the United States, Vietnam, and other places; his convictions about the goodness of the universe and the sacredness of persons; and his recognition that the moral law system requires that one see all of the laws in relation. If one believes that the universe is essentially friendly and that persons are inherently and inviolably precious, it would be a moral travesty to proceed with anything less than the utmost sense of urgency to eradicate injustice and ensure that justice will be done. By adding the sense of urgency to this law in "A Time," King was able to argue against humans' tendency to adjust to or tolerate acts of injustice and de-humanization in this country and abroad. Morally obligated to break silence, King made it clear in his speech that those who understand that persons as such are infi-nitely precious to the One who calls all persons into being, also understand the need to develop both a revolutionary spirit and a sense of urgency about freeing persons from the bondage of war, poverty, classism, and racism. "Our only hope today lies in our ability to recapture the revolutionary spirit and go out into a sometimes hostile world declaring eternal hostility to poverty, racism, and militarism."[75]

In all fairness, it should be noted that in Brightman's commentary on the Law of Specification he at least implied that the sense of urgency might have an important role. He talked about this in his recognition that different persons will, once they have done all that the law requires, tend to respond differently. Some responses will be of the "passive type" and others of the "active type." The tendency of the former will be to do the best possible to accept, submit, and adjust to the situation in ques-tion, no matter how much injustice is being done and has historically been done. On the other hand, Brightman pointed out that the tendency of the active type of person is to do all in his or her power to fight against the situation in the interest of the best possible or the highest ideal (181). For example, the passive type wants to know the best way(s) of enduring an unjust situation bravely and with character. The active type, on the other hand, wants only to know what can be done—not in some distant tomor-row, but right now—to eradicate an injustice and further us along on the path to the es-tablishment of the community of love.

John Ansbro rightly asserts that King rejected Brightman's claim that the passive type of person actually respects fact and other persons when he submits to tolerating or adjusting to, say, situations of injustice, rather than acting militantly against them and taking aggressive steps to create communities of justice.[76] Unquestionably, part of the reason King rejected this aspect of Brightman's argument was because his own po-sition had a clear logic to it. That is, according to King one who is convinced that per-sons as such are infinitely valuable before God and are inherently interdependent can never be comfortable with tolerating or adjusting to injustice toward them. To King, the passive type respects neither facts nor persons whose civil and human rights are denied solely because of their race or socio-economic status. More concretely, King held that "the passive acceptance of the evil of segregation constitutes even a dis-service to the segregator since it allows him to continue in his error."[77] Herein lies yet another reason that King found Brightman's view about the passive type of person to be problematic. King knew firsthand the cruelty of racial segregation and what it meant to experience the denial of one's personhood by whites in the United States.

It should be noted that in his reflections on the role of youth in the struggle, King said that the mood of young people basically reflected that of the country, and that there were essentially three groups, reflecting three different responses to the social crisis. King likened the largest group to the passive type, for it "is struggling to adapt itself to the prevailing values of our society. Without much enthusiasm they accept the system of government, the economic relationships of the property system, and the social stratifications our system engenders."[78]

The second and smallest group of youth was totally disenchanted with militarism, poverty, and racism. These were the radicals, ranging from moderate to extreme in their sense of the extent to which the system should be changed. The one thing the entire group agrees on is that radical structural changes are needed. King said this group was clearer about what needed changing than what should replace it,[79] but it was at least a step in the right direction.

Going beyond Brightman, King added a third type of response to societal ills, one represented by the hippies, who sought to flee from the existing society and to behave in ways that expressed their rejection of it. They had no interest in changing society, but rather sought to escape, as far as possible. Like various ascetic groups throughout history, they sought to save themselves by separating from society. Frequently the means used by hippies to this end was drug usage. Although King understood what this group wanted, he did not place much confidence therein, for he knew that one cannot advocate love as the highest value while simultaneously trying to escape from reality and other persons. Love is a social category, and thus is best lived out in the communitarian setting, not among individuals and groups that have intentionally separated themselves from the larger community.

There is no question that King preferred the second, active type of response. He recognized that for oppressed people to resign themselves to their oppression is to acquiesce and to participate in their own oppression as well as the spiritual oppression of their oppressors. In the sermon, "Shattered Dreams," King said: "To co-operate passively with an unjust system makes the oppressed as evil as the oppressor."[80]

Law of the Most Inclusive End

"All persons ought to choose a coherent life in which
the widest possible range of value is realized" (183).

The new element in this law is the idea of forming a life plan, which means doing some creative construction and looking ahead. Every person is different, possessing different talents and abilities. This uniqueness opens the door to imagination and creativity in the construction of a life plan. One seeks to construct a plan that ensures a reasonable amount of definiteness, yet is fluid enough to allow for revision and correction (184, 192).

This law helps to preclude submission to social standardization. Brightman accordingly held that to disregard the person's free use of his or her imagination and creativity to build a life plan is the equivalent of "cultural and moral calamity" (184). But isn't this precisely what happens in the enforced discrimination against persons on the basis of race and class? How is one equipped to do the best possible job of formulating a reasonable life plan when systematically denied the right to the best possible education, social and cultural experiences, and meaningful and gainful employment? Indeed, how do members of the group to which one belongs form life plans if their lives are systematically stamped out because of unjust wars such as that in Vietnam? How does one form such a plan in the face of the massive proliferation of drug abuse and automatic assault weapons in urban centers throughout the United States, especially if one happens to live there? King knew that blacks and the poor were deprived of educational and other opportunities that would make it possible for them to form better life plans, which would offer them better chances to achieve their desired outcome. When, on the basis of race, resources are inequitably distributed or siphoned off to finance an unjust war, it means not that persons are denied the right to form a life plan, but that they are denied quality opportunities that would allow them to orchestrate a better life plan, which in turn could position them to live a better life as individuals and in community.

Law of Ideal Control

"All persons ought to control their empirical
values by ideal values" (194).

This is the most concrete of the Laws of Value (Axiological Laws). It is the summary value for the second group of laws in the moral law system. It seeks to make "explicit the control of life by ideals" (194). In this regard it functions similarly to the Law of Autonomy and the Law of the Ideal of Personality. In the former the point is that in order for ideals to be obligatory they must be self-imposed and "acknowledged by the will" (194). In the case of the Law of Ideal Control, the point is that empirical values ought to be judged and organized by ideal values.

The Law of the Ideal of Control is not a new law in the sense the others are. Rather, it is essentially a principle of "unification and systematization." It seeks to control value claims by ideal or true values. The aim of this law is not to become dogmatic and intransigent about ideas (201). Rather, the law is, in the best sense, "a principle of criticism—including self-criticism—and growth" (201). There is no room for value stagnation. On any given day, a person's empirical values should be tested by his or her highest values attained to that point. This is truly a principle of constant, ongoing criticism and reinterpretation by the best one knows. It is, Brightman assures us, "a process of never-ending growth" (201).

This law has clear implications for one's stance toward civil law and even what passes as "professional ethics," the moral code that governs various professions, including the ministry. To make this point, Brightman cites Theodor Lipps approvingly. "[I am] morally obligated to change my conviction, to be untrue to myself in my willing, to break a promise, a contract, an oath, if they have an immoral content, or I recognize their content as immoral" (201).[81] Brightman acknowledged the radical nature of this stance, but he concluded that it is the only one the person serious about his or her moral sense can take.

Historically, the possessors of massive unchecked power have exhibited fear of those personalities who have been serious about ideal control of empirical values by ideal values. This has often led to the most brutal forms of persecution and death. Reflecting on what is behind such fear, Brightman concluded that one firmly and genuinely committed to ideal control "is rendered only the more energetic by the presence of obstacles" (203). This seems the perfect description of King when he finally broke silence on Vietnam. He surely thought about the immediate and most foreseeable consequences for himself, the SCLC and the struggle for social justice, as well as for the war on poverty. And yet he stayed the course, deciding in favor of controlling lesser empirical values by his sense of and commitment to a higher authority and ideals.

When King was unmercifully criticized by advisors, friends, other civil rights leaders, and the White House for his public criticism against the war, he reverted to silence. It was not politically correct to criticize the war. However, during the entire period of his silence, King was a moral mess. He knew that his empirical values were not in line with, nor could stand the test of, his highest ideals about the goodness of the universe and the sacredness of human life. One might be tempted to say that by finally breaking silence, King actually violated the Logical Law, which requires that one avoid self-contradiction and be consistent in intentions (98). Instead, by choosing to speak out, King was actually abiding by the Law of Ideal Control, which focuses on development or growth. *The breaking of silence was a sign that he recognized how experience and the facts might well require the moral person to reverse an earlier stance.* Moreover, much of what has been said about King's philosophy and theology in this book is testimony to his appreciation of Brightman's contention that "devotion to ideals . . . makes life worth living" and "is the most potent force in human history" (202). In countless speeches and sermons King pointed to love as the highest moral law or the highest ideal. This ideal characterizes all major world religions, he said, and devotion to it makes life worth living.

By breaking silence, King returned to his long devotion to his highest ideals. The universe, he believed, is structured in such a way that there can be no separation between individual and public ethics. Ordinary individuals should not be held to a higher standard than those in positions of leadership in business, government, the professions, or entertainment. It was inevitable that one who held such a view would run into serious problems with government officials during the Vietnam era. Lewis Baldwin captures the sense of this: "What King had in mind was a foreign policy not based on political expediency and an arrogant show of military might, but one grounded in the biblical principle of the sacredness of all human personality and the interrelatedness of all life. His sense of what should be the true character of political ethics and government morality made conflict between him and the Washington establishment inevitable—more especially because those who ruled America came to see that he was willing to risk all for a complete restructuring of the capitalistic society."[82]

Law of Individualism

"Each person ought to realize in his own
experience the maximum value of which he
is capable in harmony with moral law" (204).

King's decision to break silence on Vietnam was not easy, but necessary and inevitable. He was committed to being true to himself, that is, to his highest values, even during the nearly two-year period he resorted to silence. From the Logical Law to the present Law of Individualism, King knew that it was only a matter of time before he had to speak and act in the light of the Best. It was a decision that *he* had to make—and make in a way that was consistent and in harmony with moral law. Only one who possessed a healthy sense of love for self, for neighbor, and for God could decide as King did.

The Law of Individualism requires persons to think highly of self and to commit themselves to achieve the best they can in harmony with the rest of the moral law system. This implies the need for each person to put a high premium on self first and foremost, although as we will see momentarily, this implies the need to comply with yet another law in order to fill out the meaning of the Personalistic Laws, for the individual person does not exist in a vacuum, but in relationship—in community. Although personalism maintains that the individual is the moral unit, there is also acknowledgment that each person is biologically, culturally, and socially connected with countless others in the family and society in which they are reared (205).

This Law, along with the Law of Autonomy, may be equated with self-respect. "Self-respect is such an appreciation of the value of one's own personal life as results in loyalty to the highest ideals and in a feeling of shame if one violates them to any extent" (219). One who works for and acknowledges this sense of self is then, and only then, positioned to think highly of the good of others and to seek it out. There is an element of obligatory egoism in this law, namely that one must seek the constant improvement of one's highest values. This egoism becomes immoral when the individual seeks the development and maximization of his or her own values at the expense of other persons or disregards the other moral laws, especially the Law of Altruism (214). And yet the individual who chooses not to live for the highest achievement of values in the wholeness of his or her life is not capable of contributing much of value to society. We will see in the next chapter that this looms large in discussions on intracommunity violence and murder among young Afrikan American males and what must be done to significantly reduce or eliminate this devastating phenomenon.

In "Three Dimensions of a Complete Life," King preached about the length, breadth, and height of life. Presently the concern is with the first of these, which he equated with the need for self-love. One who is familiar with the Law of Individualism knows that King's discussion on the length of life and its contribution to the complete life refers to the same concern. The same principles and ideas that Brightman stresses in this law appear in different language in King's sermon. The length of life, according to King, has to do with "the individual's concern about developing his inner powers." Then, in similar language that we find in Brightman's commentary on the law (206, 214), King says: "In a sense this is the selfish dimension of life. There is such a thing as rational and healthy self-interest."[83] King goes on to speak of the difficulty of loving others in healthy, meaningful ways if the individual does not possess a proper love for self. He liked Erich Fromm's idea of the interdependency of healthy self-love and love of others.[84] Without question King was in agreement with Kant's contention that "the prior condition of our duty to others is our duty to ourselves; we can fulfill the former only in so far as we first fulfill the latter."[85] Kant was critical of those who insisted that duties to self ought only to follow upon duties performed toward others. A proper concept of self-regarding duty had for too long been little more than a footnote in moral philosophy, said Kant. "All moral philosophies err in this respect."[86] This supports Brightman's view that altruism is derived from individualism, "regard for others from self-respect" (228).

Different from Brightman, King did not focus only on the need for the individual to strive to achieve his highest or maximum values in harmony with the other moral laws. One must also "feel a responsibility to discover his mission in life." Having discovered that mission, a person is then obligated to do his or her absolute best to carry it out to the fullest. King was interested in how well one actually carries out this calling. "After one has discovered what he is made for, he should surrender all of the power in his being to the achievement of this. He should seek to do it so well that nobody could do it better. He should do it as though God Almighty called him at this particular moment of history for this reason."[87]

As can be seen, King's discussion of the principle behind the Law of Individualism gave to it a different texture, inasmuch as he applied it to a real life situation of struggle. King sought to help his people recapture their lost sense of dignity and pride. It was not enough to preach to them about the need for individuals to commit themselves to achieving their highest sense of values. Just as important in their situation of oppression was that they discover their own mission in life and do all in their power to carry it out in the interest of establishing the beloved community. More than this, King was adamant that blacks must not wait until they are fully liberated before deciding to make the most creative contribution possible to the black community in particular and the United States and broader world in general. "Although you experience a natural dilemma as a result of the legacy of slavery and segregation, inferior schools, and second-class citizenship," he said, "you must with determination break through the outer shackles of circumstance."[88]

Despite blacks' predicament as a result of slavery and subsequent discriminatory practices, King was convinced that individuals who took seriously the length of life or the Law of Individualism could make significant contributions now. Although denied basic sociopolitical freedoms, King knew his peoples' fundamental freedom made it possible for them to choose the best and highest, even in the context of their situation of oppression. He also knew they would have a better best from which to choose were they not oppressed. King would be the first to say, however, that the individual is always obligated to choose the best and the highest in the specific situation, no matter how degrading their immediate context.

King was always talking about the value of the individual and his or her potential contribution to creating the beloved community. Although he believed the individual to be the fundamental moral unit and the highest value, he knew well that the individual does not exist in total isolation. And yet King was grieved by the fact that individually and collectively his people suffered primarily because of their race. It is for this reason that I say, against Ansbro, that King gave significant emphasis to the Law of Individualism, notwithstanding his recognition that there may be times when the individual should, in the interest of the larger community and the establishing of the community of love, be willing to sacrifice self. Ansbro's claim is that King gave less emphasis to this law than did Brightman, and more emphasis to the Law of Altruism.[89] Yet we can see from King's discussion on the length of life and its contribution to the complete life that he took the Law of Individualism seriously, as he did when coming to decision to break silence on the war in Vietnam. In addition, Ansbro must have missed Brightman's discussion on the limitations of the Law of Individualism. In his comment on the second limitation, Brightman says it "is that in which one is convinced that the maximum value of which he is capable is to die for others" (221). Although he names Jesus Christ as "the supreme historical illustration," Brightman also names other personalities throughout history. This is not to say that any of them had a death wish. Rather, such individuals have so maximized their values that they are willing to sacrifice their ultimate value for the enhancement of the broader community. King took the individual very seriously, but just as Brightman, he did so while also recognizing the person's place in community. Neither the person nor the community can reach full potential without the other. This limitation of the Law of Individualism points to the next law in the system.

Law of Altruism

"Each person ought to respect all other persons
as ends in themselves, and, as far as possible, to
co-operate with others in the production and
enjoyment of shared values" (223).

The previous law required that each person respect self, and strive to achieve the highest values in harmony with the rest of the moral laws. It is an acknowledgment of duties to oneself. Implicit in the call for respect and love for one's self is the obligation to love and respect other persons, while also acknowledging their obligation to achieve their highest values. Brightman refers to this as "an impartial generalization of the Law of Individualism; for, if each person ought to respect himself as a realizer of value, then each person ought to respect all others as realizers of value and so as ends in themselves" (225). This is also a recognition that the individual may expect to enjoy "shared values" as required by the Law of Altruism only as he or she acknowledges the need to cooperate with others in their achievement and enjoyment. Implied in this law is the obligation of devotion to values that can be achieved in cooperation with others. The law requires respect for persons, as well as achievement and enjoyment of shared values.

In "Three Dimensions of a Complete Life," King observed that the length of life, which focuses on the need for self-love and achieving one's highest values in harmony with other Moral Laws, points naturally to the second element in the recipe for a complete life: the breadth of life or love for others. This is the equivalent of the Law of Altruism. King knew that the mere love of self or one's own group was not sufficient, and, when seen as standing alone, would be a violation of other moral laws. He saw this as part of the tragedy of racial discrimination and segregation. Whites seemed to exhibit an inordinate amount of love for themselves at the expense of blacks. A healthy self-love and love of one's group does not preclude love for and cooperation with others, but requires it. "No man has learned to live until he can rise above the narrow confines of his individualistic concerns to the broader concerns of all humanity," said King.[90]

For King the universe itself is constructed in a way that things work best for persons—individually and collectively—when they remember that reality is fundamentally good and social. Human beings are individuals-in-community; each has moral autonomy that ought to be acknowledged and respected. Therefore, in order to achieve both individual and shared values it is necessary for one to cultivate what King calls the breadth of life. "The self cannot be self without other selves. . . . All life is interrelated, and all men are interdependent. . . . We are inevitably our brother's keeper because of the interrelated structure of reality."[91] In "A Time," King acknowledged the value of both the individual and the collective when he said: "Every nation must now develop an overriding loyalty to mankind as a whole in order to preserve the best in their individual societies."[92]

King was not only concerned about the abstract rendering of the breadth of life or the Law of Altruism. As in the length of life he was just as concerned about its concrete meaning and manifestation, especially for communities of the oppressed. Consequently, he proclaimed: "Life's most persistent and urgent question is, 'What are you doing for others?'" He considered this to be the norm for responsible Christian behavior and those who take seriously the Law of Altruism. In this regard, King appealed to the gospel of Matthew, where Jesus gave the criterion for the last judgment (25:31–41). Focusing on the importance of deeds done to others, King said: "One will not be asked how many academic degrees he obtained or how much money he acquired, but how much he did for others. Did you feed the hungry? Did you give a cup of cold water to the thirsty? Did you clothe the naked? Did you visit the sick and minister to the imprisoned? These are the questions asked by the Lord of life. In a sense every day is judgment day, and we, through our deeds and words, our silence and speech, are constantly writing in the Book of Life."[93] King was quite explicit regarding types of deeds that churches and synagogues can engage in regarding protest against the war: "We must continue to raise our voices if our nation persists in its perverse ways in Vietnam. We must be prepared to match actions with words by seeking out every creative means of protest possible." In addition, he urged that young men of draft age declare themselves conscientious objectors,[94] and that they willingly subject themselves to any legal consequences.

The Law of Altruism grants to all persons the right to "fulfill the obligation which the Law of Individualism imposes on each." Just as important, however, it implies that there are some values that are capable of achievement (or are best achieved) through sustained cooperation with other persons and groups (223). Putting an end to the war in Vietnam and poverty in the United States are two such values, according to King.

Previously, I observed that King's decision to break silence was very difficult, although necessary and inevitable. It would have been much less difficult and problematic had he sought, like most politicians and too many religious individuals, to separate political ethics and behavior from moral laws. Instead, King saw morality from a holistic standpoint, such that the same level of morality expected of the individual is also to be expected of those in positions of public leadership. He rejected the dichotomization of private and social morality. King wanted nations, in their relations to each other, to be subjected to moral law. Brightman himself made this point in his commentary on the Law of Altruism when he said that "there can be no doubt from the standpoint of ethical science that the relations of states to each other ought to be governed by the same moral laws as guide the conduct of the good individual" (238–39). For as soon as the nation is given a holiday from moral law, it quickly shows its barbaric inclinations (239).

Law of the Ideal of Personality

"All persons ought to judge and guide all of their
acts by their ideal conception (in harmony with the
other Laws) of what the whole personality ought to
become both individually and socially" (242).

This is the summary law of Brightman's system of moral laws. The law implies the need to develop a plan or goal, in harmony with the rest of the moral law system, to guide one's moral development, as well as that of the community. It goes beyond the Laws of Individualism and Altruism to "a definitely concrete unity of purpose, and aesthetic fact which calls on the individual to create out of the materials of his life the plan of a harmonious whole which he aims to realize" (242). The ideal now becomes less general than in the Law of the Most Inclusive End. "The Personalistic Laws and the whole System now find their ultimate unity and consummation in the obligation to form and to apply a conception of a life purpose, which is not only self-imposed and ideal, but also concrete and unified" (242–43). Minimally this law requires that one have "a consistent life plan" and be aware of one's "highest possibilities" (243). The ideal of personality serves the dual function of guiding one's conduct and of acting as "an instrument of criticism" (253). It helps the agent to identify the meaning of what is happening in the present situation as well as to identify strengths and limitations in it. The focus is always on a unitary and harmonious plan. The empirical basis of the law "is the experienced fact of a unity of consciousness as the immediate datum of all experience, the implications of which lead us to acknowledge a whole self—a total personality" (243).

The Law of the Ideal of Personality neither defines nor requires that an agent subscribe to a specific ideal. Rather, it requires the development of a life plan for achieving one's self-established ideal in harmony with the other laws. The form that one's ideal takes is specific to the person or group, though it must always be framed in the light of the other laws. Just here is where the elements of novelty, creativity, dynamism, and "aesthetic taste" come into play. In other words, this law "is a law of free creativity and of personal diversification. It introduces a large factor of aesthetic variety into the moral life. It also implies very clearly that the ideal is in process of development" (250–52). As free, self-determining beings, persons have the capacity for introducing novelty into experience. Every choice and act of a person is a new (or potentially new) contribution, for good or bad, in the development of personality and the achievement of ideals (282). In this sense we may say that human experience itself is fluid and processive, and therefore ideals can be made static only when the imagination and creative juices fail because persons and groups simply stop trying.

We saw in an earlier chapter that from the time King was a boy he vowed to do what he could to address and eliminate the social ills to which his people were being subjected. Once it became clear during his college days that involvement in the medical profession would not be the best way to make his contribution, and he accepted the call to ministry, he stayed the course of trying to find both a more formal theological rationale for his bourgeoning social conscience, as well as the best possible means to address social problems. In this sense, one could say that much of what King did from college through graduate school had to do with the formulation of a plan to guide and judge his contributions to the establishment of the beloved community. As King matured and had various experiences in the many civil rights campaigns from Montgomery to the delivery of "A Time to Break Silence" in 1967, the plan was altered and refined along the way.

When King began his ministry in Montgomery, he was primarily concerned about the plight of his people and what their situation ought to be. But it is important to emphasize that his calling was to Christian ministry, and not as civil rights leader as such. Accepting his call meant that he was to relentlessly apply the ethical teachings of Jesus Christ and the best in the Jewish and Christian traditions to the social ills of the day, both locally and globally.[95] Ten years later, after he began in ministry, his concern was for what the whole human race ought to be, though this does not mean that he now subordinated the interests of his people. He did not now devote less time to the civil rights struggle.[96] His experiences and his theological and moral convictions simply led to a broadening of his moral field to include concern for the well-being of all oppressed people the world over. This was augmented both by the commission of the Nobel Peace Prize to work more diligently for the brotherhood and sisterhood of all persons, as well as his commitment to the gospel. For did he not say, in "A Time," that the good news is not for a select group of persons, but for all persons, regardless of political ideology, race, nationality, and age? Did he not remind his audience that his obligation was to obey, not man, but "the one who loved his enemies so fully that he died for them?"[97] Furthermore, without undermining the importance of race, nation, and creed, King emphasized the more important idea of the "vocation of sonship and brotherhood," and the idea that the God of the universe has a special concern for the helpless and weak. Because of this, King believed he (and other ministers) had to be their voice.

In "A Christmas Sermon on Peace," King spoke passionately about the fundamental communal nature of all reality: "It really boils down to this: that all life is interrelated. We are all caught in an inescapable network of mutuality, tied into a single garment of destiny. Whatever affects one directly, affects all indirectly. We are made to live together because of the interrelated structure of reality. . . . This is the way our universe is structured, this is its interrelated quality. We aren't going to have peace on earth until we recognize this basic fact of the interrelated structure of all reality."[98] King knew that it would be illogical to continue fighting for integrated schools and other public facilities if the world itself were destroyed by war. One has to be able to see that what happens locally and nationally is affected by and affects what happens internationally. By 1967, King refused to segregate his moral concern, to work for justice only on the local and national levels. Justice, he liked to say, is indivisible, which meant that "injustice anywhere is a threat to justice everywhere."[99] He therefore vowed to fight injustice wherever he detected it, whether in the South or North in the United States, in Vietnam, or elsewhere.

This way of thinking could only lead King to conclude that militarism (more specifically the war in Vietnam), racism, and economic exploitation were but symptoms of a more serious problem. It was a moral-spiritual problem in the deepest sense. As sons and daughters of God, persons are obligated to love self and others as God loves them. For King, this meant that there was need for "a radical revolution of values." This would necessitate a fundamental reorienting of priorities, the most significant of which would be placing the value of persons above that of things. When this is done, people will begin to question in earnest social and political policies that allow the worth of specific groups of persons to be undermined. A true revolution of values will make it impossible for persons to adjust to or tolerate injustice on any level any place in the world, without protesting it. A true revolution of values would mean that one takes seriously the fundamental goodness of the world, and "will lay hands on the world order and say of war: 'This way of settling differences is not just.' This business of burning human beings with napalm, of filling our nation's homes with orphans and widows, of injecting poisonous drugs of hate into veins of peoples normally humane, of sending men home from dark and bloody battlefields physically handicapped and psychologically deranged, cannot be reconciled with wisdom, justice and love,"[100] said King. A true revolution of values will enable us to see the need to do all in our power to ensure that justice and peace are the norms rather than injustice and war.

John Ansbro was right in proclaiming that King did not have to look to personalism to determine the need to develop a life plan or ideal conception to help guide his efforts to achieve the highest values, either as an individual, or in cooperative ventures with others.[101] King had already begun this process even before entering Morehouse College. By the time he entered college he was already committed to doing what he could to help his people. He had a long line of role models in this regard, not least his parents and grandparents. And yet his formal introduction to and study of the personalistic moral laws served to strengthen his commitment and to provide a method for thinking through socio-moral issues and determining best means for addressing them.

First and foremost, Martin Luther King, Jr., considered himself to be a minister of the Christian gospel and a Baptist preacher. Because he grounded all that he did in ministry theologically, it should come as no surprise that he declared that acceptance of the call to ministry necessarily carries with it the commitment to always apply the moral-spiritual principles of Christianity to social ills of the day. King did what he did because of his recognition that all of creation is built on a moral and theological foundation.

The God of the universe, the God of Jesus Christ, was the reason behind all that King committed himself to in the civil and human rights movement and his decision to break silence on the war in Vietnam. King himself acknowledged that even though one might comply with the requirement of the length and breadth of life—to love and respect self, and to love, respect, and enhance the sense of humanity and dignity in others—one inevitably comes up short if failing to be in touch with the ground or source of all being. It is not enough to love self and others. One has also to love God and to acknowledge God's infinite love and compassion for persons and the rest of creation. In "Three Dimensions of a Complete Life," King referred to this as the height of life, that which is much more than human and is our reason for being. "We must rise above earth and give our ultimate allegiance to that eternal Being who is the source and ground of all reality. When we add height to length and breadth, we have the complete life."[102] But King observed that often persons or groups excel at the length and breadth of life, but end here. They are "earth-bound," in the sense that they see no higher reason for what they do for self and others than themselves. Such persons (e.g., atheistic existentialists like Jean-Paul Sartre), erase God from the equation altogether. Although students of the Sartrean school of thought may develop life plans to guide their lives, King would contend that such plans are too narrowly conceived if they leave out the source of all life.

King's focus on the height of life as the fulfillment of a complete life may be equated with what Muelder, following DeWolf, called the Metaphysical Law. This law requires that persons seek to know and be in touch with the ground and harmony of the moral laws and the moral order. The law states: "All persons ought to seek to know the source and significance of the harmony and universality of these moral laws, i.e., of the coherence of the moral order."[103]Although Brightman's moral law system did not explicitly name the Metaphysical Law, the need for it was implied (chapter 16), as were the Communitarian Laws (chapters 14–15) supplied by DeWolf and Muelder. I include a brief discussion of the Metaphysical Law because as a philosophical theologian–social ethicist, King was clear about the need to provide theological grounding for one's ideas and behavior. Clear in his own mind that God should not be eliminated or erased from the picture, King declared:

> God is still in his universe. Our new technological and scientific developments can neither banish him from the microcosmic compass of the atom nor from the vast, unfathomable ranges of interstellar space. . . .
>
> I would urge you to give priority to the search for God. Allow his spirit to permeate your being. To meet the difficulties and challenges of life you will need him. Before the ship of your life reaches its last harbor, there will be long, drawn-out storms, howling and jostling winds, and tempestuous seas that make the heart stand still. If you do not have a deep and patient faith in God, you will be powerless to face the delays, disappointments, and vicissitudes that inevitably come. Without God, all of our efforts turn to ashes and our sunrises into darkest nights. Without him, life is a meaningless drama in which the decisive scenes are missing. But with him, we are able to rise from tension-packed valleys to the sublime heights of inner peace, and find radiant stars of hope against the nocturnal bosom of life's most depressing nights.[104]

King saw the need for an ultimate unifying principle of all life. This for him was Love, or more explicitly, the God of Jesus Christ. Love is the key to unlock the secrets of reality and the solutions to social ills in the world.

It is now time to consider the significance of King's doctrine of human dignity, personalism, theology, and ethics for us today by applying that doctrine to a current, destructive social problem. How does one who takes King's ethics seriously respond to an issue such as intracommunity violence and murder among young Afrikan American males?

CHAPTER 9

The Universe Is Friendly

Social-Ethical Implications

Gandhi once said that although he was a Hindu and not a Christian, he had more love in his heart for Jesus Christ than most people who have the audacity to proclaim themselves Christians.[1] Martin Luther King, Jr., was first and foremost "a clergyman, a Baptist preacher,"[2] a Christian, called to serve God and God's people. In light of his witness and steady faith, we may say that King had more love in his heart for God and Jesus Christ than most proponents of the Christian faith—then or now. This is not to say that King was perfect or pretended to be. We have seen that he was not. And yet, unlike many Christians, he stayed the course, despite some moral shortcomings, never failing to remember what the *call* to ministry meant and required of him. He made mistakes like all human beings, and there were obvious limitations in his practice. The most glaring of these was his sexism and his failure to acknowledge and identify it as one of the great menaces of his day and a contradiction of his personalism and his doctrine of human dignity. To be sure, the term "sexism" was not in vogue in those days, but various feminist groups were being very outspoken about gender discrimination and male chauvinism, especially in the public arena. Because of the person King was, as well as his devotion to his own homespun personalism and thoroughgoing personalism, he likely would have identified and sought to rectify this limitation had he lived into the 1970s, when the women's movement was gaining momentum. Indeed, throughout his career he showed an amazing propensity to broaden the moral field to include those who had traditionally been left out. Having initially begun his ministry focusing on the race problem, King's faith, experience, and conviction about the inherent and inviolable dignity of persons as such caused him to broaden his focus to include the cries of the impoverished in general, global liberation struggles, militarism, and war. In my estimation, it would only have been a matter of time before he would have heard and responded to women's cries for just and equal treatment in the public and private sphere.

In a way that most Christians and others are not, Martin Luther King, Jr., was faithful to God's call. He believed that in the end, that is what will matter—that he was faithful to his God and to the powerless and least fortunate. He tried to be their voice before the powers, and he gave his life in the quest for the realization of that community in which every person, regardless of race, gender, sexuality, and class will be treated with dignity and respect, for no other reason than the one God of the universe willingly, lovingly, and thoughtfully called them into existence. Although King did not believe that persons are the only intrinsic values in the world, he was convinced that they are the highest, most precious values to God. It therefore followed for King that every person ought to be treated as a being of worth. This and related ideas were grounded in his fundamental conviction that the universe is friendly to persons and friendly to the achievement of value. This conviction was important for how King thought about ministry, social ethics, and the possibility of establishing the beloved community. It also has important socioethical implications. Therefore, this concluding chapter focuses on several of these implications, especially in light of the tragic phenomenon of black against black violence and murder in many urban areas today.

Social Activist Personalism

As we have seen, King grew up in loving, secure surroundings, an experience that contributed to the way he early began to think about the nature of persons, God, and the universe. The love, care, and concern that his parents displayed toward each other, their children, and the love and nurture provided by extended family members—churched and un-churched—made an indelible impression on the young King, one which made it fairly easy for him to arrive at the conclusion—long before arriving at seminary—that God is personal and loving, and that the universe is friendly toward persons and their efforts to achieve good. Indeed, in part, King came to this conclusion because of his fundamental belief that God is love. The immediate, empirical evidence of this was the love he witnessed between his parents.

By the time King arrived at seminary, he already had a good sense that because God is love, it was reasonable to conclude that persons and the world have eternal cosmic support. God did not create persons to be left alone in the world, but like a loving and compassionate parent, God is present with them in every moment. Moreover, as a

boy, King heard about the social gospel activities of his maternal grandfather and witnessed similar activities in Daddy King's ministry. Early on, he knew that any relevant
religion must be concerned not only about the saving of souls but about everything
that adversely affects people in their whole lives. Not only are the more spiritual
aspects of the person sacred, but the bodily ones as well. The whole person, in other
words, is sacred. By observing his father, King also learned that meaningful social
change does not come about inevitably or merely through the preaching of sermons,
but as a result of relentless struggle and action on the part of persons and groups.

The foregoing chapters have sought to show that while the seeds of many of
King's basic intellectual ideas may be traced to his family and religious upbringing,
he had the good fortune to engage in the formal study of many of these ideas in seminary and graduate school. King was not the first Afrikan American to formally study
personalism at Boston University. That honor goes to John Wesley Edward Bowen, who
studied an earlier form of personalism (objective idealism) under Bowne in the latter
part of the nineteenth century.[3] The next Afrikan American of note to study personalism at Boston University was Willis Jefferson King (1886–1976), who studied under
Albert C. Knudson. But more than any other, Martin Luther King, Jr., made this philosophy his own. When King was formally introduced to the ideas of personalism
under Davis, he was a quick and easy study, as he found that this philosophical framework adequately grounded his deepest faith claims. One can hardly read any of King's
writings and not see reference to one or more personalistic ideas.

One of the primary reasons King embraced personalistic idealism is its un-
ashamedly fundamental focus on the person. This is not difficult to understand when
it is remembered that throughout the history of their presence in the United States,
the humanity and dignity of King's people have been systematically undermined
through the social, educational, religious, economic, and political apparatus. Like his
personalist forebears, King had a deep sense of appreciation for other areas of God's
creation, but he unquestionably considered persons to be the central or most precious values. God stamps the seal of preciousness on each person, thus making each
more significant to God than anything else, a point that Bowne highlighted, and King
accepted: "We are not simply the highest in the animal world, we are also and more
essentially children of the Highest, made in his image likewise, and to go on forever
with him; made, as the old catechism had it, to glorify God and to enjoy him forever,
growing evermore into his likeness and into ever deepening sympathy and fellowship
with the eternal as we go on through the unending years, until we are 'filled with all
the fullness of God.'"[4]

King was without peer when it came to applying the basic principles of personalism to concrete social issues such as racism, economic exploitation, and militarism.
If his personalism and doctrine of human dignity mean anything for us today, it is

that these must be *lived* each and every day. What is important is not the theory of personalism and dignity, but what these require of us in our interpersonal and communal relations, locally, nationally, and internationally. Unquestionably, we see socioethical personalism at work in King's thought and his practice of ministry. In part, King was able to apply the principles of personalism as he did because, not long after his formal academic training, he began to live and breathe personalism. It was no longer a theory to be studied and written about, as he did many times in graduate school. For King, personalism, like his ethic of nonviolence, became an attitude, a disposition, a way of living and behaving in the world, which is grounded in the principle of respect for the absolute dignity of persons, and in the universe, which is friendly to all efforts to achieve value and to enhance the worth of persons and establishing the community of love. Of course for King, the God of the Hebrew prophets and Jesus Christ is the source of these convictions. King's personalism is, then, thoroughly theistic.

The question before us now centers on the meaning of King's conviction that the universe is friendly to persons, especially in relation to the tragic phenomenon of intra-community violence and homicide perpetrated by young Afrikan American males, and what might be reasonable responses in light of that conviction. In other words, what does King's doctrine of human dignity, philosophy of personalism, and his faith that the universe is built on morality have to say about this human tragedy? In addition, what is the socioethical importance of King's doctrine of human freedom in relation to it? Is his personalism a reasonable ground for the ideal of the community of love, or what he called the beloved community? Just how relevant is King's homespun personalism in the twenty-first century?

THE UNIVERSE IS BUILT ON MORALITY

King's firm conviction that the universe is friendly, or that it hinges on a moral foundation, is fundamental to his theology, his social ethics, and his ethic of the beloved community. Although essentially a claim of faith for King, it is also a metaphysical claim, inasmuch as it is not a statement about empirical occurrences as such, but about the universe. It is about the nature of reality itself, whether it is based on impersonal and blind mechanism, or on teleology or intelligence and purpose. It says something about the structure of things.

As important as this point is, it is one that is most often misunderstood by scholars as well as students. When one is told that King believed the universe is situated on a moral foundation, and thus is friendly to the world, the temptation, frequently, is to take this to mean that the world as we know it in our day-to-day experience is good or friendly. This clearly contradicts the experience of many. What one has to remember is that when King says that the universe is friendly, he is making a statement about its fundamental nature and not about the daily experiences of persons and groups in the world. This point was frequently misunderstood by liberation theologians who, throughout much of the 1970s, declared a moratorium on metaphysics and epistemology.[5] In addition, the contention that the universe is friendly has much to say about what God intends for the world to be and about who one understands God to be. To create the universe as essentially good is to imply that the Creator is fundamentally good, loving, and caring as well.

King's belief also says something about what God expects in terms of the behavior of persons toward each other, the world, and their Creator. But such a claim also implies something about how things will best function in the world, that is, when people seek to live by the objective moral laws of the universe. To behave in ways that are consistent with the requirements of the moral laws puts one on the path to the community of love, for love, we have seen, is the highest moral law. To behave in any other way contradicts God's expectations, generally disrupts community, and undermines community making, as well as unnecessarily delays the attainment of the beloved community. Virtually any Afrikan American, Latino/a, or Native American knows that the world (the United States) is often not friendly or good toward them. However, the claim that the universe is friendly implies that because the purposes of the world originate in the mind of God, both the purposes and the foundation of the world must be good, and therefore must be friendly to divine purposes. An individual or group who has faith in such a conviction has reason to be optimistic about what is possible to achieve through relentless cooperative endeavor between persons and God. This was unquestionably part of what drove King to persist in his faith that the beloved community could be achieved.

To say that the universe is grounded on a moral foundation, and thus is fused with value is to suggest that right and truth are grounded in the structure of things. This in turn means there are moral absolutes, things that are absolutely right and things that are absolutely wrong. This was clearly King's sense of the matter. If the universe is fused with value or good, then it must be the case that love is a moral absolute that ought to guide human behavior and living; hatred toward persons and groups is to be avoided at all costs.

The conviction that the universe is friendly is not a conclusively provable postulate, any more than the scientist's postulate of the uniformity or orderliness of nature. However, it is a reasonable postulate precisely because it is in line with the evidence and because without it one must wonder where comes the hope or expectation that with the best human cooperative endeavor things can get better. It is true that there is much that has happened throughout history that has been indifferent to and downright antagonistic toward human progress and the making good of persons and communities. And yet, it is equally true that much has happened that contributes toward human and community development in the best sense. King chose to put his faith in the latter, primarily because of his faith in the existence of a personal, loving, and compassionate God who "has stamped on all of his children a seal of preciousness." This God is concerned about the welfare of every person, regardless of class, and regardless of how disobedient one has been. This is the conclusion that King came to in his sermon, "Lost Sheep." Here he said that every lost child is both "significant" and "worthful" to God.[6] It does not matter to God that a person knows "the difference between 'you does' and 'you don't,'" said King. Furthermore, when the lost person is finally found, all of "heaven rejoices," indeed, "something happens in the universe. It becomes beautiful and joyous."[7] It means that a new, positive occurrence has happened in the universe. This happens every time just one lost person is found. It is a reminder of the hope that it can happen again and again, when one lives by the faith that the universe is friendly. Although fundamentally a metaphysical claim, there has been empirical evidence of the validity of this stance. There were glimpses of this, for example, during various of the civil rights campaigns, when persons, regardless of race, class, and gender were willing to organize and to protest together against injustice and inhumane treatment of fellow human beings. Herein lies hope for continued human progress.

In chapter 8, we saw that the Law of Autonomy says that only ideals that are self-imposed are morally obligatory on the moral agent, and thus are not imposed from the outside, whether by moral-legal codes or commands such as the Ten Commandments or even by God. Part of the significance of this claim is that it is a reminder that the good or the good life is valuable in itself and quite apart from one's belief or disbelief in God or some other superior force. One does the good simply because it is good and the right thing to do. One does not do it as a way of conforming to a belief required by some greater, external force.

We have seen that the atheistic existentialist and personalist, Jean-Paul Sartre, had no use for a God-concept or for the idea that persons have cosmic companionship. And yet this stance does not mean that persons should not be concerned about the life good to live, and doing all in their power to achieve their highest interpersonal and communal values. It just means that persons have only themselves to look to, and not to cosmic or other outside support, to realize their highest values. According to the Sartrean school of thought, persons only are responsible for the realization of the life good to live. There are no divine or other crutches on which to depend. It goes without saying, that members of this school of thought reject the idea that the universe is founded on morality, or that there is at the center of the universe a power that is akin to but greater than persons, and who works cooperatively with them to both conserve and increase values.

The theist, on the other hand, believes fervently that intelligence and morality are ingrained in the structure of the universe. Therefore, if persons are to achieve the life good to live and their highest values they will need to work rationally, cooperatively, and relentlessly with each other and with that force in the universe that is greater than themselves and is making for good. In fact, according to the theistic view even persons' highest ideals do not come from them alone, but from the same source that summons persons into existence. The universe produces nature, persons, and values. What we find in persons—rationality, a moral nature, an urge toward value, and will—is not all there is, but is an important part of what is ingrained in the universe. If persons are formed from the earth as we are told in the creation stories in the Bible, then what is in persons must also be in nature. This is a way of saying that persons are made of the "stuff" of the universe. Scientists seem to have this in mind when they argue that all things, including persons, are derivative of the stars.[8] Furthermore, this line of reasoning might be seen to suggest that there is something in nature that points to the significance of persons. What is more, in the creation stories in Genesis 1, we are told more than half a dozen times that God looked out on all that God created and saw that it was good, and in at least two instances we are told that God saw that it was *very* good. This lends support to the claim that the universe is founded on morality, that it is fundamentally good; not that everything that we humans do is good, but that God intends for us to do good, or to live in accordance with the best. King reminds us, however, that God cannot guarantee individual acts of goodness precisely because God created persons in freedom, thus making it possible for them to behave and live in ways that are consistent with the morality of the universe or in ways that contradict it. Because God loves us so, God allows persons to decide, even when God knows ahead of time that the consequences of some of their choices will be devastating to them, as well as to other areas of creation. The fact that massive numbers of persons suffer from oppression is the result of human contrivance or misuse of freedom. Yet, despite the prevalence of social evil, the world is still *fundamentally* good. Because morality is at the heart of the universe, there is reason to hope that when humans work cooperatively, and also try to get in touch with that force in the universe making for good, the world can be better than it is.

Of course, from a practical standpoint the critic might also ask: "If the world is fundamentally moral and God is the source, what can we humans do to make it better? What can we do that would be better than what God has already done from the foundation of the world?" This is precisely the type of question that may be raised by one who believes God to be perfect in every way. King agreed with the response that Brightman gave to similar queries:

Personalism does not believe that now, or at any point in time, the universe is perfect. It finds in God a being of perfect goodness, but not of mechanical perfection. His perfection is perfection of purpose, a teleological perfection. In its practical bearing on human beings this means not that the universe is perfected, but that it is perfectible; not that nothing can be improved, but that real change, real improvement, is the purpose of life. The sufferings of man and the ideal obligation to attain the highest values are stern factors in life, rendered more stern by the personalistic interpretation of suffering and obligation as entailed by the divine purpose. Personalism, therefore, is not too delicate and beautiful to face the facts. It too sees life as a tragedy; there is the shadow of a cross on the face of the personalistic universe. Humanity suffers and dies. Many fail to see the suffering in the light of ideal values. . . . The secret of the practical significance of personalism is that it faces the tragedy and sees that it is not all. There is tragedy, but there is also meaning; and the meaning includes and transforms the tragedy.[9]

To say that God's goodness is perfect is not the same as saying that God ensures the perfect outcome of every detail of daily living in the world. God's purpose for the world must at least be "perfection of purpose," which leaves open the door to unlimited progress and development in the world when persons choose to work cooperatively with each other and God.

Notice that it is not that the world is already perfect, but that it is perfectible. This is the message behind the conviction that the universe is built on morality. The task of the remainder of this chapter is to examine some practical implications of this conviction about the friendliness of the universe regarding black against black violence and murder among young Afrikan American males. What is the importance of human freedom in relation to this phenomenon? A consideration of some practical implications of King's ideas is a good way to end this study, since King was a practical, as well as a theoretical personalist who was primarily concerned about how this philosophy could contribute toward making the world a gentler, sweeter place for every person.

BLACK AGAINST BLACK VIOLENCE AND HOMICIDE

In the mid-1980s, Jewelle Taylor Gibbs and her collaborators found that intra-community homicide is the number one killer of Afrikan American males between the ages of 15 and 24. Having reached epidemic proportion, there is no evidence of abatement as of this writing. Virtually every major city in the United States is infected with this tragic phenomenon.[10] Indeed, the tendency of young Afrikan American males to commit violence and homicide against each other and other members of the black community was noticed by King.

In fact, King was aware that the quantity and quality of alternatives available to young black males are so limited and poor that no matter what they choose, the consequences are frequently self-defeating, demeaning, and even destructive. King saw this as especially the plight of young black males in the northern ghettos. When he lived for some weeks in Chicago in 1966, he met and got to know a number of the angry young black males who exhibited low self-esteem, virtually no sense of hope that things would or could get better, and little to no sense of purpose in life because this society offered them nothing of substance. Many of these young men organized themselves into gangs and frequently resorted to violence against each other and other members of the Chicago black ghetto. What King said, on reflection, about these young men was no different from what he would have said regarding many young black males in Cleveland, Oakland, Los Angeles, Harlem, or Detroit. Reflecting on his experience in Chicago, King lamented:

> I met these boys and heard their stories in discussions we had on some long, cold nights last winter at the slum apartment I rented in the West Side ghetto of Chicago. I was shocked at the venom they poured out against the world. At times I shared their despair and felt a hopelessness that these young Americans could ever embrace the concept of nonviolence as the effective and powerful instrument of social reform.
>
> All their lives, boys like this have known life as a madhouse of violence and degradation. Some have never experienced a meaningful family life. Some have police records. Some dropped out of the incredibly bad slum schools, then were deprived of honorable work, then took to the streets.
>
> To the young victim of the slums, this society has so limited the alternatives of his life that the expression of his manhood is reduced to the ability to defend himself physically. No wonder it appears logical to him to strike out, resorting to violence against oppression. That is the only way he thinks he can get recognition.
>
> And so, we have seen occasional rioting—and, much more frequently and consistently, *brutal acts and crimes by Negroes against Negroes.* In many a week in Chicago, as many or more Negro youngsters have been killed in gang fights as were killed in the riots here last summer.[11]

King's characterization of those young Afrikan American males in 1966 is frighteningly similar to how many may be described even today. He was deeply moved by this experience, as well as the experience of watching young gang members remain nonviolent as they participated (without retaliation when rocks and bottles were thrown at them) in demonstrations in some of Chicago's most blatantly racist communities, such as Marquette Park.

Overall, in Chicago King saw forces making for evil as well as forces making for good. On the one hand, he saw the deleterious effects of racism, the educational system, and economic deprivation on young black males, as well as how it left many of them with a sense of hopelessness, aimlessness, and mean-spiritedness. On the other hand, King saw a hidden goodness in many of these boys as they were willing, if only for a brief period, to protest nonviolently and without returning blows, in the hope that such activity would make a meaningful difference in the movement toward justice and the beloved community. King even recalled that during Freedom Summer, in 1966, Chicago gang members went to Mississippi "in carloads." Initially apprehensive about how they might react when confronted by white racists in Mississippi, King and other leaders were stunned by their behavior. "Before the march ended, they were to be attacked by tear gas. They were to be called upon to protect women and children on the march, with no other weapon than their own bodies." King recalled that "they reacted splendidly! They learned in Mississippi, and returned to teach in Chicago, the beautiful lesson of acting against evil by renouncing force."[12] Despite their immediate daily circumstances, the young gang members were willing to participate with those forces making for good in this country in the hope of making it a better place for all people. Their participation in the protest marches—in Chicago and Mississippi—was a reminder that by virtue of their fundamental freedom, persons choose, inevitably, and forever. Persons choose to get in touch with the forces making for good, or with the forces that undermine and frustrate good. This is essentially the message of one who lives by the conviction that the universe is friendly. Granted that King believed that his people could not solve their problems without the staunch ongoing participation of whites of goodwill, he also believed that inasmuch as blacks were the chief victims of the social problems that undermined their humanity and dignity, the onus is on them to initiate and take the leading roles in the fight against injustice.

Precisely because King's personalism is thoroughly theistic, we may say that for him every person, regardless of race or gender, class or health, age or sexuality, has been imbued with the image, fragrance, and voice of God. To say, as King did on countless occasions, that God has stamped the seal of preciousness on persons is a claim not about black people or white people, brown people, or red and gold people. Rather, it is a statement about both God and persons as such. Every person is precious and infinitely valuable to God, the Creator of all, including the person(s) convicted of the most heinous crimes imaginable (e.g., American slavery, genocide against Native Americans, and the Jewish Holocaust). Because God willingly, thoughtfully, and lovingly calls persons into existence, each has absolute value. From the divine perspective, this means that all owe respect to self and to each other. The person who has been taught, and has learned to love self, will have little difficulty knowing how to love others. Experience has frequently shown that the person who mistreats and disrespects others, generally is found to think little of self and to be without proper love for self. At any rate, because of the absolute value of persons, no person or group should be easily sacrificed for the well-being of another, although we have seen that there may be times when a person or group chooses to sacrifice self for the greater good of the larger community.

King's personalism is particularly important for Afrikan Americans, especially at a time when such large numbers of young black males exhibit by their behavior toward each other that they have little love for self and for others in their community. In addition, far too many see no meaning for which to go on living. The consequences of this state of affairs are simply devastating. At a time when many whites still do not believe that Afrikan Americans are as fully human as they are,[13] it is important that blacks rediscover and reassert their own sense of humanity and dignity.

King himself would remind Afrikan Americans of their infinite worth and the necessity of their coming to terms with this and living their lives accordingly. He would emphasize that it is not merely the spiritual aspect of the black self that is so precious and valuable to God, but the whole self. Mind and body are as two sides of a single coin. According to King, the Bible teaches that everything that God created, including the human body, is good. He said that "the body in Christianity is sacred and significant. That means in any doctrine of man that we must be concerned with man's physical well-being."[14]

King's conviction that the universe hinges on a moral foundation, and his sense that his people were developing a new sense of somebodyness is a reminder to young Afrikan American males that their bodies, indeed everything that makes them persons, are precious and sacred. It is through the body that we humans come to know and understand life; that we know about emotions; that we are able to see, hear, touch, receive, give, separate, and procreate. A person has no better means, no better instrument for communicating love (or anything else for that matter) than the body.

The message of King's doctrine of human dignity and personalism to Afrikan Americans is that their bodies have an inviolable sacredness of their own, and therefore should be cared for and protected, not devastated by drugs or riddled with bullets. In this regard, King's personalism is more ethical than metaphysical. As we have seen in earlier chapters, because of the almost uncritical adoption of idealism, metaphysical personalism has not seemed to know what to do with the body. Although King was uncritical of this point, he was, nevertheless, just as adamant that it is not just the invisible part of the self that one should care about, but the body-mind. Thus, young Afrikan American males should be taught from a very early age to love, care for, and respect not only their own bodies, but those of others in their community as well.

This means that Afrikan American adults in the homes, schools, churches, and civic and recreational organizations must provide such instruction. Children do not know, and may never know what they should about what it means to be responsible persons if they are not taught by those charged with their care.

Love your whole self! That is the message of King's doctrine of dignity and personalism to young Afrikan American males in particular, and the Afrikan American community in general. In part, this means that the black community itself will have to find ways to take immediate steps to eradicate the phenomenon of black against black violence and homicide. The conviction that the universe hinges on morality must also mean that all being has intrinsic dignity and ought to be treated and respected accordingly. Throughout every stage of maturation, it will be necessary to teach the importance of honoring, loving, and respecting the whole self, as well as others in the community. Such instruction needs to begin while the Afrikan American child is still in the cradle.

Socio-Ethical Importance of Human Freedom

Even if it could be demonstrated once and for all that the universe is in fact friendly to value and the achievement of good, it would be of little consequence if persons were not equipped to behave accordingly. That is, what does it matter if the universe hinges on a moral foundation if persons are not able to decide whether to live in line with such a principle, or not? Martin Luther King, Jr., understood perfectly the need for moral agents in the world God has summoned into existence. Persons need the capacity to form plans to achieve what they have decided. This requires the potential to be rational. Indeed, one who lacks such potential has no way of even hypothesizing that the universe is friendly. However, King reminds us that one who lives by the conviction that the universe supports goodness and justice must also be committed to taking steps to help actualize such things. Progress, goodness, and justice do not roll in on the wheels of inevitability, King liked to remind his audiences. There must be a decision, followed by decided efforts toward the achievement of progress.

As King understood and sympathized with the plight of young Afrikan American males in the northern ghettos of Chicago and Cleveland, he would sympathize with those in the ghettos and battle zones of inner cities today. He would, as he did with those young men in Chicago and Cleveland, shed tears as he listened to their stories of abuse and neglect. Nevertheless, King would be just as adamant that while these young men are not responsible for the causes of the conditions that radically reduce reasonable and life-enhancing alternatives for them in this society, as persons, as moral agents, they are in fact responsible for how they respond to what has been and is being done to them and their chances in life. As agents they have the capacity to do, to act, either for, or against themselves and their community. On the moral plane it is precisely this for which they are responsible. *They can decide how to respond to what is being done to them.* And we should be clear about one thing: Martin Luther King, Jr., would hold these young men accountable for what they decide. And, of course, this must be part of his message to the Afrikan American community today.

Moreover, King frequently reminded his people that they are heirs to a legacy of dignity and worth; heirs to a legacy of parents, grandparents, great-grandparents, and other ancestors who, against the most horrendous odds, fought for their own and the dignity of their people and their posterity. For example, many of the old Afrikan Americans who marched in Montgomery and refused to ride in cars even when it was clear that they could barely make it on their feet, did so not for themselves. Some walked on tired feet and in old broken down bodies for their children and their grandchildren. "You are heirs to a legacy of stubborn determination, dignity, and worth." That would be King's message to young Afrikan Americans today.

King maintained that persons are not first created, and then *given* freedom. Rather, the nature of person is freedom. People are created in freedom. In chapter 4 we saw that King frequently said, paraphrasing Paul Tillich, that to be a person is to be free. The emphasis here is not on a will that is free, for this in itself is too abstract. Rather, the emphasis is on the actual knowing, wanting, willing woman or man. King accepted Bowne's definition of freedom as the power of self-direction and the power to formulate and carry out plans, purposes, and ideals.[15] This was little different from the view espoused by King's father and maternal grandfather, both of whom insisted on the need for Afrikan Americans to be self-determined and to depend first and foremost on themselves and on God.

That some persons lack moral agency because they are mentally retarded and otherwise challenged, clearly raises the theodicy question. That the extent of the presence of moral agency in some persons appears to be limited or reduced because of the denial of education, meaningful and gainful employment, or adequate housing, also raises fundamental questions—questions that have both moral and sociopolitical implications. It is precisely here that we are forced to return to an issue that was only named earlier in this book. The question is this: To what extent can we say that young Afrikan American males who engage in intracommunity violence and homicide are *morally* responsible for their behavior? The issue is not that of civil or legal culpability. There is generally no question that the one who pulls the trigger in a drive-by shooting, for example, is legally responsible for his action. However, the issue that needs to be examined, but is frequently suppressed or ignored, is the extent of moral culpability. To make some sense of the issue being raised, it may be helpful to first consider criteria for moral responsibility. What makes a decision or action moral?

Moral responsibility for an action requires the presence of at least two factors. The first is that one must be free to make the choice. If it can be shown that a person is constrained to behave in a certain way, the question must be raised as to whether he was truly free in choosing to behave as he did. Take for example, the young man who, against all rules and laws, takes a loaded pistol to school because he has been threatened with bodily harm multiple times by one or more of his peers. The young man has told school authorities of such threats and they have vowed to keep him safe on school grounds. This, however, is not his concern. His real concern and fear have more to do with what may happen beyond school grounds and even in his neighborhood. Neither school officials nor the police have given him reasonable assurance of protection. Having grown up where he did, he knows full well that under the circumstances it is his life or that of those who continue to threaten him that is at stake. This is the law of the urban battle zones. So he carries a gun to school, is promptly discovered by the authorities, and suspended from school. The question is: To what extent can we say that the young man was truly free in making the decision to carry the gun to school? Had he not been constrained by conditions beyond his choosing and control, might he have decided differently? The point here is not to deny the existence of some level of culpability on the part of the student, but to suggest that if he was compelled by outside factors to choose and behave as he did, the level of responsibility must vary, as must the punishment for his action. The same must be said regarding the second element that must be present if there is to be moral responsibility.

The second criterion for moral responsibility is that one must have the capacity to rationally or intelligently choose. There must be concrete evidence that a specific individual possesses this capacity. In the most general sense, we know that persons are created with the capacity to be rational and moral, but we also know that frequently this capacity may be underdeveloped as a result of a person being denied moral and other kinds of instruction. In the case of far too many young Afrikan American males, even if one is successful in showing that they are fundamentally or metaphysically free to make choices, there is still the question of whether in many cases their rational faculty or intellect has been trained and developed to the point that they can consistently make intelligent or informed moral choices. If they are not trained in the home to do this, or in the schools or churches, where would they receive such training? Why would they *think* even once, let alone twice, about taking the life of another young black male or some other innocent member of the Afrikan American community for something as insignificant as an accidental bump or for having looked at them in a certain way? Indeed, what is there to think about when it is remembered that many of these young men either drop out or are expelled indefinitely from school, and many who remain have no sense of the importance of the training of their rational faculty?

In light of this scenario and King's personalistic ethic, what is the responsibility of the Afrikan American community? As serious as is the incidence of black on black violence and murder among young Afrikan American males, precisely the type of ethic espoused and practiced by King would still insist that it is incumbent upon his people to find ways of responding to it that will ultimately lead to real solutions and the creation of openings for the emergence of the beloved community. Indeed, King's ethic of human dignity requires that Afrikan Americans actively take the necessary steps to prevent this genocidal practice in black communities. This is also an ethic that requires that the truly committed trust that if they do their part, God will help them to make a way out of no way to solve this problem. On the practical level, this means that Afrikan Americans who are more fortunate have to be willing to set the example for others as a reminder that no matter what obstacles confronts the community, they have been bequeathed a legacy of overcoming, and thus must carry that forward for future generations. This goes to the issue of self-determination, as well as finding ways to teach blacks from a very young age to think differently about who they are as a people, where they came from, and where they ought to be going. What young Afrikan American males need to develop—through wise, relentless instruction, and discipline—is the *will* to overcome. King taught that to develop the will to overcome injustice and other forms of dehumanization puts one well on the road to eradicating the problem. One has first to acknowledge that there is a problem, and then develop the determined will to overcome it.

Moreover, what is important is not what those outside the black community think about Afrikan Americans. In this regard, King was in agreement with Malcolm X. What is necessary is that Afrikan Americans look to themselves. King would not have disagreed with Malcolm's assertion: "We've got to change our own minds about each other. We have to see each other with new eyes. We have to see each other as brothers and sisters. We have to come together with warmth so we can develop unity and harmony that's necessary to get this problem solved ourselves."[16] Afrikan Americans alone must do this.

King understood better than most the difficult circumstances that confronted his people. He knew that historically a central quality of blacks' experience in the United States has been pain that is "so old and so deep that it shows in almost every moment of [their] existence. It emerges in the cheerlessness of his sorrow songs, in the melancholy of his blues and in the pathos of his sermons. The Negro while laughing sheds invisible tears that no hand can wipe away."[17] King knew that all of this was a consequence of long years of dehumanizing enslavement and discrimination on all levels of American society. Yet he still insisted on the need for cultivating black self-determination and the will to overcome injustice and dehumanizing practices. Unlike white social gospelers, King was not willing to ignore the element of agency in his people, since he was convinced that it is a central element of what it means to be a person. Afrikan Americans were not responsible for the causes of their plight, but he was convinced that they and they alone are responsible for how they respond to what had been (and was being) done to them. No matter how violently their personhood is assaulted by powerful and racist whites, King maintained that it is still within Afrikan Americans' power as persons to accept it or not; to fight against it or not. He did not excuse what racist whites had done and were doing. He was too good a personalist for that. Being responsible is one of the key elements of what it means to be free and to exercise one's freedom. One has to be willing to accept responsibility for what one does, including responding to those bent on dehumanization. As a moral agent a person is responsible for how he or she responds.

King's primary focus was to help his people to recover their lost sense of humanity and dignity, and to encourage them to contribute toward the establishment of the beloved community. King was confident that because of the long history of the black protest tradition, his people had in them what it takes to regain their sense of worth. This sense was never taken away from them, despite systematic efforts to do so, for what God implants in persons is not theirs to give away, nor can it be taken away by others. The lost sense of dignity needed only to be awakened in Afrikan Americans, and only they could do it.

And yet, it should be borne in mind that King's emphasis on the idea that human beings are persons-in-community must also mean that the individual or group is not alone responsible for a crime committed. The young black male in present-day society who mercilessly and easily takes another life is not alone morally culpable, especially since little that is worth having in this society favors him. In his sermon "Is the Universe Friendly?" King made this point as he commented on the immorality of capital punishment. Not willing to let the individual criminal off the hook, King nevertheless made it unequivocally clear that in a society in which certain groups are exploited because of their race and social class, society itself shares in the crime committed because it allows the conditions that lead to the commission of various types of crimes. "And while the individual who commits the act of crime must take the greatest part of the responsibility, society itself must take some of the responsibility. And by and large, people would not steal if economic security was made real for all of God's children."[18] King also made the point that the systematic economically deprived social conditions that blacks are forced to endure breeds crime.[19] To promise life, liberty, and happiness to Americans, and then systematically deny these to Afrikan Americans for generations, is a great contributor to the phenomenon of intracommunity violence and murder.

King's experience taught him that there was not a lack of human and other resources to solve social problems. What was lacking, he believed, was the will and courage to make the effort. In this, he was in agreement with Bowne, who argued that "the greatest need in ethics is the impartial and unselfish will to do right. With this will, most questions would settle themselves; and, without it, all theory is worthless. . . . One bent on doing wrong never lacks an excuse; and one seeking to do right can commonly find the way."[20] However, Bowne conceded, as King did, that the mere possession of a good will was not sufficient to solve social problems, although such a will must be the basis of all ethics—a necessary first step toward solving social problems and the enhancement of human dignity. King went well beyond Bowne's individualistic emphasis, for he knew (as Bowne apparently did not) that both the cause and the solution to his peoples' problems were both individual and systemic. In King's personalism, then, it is not just a matter of individual will, important as that is. It is also a matter of institutional will and resolve. For example, King declared the need for the church to "affirm that every human life is a reflection of divinity, and that every act of injustice mars and defaces the image of God in man."[21]

King was convinced that Afrikan Americans would regain neither their lost sense of dignity nor their freedom without an adamant determination and willingness to struggle—individually and collectively—to overcome and to stand up. He frequently reminded his people that a new sense of dignity would come about only through determined struggle, persistence, and hard work. Recognizing that on the deeper metaphysical plane his people are, like all people, heirs to a legacy of inherent dignity, King also knew that the debilitating, dehumanizing, and depersonalizing practice of American slavery and racial discrimination caused many blacks to think of themselves as many whites did, namely as inferior persons, and consequently with no inherent dignity. In speech after speech, King reminded his people and the nation of how blacks' sense of worthlessness came about and what they would have to do to regain what systematic racial oppression and economic deprivation took away from them. "The tragedy of slavery and segregation," he said, "is that they instilled in the Negro a disastrous sense of his own worthlessness. To overcome this terrible feeling of being less than human, the Negro must assert for all to hear and see a majestic sense of worth."[22] Agency makes it possible for Afrikan Americans to assert (for all to hear) their inherent dignity.

For as long as he could remember, King rejected racism in all its ugly forms. He did so because it implied the superiority of one race over another, as well as the idea that there is more of the image of God in some persons than in others. King was adamant that God's image is "universally shared in equal portions by all men."[23] King believed that only a renewed sense of dignity, self-respect, and self-esteem could repel the adverse and disastrous effects of American slavery and racism. The Afrikan American must do the hard, sustained work of asserting his or her own self-worth.

The Negro will only be truly free when he reaches down to the inner depths of his own being and signs with the pen and ink of assertive selfhood his own emancipation proclamation. With a spirit straining toward true self-esteem, the Negro must boldly throw off the manacles of self-abnegation and say to himself and the world: "I am somebody. I am a person. I am a man with dignity and honor. I have a rich and noble history, however painful and exploited that history has been. I am black *and* comely." This self-affirmation is the black man's need made compelling by the white man's crimes against him.[24]

King's was a tough, realistic personalism. King nonetheless held that his people are responsible for the way they respond to efforts to demean and dehumanize them. This ethic condemns the causes and forces that produce the conditions that open the door to intracommunity violence and homicide, as well as the fact that so many young black males so easily opt for this alternative. The systematic denial of reasonable life chances for many young Afrikan American males is worse than disheartening to any with even the least developed moral sense. The logic of King's personalistic ethic, however, is that some of the moral onus must remain on the oppressed themselves, inasmuch as they are inherently moral agents, and can, if nothing else, decide how to respond to what is systematically being done to undermine their humanity and dignity. In a universe deemed to be friendly toward the achievement of value, even the "victimized" must not succumb to a sense of not being able to do anything at all to assert a sense of humanity and dignity. A universe founded on morality must, as King surmised, lead to optimism in the arena of theological social ethics and social activism.

Afrikan Americans have to reach deep within to find the resources to reassert themselves. "This spirit, this drive, this rugged sense of somebodyness," King said, "is the first and most vital step that the Negro must take" in order to recapture their sense of self-worth.[25] This will not happen either automatically or inevitably, but will take determined initiative and cooperation, individually and collectively, on the part of Afrikan Americans. Self-determination is the key ingredient to progress toward the achievement of the beloved community. Essentially it comes down to blacks having to do, what on the surface, appears impossible: to overcome both enslavement and its long history of consequences—consequences that continue to this day. To overcome them, will likely require the cooperative efforts and determination of well-meaning whites who are as committed to the beloved community as their counterparts who endured beatings, and in too many instances were murdered, as a result of their courageous participation in the civil and human rights movements.

One who lives by the conviction that at the core of the universe is goodness must be able to see that freedom, self-determination, and recovery of the sense of human dignity among Afrikan Americans will come only through struggle, struggle that is intended to *make* unearned suffering redemptive or worthy of redemption. This became a concrete reality for King during his leadership in the civil rights movement, but the idea was not new to him. Indeed, although in graduate school he studied and was deeply influenced by Hegel's doctrine that progress comes only through struggle, King first encountered this idea through his father and maternal grandfather. He knew that struggle against injustice roots deep in the black protest tradition in this country, and that much of that protest was spearheaded by black churches or individuals affiliated with them. Here we need only recall the struggles of the Afrikans to free themselves from their white captors, even before they were forced onto the slave ships on the shores of West Afrika.[26] Or, we need merely recall the protests of David Walker, Maria Stewart, Henry Highland Garnet, Frederick Douglass, Anna Julia Cooper, Henry Bibb, Harriet Jacobs, Ida B. Wells-Barnett, and others during the nineteenth century.

Because of its emphasis on human dignity, King's personalism would admonish present-day Afrikan American youth to learn about, and celebrate their heritage and their race. If Afrikan American youth possess a healthy sense of the dignity and preciousness of their mind-body, this will open the way to a heightened sense of self-esteem and being proud, and not ashamed, of their blackness. This can only lead to a greater sense of self-love, which would also mean less temptation to abuse either their own bodies, or those of others in their community. For in accordance with King's doctrine of human dignity, no one who truly loves self, his people, and his heritage intentionally seeks their destruction. In his final presidential address to the SCLC board, King, almost pleading, said that "we must massively assert our dignity and worth. We must stand up amidst a system that still oppresses us and develop an unassailable and majestic sense of values. We must no longer be ashamed of being black."[27] This admonition implies the need to make a conscious effort to learn about black history, including both Afrikan and Afrikan American contributions. For King insisted that whether they like it or not, Afrikan Americans are an amalgam of Afrika and America,[28] and in the late 1960s King urged that his people take more seriously the Afrikan side of their heritage and culture.[29] However, realistically it is questionable whether black youth will soon learn about their heritage and history in this nation's educational institutions, because the vast majority of those who control these institutions see no value in this either for themselves and their children, or for Afrikan Americans and theirs. This means that the responsibility of so educating black youth falls squarely on the Afrikan American community: black families, churches, and civic groups.

King put racial prejudice at the top of the list of major social issues to be addressed and solved. He believed that racial prejudice was morally wrong because it denies the humanity and the image of God in select groups of persons. It assumes that one group is innately inferior to another, which in turn implies that God is a respecter of persons, favoring one group over another. This contradicts the idea that the universe is founded on morality. Believing all racial prejudice to be evil, King was consistent in maintaining that any prejudice which rejects persons on the basis of skin color "is the most despicable expression of man's inhumanity to man,"[30] and in this sense it has nothing but contempt for human life as such. Left unchecked, racism destroys the racist, his supporters, as well as those who are its victims.

King knew well the history of black-white relations and did not hesitate to remind the nation of it. He was aware, for example, that despite how noble were Thomas Jefferson's words that "all men are created equal," Jefferson essentially meant *all white men*. King knew that not one of the "Founding Fathers," even those who later occupied the White House, "ever emerged with a clear, unambiguous stand on Negro rights."[31] Even Abraham Lincoln at best vacillated on the issue of the full emancipation of blacks from slavery.[32]

King's personalism places yet another expectation before the Afrikan American community. The community must own responsibility for all that happens and is allowed to happen there. This once again raises the issue of moral agency, that has been so very difficult for Afrikan Americans to discuss openly before the white public, for fear that they will use what is said to appease their own conscience. "After all," some whites will invariably ask, "aren't blacks also culpable and responsible for what happens in their communities?" However, King's personalism and doctrine of human dignity forces the issue by pointing out that there is too much at stake for Afrikan Americans to continue to remain silent about moral agency and the importance of owning responsibility. Based on King's ethic, then, it is necessary for blacks to risk breaking silence on the issue of moral agency.

Afrikan Americans can, and should, blame the powerful and privileged people (who manage, control, and benefit from racist institutions) for the conditions that have created in so many black male youth a sense of hopelessness, lovelessness, and mean-spiritedness. But as for the specific acts of violence, those in the black community who take King's doctrine of dignity seriously, must find in themselves the courage to say that inasmuch as black boys pull the trigger of automatic assault weapons that maim and take the lives of others in the black community, they must answer, *not* to white America, but to the black community. For both they and their victims belong to that community, and at the end of the day, it is the black community that cares about their well-being. On the other hand, inasmuch as Afrikan American adults allow incidents of black against black violence and murder to continue unabated, they must be able to muster the courage to admit their moral culpability and to realize that they alone can put a stop to the violence. They alone can and must take back from Afrikan American boys the streets of their neighborhoods. King has left the method to do so—nonviolent resistance—although such a method will have to be creatively adapted for the situation at hand. After all, this would be a case of massive and militant nonviolent resistance not against forces external to the black community but to those internal to it.

Beyond the work that Afrikan Americans still must do among themselves, it will be necessary to develop new sociopolitical alliances, a point that King stressed during the last two years of his life.[33] At the very least, Afrikan Americans should find ways to unite in true alliance with Latinos/as and Native peoples. Politically the absolute best thing that Afrikan Americans and Latinos/as can do is form a coalition such that the powers that be will know with certainty that an attack upon either group is perceived as an attack upon both. This is a significant point made by Theodore Cross in his massive book, *The Black Power Imperative: Racial Inequality and the Politics of Nonviolence* (1987). The dominant white group has effectively played the two largest so-called minority groups in this country against each other. The Latino/a community is now the largest such group in the country, having recently eclipsed the Afrikan American community in this regard. In any event, by keeping the two communities at odds with each other and consequently disunited and divided, they have been forced to fight for the same meager crumbs from the political, economic, judicial, and educational apparatus. Wrong about a number of things in his extensive analysis, Cross is right in calling for a true alliance between Afrikan Americans and Latinos/as, which means they will have to find ways to set aside enough of their differences in order to unite around the common goal of achieving the beloved community for all. Theologian and church historian Justo González is equally adamant in making this point. He rejects the tendency to play one of these communities against the other. González puts it thusly: "Justice would not be served if some of the meager resources in the hands of blacks and other minorities were put in the hands of Hispanics while the present institutionalized racism persists. Our cause, we have come to realize, is a Hispanic cause because that is who we are, but it is above all a cause of justice, because of what we are all called to be."[34] González wants nothing to do with potentially polarizing, contrasting and comparing of the meager material advantages of one or the other community that we see in the writings of some.[35] At any rate, Cross makes an instructive comment about the political importance of the Latino/a and Afrikan American communities forging a true alliance:

> If either blacks or Hispanics are to address the issue of their powerlessness in America, they must end the competitive pressures now enervating both groups. A formal political alliance must be reached. They must collectively refuse to strengthen further the hands of political incumbents by playing out the script that calls for blacks and Hispanics to compete for government handouts. There

must be joint black-Hispanic political efforts to elect agreed-on minority political candidates; combined efforts must be launched to defeat majority candidates who attack the interests of either group; flying under a bipartisan banner, blacks and Hispanics must press for greater employment opportunities for both groups, followed by joint control over how these advantages are shared. . . . Mutually assured impotence for both ethnic groups is the expectable outcome of current conflicts where whites in industry, education, and government negotiate separately with blacks and Hispanics over the minor spoils of ethnic allotments.[36]

Even though the forces that seem to drive the two groups toward effective alliance are much stronger than those that continue to keep them apart, true coalition continues to be only a remote possibility. And yet "the political advantages that argue for a united black-Hispanic front are compelling."[37] In any case, King would have been in total agreement with this call for coalition building. However, because his personalism seeks the establishment of the beloved community, the objective is to develop alliances with people of all racial-ethnic backgrounds who are committed to mutual cooperative endeavor in efforts to establish the community of love.

King's conviction that the universe is friendly to persons fosters an optimistic, but realistic, social ethics. Built on such a foundation, the theological social ethicist would see unlimited possibilities for human achievement toward the life good to live when persons acknowledge and respect the inherent dignity in themselves and others, and agree to work together toward the establishment of the beloved community. And yet at every stage of development, persons and groups will need to acknowledge human limitations that come about because of sin. However, a social ethics based on King's personalism and conviction that the universe hinges on a moral foundation does not see the manifestations of sin as all there is in the world. Rather, it also sees that throughout history God has always had witnesses who, despite the prevalence of sin on every level of human achievement, forge ahead toward the life good to live, not only for individuals, but for individuals-in-community, recognizing both the availability of divine grace and cosmic companionship.

King's personalism requires that persons and groups take responsibility for what happens to them in God's world. He would have agreed with what Malcolm X said in an interview with Kenneth Clark. Recalling the fact that he had been imprisoned, Malcolm said emphatically that no one framed him when he was arrested and incarcerated before he was converted to the Nation of Islam. "I went to prison," he said, "for what I did."[38] "For what *I* did!" Malcolm owned responsibility for what he did, even though he knew the American judicial and prison system to be unjust and racist. He was not guilty of creating the conditions of racism and economic deprivation that led to his vulnerability as an Afrikan American male. However, he was able to see that as an autonomous being, and thus a moral agent, he chose to respond as he did. Consequently, he was responsible for how he responded to what was done to him and his people. Similarly, his conversion to Islam during his imprisonment was evidence of his recognition that a different type of response could have been given than that which landed him in prison, thus making it easy for a racist system to further dehumanize him.

A social ethics based on King's conviction that the universe is friendly can only provide a stimulus of hope and optimism for those who are committed to eradicating the phenomenon of intracommunity violence and homicide among young Afrikan American males. It puts the responsibility for addressing the immediate problem squarely on the shoulders of the Afrikan American community. But at the same time, because it is a thoroughly communal ethic, it obligates the broader human community, because what adversely affects one group is detrimental to the entire human family by virtue of the interrelated structure of reality. In addition, since such an ethic requires that persons—individually and collectively—take steps to address injustice on every level, the element of hope that things will get better will always be present. Moreover, to believe that God has established the universe on a moral foundation and is always working with persons toward the achievement of the beloved community, can only leave the committed in a state of faith and hopefulness.

An Appreciation

It is fitting to close this book with a word about Walter George Muelder (1907–2004), who was Dean and Professor of Social Ethics at Boston University for twenty-seven years (1945–72). Dean Muelder read and commented on several drafts of the manuscript version of this book, but he died before it went to press. Any who have been his students will recognize his imprint on the book.

Although Martin Luther King, Jr., did not have courses under Dean Muelder when he was a graduate student at Boston University, he was befriended and mentored by him. The two had numerous conversations, and it was Muelder who helped King to better understand Reinhold Niebuhr's doctrines of human nature and human destiny, as well as his critique of pacifism. In *Stride Toward Freedom* King paid tribute to Muelder when he wrote: "Boston University School of Theology, under the influence of Dean Walter Muelder and Professor Allan Knight Chalmers, had a deep sympathy for pacifism. Both Dean Muelder and Dr. Chalmers had a passion for social justice that stemmed, not from a superficial optimism, but from a deep faith in the possibilities of human beings when they allowed themselves to become co-workers with God."[1] It is of no small moment that King, the recipient of the Ph.D. degree in systematic theology, considered himself first and foremost a pastor and a social ethicist (the field Muelder pioneered). In this he was only being consistent with his calling to ministry, the rudiments of which dated back to his childhood and formative experiences in his family and the black church.

I took nearly half of my graduate school course work under Dean Muelder twenty years after King earned his degree. I have no doubt that Muelder's passion for and witness to social justice had an indelible influence on King. He saw in Muelder one who was both a man of ideas and an action-oriented personalist. Moreover, King was most assuredly impressed and encouraged to know that more than any other dean of predominantly white seminaries in the United States, Muelder essentially practiced affirmative action long before it became a short-lived official policy and practice in this nation from the late 1960s into the 1980s. Under Muelder's deanship, Boston University School of Theology graduated more Afrikan Americans with academic doctorates than any white institution in the country between 1953 and 1968. In addition, thirteen doctorates were awarded to Afrikan Americans between 1945 and 1952, and two more in 1969 and 1970, respectively. Not only was Muelder proactive in bringing Afrikan American students to the School of Theology, but he took the necessary measures to see that financial and other assistance was available to help them stay until degree requirements were met.[2]

Muelder's contributions have not been forgotten—neither by some of his students, including Dean Lawrence Carter of Morehouse College, nor by King's widow, Coretta Scott King. In 1983, at Carter's invitation, he lectured on "Martin Luther King, Jr., and the Moral Laws" at Morehouse. Two years later Mrs. King invited him to the Martin Luther King, Jr. Center for Social Change in Atlanta, where he lectured on "Martin Luther King, Jr.'s Ethics of Nonviolent Action." In a conversation with me in the late 1980s, Muelder related his deep sense of satisfaction that in her response to the scholars invited to present papers at the King Center, Mrs. King said that his understanding and interpretation of King's doctrine of nonviolent direct action was right on target. Moreover, in a letter sent to the Muelder family on hearing of his death, Mrs. King paid tribute to Muelder, his contributions, and the impact he had on Martin Luther King, Jr. She wrote: "Dr. Walter Muelder was one of the world's most eminent theologians and an educator of extraordinary vision and humanity. His pioneering work in behalf of social ethics, ecumenicism, racial diversity and personalism in theological education had a profound influence on the views of my husband, Martin Luther King, Jr., who regarded Dr. Muelder with great respect and admiration."[3]

Right up to the end, Dean Muelder was in his own right an ethical prophet, one who sought to be faithful to God's expectation that justice be done in righteous ways. Three days before he died, in an address to retirees at the New England Conference of the United Methodist Church, Muelder said that even as retired ministers we still "have an ongoing role to play in the conflicts, such as those on homosexuality."[4] For Muelder, those called to ordained ministry are obligated to speak and stand for justice as long as they are mentally and physically able. His life, in and beyond the academy, was a testimony to his commitment in this regard. He was truly the champion of the least of the sisters and brothers, as he sought ways throughout his long and productive life to contribute to the establishment of the beloved community. The quintessential teacher, Walter George Muelder influenced the development of countless students throughout the world. However, he would be the first to say that his own ideas and outlook on life were as much influenced and transformed by the witness of Martin Luther King, Jr., and others of his students. This must be the case for the staunch personalist, like Muelder, who is committed—as King was—to the belief that truth grows and that one should have the courage to alter one's views and practice in the face of new evidence and facts. There must always be give and take in the adventure we call life if one is truly serious about being a better person and contributing to the development of a more gentle and just world. Dean Muelder modeled this for Martin Luther King, Jr., this writer, and numerous others who had the good fortune to be his students, both in the classroom and outside it. He was, after all, the beloved teacher, who showed so many of us what it really means to be a person-in-community.

Introduction

1. Ernest Shaw Lyght, *The Religious and Philosophical Foundations in the Thought of Martin Luther King, Jr.* (New York: Vantage Press, 1972).

2. Kenneth L. Smith and Ira G. Zepp, Jr., *Search for the Beloved Community: The Thinking of Martin Luther King, Jr.* (Valley Forge, Pa.: Judson Press, 1974).

3. Ervin Smith, *The Ethics of Martin Luther, Jr.* (New York: Mellen Press, 1981). It is of interest to note that Smith and Lyght are not generally cited by white scholars who have written on King. I have seen references to Smith in Lewis V. Baldwin's work on King. See Baldwin's *To Make the Wounded Whole: The Cultural Legacy of Martin Luther King, Jr.* (Minneapolis: Fortress Press, 1992), 3, 67, 115, 126–32, 144. Baldwin, however, is Afrikan American.

4. John J. Ansbro, *Martin Luther King, Jr.: The Making of a Mind* (Maryknoll, N.Y.: Orbis Books, 1982). This book was reissued in 2000 by Madison Books as *Martin Luther King, Jr.: Nonviolent Strategies and Tactics for Social Change*. A new introduction by Ansbro chronicles King's major civil rights campaigns from Montgomery to Memphis. No new information is provided. It is a disappointment, however, that Ansbro included nothing in the introduction about the tensions between King, Ella Baker, and other black women in some of the campaigns.

5. See Stephen B. Oates, *Let the Trumpet Sound: The Life of Martin Luther King, Jr.* (New York: Harper & Row, 1982). Oates discusses the availability of sources—sources that were not available to King scholars prior to 1980 (p. x).

6. Ansbro, *Martin Luther King, Jr.*, xiii.

7. See Martin Luther King, Sr., *Daddy King: An Autobiography*, with Clayton Riley (New York: William Morrow, 1980), 32–36, 41–43.

8. Garth Baker-Fletcher, *Somebodyness: Martin Luther King, Jr., and the Theory of Dignity* (Minneapolis: Fortress Press, 1993).

9. I am also completing a second book on personalism, one that focuses on the Afrikan traditional and Afrikan American contributions. I was early encouraged in this work by Randall

Auxier (a fifth-generation personalist who teaches philosophy at the University of Southern Illinois) and Tom Buford (a fourth-generation personalist who teaches philosophy at Furman University).

10. Baker-Fletcher, *Somebodyness*, chap. 3, "Philosophical Influences: Boston Personalism." This book is a revision of Baker-Fletcher's doctoral dissertation. Since we were colleagues on the faculty at Christian Theological Seminary when he received the contract to publish the manuscript, he asked me to read and comment on the aforementioned chapter. I did so and noted several places where the interpretation of personalistic principles was not as sharp and accurate as it could be. Unfortunately, whether due to pressure of the manuscript deadline or something else, these were not attended to. Even his use of the term "Boston personalism" to designate the type of personalism which most influenced King, is problematic, for it implies that those who were influenced by Bowne were in general agreement at every point. They were not, which is not uncommon regardless of the school of thought. The truth is that disciples of Bowne clearly agreed with the basic outlines of his personalism, but there were significant points of divergence (e.g., in ethics, philosophy of religion, and philosophical psychology), as evidenced in the work of Edgar S. Brightman, Georgia Harkness, Peter A. Bertocci, Walter G. Muelder, and S. Paul Schilling. Indeed, William Werkmeister's designation of personalism as a way of thinking is also applicable to the so-called Boston Personalists. Said Werkmeister: "But as a broad point of view concerning the facts of human existence, personalism can and does tolerate differences in detail. Revealing the outstanding landmarks by way of a general orientation, it leaves to the individual investigator the tasks of analysis and of critical evaluation of the facts in question. Thus, and thus only, is it possible to tolerate atheistic, agnostic, and fervent theists alike among the personalists and, among the theists, to accept with equanimity as fellow personalists thinkers who believe in a finite God and thinkers who maintain that God is infinite in every respect" ("Some Aspects of Contemporary Personalism," *Personalist* 32 [October 1951]: 349). Personalists influenced by Bowne are among the "fervent theists," but we find among them absolutists as well as finitists.

11. Major J. Jones, *The Color of God: The Concept of God in Afro-American Thought* (Macon, Ga.: Mercer University Press, 1987). Jones introduces the term "black personalism," but without ever once acknowledging that he himself was influenced by the personalism of Walter G. Muelder and L. Harold DeWolf when he was a doctoral candidate at Boston University. In addition, his discussion on the doctrine of the finite-infinite God, introduced by Edgar S. Brightman and interpreted by Peter A. Bertocci, is flawed in a number of instances.

12. James H. Cone, "The Theology of Martin Luther King, Jr.," *Union Seminary Quarterly Review* 40, no. 4 (January 1986): 21–39, 39n.30; and David J. Garrow, "The Intellectual Development of Martin Luther King, Jr.: Influences and Commentaries," in *Martin Luther King, Jr.: Civil Rights Leader, Theologian, Orator*, ed. Garrow (New York: Carlson Publishing, 1989), 2:437. Garrow was most assuredly right in his claim during this period that "few if any commentators have fully appreciated the underlying link that existed between the predispositions King drew from his youth and the ideas he was drawn to as a young man" (p. 441). In order to highlight this crucial point, however, Garrow erroneously undermines the significance of personalism on King's intellectual development. The truth is that both were major influences on his thought.

13. Lewis V. Baldwin, *There Is a Balm in Gilead: The Cultural Roots of Martin Luther King, Jr.* (Minneapolis: Fortress Press, 1991), 11–14. At an earlier period Baldwin himself showed an appreciation for Garrow's claim in this regard. In 1987 Baldwin wrote:

> In order to give proper emphasis to the black sources of King's thought and activism, careful attention has been given to the trove of his largely unpublished, spontaneously delivered sermons in black churches and mass meeting speeches to black community rallies. These materials, housed at the Martin Luther King, Jr. Center for Nonviolent Social Change in Atlanta, Georgia, are extremely valuable for our purpose because they—to a greater extent than some of King's books which were ghostwritten for presentation to a largely northern, white, well-educated audience of potential contributors—reveal so much about King's southern style and manner of speech ["Understanding Martin Luther King, Jr., within the Context of Southern Black Religious History," *Journal of Religious Studies* 13, no. 2 (Fall 1987): 2].

In a footnote Baldwin credits David Garrow "for this information and direction." However, he does not then fall into the trap of emphasizing one or the other of these influences on King as Garrow did. Instead, Baldwin acknowledged that each plays a prominent role.

14. Baldwin, *There Is a Balm in Gilead*, 13.

15. Baker-Fletcher, *Somebodyness*, 61.

16. James H. Cone stresses this point in *Martin & Malcolm & America* (Maryknoll, N.Y.: Orbis, 1991), as does Baker-Fletcher in *Somebodyness*. See also Baldwin, *There Is a Balm in Gilead*, 168–69, 171–72.

17. See my "Martin Luther King, Jr., and the Objective Moral Order: Some Ethical Implications," *Encounter* 61, no. 2 (Spring 2000): 221–30.

18. Oates, *Let the Trumpet Sound*, 35.

19. See the list of courses taken at Morehouse College, in Ralph Luker and Penny Russell, eds., *The Papers of Martin Luther King, Jr.: Called to Serve* (Berkeley: University of California Press, 1992), 1:40.

20. Kelsey earned the Ph.D. at Yale, where he could well have been introduced to the personalism of George T. Ladd, and that of Bowne and Brightman as well.

21. Baldwin, *There Is a Balm in Gilead*, 124.

22. King, *Stride Toward Freedom* (New York: Harper & Row, 1958), 100.

23. Coretta Scott King, *My Life with Martin Luther King, Jr.* (New York: Holt Rinehart & Winston, 1969), 92.

24. See my *Personalism: A Critical Introduction* (St. Louis: Chalice Press, 1999), 258 n.5, where I list more than a dozen types of personalisms.

25. Luker and Russell, eds., introduction, in *The Papers of Martin Luther King, Jr.*, 1:127.

26. Clayborne Carson is professor of history and the director of the King Papers Project at Stanford University. Although the discovery of the extensive pattern of plagiarizing was made by research assistants in the late 1980s, the story actually broke in 1990. Clayborne Carson et al., "The Student Papers of Martin Luther King, Jr.: A Summary Statement on Research," *Journal of American History* 78, no. 1 (June 1991): 24.

27. L. Harold DeWolf, "Martin Luther King, Jr. as Theologian," *Journal of the Interdenomi-national Theological Center* 4, no. 2 (Spring 1977): 10.

28. Theodore Pappas, *Plagiarism and the Culture War: The Writings of Martin Luther King, Jr., and Other Prominent Americans* (Tampa, Fla.: Hallberg Publishing, 1998); Michael Eric Dyson, *I May Not Get There with You: The True Martin Luther King, Jr.* (New York: Free Press, 2000); Richard Lischer, *The Preacher King: Martin Luther King, Jr. and the Word that Moved America* (New York: Oxford University Press, 1995); and Keith D. Miller, *Voice of Deliverance: The Language of Martin Luther King, Jr., and Its Sources* (New York: Free Press, 1992).

29. "Becoming Martin Luther King, Jr.—Plagiarism and Originality: A Round Table," *Journal of American History* 78, no. 1 (June 1991): 11–123.

30. Quoted in Peter Waldman, "To Their Dismay, Scholars of Martin Luther King Find Troubling Citation Pattern in Academic Papers," *Wall Street Journal* (November 9, 1990): 1.

31. Dyson, *I May Not Get There with You*, 144, 147, 151.

32. Ibid., 150.

33. This is the verbatim statement that Bundy wrote by hand and inserted at the bottom of my typewritten note to him, September 11, 1991. This document remains in my file on King and the plagiarism issue.

34. Ralph Abernathy, *And the Walls Came Tumbling Down: An Autobiography* (New York: Harper & Row, 1989), 310, 434–36, 470–75. Interestingly, Taylor Branch reports that "King confided to a colleague that he not only had known of Abernathy's extramarital liaisons in Montgomery but had joined in some of them himself" (Branch, *Parting the Waters: America in the King Years, 1954–63* [New York: Simon and Schuster, 1988], 239). Branch does not include the source of this revelation.

35. See Stewart Burns, *To the Mountaintop: Martin Luther King, Jr.'s Sacred Mission to Save America, 1955–1968* (San Francisco: HarperSanFrancisco, 2004), 422, 427.

36. Abernathy, *And the Walls Came Tumbling Down*, 434–35. That King was with a woman at the Lorraine Motel the night before he was assassinated is corroborated by Georgia Davis Powers, then in her first term as a Kentucky state senator. The relationship lasted for about a year, ending only at King's death. The first Afrikan American and first woman to be elected senator to the Kentucky legislature, Powers has written of her close friendship and intimate relationship with King in her autobiography, *I Shared the Dream: The Pride, Passion and Politics of the First Black Woman Senator from Kentucky* (Far Hills, N.J.: New Horizon Press, 1995). See especially chaps. 9–10, 18–19. Powers writes that Abernathy "was not the straight-laced person he claimed to be," and that "he didn't relate the whole truth about the evening before King's assassination" (244). Powers and King first became something more than friends in March 1967 (146). After the march with sanitation workers in Memphis turned violent on March 28, 1968, Powers phoned King's office in Atlanta and left a message. When King received the message he phoned her and expressed his need to have her in Memphis. She recalled him saying: "Senator, please come to Memphis, I need you" (222). There is no attempt in Powers' book to malign King and his legacy in any way. According to Powers, her relationship with King "began as a close friendship between two people sharing the same dream, working for the same goals, and it crossed the line into intimacy." She said that she "tried to be candid and not explicit, but if you are going to do an

honest book it would be dishonest to leave out an important part of your life. It's part of my history and part of Black history and part of American history" (323). Powers said elsewhere that it was not that she was in love with King, or he with her. She said: "It was not a love affair, really, it was just a relationship." At the time they met he was a man who had no peace and was distraught over the way the movement was going. He was seeking peace of mind. He wanted to just sit at times and shoot the breeze as a way of getting his mind off a troubled nation and world. A deeply "spiritual person," Powers says that it took her a very long time to forgive herself. See Tom McDonald, "More than a Dream," *Springfield Sun*, August 18, 2004.

37. King often characterized Abernathy as "my alter ego," and "the best friend that I have in the world." Whether Abernathy was or was not King's alter ego, Georgia Davis Powers contends that he wanted to be, and that he was "jealous" of King and "had an inferiority complex about being second-in-command" (*I Shared the Dream*, 244).

38. Abernathy, *And the Walls Came Tumbling Down*, 470–71.

39. John A. Williams, *The King God Didn't Save: Reflections on the Life and Death of Martin Luther King, Jr.* (New York: Coward-McCann, 1970), 196–221; Jim Bishop, *The Days of Martin Luther King, Jr.* (New York: G. P. Putnam's Sons, 1971), 358–61; and David L. Lewis, *King: A Critical Biography* (New York: Praeger Publishers, 1970), 256–58.

40. Oates, *Let the Trumpet Sound*, 282–85.

41. David J. Garrow, *Bearing the Cross: Martin Luther King, Jr., and the Southern Christian Leadership Conference: A Personal Portrait* (New York: William Morrow, 1986), 374–76; Branch, *Parting the Waters*, 239, 812, 860; and Dyson, *I May Not Get There with You*, chap. 8, "There Is a Civil War Going on Within All of Us: Sexual Personae in the Revolution."

42. Powers, *I Shared the Dream*, 323.

43. Michael G. Long, *Martin Luther King, Jr., on Creative Living* (St. Louis: Chalice Press, 2004), 5.

Chapter 1. King's Intellectual Odyssey: From Morehouse to Crozer

1. Quoted in Lerone Bennett, Jr., *What Manner of Man: A Biography of Martin Luther King, Jr.* (Chicago: 1964; reprint, Johnson Publishing, 1968), 26.

2. Clayborne Carson, ed., *The Autobiography of Martin Luther King, Jr.* (New York: Warner Books, 1998), 13.

3. Ralph Luker and Penny Russell, eds., *The Papers of Martin Luther King, Jr.: Called to Serve* (Berkeley: University of California Press, 1992), 1:39–40. Hereafter *The Papers*.

4. David Garrow, "King's Intellectual Development," in *Martin Luther King, Jr. and the Civil Rights Movement*, ed. Garrow (New York: Carlson Publishers, 1989), 2:438–39 (emphasis added).

5. Branch, *Parting the Waters*, 60.

6. King, "An Autobiography of Religious Development," in *The Papers*, 1:363.

7. Carson, *Autobiography of Martin Luther King, Jr.*, 13.

8. See Martin Luther King, Sr., *Daddy King*, 107–9.

9. Ibid., 82–83.

10. Ibid., 105, 125.

11. Carson, *Autobiography of Martin Luther King, Jr.*, 179.

12. Ibid., 19.

13. King, *Daddy King*, 131.

14. See Stephen B. Oates, *Let the Trumpet Sound*, 18.

15. See King, "Letter from Birmingham City Jail," in his *Why We Can't Wait* (New York: Harper & Row, 1963), 79. Here King points out that fact gathering is one of four elements that precede every nonviolent campaign.

16. Carson, *Autobiography of Martin Luther King, Jr.*, 14.

17. Ibid., 15.

18. Branch, *Parting the Waters*, 70.

19. Carson, *Autobiography of Martin Luther King, Jr.*, 6.

20. Ibid., 17.

21. Branch, *Parting the Waters*, 79.

22. Oates, *Let the Trumpet Sound*, 33.

23. Branch, *Parting the Waters*, 88.

24. Ibid., 89.

25. Oates, *Let the Trumpet Sound*, 34.

26. Martin Luther King, Jr., *Stride Toward Freedom* (New York: Harper & Brothers, 1958), 94.

27. Carson, *Autobiography of Martin Luther King, Jr.*, 18.

28. Ibid., 32.

29. See King, *Daddy King*, 82. I have found no evidence that either A. D. Williams or Daddy King studied Hegel in college or independently. It is reasonable to conclude that Williams arrived at the principle (that growth comes through struggle) through his own experience.

30. It is important to acknowledge and distinguish between the Social Gospel in black and in white. Early scholars on the Social Gospel assumed this was a movement led primarily by white pastors and scholars such as Washington Gladden and Walter Rauschenbusch. We now know that parallel to this movement was one led by Afrikan American pastors, scholars, and lay persons such as George Washington Woodbey, Reverdy Ransom, Ida B. Wells-Barnett, Fannie Barrier Williams, Anna Julia Cooper, Henry McNeal Turner, W. E. B. DuBois, John Wesley Edward Bowen, and George W. Slater. I address this topic more extensively in the next chapter.

31. Davis likely came under the influence of the personalistic idealism of George T. Ladd at Yale. Ladd knew, respected, and cited the work of Bowne in a number of his books. In fact, during his tenure at Boston University, Bowne was sought after by the presidents of both Yale and the University of Chicago, although he remained faithful to Boston. Francis J. McConnell reports on this in his *Borden Parker Bowne: His Life and His Philosophy* (New York: Abingdon Press, 1929), 9. It is likely that Davis studied the work of both Bowne and Brightman at Yale.

32. Kenneth L. Smith and Ira G. Zepp, Jr., *Search for the Beloved Community*, 26.

33. Ira G. Zepp, Jr., *The Social Vision of Martin Luther King, Jr.* (New York: 1971; reprint, Carlson Publishing, 1989), 12.

34. Smith and Zepp, *Search for the Beloved Community*, 22.

35. Kenneth Smith and Ira Zepp overstate their point about the influence of Davis on King. In 1974 they wrote: "Davis was a pivotal figure in King's intellectual pilgrimage, and it is impossible to understand the intellectual sources and the intellectual categories of King's thought without a thorough knowledge of George Washington Davis and the place he occupied on the Crozer Seminary faculty between 1938 and 1960" (Smith and Zepp, *Search for the Beloved Community*, 22). The authors seem not to have considered that upon arrival at Crozer, King's mind was not a *tabula rasa*. There were already some intellectual categories in place from his days at Morehouse College. It was there that he was inspired to think about the reasonableness (or lack thereof) of the "strict fundamentalist tradition" in which he was reared (see Carson, *Autobiography of Martin Luther King, Jr.*, 24). King's experience at Morehouse more than adequately prepared him for the contributions that Davis would make to his ongoing intellectual development.

36. King, "A View of the Cross Possessing Biblical and Spiritual Justification," in *The Papers*, 1:266. The work of Knudson's not named by King is *The Doctrine of Redemption* (New York: Abingdon Press, 1933).

37. King, "War and Pacifism," in *The Papers*, 1:434.

38. See Gary Dorrien, *The Making of American Liberal Theology: Idealism, Realism, & Modernity, 1900–1950* (Louisville, Ky.: Westminster John Knox Press, 2003), 511.

39. I am indebted to Gary Dorrien of Union Theological Seminary in New York City.

40. See Smith and Zepp, *Search for the Beloved Community*, 24–27.

41. See Bennett, *What Manner of Man*, 28–29.

42. King, *Stride Toward Freedom*, 96.

43. Bennett, *What Manner of Man*, 30.

44. Carson, *Autobiography of Martin Luther King, Jr.*, 14.

45. M. K. Gandhi, *Nonviolent Resistance*, ed. Bharatan Kumarappa (New York: Schocken Books, 1961), 3–4.

46. See King, "The Answer to a Perplexing Question," in *Strength to Love* (New York: Harper & Row, 1963), 126; and Branch, *Parting the Waters*, 702.

47. Branch, *Parting the Waters*, 75.

48. Ibid., 76.

49. Carson, *Autobiography of Martin Luther King, Jr.*, 18.

50. Branch, *Parting the Waters*, 76.

51. Baldwin, *There Is a Balm in Gilead*, 301.

52. Coretta Scott King, *My Life with Martin Luther King, Jr.* (New York: Holt, Rinehart and Winston, 1969), 59.

53. Baldwin, *There Is a Balm in Gilead*, 299. See also William E. Hatcher, *John Jasper: The Unmatched Negro Philosopher and Preacher* (New York: Fleming H. Revell, 1908).

54. Baldwin, *There Is a Balm in Gilead*, 29.

55. Branch, *Parting the Waters*, 119 (emphasis added).

56. For example, Lerone Bennett, Jr., wrote that "he was a perfect student at Crozer, maintaining an A average for the three-year course" (Bennett, *What Manner of Man*, 35). David L. Lewis said only that King graduated at the top of his class and gave the valedictory address (Lewis, *King: A Critical Biography* [New York: Praeger Publishers, 1970], 37–38). Jim Bishop wrote

that "King was the perfect student" at Crozer (Bishop, *The Days of Martin Luther King, Jr.* [New York: G. P. Putnam's Sons, 1971], 104). In addition, Coretta Scott King wrote that he had a "straight A average" at Crozer (King, *My Life with Martin Luther King, Jr.*, 88). These claims are misleading inasmuch as they imply that the vast majority of his grades were A's, a claim not supported by his academic transcript at Crozer. See the list of courses taken and grades earned at Crozer, in *The Papers*, 1:48.

57. See Lawrence D. Reddick, *Crusader without Violence: A Biography of Martin Luther King, Jr.* (New York: Harper & Brothers, 1959), 86.

58. Branch, *Parting the Waters*, 72.

59. Oates, *Let the Trumpet Sound*, 14.

60. Branch, *Parting the Waters*, 73.

61. See confidential evaluation of King by Morton Scott Enslin, in *The Papers*, 1:354.

62. Confidential evaluation of King by Charles E. Batten, in *The Papers*, 1:406–407.

63. *The Papers*, 1:391.

64. Ibid., 1:392.

65. Branch, *Parting the Waters*, 75.

66. See King's letter to Sankey L. Blanton in, *The Papers*, 1:391. King's comment about Yale is interesting in light of his strong interest in studying personalism under Brightman at Boston University. See "Fragment of Application to Boston University," in *The Papers*, 1:390.

67. Branch, *Parting the Waters*, 81. David Garrow reports that King was accepted at Yale. See his *Bearing the Cross*, 44. Coretta King reports this as well (see *My Life with Martin Luther King, Jr.*, 88). Luker, Russell, and Holloran maintain that King was not accepted at Yale. See their introduction in *The Papers*, 2:4.

68. See his letter to Sankey L. Blanton, in *The Papers*, 1:391.

69. Branch, *Parting the Waters*, 90.

70. *The Papers*, 1:390.

71. See ibid.

Chapter 2. Social Gospel and Walter Rauschenbusch

1. Not only was there no place for racism in Woodbey's socialism, but he argued just as vehemently that there was no place in it for the denial of women's rights. Arguing that "the working man is a slave and his wife is the slave of a slave," Woodbey quoted approvingly the socialist platform regarding women: "We demand the absolute equality of the sexes before the law, and the repeal of all law that in any way discriminates against women" (George Washington Woodbey, *What to Do and How to Do It, or Socialism vs. Capitalism*, in *Black Socialist Preacher*, ed. Philip S. Foner [San Francisco: Synthesis Publications, 1983], 80). We will see in chapter 5 that in principle King affirmed women's rights, but his practice in the public arena left much to be desired.

2. Darryl M. Trimiew, "The Social Gospel Movement and the Question of Race," in *The Social Gospel Today*, ed. Christopher H. Evans (Louisville, Ky.: Westminster John Knox Press, 2001), 36.

3. Robert T. Handy, ed., *The Social Gospel in America: Gladden, Ely, Rauschenbusch* (New York: Oxford University Press, 1966), 11.

4. Ibid., 5.

5. Walter Rauschenbusch, *A Theology for the Social Gospel* (New York: Macmillan, 1917), 5–6.

6. See the massive classic study by Cecil J. Cadoux, *The Early Church and the World: A History of the Christian Attitude to Pagan Society and the State Down to the Time of Constantinus* (1925; reprint, Edinburgh: T. & T. Clark, 1955).

7. Rauschenbusch, *Theology for the Social Gospel*, 5.

8. Shailer Mathews, *New Faith for Old: An Autobiography* (New York: Macmillan, 1936), 122.

9. Handy, *Social Gospel in America*, 4.

10. Charles Howard Hopkins, *The Rise of the Social Gospel in American Protestantism* (New Haven, Conn.: Yale University Press, 1940), 318.

11. Ibid., 320.

12. Ibid., 321.

13. See E. Clinton Gardner, *Biblical Faith and Social Ethics* (New York: Harper & Row, 1960), 9.

14. I am indebted to Lewis V. Baldwin for sharing these Social Gospel emphases with me when he read this manuscript. Baldwin said that these general characteristics of the Social Gospel movement were obtained in a course he had with Kenneth Smith in 1974.

15. See Josiah Royce, *The Problem of Christianity* (New York: Macmillan, 1913), vol. 1.

16. Brightman, "Values, Ideals, Norms, and Existence," in *Studies in Personalism: Selected Writings of Edgar Sheffield Brightman*, ed. Warren Steinkraus (Utica, N.Y.: Meridian Publishing, 1984), 30.

17. Henry Churchill King discusses personalistic principles at length in several of his books and also reveals a familiarity with the personalism of Bowne. King also consistently applied these principles to racism in such works as: *Reconstruction in Theology* (New York: Macmillan, 1901), *Theology and the Social Consciousness* (New York: Macmillan, 1902), *The Ethics of Jesus* (New York: Macmillan, 1910), *The Moral and Religious Challenge of Our Times* (New York: Macmillan, 1911), and *Seeing Life Whole: A Christian Philosophy of Life* (New York: Macmillan, 1925). One has to wonder why Bowne, the father of American personalism (who clearly influenced Henry Churchill King), failed to explicitly apply personalistic principles to racism.

18. Mathews, *New Faith and Old*, 122.

19. King, "Pilgrimage to Nonviolence," in *Stride Toward Freedom*, 91.

20. Ibid.

21. King, *Stride Toward Freedom*, 197.

22. See King, "Plirimage to Nonviolence," in *Stride Toward Freedom*, 91.

23. Rauschenbusch, *Theology for the Social Gospel*, 50.

24. Ibid., 54.

25. Ibid., 111, 113.

26. Ibid., 114.

27. Ibid., 66 (emphasis added).

28. Ibid., 67.

29. See Reinhold Niebuhr, *The Nature and Destiny of Man: A Christian Interpretation*, one-volume edition (New York: Charles Scribner's Sons, 1941), 1:199–200.

30. Hopkins, *Rise of the Social Gospel*, 319. See also Handy, *Social Gospel in America*, 4.

31. Paul A. Carter, *The Decline and Revival of the Social Gospel: Social and Political Liberalism in American Protestant Churches, 1920–1940* (Ithaca, N.Y.: Cornell University Press, 1954), 195.

32. Ibid., 196.

33. Handy, "Washington Gladden: An Introduction," in *Social Gospel in America*, 29.

34. Jacob H. Dorn, *Washington Gladden: Prophet of the Social Gospel* (Columbus: Ohio State University Press, 1966), 291.

35. See Mervin A. Warren, *King Came Preaching: The Pulpit Power of Dr. Martin Luther King, Jr.* (Downers Grove, Ill.: InterVarsity Press, 2001), 123.

36. Members of the earlier generation of social gospel scholars who argued that the social gospelers devoted little attention to racism include: Charles White Hopkins, *Rise of the Social Gospel*; Thomas F. Gossett, "The Social Gospel and Race" (chap. 7), in *Race: The History of an Idea in America* (Dallas: Southern Methodist University Press, 1963); Carter, *Decline and Revival*, 130–32, 195–99; Preston Williams, "The Social Gospel and Race Relations: A Case Study of a Social Movement" (chap. 10), in *Toward a Discipline of Social Ethics: Essays in Honor of Walter George Muelder*, ed. Paul Deats, Jr. (Boston: Boston University Press, 1972).

37. See Ronald C. White, Jr., *Liberty and Justice for All: Racial Reform and the Social Gospel (1877–1925)* (New York: Harper & Row, 1990), and Ralph E. Luker, *The Social Gospel in Black and White: American Racial Reform, 1885–1912* (Chapel Hill: University of North Carolina Press, 1991).

38. Luker, *Social Gospel in Black and White*, 322.

39. Ibid., 177.

40. Ronald C. White, Jr., and C. Howard Hopkins, "What Is the Social Gospel?" in their *The Social Gospel: Religion and Reform in Changing America* (Philadelphia: Temple University Press, 1976), xii.

41. Quoted in Luker, *Social Gospel in Black and White*, 270.

42. Ibid.

43. Ibid., 273.

44. Quoted in White, *Liberty and Justice for All*, 20. From Josiah Strong, "Brothers and a Story," *American Missionary* 49 (December 1895): 423; *Congregationalist* 80 (October 31, 1895): 661.

45. Luker, *Social Gospel in Black and White*, 274.

46. White, *Liberty and Justice for All*, 212–13.

47. Ibid., 214.

48. Quoted in Luker, *Social Gospel in Black and White*, 274.

49. White, *Liberty and Justice for All*, 26.

50. Luker, *Social Gospel in Black and White*, 318–19.

51. Quoted in ibid., 319.

52. Ibid., 215–16.

53. Trimiew, "The Social Gospel Movement," 180n7.

54. Manning Marable, *Speaking Truth to Power: Essays on Race, Resistance, and Radicalism* (Boulder, Colo.: Westview Press, 1996); Marable, *Black Liberation in Conservative America* (Boston: South End Press, 1997); Joe R. Feagin, *Racist America: Roots, Current Realities, and Future Reparations* (New York: Routledge, 2000); Andrew Hacker, *Two Nations: Black and White, Separate, Hostile, Unequal* (1992; reprint, New York: Ballentine Books, 1995); Paula S. Rothenberg, ed., *White Privilege: Essential Readings on the Other Side of Racism* (New York: Worth Publishers, 2002); C. Eric Lincoln, *Coming through the Fire: Surviving Race and Place in America* (Durham, N.C.: Duke University Press, 1996); and Derrick Bell, *Confronting Authority: Reflections of an Ardent Protester* (Boston: Beacon Press, 1994).

55. Dinesh D'Souza, *The End of Racism: Principles for a Multiracial Society* (New York: Free Press, 1995); and Paul M. Sniderman and Thomas Piazza, *The Scar of Race* (Cambridge, Mass.: Harvard University Press, 1993).

56. Feagin, *Racist America*, 5.

57. Ibid., 14.

58. Rauschenbusch did not submit this manuscript for publication. The manuscript was "discovered in the archives of the American Baptist Historical Archives." It was edited and introduced for publication by Max L. Stackhouse in 1968. See *The Righteousness of the Kingdom* (Nashville, Tenn.: Abingdon Press, 1968), 17.

59. Rauschenbusch, introduction, *Righteousness of the Kingdom*, 67.

60. Rauschenbusch, *Dare We Be Christians?* (1914; reprint, Cleveland: Pilgrim Press, 1993), 46.

61. Dores Sharpe, *Walter Rauschenbusch* (New York: Macmillan, 1942), 166.

62. See Rauschenbusch, *Righteousness of the Kingdom*, 67, 167, 194.

63. See Roi Ottley and William J. Weatherby, ed., *The Negro in New York: An Informal History, 1626–1940* (New York: Praeger Publishers, 1969), especially chap. 10, "Social Emergence." See also Joel Tyler Headley, *The Great Riots of New York, 1712–1873* (1873; reprint, Indianapolis: Bobbs-Merrill, 1970).

64. White and Hopkins, "What Is the Social Gospel?," xvi.

65. Luker, *Social Gospel in Black and White*, 317. Interestingly, White contends that the speaking engagements actually occurred earlier in 1913. See his *Liberty and Justice for All*, 211.

66. White, *Liberty and Justice for All*, 211.

67. Sharpe, *Rauschenbusch*, 167.

68. Rauschenbusch, *The Social Principles of Jesus*, ed. Henry H. Meyer (New York: Methodist Book Concern, 1916), 17.

69. Ibid., 27.

70. Quoted in Rauschenbusch, *Social Principles of Jesus*, 14.

71. Henry Churchill King, like Borden P. Bowne, was much influenced by the German idealist Rudolph Hermann Lotze. Unlike Bowne, however, King saw both the clear implications between Lotze's emphasis on reverence for persons and racism in the United States, and consistently applied this principle to that problem. For discussions on his application of the principle of reverence, see Donald M. Love, *Henry Churchill King of Oberlin* (New Haven, Conn.: Yale University Press, 1956), 155–56. One also sees in this text the clear influence of Lotze (28, 72, 77, 115, 169, 170). King was, more than anything, interested in the practical application of Lotze's idealism,

and thus, like his teacher, made ethics a significant category of theology. The principle of reverence for persons meant nothing to him if it contributed nothing to solving problems that demean persons. In more than half a dozen of his books he consistently applied the principle of reverence for persons to the problem of racism. Four of these include: *Construction in Theology* (New York: Macmillan, 1901), *Theology and the Social Consciousness* (New York: Macmillan, 1902), *The Ethics of Jesus* (New York: Macmillan, 1910), and *The Moral and Religious Challenge of Our Times* (New York: Macmillan, 1911).

72. Quoted in White, *Liberty and Justice for All*, 209. From Rauschenbusch, *The Belated Races and the Social Problems* (New York: American Missionary Association, 1914), 11. Also published as "Belated Races and the Social Problems," *Methodist Review Quarterly* (South) 63 (April 1914): 252–59.

73. Gary J. Dorrien, *Soul in Society: The Making and Renewal of Social Christianity* (Minneapolis: Fortress Press, 1995), 43.

74. Quoted in Paul M. Minus, *Walter Rauschenbusch: American Reformer* (New York: Macmillan, 1988), 105. This is quoted from an article attributed to Rauschenbusch, "The German Seminary in Rochester," pamphlet, 1897. Minus notes that although no author was listed internal evidence suggests that Rauschenbusch "was the primary author." (215n4).

75. Minus, *Walter Rauschenbusch: American Reformer*, 105.

76. Dorrien, *Soul in Society*, 43–44.

77. See Rauschenbusch, *Christianity and the Social Crisis* (New York: Macmillan, 1907), 253–56. See also 265.

78. Dorrien, *Soul in Society*, 43.

79. Rauschenbusch, *Christianity and the Social Crisis*, 150.

80. White, *Liberty and Justice for All*, 209, 16.

81. Dorn, *Washington Gladden*, 298.

82. See King, "Honoring Dr. DuBois," in *Black Titan: W. E. B. DuBois* (Boston: Beacon Press, 1970), 180.

83. Ibid., 181.

84. See King, *Where Do We Go From Here: Chaos or Community?* (Boston: Beacon Press, 1967), 110–11.

85. Luker, *Social Gospel in Black and White*, 323.

86. Ibid., 427.

87. Indeed, Reverdy Ransom, an alumnus of Oberlin, reported just such an experience. Ransom reported that he "soon found that I, with other colored students, while not treated as an outsider, was held within definite boundaries upon the outer fringes of college life which embraces, mental, social and recreational contacts." He further noted that his "scholarship was taken from me by the faculty when I addressed a meeting I had helped to organize to voice a protest against a new regulation segregating colored girls at a separate table in the 'Ladies Dining Hall' of the college." It is of interest to point out that one of Ransom's peers at Oberlin, Mary Church (Terrell), a forerunner of the present-day womanist movement, reported neither being aware of, nor experiencing racism at Oberlin. In fact, she insisted that during her time there college officials would not have

tolerated it. However, without providing details, she went on to say: "Later on, however, conditions affecting colored students changed considerably." See Reverdy Ransom, *The Pilgrimage of Harriet Ransom's Son* (Nashville, Tenn.: Sunday School Union, 1949), 33; and Mary Church Terrell, *A Colored Woman in a White World*, introduction by Nellie V. McKay (New York: G. K. Hall, 1996), 39, 40.

88. Rauschenbusch, "The Revolutionary Power," in *Righteousness of the Kingdom*, 167.

89. Rauschenbusch, "The New Law," in *Righteousness of the Kingdom*, 194.

90. Luker, *Social Gospel in Black and White*, 320.

91. See Reinhold Niebuhr, *Moral Man and Immoral Society* (New York: Charles Scribner's Sons, 1932), 252, 253–54.

92. Dorrien, *Soul in Society*, 44.

93. Coretta Scott King, *My Life with Martin Luther King, Jr.*, 59.

94. See David R. Collins, *Not Only Dreamers: The Story of Martin Luther King, Sr., and Martin Luther King, Jr.* (Elgin, Ill.: Brethren Press, 1986), 67.

95. King, *Daddy King*, 86, 100–101.

96. Quoted in *The Papers*, 1:34.

97. Quoted in Collins, *Not Only Dreamers*, 91.

98. King, *Daddy King*, 107.

99. Ibid., 121–22.

100. Ibid., 96.

101. Michael G. Long, *Martin Luther King, Jr. on Creative Living* (St. Louis: Chalice Press, 2004), 11–12, 13n14, 40n17.

102. King, "Letter from Birmingham Jail," 87, 89.

103. "*Playboy* Interview: Martin Luther King, Jr.," in *A Testament of Hope*, ed. James M. Washington (New York: Harper & Row, 1986), 345.

104. Carson, *Autobiography of Martin Luther King, Jr.*, 47.

105. Stewart Burns, ed., *Daybreak of Freedom: The Montgomery Bus Boycott* (Chapel Hill: University of North Carolina Press, 1997), 132.

106. See Baldwin, *There Is a Balm in Gilead*, 276.

107. Taylor Branch, *Parting the Waters* (New York: Simon & Schuster, 1988), 54, 64.

108. Ibid., 64.

109. See James W. English, *The Prophet of Wheat Street* (Elgin, Ill.: David C. Cook Publishing, 1967, 1973), 21–22.

110. Ibid., 56.

111. See King, *Daddy King*, 82.

112. English, *Prophet of Wheat Street*, 69.

113. Quoted in ibid., 70.

114. Ibid., 161.

115. Quoted in ibid., 155.

116. King, *My Life with Martin Luther King, Jr.*, 86.

117. Luker and Russell, "Introduction," in *The Papers*, 1:42. The citation from Kelsey is from his "Protestantism and Democratic Intergroup Living," *Phylon* 7 (1947): 77–82.

118. Branch, *Parting the Waters*, 73. See also King, *Stride Toward Freedom*, where King writes that in seminary he "came early to Walter Rauschenbusch's *Christianity and the Social Crisis*," 91.

119. Ronald C. White, Jr., and C. Howard Hopkins assure us that not all social gospelers were liberals; nor were all liberals proponents of the social gospel. See "What Is the Social Gospel?" xvii.

120. Even if King said this to Smith, it would not prove that he in fact read *all* of Rauschenbusch's major works, including *A Theology for the Social Gospel*. It would mean only that this is what King told Smith. For if King in fact read this text, how do we explain the fact that he criticized Rauschenbusch for what the latter corrected in his last published book? In addition, why did King name *Christianity and the Social Crisis* as the text that had such a significant impact on him rather than *A Theology for the Social Gospel*, or both?

On the basis of Smith's claim John Ansbro rejects Lois Wasserman's claim that "King's critique of what he had regarded as Rauschenbusch's 'superficial optimism' revealed that he had not read Rauschenbusch's later works." Wasserman, Ansbro maintains, was not aware of what King allegedly told Smith regarding his familiarity with all of Rauschenbusch's major writings. See John Ansbro, *Martin Luther King, Jr.*, 313n66.

121. King, *Stride Toward Freedom*, 91.

122. See Rauschenbusch, *Social Principles of Jesus*, 75.

123. See King, "Pilgrimage Toward Nonviolence," in his *Strength to Love* (New York: Harper & Row, 1963), 138. Criticisms listed here are those we find in early social gospel historians, e.g., Hopkins, *Rise of the Social Gospel*.

124. Rauschenbusch, *Theology for the Social Gospel*, 131.

125. Quoted in Sharpe, *Walter Rauschenbusch*, 228.

126. Rauschenbusch, *Christianity and the Social Crisis*, 60, 61, 65.

127. Ibid., 77.

128. Ibid., 67.

129. It is questionable, however, that Kant intended to include blacks in this claim. See Emmanuel Chukwudi Eze's discussion of this in his selection, "Western Philosophy and African Colonialism," in *African Philosophy: An Anthology* (Oxford: Blackwell Publishers, 1998), 215. Indeed, in *Observations on the Feeling of the Beautiful and Sublime*, Kant said that by nature blacks have "no feeling that rises above the trifling." He goes on to summarize David Hume's racist stance on black Afrikans. "Mr. Hume challenges anyone to cite a single example in which a Negro has shown talents, and asserts that among the hundreds of thousands of blacks who are transported elsewhere from their countries, although many of them have even been set free, still not a single one was ever found who presented anything great in art or science or any other praiseworthy quality, even though among the whites some continually rise aloft from the lowest rabble, and through superior gifts earn respect in the world. So fundamental is the difference between these two races of man, and it appears to be as great in regard to mental capacities as in color. The religion of fetishes so widespread among them is perhaps a sort of idolatry that sinks as deeply into the trifling as appears to be possible to human nature" (*Observations on the Feeling of the Beautiful and the Sublime*, trans. John T. Goldthwait [1764; reprint, Berkeley: University of California Press, 1960], 110–11). There is no evidence that Kant criticized Hume's racism. This is

interesting in light of his declaration that it was Hume who snapped him out of his dogmatic slumber and gave his "investigations in the field of speculative philosophy a quite new direction" (Kant, *Prolegomena to Any Future Metaphysics*, ed. Lewis White Beck [1783; reprint, Indianapolis: Bobbs-Merrill, 1950], 8). Hume clearly did not snap Kant out of his race slumber. Of course he could not, considering his own racism. That a person was "quite black from head to foot," Kant maintained was proof enough that "what he said was stupid" (*Observations on the Feeling of the Beautiful*, 113). One wonders how men of such great philosophical insight and acumen seemed to have no insight at all when it came to acknowledging the humanity and dignity of persons of black Afrikan descent.

130. Rauschenbusch, *Social Principles of Jesus*, 14.

131. Niebuhr, *Moral Man and Immoral Society*, 252.

132. Rauschenbusch was virtually silent on the matter of white violence against blacks.

133. Rauschenbusch, *Christianity and the Social Crisis*, 151–52.

134. Ibid., 151.

135. Rauschenbusch, *Social Principles of Jesus*, 50.

136. Ibid., 76.

137. Rauschenbusch, *Christianity and the Social Crisis*, 145.

138. Ibid., 24, 210.

139. "*Playboy* Interview," 346.

140. Sherwood Eddy, *The Kingdom of God and the American Dream* (New York: Harper & Brothers, 1941), 268.

141. Ibid., 268.

142. Quoted in Rauschenbusch, *Righteousness of the Kingdom*, 16, taken from the *Rochester Democrat and Chronicle*, January 25, 1913.

143. See King's discussion of his family's experience in Lawndale and the adverse effects on his children. See his *Where Do We Go From Here?* 113–16.

144. Rauschenbusch, *Righteousness of the Kingdom*, 17.

145. H. Shelton Smith, Robert T. Handy, and Lefferts A. Loetscher, *American Christianity: An Historical Interpretation with Representative Documents* (New York: Charles Scribner's Sons, 1963), 2:401, 402.

146. Quoted in Sharpe, *Walter Rauschenbusch*, 233.

147. Ibid., 232.

148. Ibid., 231.

149. Rauschenbusch, *Christianity and the Social Crisis*, 2.

150. Ibid., 27.

151. Ibid., 150.

152. Ibid., 90.

153. Ibid., 91.

154. See Walter Rauschenbusch, *Christianizing the Social Order* (New York: Macmillan, 1913).

155. Ibid., Part 3, "Our Semi-Christian Social Order."

156. King, *Stride Toward Freedom*, 91.

157. Handy, *Social Gospel in America*, 15.

Chapter 3. King and Personalism

1. David L Chappell makes this error in his recently published *A Stone of Hope: Prophetic Religion and the Death of Jim Crow* (Chapel Hill: University of North Carolina Press, 2004), 53, 222n32.

2. Mays, *The Negro's God: As Reflected in His Literature* (1938; reprint, New York: Atheneum, 1969).

3. I develop this discussion in my book length manuscript in progress, *Afrikan Personalism: God, Person, and Community*; Burrow, "Personalism and Afrikan Traditional Thought," *Encounter* 61, no. 3 (Summer 2000): 321–48.

4. Albert C. Knudson, *The Philosophy of Personalism* (New York: Abingdon Press, 1927), 85, 87, 433.

5. Ibid., 85–86.

6. See Borden P. Bowne, *The Philosophy of Herbert Spencer* (New York: Hunt & Eaton, 1874).

7. See Ralph Tyler Flewelling, *Personalism and the Problems of Philosophy: An Appreciation of the Work of Borden Parker Bowne* (New York: Methodist Book Concern, 1915), 195.

8. For a thorough discussion of this and related matters see my *Personalism*, chap. 1, "What Is Personalism?"

9. See David J. Garrow, *Martin Luther King, Jr., and the Civil Rights Movement* (New York: Carlson Publishing), 1:xiv; and Keith D. Miller, *Voice of Deliverance: The Language of Martin Luther King, Jr., and Its Sources* (New York: Free Press, 1992), 7, 17.

10. Peter Paris, *Black Leaders in Conflict: Martin Luther King, Jr., Malcolm X, Joseph H. Jackson, Adam Clayton Powell* (New York: Pilgrim Press, 1978), 72.

11. King, *Stride Towarrd Freedom* (New York: Harper and Row, 1958), 100.

12. Garrow, "The Intellectual Development of Martin Luther King, Jr.: Influences and Commentaries," in his *Martin Luther King, Jr.*, 2:445.

13. Ibid., 2:451n23.

14. Garrow, *King and the Civil Rights Movement*, 1:xi–xii.

15. See Garrow, "Intellectual Development of Martin Luther King, 2:451n23.

16. King, *Stride Toward Freedom*, 137–38.

17. See Branch, *Parting the Waters*, 653–54.

18. See Abernathy, *And the Walls Came Tumbling Down*, 314–15, 332.

19. King, *The Trumpet of Conscience* (New York: Harper and Row, 1968), 72.

20. For an explicit reference in this regard, see King, *Stride Toward Freedom*, 100. Moreover, personalistic ideas are pervasive in King's sermons and speeches from 1954 throughout the 1950s. See his first three sermons in *A Knock at Midnight*, ed. Clayborne Carson and Peter Halloran (New York: Warner Books, 1998), 1–60, and his first two speeches in *A Call to Conscience*, ed. Carson and Kris Shepard (New York: Warner Books, 2001), 7–12, 17–41.

21. See Baker-Fletcher, *Somebodynes*, 61.

22. King, "A Comparison of the Conceptions of God in the Thinking of Henry Nelson Wieman and Paul Tillich" (Ph.D. dissertation, Boston University 1955), 269.

23. Ibid., 270.

24. Rudolph Hermann Lotze, *Microcosmus: An Essay Concerning Man and His Relation to the World* (first published in 3 vols., 1856–64), trans. Elizabeth Hamilton and E. E. Constance Jones, 4th ed. (single-volume edition in two volumes) (Edinburgh: T&T Clark, 1885), 2:688.

25. Borden P. Bowne, *Studies in Theism* (New York: Phillips and Hunt, 1879), 275.

26. King, "Comparison of the Conceptions of God," 270. See also Bowne, *Personalism* (Boston: Houghton Mifflin, 1908), where he characterizes essential person as selfhood, self-consciousness, self-control, and the power to know, 266).

27. King, *The Measure of a Man* (1959; reprint, Philadelphia: Fortress Press, 1988), 54.

28. Bowne wrote in *Theism*: "By personality, then, we mean only self-knowledge and self-control. Where these are present we have personal being; where they are absent the being is impersonal. Selfhood, self-knowledge and self-direction are the essence of personality; and these have no implication of corporeality or dependent limitation" (Bowne, *Theism* [1876; reprint, New York: American Book Company, 1902], 162). Bowne also wrote: "Man himself in his essential personality is as unpicturable and formless as God. Personality and corporeality are incommensurable ideas" (see his *Personalism*, 266). King uses strikingly similar language to describe essential person in "Pligrimage to Nonviolence," in *Strength to Love* (New York: Harper & Row, 1963), 141–42.

29. King, "What Is Man?" sermon, preached on WAAF-AM in Chicago, April 17, 1966, King Library and Archives, 3.

30. See my discussion on "Meaning of Person," in my *Personalism*, 240–43.

31. Quoted in King, "Comparison of the Conceptions of God," Nelson Wieman and Paul Tillich," 268 (from Albert C. Knudson, *The Doctrine of God* [Nashville, Tenn.: Abingdon Press, 1930], 300).

32. King, *Stride Toward Freedom*, 100.

33. See my discussion on Bowen and Bowne in *Personalism*, 78–80.

34. See for example, King, "Pilgrimage to Nonviolence," in *Stride Toward Freedom*, chap. 6. King does not expressly mention the influence of his family and the black church. But he did imply these when he said that personalism provided the metaphysical grounding for his long-held beliefs in a personal God and the dignity of persons. Having grown up in a black family with proud black parents, and having grown up in his father's church, it is clear that these were primary sources of such beliefs.

35. King, "The American Dream," in *A Knock at Midnight*, ed. Clayborne Carson and Peter Holloran (New York: Warner Books, 1998), 88.

36. King, "How Modern Christians Should Think of Man," in *The Papers*, 1:274.

37. For example, Howard Thurman reported that his grandmother told the story to him when he was a boy. See his *With Head and Heart: The Autobiography of Howard Thurman* (New York: Harcourt Brace Jovanovich, 1979), 21.

38. King, "What a Christian Should Believe About Himself," in *The Papers*, 1:281.

39. Luker and Russell, "Introduction," in *The Papers*, 1:54n172.

40. King, "An Autobiography of Religious Development," in *The Papers*, 1:363.

41. Carson, *Autobiography of Martin Luther King, Jr.* (New York: Warner Books, 1998), 5.

42. Ibid., 8.

43. Quoted in Walter Kaufmann, "Existentialism from Dostoevsky to Sartre," in his *Existentialism from Dostoevsky to Sartre* (New York: World Publishing, 1969), 47.

44. King conveyed this information in "Autobiography of Religious Development," in *The Papers*, 1:259–63.

45. Carson, *Autobiography of Martin Luther King, Jr.*, 3, 4. My parents grew up in Alabama and West Virginia. We moved to the North when I was four years old. I have a vivid memory of being told these words numerous times by my mother when I was a boy. I also remember that the words were usually uttered when racial incidents occurred.

46. King, *Stride Toward Freedom*, 20.

47. Baldwin, *There Is a Balm in Gilead*, 116–17.

48. Carson, *Autobiography of Martin Luther King, Jr.*, 11–12.

49. Luker and Russell, *The Papers*, 1:38.

50. King, *Stride Toward Freedom*, 145.

51. Mays, *The Negro's God*, 188.

52. Baldwin, *There Is a Balm in Gilead*, 117–18.

53. King, "Autobiography of Religious Development," in *The Papers*, 1:360.

54. Coretta Scott King, *My Life with Martin Luther King, Jr.* (New York: Holt Rinehart and Winston, 1969), 92.

55. Ralph Luker was only partially correct when he said that when King studied personalism at Boston University it was "the last remaining citadel" of personalistic studies. See Luker, *Social Gospel in Black and White*, 323.

56. Upon Bowne's death, Brightman and Knudson significantly broadened the range of influence of Bownean personalism throughout the country and other parts of the world. Brightman was particularly successful in influencing philosophers from Puerto Rico and Latin America, e.g., José A. Fránquiz and Francisco Romero, respectively. Knudson's greatest contribution was that he situated Bowne's personalism in the history of western thought and also became its first systematic theologian.

57. King took two courses under Peter A. Bertocci: Seminar in History of Philosophy, and Seminar in Philosophy. The latter course was a year-long seminar on Hegel that King began with Brightman in the fall of 1952. When Brightman died suddenly, Bertocci assumed responsibility for the seminar.

Jannette Newhall was the instructor for the thesis and dissertation writing course King was required to take during the 1952–53 school year. Newhall was associate professor in the Department of Philosophy. A close friend of Brightman's, Newhall wrote a brief biographical sketch of him not long after his death. In addition, using the complete bibliography prepared by Brightman himself, she compiled the bibliography for his posthumously published magnum opus, *Person and Reality: An Introduction to Metaphysics*, ed. Peter A. Bertocci in collaboration with Janette Elthina Newhall and Robert Sheffield Brightman (New York: Ronald Press, 1958), 367–70.

In 1952 King took History of Recent Philosophy under Millard, an avowed personalist in the tradition of Bowne and Brightman. Millard coauthored with Bertocci the massive, outstanding work in philosophical ethics, *Personality and the Good: Psychological and Ethical Perspectives* (New York: David McKay Company, 1963). The text is clearly written by men who took personalism as their fundamental point of departure. (For the complete list of courses King took as a graduate student, see *The Papers*, 2:18).

58. Taylor Branch wrongly asserts that King took a course from Muelder. He did not, although Muelder was an important mentor, conversation partner, and friend. See Branch, *Parting the Waters*, 94.

59. King alludes to this in *Stride Toward Freedom*. "It was at Boston University that I came to see that Niebuhr had over-emphasized the corruption of human nature. His pessimism concerning human nature was not balanced by an optimism concerning divine nature" (p. 100). In addition, in graduate school King cited articles that Muelder wrote on Niebuhr (see *The Papers*, 2:150–51).

60. King, "Professor Brightman," *Bostonia* (Spring 1957): 7; King, "Lost Sheep" or "The God of the Lost," sermon preached at Ebenezer, King Library & Archives, 1966, 2.

61. Oates, *Let the Trumpet Sound*, 47.

62. Smith and Zepp, *Search for the Beloved Community*, 115.

63. Ibid.

64. Gary Dorrien reacted strongly to this "one-dimensional thesis-antithesis-synthesis" characterization of Hegel's dialectic. He rightly contends that this was not only the tendency of Smith and Zepp, but of Brightman as well. And of course, King shared Brightman's view. Dorrien claims, however, that, "Hegel's dialectic was three-dimensional, involving three simultaneous cases of reduplicated relation." From page two of his letter to me, October 21, 2002, in which he responded to the manuscript form of this book. The letter is in my possession.

65. King, *Strength to Love* (New York: Harper & Row, 1963), 1.

66. King, "What Is Man?" 2.

67. See Ansbro, *Martin Luther King, Jr.*, 298n63.

68. Bertocci wrote to King while he was providing leadership in the Montgomery struggle (as did S. Paul Schilling, the second reader of King's dissertation). He wanted his former student to know that he believed his work was very important, and that he was aware that it was also quite trying and dangerous (see Bertocci to King, February 24, 1956, in *The Papers* 3: 142–43). I say it is not surprising that Bertocci wrote to King because it is characteristic of those in the Bowne-Brightman tradition of personalism to express its chief tenets through all that they do. That is, this type of personalism is not just a philosophy and worldview. It is a way of life, a way of living toward enhanced personhood and community. To be sure, one may teach, preach, and write about it, as did the first three generations of personalists. However, one misses the true essence of personalism if one does not also *live* its meaning, including not disregarding or otherwise mistreating people because of their race, ability, or sexuality. Indeed, from the time of Bowne, personalists have generally behaved like persons who believe in the dignity of persons and live by the conviction that God is personal. This is not to say, however, that the witness and life of some personalists were not marred by contradictory behavior. For example, we know that some personalists, e.g., Albert C. Knudson, were at best racially and culturally insensitive, and that is putting it mildly.

69. King, *Stride Toward Freedom*, 101.

70. King, *Daddy King*, 82.

71. Lewis Baldwin makes a similar point in his discussion on major themes in Kings' thought. See Baldwin, *There Is a Balm in Gilead*, 168–74. Baldwin does not include the objective

moral order, which I take to be absolutely crucial to understanding King's theology and social ethics and his hope for the establishment of the beloved community.

72. See King, "A New Sense of Direction," *Worldview* (April 1972): 11; King, *Where Do We Go From Here?* 250.

73. Ibid., 123.

Chapter 4. King's Conception of God

1. See James Cone, *God of the Oppressed* (New York: Seabury Press, 1975), 163.

2. I should call attention to a glaring error that has been made regarding Bowne's doctrine of God. In his dissertation King quotes Bowne, against Tillich and Wieman, a number of times. Indeed, in the dissertation King essentially concluded with Bowne, Knudson, and DeWolf regarding God. But for a nuance here and there each man concluded in favor of an omnipotent-omnibenevolent God. In this regard they were theistic absolutists. This notwithstanding, at least one writer on King's doctrine of God, Thomas Jarl Sheppard Mikelson, has made the egregious error of concluding that both Bowne and Brightman were theistic finitists. In his doctoral dissertation, Mikelson writes: "For Bowne and Brightman, God could not be both all powerful and all good, since an omnipotent God would control evil as well as good. *They both solved the problem of theodicy by arguing for a limited God. They were what King called finitistic theists.* Knudson and DeWolf followed a different path of reasoning; for them, God was not limited in any way. They both affirmed God's complete power and complete goodness." (See Mikelson, "The Negro's God in the Theology of Martin Luther King, Jr.: Social Community and Theological Discourse" [Th.D. dissertation, Harvard University, April 1988], 123), emphasis added.

It is true that I have myself argued that there are openings for theistic finitism in Bowne's philosophy. (See my discussion in "Borden P. Bowne's Contribution to Theistic Finitism," *Personalist Forum* 13, no. 2 (Fall 1997): 122–42.) However, I did not argue that Bowne was a theistic finitist, for there is no evidence in his writing that he was. In any case, Mikelson could not have been familiar with what I wrote, inasmuch as his dissertation was completed in 1988 and my article appeared in 1997. My argument is that Bowne sometimes wrote like a theistic finitist, but he considered himself a theistic absolutist. Brightman was the first of Bowne's students to diverge from this stance, and he was quite intentional about characterizing his new theory the finite-infinite God. Moreover, Mikelson is not completely accurate when he claims that for Knudson and DeWolf "God was not limited in any way." The truth is that both men acknowledged the divine self-imposed limitation that results from God having created persons in freedom. In addition, it should be noted that Mikelson includes not a single work by either Bowne or Brightman in his bibliography, a curious omission to say the very least.

3. For a thorough discussion of Brightman's doctrine of the Given see my *Personalism*, chap. 7, "Edgar S. Brightman's Theism."

4. Edgar S. Brightman, "Religion as Truth," in *Contemporary American Theology: Theological Autobiographies*, ed. Vergilius Ferm (New York: Round Table Press, 1932), 57.

5. Brightman, *Religious Values* (New York: Abingdon Press, 1925), 68, 236.

6. Brightman, "The Finite-Infinite God" (chap. 3), in his *Personality and Religion* (New York: Abingdon Press, 1934).

7. Brightman, "An Empirical Approach to God," in *The Development of American Philosophy: A Book of Readings*, 2nd ed., ed. Walter G. Muelder, Laurence Sears, and Anne W. Schlaback (1940; reprint, Boston: Houghton Mifflin, 1960), 314–25. Article reprinted by permission from the *Philosophical Review* 46 (1936): 147–60.

8. Brightman, "The Finite-Infinite God," 85–86.

9. Ibid., 100.

10. Brightman, *The Problem of God* (New York: Abingdon Press, 1930), 122, 137–38 (emphasis added).

11. See Martin Luther King, Jr., "The Personalism of J. M. E. McTaggart Under Criticism." This was a paper King wrote in Brightman's course on philosophy of religion in 1951. It is included in *The Papers*, 2:61–76.

12. See King, "A Comparison and Evaluation of the Philosophical Views Set Forth in J. M. E. McTaggart's *Some Dogmas of Religion* and William E. Hocking's *The Meaning of God in Human Experience* with Those Set Forth in Edgar S. Brightman's Course on 'Philosophy of Religion,'" in *The Papers*, 2:76–92.

13. Paris, *Black Leaders in Conflict*, 72.

14. Bowne, *Theism*, 167–68.

15. Ibid., 168.

16. Ibid., 161–62.

17. Ibid., 162.

18. Brightman gave an instructive commentary on Bowne's view of essential person and what would be needed to arrive at a view of it as a clue to objective reality. One would need to remove all limiting traits of the human person. Brightman put it thusly: "Remove from personality those aspects that are peculiar to man and consider it in its essential nature: is there not left a universal essence which man and God and every possible real being may share? Remove desire for victory in war, but leave desire for the highest and best; remove the particular local environment of this or that man's experience, but leave the power to interact with any environment; remove the memories of this man's particular weaknesses and sins, but leave memory as the unifying power binding past and present; remove petty and selfish purposes, but leave purpose as the movement of reality into the future: remove the traits of my partly-integrated personality, but leave the experience of the unity of consciousness as indivisible wholeness—and one then has in personality a clue to universal being." See Brightman, "Personality as a Metaphysical Principle," in *Personalism in Theology*, ed. Brightman (Boston: Boston University Press, 1943), 55–56.

19. Francis J. McConnell, *Is God Limited?* (New York: Abingdon Press, 1924), 256–57. See also McConnell, *The Christlike God* (New York: Abingdon Press, 1927), 44–45. Here McConnell writes: "I was not thinking, however, of the more-than-personality idea when I spoke of the many who accept Christ while denying personality to God. I had in mind those who conceive of the forces of the universe as at bottom impersonal, the forces themselves being either materialistic, or idealistic, or, in the latest terminology, 'neutral.' They would be willing, many of them, to

pronounce Christ the finest flower of the universe, the apex and climax of creation, but they would make him nevertheless the outcome of an impersonal process."

20. See William R. Jones, *Is God a White Racist?* (Garden City, N.Y.: Doubleday, 1973).

21. Cone, *Martin & Malcolm & America*, 131–35.

22. Coretta Scott King, *My Life with Martin Luther King, Jr.*, 59.

23. Luker and Russell, *The Papers*, 1:432.

24. Ibid., 1:426.

25. Ibid., 1:432.

26. Luker and Russell, *The Papers*, 2:84–85.

27. Quoted in Luker, Russell, and Holloran, *The Papers*, 2:85n (emphasis added).

28. See Luker and Russell, *The Papers*, 1:426n24. Here Luker and Russell cite the Rall passage: "Both he [i.e., Montague] and Brightman escape a cosmic dualism by introducing a dualism into the nature of God" (from Rall, *Christianity*, 321). This shows that King's critique of Brightman was not original.

29. This actually goes to the matter of plagiarism. It is now a well-established fact that during both seminary and graduate school King often plagiarized in written assignments, including the dissertation. It is still not clear to this writer that King was always aware that he was in fact plagiarizing. I have had too many students over the past twenty years who, as King did on many occasions, deleted, added, or changed the order of terms and phrases in another's work but did not recognize this practice as plagiarism until informed by the professor. See "Becoming Martin Luther King, Jr.—Plagiarism and Originality, 11–123; Pappas, *Plagiarism and the Culture War*.

30. Luker, Russell, Holloran, *The Papers*, 2:109 (emphasis added).

31. Carson, *Autobiography of Martin Luther King, Jr.*, 32.

32. King, "Comparison of the Conceptions of God," 297.

33. Ibid., 298.

34. Ibid., 297.

35. Ibid., 298–99 (emphasis added).

36. Ibid.

37. Borden P. Bowne, *Metaphysics* (1882; rev. ed, New York: Harper & Brothers, 1898), 93.

38. Bowne, *Theism*, 60–61, 163, 164, and 246.

39. King, "Comparison of the Conceptions of God," 95.

40. I have argued elsewhere that there are a number of openings for theistic finitism in Bowne's thought. See my article, "Borden P. Bowne's Contribution to Theistic Finitism," 122–42.

41. Edgar S. Brightman, *A Philosophy of Religion* (Englewood Cliffs, N.J.: Prentice Hall, 1940), 337.

42. Luker and Russell, *The Papers*, 1:428 (emphasis added).

43. Brightman, *The Finding of God* (New York: Abingdon Press, 1931), 189 (emphasis added).

44. Ibid., 91.

45. See Bowne, *Theism*, 287, and Brightman, *Nature and Values* (New York: Abingdon-Cokesbury Press, 1945), 117.

46. Brightman, *Finding of God*, 173.

47. Brightman, *Personality and Religion* (New York: Abingdon Press, 1934), 85.

48. Quoted in Branch, *Parting the Waters*, 141.

49. See King, "The Drum Major Instinct," in *A Testament of Hope*, ed. James M. Washington (New York: Harper & Row, 1986), 259–67.

50. Borden P. Bowne, *Studies in Theism* (New York: Phillips & Hunt, 1879), 4.

51. King, "Pilgrimage to Nonviolence," in *Strength to Love* (New York: Harper & Row, 1963), 141.

52. Ibid.

53. Quoted in Garrow, *Bearing the Cross*, 89.

54. King, "Why Jesus Called a Man a Fool," in *A Knock at Midnight*, ed. Clayborne Carson and Peter Holloran (New York: Warner Books, 1998), 159.

55. King, *Stride Toward Freedom*, 134–35.

56. Garrow, *Bearing the Cross*, 57, 89.

57. King, "Thou Fool," sermon, preached at Mount Pisgah Missionary Baptist Church, Chicago, August 22, 1967, King Library and Archives, 3.

58. Quoted in Branch, *Parting the Waters*, 164.

59. Quoted in Oates, *Let the Trumpet Sound*, 76.

60. Quoted in King, "The Three Dimensions of a Complete Life," in *A Knock at Midnight*, 136.

61. King, "Comparison of the Conceptions of God," 272.

62. King, "The Answer to a Perplexing Question," in *Strength to Love*, 125–26.

63. King, "Comparison of the Conceptions of God," 273.

64. See Samuel K. Roberts, *An African American Christian Ethics* (Cleveland: Pilgrim Press, 2001).

65. It is not my intention to take up the issue of King's plagiarism in his treatment of Tillich in the dissertation. Those interested in this topic may wish to review the sources listed in the introduction of this book. See also note 29 of this chapter.

66. Paul Tillich, *Systematic Theology* (Chicago and New York: University of Chicago Press and Harper & Row, 1967), 1:245.

67. King, "Comparison of the Conceptions of God," 262.

68. Paul Tillich, *Theology of Culture*, ed. Robert C. Kimball (New York: Oxford University Press, 1959), 131–32.

69. Paul Tillich, *Biblical Religion and the Search for Ultimate Reality* (Chicago: University of Chicago Press, 1955), 85.

70. See Alexander J. McKelway, *The Systematic Theology of Paul Tillich: A Review and Analysis* (Richmond, Va.: John Knox Press, 1964), 126n10.

71. Paul Tillich, *Dynamics of Faith* (New York: Harper & Brothers, 1957), 42.

72. See Étienne Gilson, *God and Philosophy* (New Haven, Conn.: Yale University Press, 1941), chap. 1, "God and Greek Philosophy," esp. 34–37.

73. Paul Tillich, *The Protestant Era*, trans. James Luther Adams (Chicago: University of Chicago Press, 1948), 61.

74. Tillich, *Systematic Theology*, 1:240–41.

75. King, "Comparison of the Conceptions of God," 266.

76. Tillich, *Systematic Theology*, 1:242.

77. King, "Comparison of the Conceptions of God," 158–59.

78. Cone, *Martin & Malcolm & America*, 29–30.

79. Baldwin, *There Is a Balm in Gilead*, 169.

80. King, "An Experiment in Love," in *A Testament of Hope*, 20. Also in King, *Stride Toward Freedom*, 107.

81. King, "How Should a Christian View Communism?" in *Strength to Love*, 94.

82. King, "A Tough Mind and a Tender Heart," in *Strength to Love*, 7 (emphasis added).

83. King, "Our God Is Able," 101.

84. King, "Why Jesus Called a Man a Fool," 162.

85. King, "Thou Fool," 1.

86. King, "Desirability of Being Maladjusted," sermon, preached in Chicago, January 13, 1958, King Library Archives, 1.

87. King, "The Death of Evil upon the Seashore," in *Strength to Love*, 64.

88. Borden P. Bowne, *Studies in Christianity* (Boston: Houghton Mifflin, 1909), 322–23.

89. Edgar S. Brightman, *Nature and Values* (Nashville, Tenn.: Abingdon-Cokesbury, 1945), 117.

90. Brightman, *Nature and Values*, 165.

91. See Abraham J. Heschel, "God Is in Need of Man," in *Between God and Man: An Interpretation of Judaism*, ed. Fritz A. Rothschild (New York: Harper & Brothers, 1959), 140–45. Also, Heschel, *God in Search of Man* (New York: Harper Torchbooks, 1955); Heschel, *The Prophets* (New York: Harper & Row, 1962), chaps. 11–15.

92. See Gilson, *God and Philosophy*, chap. 1, "God and Greek Philosophy."

93. See Mays, *The Negro's God*, 45.

94. Mays, *The Negro's God*, 91–92.

95. Martin Luther King, Jr., *Where Do We Go From Here?* 148–59.

96. See King, "Testament of Hope," and "*Playboy* Interview," 314, 375.

97. King, *Where Do We Go From Here?* 150–51.

98. King, "Negroes Are Not Moving Too Fast," in *A Testament of Hope*, 180.

99. King, "Give Us the Ballot—We Will Transform the South," in *A Testament of Hope*, 200.

100. King, "Facing the Challenge of a New Age," in *A Testament of Hope*, 144.

101. See "*Playboy* Interview," 375.

102. King, "Antidotes for Fear," in *Strength to Love*, 115 (emphasis added).

103. Borden P. Bowne, *Personalism* (Boston: Houghton Mifflin, 1908), 297.

104. Ibid., 298.

105. Ibid., 293–99.

106. Borden P. Bowne, *The Essence of Religion* (Boston: Houghton Mifflin, 1910), 250, 253.

107. Ibid., 247.

108. Mays, *The Negro's God*, 219.

109. Quoted in ibid., 220. From W. E. B. DuBois, *Darkwater* (New York: Harcourt, Brace & Howe, 1920), 275, 276.

110. Mays, *The Negro's God*, 220–24. See Nella Larsen, *Quicksand* (New York: Alfred A. Knopf, 1928).

111. Mays, *The Negro's God*, 226–38.

112. When a Cuban priest asked DuBois whether he believed in a personal God he responded in a letter that he did not believe God to be "a person of vast power who consciously rules the universe for the good of mankind." He went on to say: "I cannot disprove this assumption, but I certainly see no proof to sustain such a belief, neither in History nor in my personal experience." And then this: "[If] you mean by 'God' a vague Force which, in some uncomprehensible way, dominates all life and change, then I answer, Yes; I recognize such Force, and if you wish to call it God, I do not object." The source of these quotes is DuBois's letter to E. Peña Moreno, November 15, 1948, in *The Correspondence of W. E. B. DuBois*, ed. Herbert Aptheker (Amherst: University of Massachusetts Press, 1978), 3:223.

113. Mays, *The Negro's God*, 243.

114. Ibid., 239.

115. James Baldwin, "In Search of a Majority," in his *Nobody Knows My Name* (1954; reprint, New York: Dell, 1961), 113.

116. Cone, *Martin & Malcolm & America*, 29–30.

117. See J. DeOtis Roberts, "Black Consciousness in Theological Perspective" in *Quest for a Black Theology*, ed. Roberts and James J. Gardiner (Philadelphia: Pilgrim Press, 1971), 73. See also Roberts, *A Black Political Theology* (Philadelphia: Westminster Press, 1974), 110–16.

118. James Cone, *God of the Oppressed* (New York: Seabury, 1975), 163.

119. Charles Hartshorne, *Omnipotence and Other Theological Mistakes* (New York: State University of New York Press, 1984), 26.

120. Roberts, "Black Consciousness in Theological Perspective," in *Quest for a Black Theology*, 73.

121. Ibid.

122. Burrow, *Personalism*, 178. See Schilling's critique of Brightman's characterization of the nonrational Given in his *God and Human Anguish* (Nashville, Tenn.: Abingdon Press, 1977), 241–45.

123. Brightman, *A Philosophy of Religion* (New York: Prentice Hall, 1940), 338.

124. Brightman, *Problem of God*, 137–38.

Chapter 5. The Dignity of Being and Sexism

1. In principle Bowne's personalism was against racism. The problem is he did not address this in any of his published writings, including his excellent book on ethics. All efforts to locate unpublished papers by Bowne where he might have addressed racism have failed to date. Although Mrs. Bowne implied in a letter to their godson, Borden Bowne Kessler (January 6, 1912) that her husband's library and papers went to Drew University Library, officials there have insisted that his papers were not included with his library. The letter to Kessler is in the Borden Parker Bowne collection at the Boston University School of Theology Library.

2. King, "A Time to Break Silence," in *Testament of Hope*, 232–33.

3. Bowne, *Metaphysics*, 423.

4. King, "On Being a Good Neighbor," in *Strength to Love* (New York: Harper & Row, 1963), 19.

5. King, "Three Dimensions of a Complete Life," in *Strength to Love*, 75.

6. Equally important, King could make a claim that many environmentalists cannot make: that throughout his campaign to reestablish the sense of black dignity and self-worth, neither he nor groups of Afrikan Americans engaged in practices that had massive, systematic, long-term debilitating effects on the environment. Many environmentalists today are calling for repentance for the way the environment has been treated on a massive scale for many years. But in truth, they should call for the repentance of those who have masterminded the destruction of the environment and who continue to benefit mightily from it. We need to be clear about one thing. These would not be Afrikan Americans. King's focus on the human rights and the dignity of blacks did not mean, conversely, a total disrespect for, and destruction of, other life forms. On the other hand, many environmentalists seem to demand that nonhuman life forms be respected, while they simultaneously benefit from the ongoing systematic oppression and dehumanization of Afrikan Americans and other people of color. Nor is there enthusiasm among many environmentalists and animal rights activists to admit culpability in this regard.

7. This is the sense I get from some of Peter Singer's work in this area. See his *Animal Liberation: A New Ethics for our Treatment of Animals* (New York: Avon Books, 1975).

8. Baker-Fletcher, *Somebodyness*, 171–72.

9. King, *Where Do We Go from Here?* 38.

10. Ibid., 80.

11. Ibid., 119.

12. See Louise Derman-Sparks and Carol Brunson Phillips, *Teaching/Learning Anti-Racism: A Developmental Approach* (New York: Teachers College Press, Columbia University, 1997), 25–28.

13. King, *Where Do We Go From Here?* 119–20.

14. In "Some Reflections on King, Personalism, and Sexism," I try to make the case that in light of King's understanding and acceptance of personalistic method; his overwhelming capacity to change his point of view and his practice in light of facts and current events; and his pattern of expanding his moral sphere to include those things and persons he had previously left out, his attitude and practice toward women in the public arena would very likely have changed had he lived into the 1970s and experienced the full brunt of the women's movement. See *Encounter* 65, no. 1 (Winter 2004): 9–38.

15. See Carson, *Autobiography of Martin Luther King*, 160–65.

16. Cone, *Martin & Malcolm & America*, 277–78.

17. Mary Fair Burks, close friend and predecessor of Robinson as president of the WPC reminds us that the boycott was not solely the latter's idea, and that in any case the important thing is that it occurred and had a successful outcome. See Burks, "Trailblazers: Women in the Montgomery Bus Boycott," in *Women in the Civil Rights Movement: Trailblazers and Torchbearers, 1941–1965*, ed. Vicki L. Crawford, Jacqueline Anne Rouse, and Barbara Woods (Bloomington: Indiana University Press, 1993), 75.

18. See King, *Stride Toward Freedom*, 30, 34, 118; and Branch, *Parting the Waters*, 132.

19. See my manuscript, "Martin Luther King, Jr.: The Person," for an extensive discussion of this and related matters. In author's possession.

20. Jo Ann Gibson Robinson, *The Montgomery Bus Boycott and the Women Who Started It*, ed. David Garrow (Knoxville: University of Tennessee Press, 1987), 40.

21. Burks, "Trailblazers," 76.

22. Ibid., 71.

23. Pauli Murray, *Song in a Weary Throat* (New York: Harper & Row, 1987), 377.

24. Quoted in Lynne Olson, *Freedom's Daughters: The Unsung Heroines of the Civil Rights Movement from 1830 to 1970* (New York: Simon & Schuster, 2001), 129.

25. Quoted in Rosa Parks, *Rosa Parks: My Story*, with Jim Haskins (New York: Dial Books, 1992), 139.

26. Ibid., 139.

27. Olson, *Freedom's Daughters*, 116.

28. Paula Giddings puts Baker's birth at 1905. See Giddings, *When and Where I Enter: The Impact of Black Women on Race and Sex in America* (New York: William Morrow, 1984), 268. Others who have written on Baker put her birth at 1903. See Joanne Grant, *Ella Baker: Freedom Bound* (New York: John Wiley & Sons, 1998), 12, and Shyrlee Dallard, *Ella Baker: A Leader behind the Scenes* (New York: Silver Burdett Press, 1990), 8.

29. Barbara Ransby, *Ella Baker and the Black Freedom Movement: A Radical Democratic Vision* (Chapel Hill: University of North Carolina Press, 2003), 39.

30. Ibid., 164.

31. Giddings, *When and Where I Enter*, 268.

32. Quoted in ibid., 268.

33. See Garrow, *Bearing the Cross*, 84, and the entirety of chap. 2, "The Birth of SCLC, 1957–1959."

34. See ibid., 645n2.

35. Ransby, *Ella Baker*, 173.

36. See Zita Allen, *Black Women Leaders of the Civil Rights Movement* (New York: Grolier Publishing, 1996), 68.

37. Ransby, *Ella Baker*, 180.

38. Ibid., 175.

39. Ibid., 189. John Lewis implies that Baker was not alienated from King as much as Wyatt Tee Walker, Ralph Abernathy, "and the male structure of that organization in general." See John Lewis, *Walking with the Wind: A Memoir of the Movement*, with Michael D'Orso (New York: Simon and Schuster, 1998), 212.

40. See Darlene Clark Hine and Kathleen Thompson, *A Shining Thread of Hope: The History of Black Women in America* (New York: Broadway Books, 1998), 262, 242. It is worth noting that Baker did not receive significant treatment in what is arguably the best Afrikan American history text since it was first published in 1947: see John Hope Franklin, *From Slavery to Freedom*. Now in its eighth edition, the book makes its first reference to Baker in the seventh edition (1994). Alfred A. Moss, Jr., joined Franklin as coauthor with the publication of the sixth edition (1988). The authors attribute but one sentence to Baker. The information they give is not entirely accurate. In the seventh and eighth editions we find: "Ella Baker, who was an NAACP field organizer in the 1940s, served as executive secretary of the Southern Christian Leadership Conference (SCLC)

during the 1960s and was the 'political and spiritual midwife for the Student Nonviolent Coordinating Committee (SNCC)'" (Franklin and Moss, *From Slavery to Freedom* 7th ed. [New York: Alfred A. Knopf, 1994], 497, and 8th ed. [New York: Alfred A. Knopf, 2000], 527). This implies that Baker served with the SCLC for a number of years during the 1960s, but this is not quite accurate since we know that she began in 1957 and devoted about two and a half years of service.

41. Howard Zinn, *SNCC: The New Abolitionists* (Boston: Beacon Press, 1964, 1965).

42. Lewis, *Walking with the Wind*, 212.

43. James Forman, *The Making of Black Revolutionaries: A Personal Account* (New York: Macmillan, 1972), 215.

44. Alice Walker, "Duties of the Black Revolutionary Artist," in her *In Search of Our Mothers' Gardens: Womanist Prose* (New York: Harcourt Brace Jovanovich, 1983), 135.

45. Ransby, *Ella Baker*, 136 (emphasis mine).

46. Ibid., 181.

47. Quoted in Chana Kai Lee, *For Freedom's Sake: The Life of Fannie Lou Hamer* (Urbana: University of Illinois Press, 1999), 23.

48. Forman, *Making of Black Revolutionaries*, 215.

49. Ransby, *Ella Baker*, 142.

50. Forman, *Making of Black Revolutionaries*, 217.

51. Ransby, *Ella Baker*, 106.

52. Ibid., 170–71, 178.

53. See the excellent discussion on Clark's stance in Rosetta E. Ross, *Witnessing and Testifying: Black Women, Religion, and Civil Rights* (Minneapolis: Fortress Press, 2003), 85–86.

54. Ransby, *Ella Baker*, 172.

55. Ella Baker, "Developing Community Leadership," in *Black Women in White America: A Documentary History*, ed. Gerda Lerner (New York: Vintage Books, 1973), 351.

56. Ransby, *Ella Baker*, 184.

57. Ibid., 143.

58. It was not unusual in Baker's time (and perhaps today as well) for men (as well as some women) to characterize women like Baker as "difficult." This was but one tactic used to silence or minimize the importance of the contributions of such women. See Ransby, *Ella Baker*, 142–46.

59. Coretta Scott King, *My Life with Martin Luther King, Jr.*, 142. (emphasis added).

60. Ransby, *Ella Baker*, 257.

61. Quoted in Grant, *Ella Baker*, 111.

62. Septima Clark and Diane Nash had similar experiences with the all-male leadership of the SCLC. When Clark was hired as an executive of the organization the men frequently questioned her role, and like Baker she found that her suggestions and contributions were frequently undervalued by them. "I was on the executive staff of the SCLC," she said, "but the men on it didn't listen to me too well." She recalled that some even questioned why she was on the staff, and had no faith or confidence in women's abilities in the public sphere. "Rev. Abernathy would say continuously, 'Why is Mrs. Clark on the staff?' Dr. King would say, 'Well, she has expanded our program. She has taken it into eleven deep south cities.' Rev. Abernathy'd come right back the next time and ask again" (quoted in Ross, *Witnessing and Testifying*, 85.) Clark acknowledged

King's support of her work with the citizenship schools, but concluded that he was no different from other black ministers in that he did not place much stock in women's ability to contribute in the public arena.

63. Ransby, *Ella Baker*, 185.

64. Lewis, *Walking with the Wind*, 212.

65. Ransby, *Ella Baker*, 370. See also 422n60 for an explanation of Patricia Hill Collins' concept of the "conditional insider."

66. Ibid., 371.

67. Ibid., 135.

68. Ibid.

69. Grant, *Ella Baker*, 122.

70. Ransby, *Ella Baker*, 112.

71. Quoted in Garrow, *Bearing the Cross*, 141.

72. Quoted in ibid., 655n12.

73. Quoted in Carol Mueller, "Ella Baker and the Origins of Participatory Democracy," in *Women in the Civil Rights Movement*, 64.

74. See Rosemary Radford Ruether, "Sexism," in *Dictionary of Feminist Theologies*, ed. Letty M. Russell and J. Shannon Clarkson (Louisville, Ky.: Westminster John Knox Press, 1996), 256–57.

75. Michael Eric Dyson claims that King "allegedly got physical with at least one woman." See his *I May Not Get There with You*, 177. Whether true or not, Ralph Abernathy wrote of an incident in which King was involved in an altercation with a lover and violently pushed her onto the bed in a motel. Abernathy claims that King and the young woman literally fought each other. This is quite possibly the undocumented incident to which Dyson refers in his book. See note 74. Abernathy reports the incident in *And the Walls Came Tumbling Down*, 436.

76. See my *Personalism*, 85–86, 106–8.

77. Bowne writes: "No logical subtlety would enable a man to judge in the court of aesthetics, who was lacking in the aesthetic sense. Such a one would likely decide that there is no proof that the Hottentot Venus is any less fair than the Venus of Milo; and he might even boast of the acumen and impartiality of his decision." See Bowne, *Theism*, 260. The Hottentots were dark-skinned Afrikans.

78. One would expect to find some discussion on the problem of race in Bowne's writings on ethics. Nowhere does this occur in any of his published writings, including *The Principles of Ethics* (1892) where he includes an extensive discussion on child labor laws and the rights of (white) women. There is at this writing no evidence that any of Bowne's unpublished writings on ethics are extant.

79. See McConnell, *Borden Parker Bowne*, 176, 259.

80. Étienne Gilson, *The Spirit of Medieval Philosophy* (New York: Scribners, 1936), 190.

81. Bowne, *Principles of Ethics*, 161.

82. Howard Thurman, "The New Heaven and the New Earth," *Journal of Negro Education* 27 (1958): 116.

83. Thurman, "The Christian Minister and the Desegregation Decision," *Pulpit Digest* 37, no. 229 (May 1957): 13.

84. Thurman, "New Heaven and the New Earth," 117. One had to do essentially what President Harold Case of Boston University did when he invited Thurman to be Dean of Marsh Chapel and Professor of Spiritual Disciplines and Resources in 1953. See Thurman, *With Head and Heart: The Autobiography of Howard Thurman* (New York: Harcourt Brace Jovanovich, 1979), 166–67.

85. Bowne, *Principles of Ethics*, 133.

86. King, "A Time to Break Silence," in *A Testament of Hope*, 232.

87. Bowne, *Principles of Ethics*, 147.

88. Ibid., 148.

89. Ibid., 150–51. See also his important article on the subject in "Woman and Democracy," *North American Review* 119 (April 1910): 527–36.

90. Borden P. Bowne, *The Philosophy of Theism* (New York: Harper & Brothers, 1887), 249.

91. On Douglass, see my article, "Some African American Males' Perspectives on the Black Woman," in *Black Men on Race, Gender, and Sexuality: A Critical Reader*, ed. Devon W. Carbado (New York: New York University Press, 1999), 390–407. On DuBois, see my essay, "W. E. B. DuBois and the Intersection of Race and Sex in the Twenty-First Century," in *W. E. B. DuBois and Race: Essays Celebrating the Centennial Publication of* The Souls of Black Folk, ed. Chester J. Fontenot and Mary Alice Morgan, with Sarah Gardner (Macon, Ga.: Mercer University Press, 2001), 122–41. It should be noted, however, that DuBois biographer David L. Lewis has written about his less than admirable treatment of his wife and daughter in the home. This is a clear contradiction of DuBois's strong and persistent support of *all* women's rights in the public sphere. See Lewis, *W. E. B. DuBois: Biography of Race, 1868–1919* (New York: Henry Holt, 1993), chap. 16, "Connections at Home and Abroad."

92. Bowne, *Principles of Ethics*, 161.

93. Ibid., 161. See also 193–94, 201.

94. L. D. Reddick, *Crusader without Violence: A Biography of Martin Luther King, Jr.* (New York: Harper & Brothers, 1959), 5.

95. Coretta Scott King, *My Life with Martin Luther King, Jr.*, 57–58.

96. Ibid., 88.

97. Ibid.

98. See my *James H. Cone and Black Liberation Theology* (Jefferson, N.C.: McFarland, 1994), chap. 5, "Developing Perspective on Oppression;" and Manning Marable, "Grounding with My Sisters: Patriarchy and the Exploitation of Black Women" (chap. 3), in his *How Capitalism Underdeveloped Black America*; and Marable, *Speaking Truth to Power*.

99. Baker-Fletcher has only written one book on King to date, but this is a significant and groundbreaking text inasmuch as it is the first attempt at a systematic study on King's doctrine of dignity. Baker-Fletcher examined the cultural, black family, and black church roots of King's theory of dignity, as well as contributions of King's personalist teachers. See his *Somebodyness*.

100. I find it interesting that Manning Marable, one of the most clearheaded progressive social analysts around, did not name King as a sexist in his chapter, "Groundings with My Sisters" (chap. 3), in *How Capitalism Underdeveloped Black America*. He named Malcolm X, Stokely Carmichael, and Eldridge Cleaver, among others. True, Marable was here focusing on represen-

tatives in the Black Power Movement, but he also makes references to the civil rights movement, which was the opening to mention King's sexism. I have looked in vain in Marable's many other books, but as of this writing there is no reference to King as sexist.

101. Baker-Fletcher, *Somebodyness*, 184.

102. For example, the claim that Afrikan American males generally benefit from sexism in the wider society, or more specifically from sexism in the white community is not legitimate, by virtue of the existence of embedded racism. However, there is no question that black men benefit from sexism in the context of the Afrikan American community.

103. Baldwin, *There Is a Balm in Gilead*, 270n137.

104. See King's letter to Mrs. Katie E. Whickam, July 7, 1958, King Library and Archives, 1. Whickam was elected as the first woman staff officer at the SCLC. See Belinda Robnett, *How Long? How Long?: African-American Women in the Struggle for Civil Rights* (New York: Oxford University Press, 1997), 93.

105. Baldwin acknowledges that women in South Afrika represent three different perspectives regarding the struggle for liberation. One group thinks that only women can fight the struggle for women's liberation. A second believes that black women's struggle should be kept separate from that of white women. A third group, representative of the largest number of black South Afrikan women, prefer that their struggle remain a part of the struggle to eradicate all semblances of apartheid. Baldwin argues that the ongoing struggle for total liberation in South Afrika will "reflect more adequately the beloved community ideal as articulated by King" only if it draws on the experiences of women in general, not just black South Afrikan women (*Toward the Beloved Community*, 173). He rightly sees that in principle King's beloved community ethic is inclusive, and therefore has no place for absolute separation between the races.

In principle, Baldwin is right to insist on the need for the inclusion of *all* women in the continuing struggle in South Afrika. Aware of the need for South Afrikans to adapt King's ideas to their context, Baldwin could have been much more explicit about this in his discussion on the three views represented by women. That is, we know that the beloved community ethic is an inclusive one. However, even King acknowledged (ten days before he was murdered) that at the point of strategy, i.e., on the way to the beloved community, temporary separation *might* be needed in order for blacks to organize and to solidify a power base capable of confronting ongoing oppression and achieving the "truly integrated society where there is shared power" ("Conversation with Martin Luther King," in *Testament of Hope*, 666). King was essentially supporting the emergence of the black caucus idea as a political weapon. At any rate, he understood that the means to the beloved community might call for a kind of *way station ethic* based on the temporary separation of the races. On the other hand, he passionately rejected the Black Muslim's call for the absolute separation of whites and blacks (ibid., 662–63). King lived by the conviction that the universe itself is built on a moral foundation, and thus is fundamentally good (a point to be discussed in detail in the next chapter). In addition, King's experience and his theology convinced him that reality is essentially social, and therefore persons are created in a way that makes them interrelated and interdependent beings. To be is to be in community. Furthermore, the history of black-white relations in the United States is such that it is impossible for the two groups to live apart from each other in a permanent way. What is important here is that King's was to be a temporary or interim ethic—a means or strategy to the much higher end of inclusion within the whole. In this regard, I would argue that in light of hundreds of years of legalized systematic apartheid, it is reasonable that some black South Afrikan women would prefer a period of time to work among themselves and-or with sympathetic black men before joining with sympathetic white women and men who, whether they wanted to or not, benefited from the oppression of black South Afrikans. In other words, the opening should be left for black South Afrikan women to adapt King's beloved community ethic to their situation, or to at least include his idea of temporary (not absolute!) separation as a matter of strategy. Aware of King's male chauvinism, Baldwin rightly proclaims the need for South Afrikan women to read King's works with a critical eye and that they reject those ideas which are not applicable to their situation (*Toward the Beloved Community*, 174).

106. Letter from Lewis V. Baldwin to Rufus Burrow, Jr., 28 April 1996, 1. My review article of Baldwin's book was published in the *Journal of Religion* 77, no. 3 (July 1997): 442–48.

107. Baldwin, *There Is a Balm in Gilead*, 270. David Garrow reports that Coretta King "openly complained about her husband's insistence that she take care of the home and family and not become involved in movement activities. 'I wish I was more a part of it,' she told one interviewer. 'Martin didn't want her to get too active,' Andrew Young recalled. Bernard Lee put it more bluntly. 'Martin . . . was absolutely a male chauvinist. He believed that the wife should stay home and take care of the babies while he'd be out there in the streets.' Dorothy Cotton saw it regularly. 'He would have had a lot to learn and a lot of growing to do' concerning women's rights. 'I'm always asked to take the notes, I'm always asked to go fix Dr. King some coffee.'" See Garrow, *Bearing the Cross*, 375–76.

108. Baldwin, *There Is a Balm in Gilead*, 270.

109. Ibid.

110. Baldwin, *To Make the Wounded Whole* (Minneapolis: Fortress Press, 1992), 311.

111. Ibid.

112. See Lewis V. Baldwin and Amiri YaSin Al-Hadid, *Between Cross and Crescent: Christian and Muslim Perspectives on Malcolm and Martin* (Gainesville: University Press of Florida, 2002), 3, 6, 168, 170, 403n48.

113. See Cone, *Martin & Malcolm & America*, 273, and the entirety of chap. 10, "Nothing But Men."

114. Andrew Billingsley, *Mighty Like a River: The Black Church and Social Reform* (New York: Oxford University Press, 1999), 142.

115. For a thorough discussion on Cone's movement toward sexual analysis in his theological project, see my *James H. Cone and Black Liberation Theology* (Jefferson, N.C.: McFarland, 1994), chap. 5, "Developing Perspective on Oppression."

116. Cone, "New Roles in the Ministry: A Theological Appraisal," in *Black Theology: A Documentary History, 1966–1979*, ed. Cone and Gayraud Wilmore (Maryknoll, N.Y.: Orbis Books, 1979), 394–97.

117. Billingsley, *Climbing Jacob's Ladder: The Enduring Legacy of African-American Families* (New York: Simon & Schuster, 1992), 66, 159, 162, 243.

118. Billingsley, *Mighty Like a River*, 143.

119. Walter G. Muelder, "Communitarian Dimensions of the Moral Laws," in *The Boston Personalist Tradition in Philosophy, Social Ethics, and Theology,* ed. Paul Deats, Jr., and Carol Robb (Macon, Ga.: Mercer University Press, 1986), 250.

120. See my essay "W. E. B. DuBois and the Intersection of Race and Sex," 132–37.

121. See Angela Y. Davis, *Women, Race & Class* (New York: Vintage Books, 1983), 77–79, 85, 145.

122. Burns, *To the Mountaintop,* 374.

123. Rufus Burrow, Jr., "Some Reflections on King, Personalism, and Sexism," *Encounter* 65, no. 1 (Winter 2004): 9–38.

Chapter 6. Personal Communitariaism and the Beloved Community

1. See Walter G. Muelder, *Moral Law in Christian Social Ethics* (Richmond, Va.: John Knox Press, 1966), 29, 113, and chap. 2, "Person and Community."

2. See John S. Mbiti, *African Religions and Philosophy* 2d ed. (1969; 2d ed., Oxford: Heinemann Educational Publishers, 1989) 106 and chap. 10, "Ethnic Groups, Kinship and the Individual."

3. See Kwame Gyekye, *An Essay on African Philosophical Thought: The Akan Conceptual Scheme* Revised Edition (1987; reprint, Philadelphia: Temple University Press, 1995), chap. 10, "The Individual and the Social Order."

4. Mays, *The Negro's God,* 78, 115–16, 188.

5. Edgar S. Brightman, *Nature and Values* (New York: Abingdon, 1945), 117.

6. Ibid.

7. John S. Pobee, *Toward an African Theology* (Nashville: Abingdon, 1979), 49.

8. Bowne, *Philosophy of Theism,* 50.

9. Ibid.

10. Ibid., 52–53.

11. Francis J. McConnell, *Personal Christianity* (New York: Fleming H. Revell, 1914), 48.

12. Muelder, *Moral Law in Christian Social Ethics,* 124.

13. Brightman, *An Introduction to Philosophy,* 3rd ed. rev. by Robert N. Beck (New York: Holt Rinehart Winston, 1963), 353.

14. Albert C. Knudson, *The Principles of Christian Ethics* (New York: Abingdon Press, 1943), 118.

15. See Lotte Hoskins, ed., *"I Have a Dream": The Quotations of Martin Luther King, Jr.* (New York: Grosset & Dunlap, 1968), 71.

16. Mays, *The Negro's God,* 162, and all of chap. 6, "The Impartiality of God and the Unity of Mankind."

17. Martin Luther King, Jr., "A Christmas Sermon on Peace," in *Testament of Hope,* 254.

18. King, "Three Dimensions of a Complete Life," in *Strength to Love,* 72.

19. Ibid.

20. Mays, *The Negro's God,* 162.

21. King, "The Birth of a New Age," in *The Papers,* 3:344.

22. Ibid., 3:458.

23. King, "An Experiment in Love" in *Testament of Hope*, 20.

24. Ibid.

25. Donald M. Chinula, *Building King's Beloved Community: Foundations for Pastoral Care and Counseling with the Oppressed* (Cleveland: United Church Press, 1997), 60.

26. Benjamin E. Mays and Joseph William Nicholson, *The Negro's Church* (1933; reprint, Salem: Ayer Company, 1988), 64.

27. Zepp and Smith, *Search for the Beloved Community*; Ansbro, *Martin Luther King, Jr.*, 187–97; and Lewis V. Baldwin, *Toward the Beloved Community: Martin Luther King, Jr., and South Africa* (Cleveland: Pilgrim Press, 1995).

28. See my *Personalism*, 40.

29. Josiah Royce, *The Religious Aspect of Philosophy: A Critique of the Bases of Conduct and of Faith* (1885; reprint, Boston: Houghton Mifflin, 1913), 175.

30. Josiah Royce, *The Problem of Christianity* (New York: Macmillan, 1913), 1:39.

31. Ibid., 1:172.

32. Perhaps this is the place to note two books, published in 1930 and 1937, that have "beloved community" in their title. The first is about a Vermont town that struggles with its own image and the place and role of seasonal tourists and the effects on that town. The author seemed to see as synonymous "beloved community" and "Kingdom of Heaven on earth." See Zephine Humphrey, *The Beloved Community* (New York: E. P. Dutton, 1930). The other book is an explicitly religious portrayal of the beloved community and how it is characterized. One can work effectively toward the achievement of such a community only if one is truly in love with it. The author equates the beloved community with the Church, and argues that "New Testament teaching about its nature suggests that the real goal of Christians and of the Church is not to be found in this world" (175). And yet on earth it is to be a community in which the freedom of every member is acknowledged, and where emphasis is placed on the spiritual nature of the universe and efforts are made to order life according to the highest spiritual values. See Roger Lloyd, *The Beloved Community* (London: Nisbet, 1937).

33. Royce, *Problem of Christianity*, 1:359, 356.

34. Ibid., 1:357.

35. King, "I See the Promised Land," in *Testament of Hope*, 286.

36. Ira Zepp, Jr., *The Social Vision of Martin Luther King, Jr.* (1971; reprint, Brooklyn: Carlson Publishing, 1989), 209.

37. Rauschenbusch, *Theology for the Social Gospel*, 126–27. Rauschenbusch also refers on 70–71 to Royce and quotes from *The Problem of Christianity*.

38. Brightman, "Religion As Truth," 1:57.

39. Ibid.

40. Jannette Newhall, "Edgar Sheffield Brightman," *Philosophical Forum* 12 (1954): 14.

41. Brightman, *Religious Values*, 221.

42. John Cartwright, "Foundations of the Beloved Community," *Debate and Understanding* 1, no. 3 (1977): 171.

43. See King, "Pilgrimage to Nonviolence" (chap. 6), in *Stride Toward Freedom*, (New York: Harper & Row, 1958); and King, "Pilgrimage to Nonviolence" (chap. 17), in *Strength to Love*.

44. King, "Philosophical Views Set Forth in Hocking," in *The Papers*, 2:88, 89n45.

45. Ansbro makes this claim in *Martin Luther King, Jr.*, 319n152.

46. See "The Southern Christian Leadership Conference: 'The Ultimate Aim is the "Beloved Community,'" in *Black Protest Thought in the Twentieth Century*, ed. August Meier, Elliott Rudwick, and Francis L. Broderick (1965; 2d ed., Indianapolis: Bobbs-Merrill, 1971), 306.

47. *Playboy* Interview, 375.

48. See John Malcus Ellison, *They Who Preach* (Nashville: Broadman Press, 1956), 37. I am indebted to my wife, Mary Alice Mulligan, a homiletics and ethics scholar, for informing me of Ellison's use of this term.

49. On p. 3, Thurman writes: "I quote from my essay published in 1965." On p. 6, he referred to the 1954 Supreme Court decision as having "precipitated a social revolution in America in the midst of which more than a decade later we are still involved." He also referred to "the recent riots in Atlanta, Georgia" (5). On p. 6 he writes: "Nearly twelve years after the Supreme Court decision. . . ." Near the end of the article he wrote of "the white heat of the long, hot summer, the angry violence of a suburban Cicero" (18). The latter reference is to the violence that broke out when King led a march through Cicero, Illinois, in 1966.

50. Howard Thurman, "Desegregation, Integration, and the Beloved Community," article, 16. Possibly written in 1966. See note 49, above.

51. Ibid., 17.

52. Ibid.

53. Ibid., 18.

54. Howard Thurman, *The Search for Common Ground: An Inquiry into the Basis of Man's Experience of Community* (New York: Harper & Row, 1971), 104.

55. Rauschenbusch, *Theology for the Social Gospel*, 142.

56. King, "Christian View of the World," in *The Papers*, 1:283.

57. See Rauschenbusch, *Social Principles of Jesus*, 63, 74, 75.

58. King, "The Christian Pertinence of Eschatological Hope," in *The Papers*, 1:272–73.

59. King, *Where Do We Go From Here?* 9.

60. Lewis V. Baldwin, *To Make the Wounded Whole* (Minneapolis: Fortress Press, 1992), 4, 286–301.

61. King, *Where Do We Go From Here?* 176.

62. See Reinhold Niebuhr, *An Interpretation of Christian Ethics* (1935; reprint, New York: Seabury Press, 1979), 112, 123; Niebuhr, *Nature and Destiny of Man*, 2:246.

63. King, "A Christmas Sermon on Peace," in his *The Trumpet of Conscience* (New York: Harper & Row, 1967), 76. Published posthumously in 1968.

64. King, "Death of Evil upon the Seashore," in *Strength to Love*, 64.

65. King, *Why We Can't Wait*, 26.

66. Smith and Zepp, *Search for the Beloved Community*, 119.

67. Baldwin, *Toward the Beloved Community*, 3.

68. Josiah Royce, *The Philosophy of Loyalty* (New York: Macmillan, 1908), 252. See also 351.

69. Ibid., 353.

70. Ibid., 357.

71. Baldwin, *Toward the Beloved Community*, 2.

72. Ibid., 175.

73. Bowne, *Principles of Ethics*, 124.

74. Peter A. Bertocci and Richard Millard introduce the term "foreseeable consequences" in their discussion of the principle of consequences in their massive *Personality and the Good: Psychological and Ethical Perspectives* (New York: David McKay, 1963), 493–98.

75. See Paul W. Taylor, *Respect for Nature: A Theory of Environmental Ethics* (Princeton, N.J.: Princeton University Press, 1986), 14–16.

76. Ibid.

77. King, *Daddy King*, 109.

78. Ibid., 82.

79. Ibid., 106, 107.

80. Ibid., 98–99.

81. Jean-Paul Sartre, "Existentialism Is a Humanism," trans. Philip Mairet, in *The Existentialist Tradition: Selected Writings*, ed. Nino Langiulli (Garden City, N.Y.: Anchor Books, 1971), 399, 410.

82. Sartre, *Being and Nothingness: An Essay on Phenomenological Ontology*, trans. and with an introduction by Hazel E. Barnes (New York: Philosophical Library, 1965), 47–49, 55–70.

83. Sartre, *The Age of Reason*, trans. Eric Sutton (New York: Bantam Book, 1968), 276.

84. Brightman, *Moral Laws* (New York: Abingdon Press, 1933), 283.

85. King, "The Ethical Demands of Integration," in *Testament of Hope*, 120.

86. King, "Shattered Dreams," in *Strength to Love*, 81.

87. See Borden P. Bowne, *The Theory of Thought and Knowledge* (New York: Harper & Brothers, 1897), 239–44, and Brightman, *Moral Laws*, 282–83.

88. King, "The Personalism of J. M. E. McTaggart Under Criticism," in *The Papers*, II:72, 73.

89. See Bowne, "The Speculative Significance of Freedom," *Methodist Review* 77 (September 1895): 681–97; *Theory of Thought and Knowledge* (New York: Harper & Brothers, 1899), 239–44; *Personalism*, 200–208; *Metaphysics* (1898), 406–409.

90. Bowne, *Theory of Thought and Knowledge*, 243.

91. King, "Personalism of J. M. E. McTaggart," in *The Papers*, 2:73.

92. King, "What is Man?," in *Strength to Love*, 90.

93. King, "The Ethical Demands for Integration," in *Testament of Hope*, 119.

94. Ibid., 120. See also Bowne, *Metaphysics*, 405, 406.

95. See Bowne's view in *Metaphysics*, 415.

96. King, "The Answer to a Perplexing Question," in *Strength to Love*, 124.

Chapter 7. Objective Moral Order and Moral Laws

1. Borden P. Bowne, *The Philosophy of Herbert Spencer* (New York: Hunt & Eaton, 1874), 264, 265.

2. Quoted in Lotze, *Microcosmus*, 2:675.

3. See Knudson, *The Principles of Christian Ethics*, 65.

4. Bowne, *Studies in Theism*, 272–73.

5. Bowne, *Philosophy of Theism*, 214–15.

6. Ibid., 216.

7. Ibid., 219.

8. Ibid.

9. Ibid., 220.

10. Ibid.

11. Ibid., 221.

12. Benjamin E. Mays, *Seeking To Be Christian in Race Relations* (New York: Friendship Press, 1946), 8.

13. Ibid., 9.

14. King, "An Autobiography of Religious Development," in *The Papers*, 1:360.

15. Quoted in Branch, *Parting the Waters*, 68. Branch tells us that Samuel DuBois Cook, a classmate of King's at Morehouse College, reported in an interview that King uttered these words in that senior sermon (*Parting the Waters*, 932n68). I wrote to Cook and Charles Willie (another of King's Morehouse peers) to ask if either man recalled hearing the term personalism or Brightman's name while at Morehouse. Cook did not respond to the two letters sent. Willie responded in an email (September 2, 2004) that he could not be helpful in this regard, but he confirmed for me that a close examination of books by and about Benjamin E. Mays may prove insightful in this regard.

16. See Oates, *Let the Trumpet Sound*, 35.

17. See Baldwin, *There Is a Balm in Gilead*, 118.

18. Brightman, *Moral Laws*, 286.

19. King, "Our God Is Able," 105.

20. Hoskins, *"I Have a Dream,"* 79.

21. Richard T. Nolan et al., *Living Issues in Ethics* (Belmont, Calif.: Wadsworth Publishing, 1982), 10.

22. Bowne, *Principles of Ethics*, 201.

23. King, "Letter from Birmingham City Jail," in *Why We Can't Wait*, 85.

24. Bowne, *Principles of Ethics*, 251.

25. George W. Davis, "Liberalism and a Theology of Depth," *Crozer Quarterly* 28, no. 3 (July 1951): 198–206.

26. Quoted in ibid., 201.

27. King, "Comparison of the Conception of God," in *The Papers*, 2:536.

28. See King, "Comparison and Evaluation of the Philosophical Views Set Forth in McTaggart and Hocking," in *The Papers* 2:89n. King failed to attribute to Brightman the quote taken from *Religious Values*.

29. Sorley was educated and taught at Cambridge. Unlike many idealists, he saw ethics as prior to metaphysics, and concluded that value is the basic key to reality. For him, only persons possess intrinsic value, a stance similar to Bowne and then to Brightman at an earlier stage of his development. Sorley was an ethical, rather than a metaphysical, theist.

30. Edgar S. Brightman, *A Philosophy of Ideals* (New York: Henry Holt, 1928), 211.

31. Ibid.

32. Brightman, *Religious Values*, 110.

33. Brightman, *An Introduction to Philosophy* (1925; reprint, New York: Henry Holt, 1951), 159.

34. Ibid., 161.

35. Ibid., 158.

36. Brightman, *Religious Values*, 168–69 (emphasis added).

37. Theodore Parker, "Of Justice and the Conscience," in *The Collected Works of Theodore Parker*, ed. Frances Power Cobbe (London: Trübner, 1879), 2:48.

38. Ibid., 2:40.

39. Ibid., 2:48 (emphasis added).

40. Hoskins, *"I Have a Dream,"* 63; King, "Love, Law, and Civil Disobedience" in *Testament of Hope*, 52; and "The Current Crisis in Race Relations," in ibid., 88.

41. Branch, *Parting the Waters*, 197.

42. John Haynes Holmes, "Salute to Montgomery," *Liberation* (December 1956): 5 (emphasis added).

43. Quoted in Branch, *Parting the Waters*, 297 (emphasis added).

44. Brightman, *Introduction to Philosophy*, 363 (see also 214, 224–29).

45. Ibid., 364 (emphasis added).

46. Mays, *The Negro's God*, 126.

47. Quoted in ibid., 54.

48. King, "Is the Universe Friendly?" sermon preached on December 12, 1965 at the Ebenezer Baptist Church in Atlanta, Georgia, King Library & Archives, 1.

49. King, "Discerning the Signs of History," sermon, King Library and Archives, November 15, 1964, 2.

50. King, "The Prodigal Son," sermon preached at Ebenezer Baptist Church in Atlanta, September 4, 1966, unpublished, King Library and Archives, 6.

51. King, "Discerning the Signs of History," 2.

52. Quoted in King, "Facing the Challenge of a New Age," in *A Testament of Hope*, 141. This is a familiar quote in King's writings, speeches, and sermons. It comes from James Russell Lowell, "The Present Crisis," in *The Complete Poetical Works of Lowell* (Cambridge Edition), ed. Horace E. Scudder (Boston: Houghton Mifflin, 1925), 67.

53. Lowell, "The Present Crisis," 67.

54. King, "A Christmas Sermon on Peace," in his *The Trumpet of Conscience*, 75 (emphasis added).

55. King, "Non-Aggression Procedures to Interracial Harmony," in *The Papers*, 3:327–28.

56. King, "Facing the Challenge of a New Age," in *The Papers*, 3:460.

57. King, *Stride Toward Freedom*, 69–70.

58. Luther D. Ivory, *Toward a Theology of Radical Involvement: The Theological Legacy of Martin Luther King, Jr.* (Nashville, Tenn.: Abingdon, 1997), 52.

59. See my article "Moral Laws in Borden P. Bowne's *Principles of Ethics*," *Personalist Forum* 6, no. 2 (Fall 1990): 161–80.

60. We get a sense of Brightman's anxiety over the use of law in his discussion on the meaning of ethics. Some illustrations of this follow. In *Moral Laws* Brightman writes: "Ethics is the normative science of the principles (or laws) of the best types of human conduct" (13). He later writes: "Since it [ethics] aims at principles or laws . . ." And this: The definition of ethics implies three basic concepts: "law (principles), value (the good), and obligation (ought, duty)." Brightman then writes that the only reasonable ethics "would give us principles by which we might confront the many conflicting value-claims of our daily experience and show us where the true value of life lies" (29). Ethics is "a normative science of ideal principles" (9). Suffice it to say that this frequent going back and forth between the use of law and principle implies Brightman's discomfort with "law," even though he settled for it in his construction of the moral law system.

61. See Bertocci and Millard, *Personality and the Good.* According to the division of labor, Millard wrote part 4, "Principles of Ethical Choice." However, the authors were careful to point out that they "worked with common aims on every part of the book" (viii). See also L. Harold DeWolf, *Responsible Freedom* (New York: Harper & Row, 1971), 144–95.

62. Brightman's disciples who addressed the subject of moral laws in their work include Peter A. Bertocci and Richard Millard, Walter G. Muelder, L. Harold DeWolf, Paul Deats, Jr., and J. Philip Wogaman.

63. Brightman, *Moral Laws*, 95.

64. Ibid.

65. Ibid., 35–45.

66. Ibid., 45.

67. Ibid.

68. In a recent text on the role of political personalism during the 1960s, James Farrell instead contends that Brightman's *Moral Laws* was essentially an effort to develop "a social ethics of personalism" (*The Spirit of the Sixties: The Making of Postwar Radicalism* [New York: Routledge, 1977, 13]). Although well intentioned, this is not completely accurate. This was Brightman's major systematic work on axiology (study of value). He was primarily concerned to develop a process for responsible moral deliberation. Indeed, in that text he opens the door to, but does not explicitly develop, the category of social cooperation or devotion, which one would expect to find in a text on social ethics. The category of social cooperation was anticipated in the work of Brightman's personalist contemporary Francis J. McConnell. (See, for example, his *Christian Ideal and Social Control* [Chicago: University of Chicago Press, 1932].) And it was two of Brightman's students, Muelder and DeWolf, who explicitly developed and added communal laws to the moral law system. Muelder was expressly concerned to develop a text on Christian social ethics, and thus devoted a considerable amount of energy and space to discussing laws of community.

69. Muelder, "Martin Luther King, Jr., and the Moral Laws," lecture, given at Morehouse College, March 24, 1983, 2.

70. Ibid.

71. See King, *Trumpet of Conscience*, 70–71.

72. Muelder, "Martin Luther King, Jr., and the Moral Laws," 3.

73. King, "Personalism of J. M. E. McTaggart," in *The Papers*, 2:72, 72n.20.

74. King *might* have known about the Metaphysical Law and the Communitarian Laws which were added by DeWolf and Muelder, although he does not mention these explicitly in his writings, speeches, and sermons. Muelder published his version of these laws in *Moral Law in Christian Social Ethics* (1966), and DeWolf in *Responsible Freedom: Guidelines for Christian Action* (1971). Since Muelder's version of the moral law system was published *before* King was murdered, it is at least conceivable, although not probable, that he knew about the introduction of communitarian laws. It is not probable because by 1966 the civil rights movement was in serious trouble, and King was increasingly being pulled into the peace movement, particularly protests against the war in Vietnam. In addition, his bouts with depression were both increasing and more frequent by this time. Peace of mind was a rare commodity for him. It is therefore not likely that King was able to keep up with formal academic changes being made to Brightman's moral law system. However, King was from the beginning to the end of his ministry adamant that God creates persons to be in relationship, and to live in the Kingdom of God or the community of love. Therefore, even if he was not aware of the newly added laws of community contributed by DeWolf and Muelder, there is no question that the idea fostered by each of these laws was very important to his ministry and leadership in the civil rights movement.

75. See Paul Deats, Jr., "Conflict and Reconciliation in Communitarian Social Ethics," in *The Boston Personalist Tradition in Philosophy, Social Ethics, and Theology*, eds. Deats and Carol Robb (Macon, Ga.: Mercer University Press, 1986), 273–85.

Note that in his otherwise instructive book on King, Luther D. Ivory misleadingly claims that the "*Moral Law System* consisted of five sets of laws," and that King was influenced by this system (*Toward a Theology of Radical Involvement*, 51). As we have seen, this goes to the issue of historical accuracy. In order to support his discussion on the moral laws and their influence on King, Ivory unfortunately appealed uncritically to the Master of Theological Studies thesis written by Brian Kane in 1985 on the Boston personalist influence on King ("The Influence of Boston Personalism on the Thought of Dr. Martin Luther King, Jr.," MTS thesis, Boston University, 1985). There is no evidence that Ivory himself actually read the primary sources on personalistic moral laws. He therefore follows, and takes as his own understanding, Kane's contention that King was influenced by five sets of moral laws plus the Metaphysical Law. Ivory based his claims on secondary source information about the moral law system. This is unfortunate, inasmuch as it skewed some aspects of his discussion on the influence of the moral law system on King. Therefore, where Kane erred, Ivory did as well. This notwithstanding, Ivory is quite correct in pointing to the influence of the moral law system, in general, on King. However, to imply that King was influenced by the Metaphysical Law and the other five sets of moral laws, implying his familiarity with them all, is misleading at best.

76. Brightman, *Moral Laws*, 204.

77. Ibid. (emphasis added).

78. McConnell was also a personalist who studied under Bowne, and was a contemporary of Brightman. See McConnell, *Personal Christianity* (New York: Fleming H. Revell, 1914), 48, and entirety of lecture 1, "The Personal in Christianity." The book comprises the Cole Lectures for 1914 delivered at Vanderbilt University.

79. Brightman, *Moral Laws*, 94 (emphasis added).

80. Muelder, *Moral Law in Christian Social Ethics*, 119.

81. Ibid., 119–20.

82. Deats, "Conflict and Reconciliation," 285.

83. Ibid.

Chapter 8.   Use of Moral Laws and the Vietnam War

1. Burrow, *Personalism*, 218–22.

2. George W. Davis, "Liberalism and a Theology of Depth," *Crozer Quarterly* 28, no. 3 (July 1951): 200.

3. See L. H. Marshall, *The Challenge of New Testament Ethics* (New York: Macmillan, 1947), 16–17. Marshall argued that one of the chief religious premises of Jesus was his assumption of the existence of God the Creator of the universe who cares about all of creation, especially persons. Jesus therefore held that the Universe is friendly, rather than hostile to persons.

4. Davis, "Liberalism and a Theology of Depth," 201.

5. King, "Rediscovering Lost Values," in *Knock at Midnight*, 12.

6. Ibid, 10.

7. See Immanuel Kant, *Critique of Practical Reason*, trans. with an introduction by Lewis White Beck (1788; reprint, Indianapolis: Bobbs-Merrill, 1956), 166.

8. King, "Rediscovering Lost Values," 11–12.

9. Ibid., 12.

10. Brightman, *Introduction to Philosophy*, chap. 2, "How Can We Distinguish Truth from Error?" esp. 50–58.

11. King, "Rediscovering Lost Values," 12–13.

12. My daughter, Sheronn Lynn, a lawyer, is the source of this information that she discovered while engaged in legal research.

13. King, "Rediscovering Lost Values," 14.

14. Parker, "Of Justice and the Conscience," 2:44.

15. King, "Facing the Challenge of a New Age," in *Testament of Hope*, 141.

16. King, "Rediscovering Lost Values," 15.

17. King, "Death of Evil Upon the Seashore," in *Strength to Love*, 64.

18. See King's examination answers for Davis's course Christian Theology for Today, September 13, 1949 to February 15, 1950, in *The Papers*, 1:294.

19. King, "Rediscovering Lost Values," 15.

20. Ibid., 18.

21. Alfred North Whitehead, *Process and Reality*, ed. David Ray Griffin and Donald W. Sherburne (1929; reprint, New York: Free Press, 1978), 351.

22. King, "Death of Evil Upon the Seashore," 64.

23. King, "A Knock at Midnight," sermon preached at All Saints Community Church, Los Angeles, June 25, 1967, King Library & Archives, 6.

24. King, "Paul's Letter to American Churches," in *Knock at Midnight*, 34.

25. King, "Loving Your Enemies," in *Knock at Midnight*, 41.

26. Quoted in King, "A Time to Break Silence," in *Testament of Hope*, 243.

27. King, "Paul's Letter to American Christians," in *Knock at Midnight*, 35.

28. King, "Our God Is Able," 105.

29. King, "Loving Your Enemies," in *Knock at Midnight*, 44.

30. King, "A Christmas Sermon on Peace," in *Testament of Hope*, 255.

31. Brightman, *Moral Laws*, 98.

32. See my *Personalism* for a discussion on Muelder's lecture on King and the moral laws, 219–20.

33. Dr. Muelder sent me a copy of this lecture.

34. King, *Stride Toward Freedom*, 95.

35. Ibid. Reflecting on this earlier stance in 1967 King said that the destructive potential of modern day weapons "eliminates even the possibility that war may serve any good at all." See King, *Where Do We Go From Here?* 183.

36. King, *Where Do We Go From Here?* 183.

37. King, "When Peace Becomes Obnoxious," sermon delivered at Dexter Avenue Baptist Church, March 18, 1956, in *The Papers*, 3:208.

38. Robert F. Williams, "Can Negroes Afford to Be Pacifists," in *Seeds of Liberation*, ed. Paul Goodman (New York: George Braziller, 1964), 277.

39. King, "The Social Organization of Nonviolence" (A Reply to Robert F. Williams), in Goodman, *Seeds of Liberation*, 286.

40. See transcription of conversation with Vincent Harding in *Voices of Freedom: An Oral History of the Civil Rights Movement from the 1950s through the 1980s* by Henry Hampton and Steve Fayer, with Sarah Flynn (New York: Bantam Books, 1990), 337.

41. See Adam Fairclough, *Martin Luther King, Jr.* (Athens: University of Georgia Press, 1990), chap. 7; Fairclough, "Martin Luther King, Jr., and the War in Vietnam," in *The African American Voice in U.S. Foreign Policy Since World War II*, ed. Michael L. Krenn (New York: Garland Publishing, 1999), 255–75, originally published in *Phylon* 45, no. 1 (1984): 19–39; Oates, *Let the Trumpet Sound*, 373–82; and Garrow, *Bearing the Cross*, 541–59.

42. Fairclough, "King and the War in Vietnam," 258; Fairclough, *To Redeem the Soul of America: The Southern Christian Leadership Conference & Martin Luther King, Jr.* (1987; reprint, Athens: University of Georgia Press, 2001), chap. 13, "The Politics of Peace."

43. Frederick Douglass, "How to End the War," in *The Life and Writings of Frederick Douglass: The Civil War*, ed. Philip S. Foner (New York: International Publishers, 1975), 3:94–96; W. E. B. DuBois, "Close Ranks," *Crisis* (July 1918): 111. See also his "A Pageant in Seven Decades," in *W. E. B. DuBois Speaks: Speeches and Addresses, 1890–1919*, ed. Philip S. Foner (New York: Pathfinder Press, 1982), 62. In this selection DuBois also expressed his disillusion once he became aware of the racism to which black soldiers were subjected by U.S. officers, as well as French and German troops.

44. Quoted in Garrow, *Bearing the Cross*, 543. It should be noted that King himself said that while he was in Jamaica working on *Where Do We Go From Here?* he read a magazine article entitled

"The Children of Vietnam." (See Carson, *Autobiography of Martin Luther King, Jr.*, 335.) Lee's version is that King read the article at the airport before boarding the plane to Jamaica.

45. Fairclough, *To Redeem the Soul of America*, 334.

46. Carson, *Autobiography of Martin Luther King, Jr.*, 335.

47. Fairclough, *To Redeem the Soul of America*, 334.

48. Carson, *Autobiography of Martin Luther King, Jr.*, 334.

49. See transcription of Dorothy Cotton's statement in *Voices of Freedom*, 341.

50. Alan F. Westin and Barry Mahoney, *The Trial of Martin Luther King* (New York: Thomas Y. Crowell, 1974), 242.

51. Abraham J. Heschel, *The Prophets* (New York: Harper & Row, 1962), 139.

52. Lewis V. Baldwin, *To Make the Wounded Whole* (Minneapolis: Fortress Press, 1992), 272.

53. Brightman, *An Introduction to Philosophy*, 41.

54. See my fuller discussion on personalistic methodology and criterion of truth in my *Personalism*, chap. 5, "Personalistic Method and Criterion of Truth."

55. Brightman, *An Introduction to Philosophy*, 42. What Alfred N. Whitehead called the "method of imaginative rationalization" is quite similar to Brightman's analogy of the flight of the arrow of intelligibility as a means of characterizing synoptic method. Reflecting on Bacon's rigid method of induction, Whitehead writes: "What Bacon omitted was the play of a free imagination, controlled by the requirements of coherence and logic. The true method of discovery is like the flight of an aeroplane. It starts from the ground of particular observation; it makes a flight in the thin air of imaginative generalization; and it again lands for renewed observation rendered acute by rational interpretation" (see Whitehead, *Process and Reality*, 5).

56. King, "Nobel Prize Acceptance Speech," in *Testament of Hope*, 226.

57. Charles E. Fager, "Dilemma for Dr. King," *Christian Century* (March 16, 1966): 332.

58. Quoted in Garrow, *Bearing the Cross*, 555.

59. While my concern is King's sense of the need to work at those things that will lead to social righteousness, I am not unmindful that some of his reflections might well have had more to do with his own sense of having fallen short in the area of personal morality. One gets this sense, for example, from statements he made in the sermon "Unfulfilled Dreams," preached on March 3, 1968 at Ebenezer Baptist Church, just one month before he was assassinated. He seemed to have been trying to put the best spin on some of his own questionable moral behaviors. He said: "In the final analysis, God does not judge us by the separate incidents or the separate mistakes that we make, but by the total bent of our lives. In the final analysis, God knows that his children are weak and they are frail. In the final analysis, what God requires is that your heart is right. Salvation isn't reaching the destination of absolute morality, but it's being in the process and on the right road" (See "Unfulfilled Dreams," in *A Knock at Midnight*, 196). See also Burns, *To the Mountaintop*, 217, 226, 260. Burns frequently returns to this and the related theme of King's deepening depression.

60. King, *Stride Toward Freedom*, 161, 187, 190.

61. Quoted in Garrow, *Bearing the Cross*, 554.

62. Ibid., 551.

63. Muelder, "Martin Luther King, Jr.'s Ethics of Non-Violent Action," lecture, King Center for Social Change, Atlanta, March 2, 1985, 9.

64. In the discussion that follows, the number in parenthesis following a law is to Brightman's text, *Moral Laws* (New York: Abingdon Press, 1933). When appropriate, reference may be made to laws contributed by Muelder in his *Moral Law in Christian Social Ethics* (Richmond, Va.: John Knox Press, 1966). The parenthetical page numbers are to this text.

65. This speech is reprinted in *A Testament of Hope*, 231–44.

66. King, "A Time to Break Silence," 233.

67. King, *Where Do We Go From Here?* 183.

68. King, "A Time to Break Silence," 234.

69. See King, "Letter from Birmingham City Jail," 84–86.

70. King, "A Time to Break Silence," 241.

71. Carson, *Autobiography of Martin Luther King, Jr.*, 336.

72. Quoted in Cone, *Martin & Malcolm & America*, 242–43.

73. King, "*Playboy* Interview," 344.

74. King, "A Time to Break Silence," 243.

75. Ibid., 242.

76. Ansbro, *Martin Luther King, Jr.*, 82.

77. Ibid.

78. King, "A New Sense of Direction," *Worldview* (April 1972): 8 (published posthumously).

79. Ibid.

80. King, "Shattered Dreams," in *Strength to Love*, 83.

81. Quoted from Theodor Lipps, *Die ethischen Grundfragen* (Leipzig: Voss, 1922), 153.

82. Lewis V. Baldwin, "American Political Traditions and the Christian Faith," in his *Legacy of Martin Luther King, Jr.: The Boundaries of Law, Politics, and Religion* with Rufus Burrow, Jr., Barbara A. Holmes, and Susan Holmes Winfield (Notre Dame, Ind.: University of Notre Dame Press, 2002), 147.

83. King, "Three Dimensions of a Complete Life," in *Strength to Love*, 69.

84. King, "Antidotes for Fear," in *Strength to Love*, 111. See Erich Fromm, *The Art of Loving* (New York: Harper & Brothers, 1956), esp. 58–59.

85. Immanuel Kant, *Lectures on Ethics*, translated Louis Infield, with an introduction by J. Macmurray (New York: Century Company, 1930), 118.

86. Ibid., 117.

87. King, "Three Dimensions of a Complete Life," in *Strength to Love*, 71.

88. Ibid., 70.

89. Ansbro, *Martin Luther King, Jr.*, 85.

90. King, "Three Dimensions of a Complete Life," in *Strength to Love*, 71.

91. Ibid., 72, 73.

92. King, "Time to Break Silence," in *A Testament of Hope*, 242.

93. King, "Three Dimensions of a Complete Life," 72.

94. King, "Time to Break Silence," 239–40.

95. King, "Face to Face," television news Interview, in *Testament of Hope*, 408.

96. See King, "Face to Face," 408. Here King tells a questioner that despite having broken silence on Vietnam, he stll spends 95 percent of his time and energy on civil rights.

97. King, "Time to Break Silence," 234.

98. King, "A Christmas Sermon on Peace," in *Testament of Hope*, 254.

99. King, "Face to Face," 408.

100. King, "A Time to Break Silence," 241.

101. Ansbro, *Martin Luther King, Jr.*, 86.

102. King, "Three Dimensions of a Complete Life," 73.

103. Muelder, *Moral Law in Christian Social Ethics*, 124.

104. King, "Three Dimensions of a Complete Life," 75.

Chapter 9. The Universe Is Friendly: Social-Ethical Implications

1. See Frederick B. Fisher, *That Strange Little Brown Man: Gandhi* (New York: Ray Long & Richard R. Smith, 1932), 99.

2. King, "The Un-Christian Christian," *Ebony* (August 1965): 77.

3. See my *Personalism*, 78–80; idem, "John Wesley Edward Bowen: First Afrikan American Personalist," *Encounter* 56, no. 2 (Summer 1995): 241–60 and "The Personalism of John Wesley Edward Bowen," *Journal of Negro History* 82, no. 2 (Spring 1997): 244–56.

4. Bowne, *Personalism*, 300–301.

5. See my discussion of the importance of metaphysics for black liberation theology in my *James H. Cone and Black Liberation Theology* (Jefferson, N.C.: McFarland, 1994), 196–202.

6. King, "Lost Sheep," sermon, Ebenezer Baptist Church, September 18, 1966, King Library and Archives, 6.

7. Ibid., 6, 8.

8. See Philip M. Dauber and Richard A. Muller, "Stars Are Us" (chap. 3), in *The Three Big Bangs* (Reading, Mass.: Addison-Wesley, 1996).

9. Brightman, *An Introduction to Philosophy* (New York: Henry Holt, 1925), 364.

10. See Jewelle Taylor Gibbs, "The New Morbidity: Homicide, Suicide, Accidents, and Life-Threatening Behaviors" (chap. 8), in *Young, Black, and Male in America: An Endangered Species*, ed. Gibbs (New York: Auburn House, 1988).

11. King, "A Gift of Love," in *A Testament of Hope*, ed. James M. Washington (New York: Harper & Row, 1986), 62–63 (emphasis added). This was a problem that Malcolm X was familiar with as well, insisting as he did on the need for blacks to be taught how to be nonviolent toward each other rather than whites. See Steve Clark, ed., *Malcolm X Talks to Young People: Speeches in the U.S., Britain & Africa* (New York: Pathfinder, 1991), 50–51, and *The Negro Protest: James Baldwin, Malcolm X, and Martin Luther King Talk with Kenneth B. Clark* (Boston: Beacon Press, 1963), 26.

12. Carson, *Autobiography of Martin Luther King, Jr.*, 313.

13. See Andrew Hacker's helpful discussion of this point in his *Two Nations*.

14. King, *Measure of a Man*, 13–14.

15. Bowne, *Metaphysics*, 405.

16. George Breitman, ed., *Malcolm X Speaks* (1965; reprint, New York: Pathfinder Press, 1989), 40.

17. King, *Where Do We Go From Here?* 102–3.

18. King, "Is the Universe Friendly?" 3.

19. King, *Where Do We Go From Here?* 119.

20. Bowne, *Principles of Ethics*, 305.

21. King, *Where Do We Go From Here?* 99.

22. Ibid., 122.

23. Ibid., 97.

24. Ibid., 43–44.

25. Ibid., 123.

26. See my discussion of this in *James H. Cone and Black Liberation Theology*, chap. 1, "The Origins of Black Theology."

27. King, "Where Do We Go From Here?" in *Testament of Hope*, 245.

28. King, "Testament of Hope," in *Testament of Hope*, 318. See also King, *Where Do We Go From Here?* 53.

29. See King, *Where Do We Go From Here?* 41–44, chap. 4, "The Dilemma of Negro Americans."

30. King, *Where Do We Go From Here?* 110.

31. Ibid., 77.

32. In his last speech, the night before he was assassinated, King characterized Lincoln in this way. See "I See the Promised Land," in *Testament of Hope*, 279.

33. King, *Where Do We Go From Here?* 150–51.

34. Justo L. González, *Mañana: Christian Theology from a Hispanic Perspective* (Nashville: Abingdon Press, 1990), 36.

35. See Ana María Díaz-Stevens and Anthony M. Stevens-Arroyo, *Recognizing the Latino Resurgence in U.S. Religion: The Emmaus Paradigm* (Boulder, Colo.: Westview Press, 1998), 20–26.

36. Theodore Cross, *The Black Power Imperative: Racial Inequality and the Politics of Nonviolence* (New York: Faulkner Books, 1987), 705–6. Cross's is a prodigious study that fosters much critical social analysis. However, there are two primary defects in his massive work. First, not in itself problematic, he is a white male progressive liberal of the 1960s era. However, when this is connected with his assumption—the assumption of many white liberal progressive types in this country—that the political-economic structure in this country is essentially sound and needs only reforms, whether minor or major, we have a serious problem. Relatedly, and the second concern with his text, is that Cross does not take seriously enough the possibility that the capitalist political economy itself needs to be replaced with a system whose vision is based on sharing and equality rather than rugged individualism. This notwithstanding, it is also appropriate to say that this book provides clear and helpful social analysis of Afrikan Americans' predicament in this country. It also provides copious empirical data to support his discussion of the causes of black oppression.

37. Ibid., 707.

38. Malcolm X, in *The Negro Protest*, 21–22.

Afterword. An Appreciation

1. King, *Stride Toward Freedom*, 100.

2. See C. Eric Lincoln and Paul Deats, Jr., "Walter G. Muelder: An Appreciation of His Life, Thought, and Ministry," in *Toward a Discipline of Social Ethics: Essays in Honor of Walter George Muelder*, ed. Paul Deats, Jr. (Boston: Boston University Press, 1972), 12–13.

3. This is quoted by permission of Mrs. Linda Muelder Schell, youngest daughter of Dr. Muelder, and dated June 16, 2004. At my request Mrs. Schell kindly sent me a copy of the letter.

4. See *The United Methodist Newscope* (the weekly newsletter for United Methodist Leaders), 32; no. 30 (July 16, 2004), 8.

S E L E C T
B I B L I O G R A P H Y

Abernathy, Ralph David. *And the Walls Came Tumbling Down: An Autobiography.* New York: Harper & Row, 1989.

Allen, Zita. *Black Women Leaders of the Civil Rights Movement.* New York: African American Experience, A Division of Grolier Publishing, 1996.

Ansbro, John J. *Martin Luther King, Jr.: The Making of a Mind.* Maryknoll, N.Y.: Orbis Books, 1982. Reissued as *Martin Luther King, Jr.: Nonviolent Strategies and Tactics for Social Change.* New York: Madison Books, 2000.

Aptheker, Herbert, ed. *The Correspondence of W. E. B. DuBois.* Vol. 3. Amherst: University of Massachusetts Press, 1978.

Baker, Ella. "Developing Community Leadership." In *Black Women in White America: A Documentary History,* edited by Gerda Lerner, 345–52. New York: Vintage Books, 1973.

Baker-Fletcher, Garth. *Somebodyness: Martin Luther King, Jr., and the Theory of Dignity.* Minneapolis: Fortress Press, 1993.

Baldwin, James. "In Search of a Majority" in *Nobody Knows My Name,* 107–14. 1954. Reprint, New York: Dell, 1961.

Baldwin, Lewis V. *The Legacy of Martin Luther King, Jr.: The Boundaries of Law, Politics, and Religion.* With Rufus Burrow, Jr., Barbara A. Holmes, and Susan Holmes Winfield. Notre Dame, Ind.: University of Notre Dame Press, 2002.

Baldwin, Lewis V. *Toward the Beloved Community: Martin Luther King, Jr., and South Africa.* Cleveland: Pilgrim Press, 1995.

———. *To Make the Wounded Whole: The Cultural Legacy of Martin Luther King, Jr.* Minneapolis: Fortress Press, 1992.

———. *There Is a Balm in Gilead: The Cultural Roots of Martin Luther King, Jr.* Minneapolis: Fortress Press, 1991.

——— and Amiri YaSin Al-Hadid. *Between Cross and Crescent: Christian and Muslim Perspectives on Malcolm and Martin.* Gainesville: University Press of Florida, 2002.

Bennett, Lerone, Jr. *What Manner of Man: A Biography of Martin Luther King, Jr.* 1964. Reprint, Chicago: Johnson Publishing, 1968.

Bertocci, Peter A., and Richard M. Millard. *Personality and the Good: Psychological and Ethical Perspectives.* New York: David McKay, 1963.

Billingsley, Andrew. *Mighty Like a River: The Black Church and Social Reform.* New York: Oxford University Press, 1999.

———. *Climbing Jacob's Ladder: The Enduring Legacy of African-American Families.* New York: Simon & Schuster, 1992.

Bishop, Jim. *The Days of Martin Luther King, Jr.* New York: G. P. Putnam's Sons, 1971.

Bowne, Borden P. *The Essence of Religion.* Boston: Houghton Mifflin, 1910.

———. "Woman and Democracy." *North American Review* 119 (April 1910): 527–36.

———. *Studies in Christianity.* Boston: Houghton Mifflin, 1909.

———. *Personalism.* Boston: Houghton Mifflin, 1908.

———. *Theism.* New York: American Book, 1902.

———. *Metaphysics.* 1882. Revised edition. New York: Harper & Brothers, 1898.

———. *The Theory of Thought and Knowledge.* New York: Harper & Brothers, 1897.

———. "The Speculative Significant of Freedom." *Methodist Review* 77 (September 1895): 681–97.

———. *The Principles of Ethics.* New York: Harper & Brothers, 1892.

———. *The Philosophy of Theism.* New York: Harper & Brothers, 1887.

———. *Studies in Theism.* New York: Phillips and Hunt, 1879.

———. *The Philosophy of Herbert Spencer.* New York: Hunt & Eaton, 1874.

Branch, Taylor. *Parting the Waters: America in the King Years, 1954–63.* New York: Simon & Schuster, 1988.

Breitman, George, ed. *Malcolm X Speaks.* 1965. Reprint, New York: Pathfinder Press, 1989.

Brightman, Edgar S. *An Introduction to Philosophy.* 1925. Reprint, New York: Henry Holt, 1951; third edition, Robert N. Beck, 1964.

———. *Nature and Values.* Nashville, Tenn.: Abingdon-Cokesbury, 1945.

———. *A Philosophy of Religion.* Englewood Cliffs, N.J.: Prentice Hall, 1940.

———. *Personality and Religion.* New York: Abingdon Press, 1934.

———. *Moral Laws.* Nashville, Tenn.: Abingdon Press, 1933.

———. "Religion as Truth." In *Contemporary American Theology: Theological Autobiographies,* edited by Vergilius Ferm, 53–81. New York: Round Table Press, Inc., 1932.

———. *The Finding of God.* New York: Abingdon Press, 1931.

———. *The Problem of God.* New York: Abingdon Press, 1930.

———. *A Philosophy of Ideals.* New York: Henry Holt, 1928.

———. *Religious Values.* New York: Abingdon Press, 1925.

Burks, Mary Fair. "Trailblazers: Women in the Montgomery Bus Boycott." In *Women in the Civil Rights Movement: Trailblazers and Torchbearers 1941–1965,* edited by Vicki L. Crawford, Jacqueline Anne Rouse, and Barbara Woods, 71–83. Bloomington and Indianapolis: Indiana University Press, 1993.

Burns, Stewart. *To the Mountaintop: Martin Luther King, Jr.'s Sacred Mission to Save America, 1955–1968.* San Francisco: HarperSanFrancisco, 2004.

Burrow, Rufus, Jr. "W. E. B. DuBois and the Intersection of Race and Sex in the Twenty-First Century." In *W. E. B. DuBois and Race: Essays Celebrating the Centennial Publication of the Souls of Black Folk*, edited by Chester J. Fontenot and Mary Alice Morgan, with Sarah Gardner, 122–41. Macon, Ga.: Mercer University Press, 2001.

———. "Martin Luther King, Jr. and the Objective Moral Order: Some Ethical Implications." *Encounter* 61, no. 2 (Spring 2000): 219–44.

———. *Personalism: A Critical Introduction.* St. Louis: Chalice Press, 1999.

———. "Some African American Males' Perspectives on the Black Woman." In *Black Men on Race, Gender, and Sexuality: A Critical Reader*, edited by Devon W. Carbado, 390–407. New York: New York University Press, 1999.

———. "Borden P. Bowne's Contribution to Theistic Finitism." *Personalist Forum* 13, no. 2 (Fall 1997): 122–42.

———. "Authorship: The Personalism of George Holmes Howison and Borden Parker Bowne." *Personalist Forum* 13, no. 2 (Fall 1997): 287–303.

———. "The Personalism of John Wesley Edward Bowen." *Journal of Negro History* 82, no. 2 (Spring 1997): 244–56.

———. "John Wesley Edward Bowen: First Afrikan American Personalist." *Encounter* 56, no. 2 (Summer 1995): 214–30.

———. *James H. Cone and Black Liberation Theology.* Jefferson, N.C.: McFarland, 1994.

———. "Borden Parker Bowne's Doctrine of God." *Encounter* 53, no. 4 (Autumn 1992): 381–400.

———. "Moral Laws in Borden P. Bowne's *Principles of Ethics*." *Personalist Forum*, 6, no. 2 (Fall 1990): 161–80.

Cadoux, Cecil J. *The Early Church and the World: A History of the Christian Attitude to Pagan Society and the State Down to the Time of Constantinus.* Edinburgh: T & T Clark, 1955.

Carson, Clayborne, ed. *The Papers of Martin Luther King, Jr.* Five vols. Berkeley: University of California Press, 1992, 1994, 1997, 2000, 2005.

Carson, Clayborne, and Peter Holloran, eds. *A Knock at Midnight.* New York: Warner Books, 1998.

Carter, Paul A. *The Decline and Revival of the Social Gospel: Social and Political Liberalism in American Protestant Churches, 1920–1940.* Ithaca, N.Y.: Cornell University Press, 1954.

Cartwright, John. "Foundations of the Beloved Community." *Debate and Understanding* 1, no. 3 (1977): 171–78.

Chinula, Donald M. *Building King's Beloved Community: Foundations for Pastoral Care and Counseling with the Oppressed.* Cleveland: United Church Press, 1997.

Clark, Steve, ed. *Malcolm X Talks to Young People: Speeches in the U.S., Britain & Africa.* New York: Pathfinder, 1991.

Collins, David R. *Not Only Dreamers: The Story of Martin Luther King, Sr., and Martin Luther King, Jr.* Elgin, Ill.: Brethren Press, 1986.

Cone, James H. *Martin & Malcolm & America: A Dream or a Nightmare.* Maryknoll, N.Y.: Orbis Books, 1991.

———. "New Roles in the Ministry: A Theological Appraisal." In *Black Theology: A Documentary History, 1966–1979*, edited by Cone and Gayraud Wilmore, 389–97. Maryknoll, N.Y.: Orbis Books, 1979.

————. *God of the Oppressed.* New York: Seabury Press, 1975.

Crawford, Vicki, Jacqueline A. Rouse, and Barbara Woods, eds. *Women in the Civil Rights Movement.* Bloomington: Indiana University Press, 1990.

Cross, Theodore. *The Black Power Imperative: Racial Inequality and the Politics of Nonviolence.* New York: Faulkner Books, 1987.

Dallard, Shyrlee. *Ella Baker: A Leader behind the Scenes.* New York: Silver Burdett Press, 1990.

Davis, Angela Y. *Women, Race & Class.* New York: Vintage Books, 1983.

Davis, George Washington. "Liberalism and a Theology of Depth." *Crozer Quarterly* 28, no. 3 (July 1951): 198–206.

Deats, Paul, Jr., "Conflict and Reconciliation in Communitarian Social Ethics." In *The Boston Personalist Tradition in Philosophy, Social Ethics, and Theology,* edited by Deats and Carol Robb, 273–85. Macon, Ga.: Mercer University Press, 1986.

Derman-Sparks, Louise, and Carol Brunson Phillips. *Teaching/Learning Anti-Racism: A Developmental Approach.* New York: Teachers College Press, Columbia University, 1997.

DeWolf, L. Harold. *Responsible Freedom: Guidelines for Christian Action.* New York: Harper & Row, 1971.

Dorrien, Gary J. *The Making of American Liberal Theology: Idealism, Realism, & Modernity, 1900–1950.* Louisville, Ky.: Westminster John Knox Press, 2003.

————. *The Making of American Liberal Theology: Imagining Progressive Religion, 1805–1900.* Louisville, Ky.: Westminster John Knox Press, 2001.

————. *Soul in Society: The Making and Renewal of Social Christianity.* Minneapolis: Fortress Press, 1995.

D'Souza, Dinesh. *The End of Racism: Principles for a Multiracial Society.* New York: Free Press, 1995.

DuBois, W. E. B. *Darkwater: Voices from within the Veil.* New York: Harcourt, Brace & Howe, 1920.

Dyson, Michael Eric. *I May Not Get There with You: The True Martin Luther King, Jr.* New York: Free Press, 2000.

Ellison, John Malcus. *They Who Preach.* Nashville, Tenn.: Broadman Press, 1956.

English, James W. *The Prophet of Wheat Street.* 1967. Reprint, Elgin, Ill.: David C. Cook, 1973.

Eze, Emmanuel Chukwudi. "Western Philosophy and African Colonialism." In *African Philosophy: An Anthology,* edited by Eze, 213–21. Oxford: Blackwell Publishers, 1998.

Fager, Charles E. "Dilemma for Dr. King." *Christian Century* (March 16, 1966): 331–32.

Fairclough, Adam. *To Redeem the Soul of America: The Southern Christian Leadership Conference & Martin Luther King, Jr.* 1987. Reprint, Athens: University of Georgia Press, 2001.

————. "Martin Luther King, Jr. and the War in Vietnam." In *The African American Voice in U.S. Foreign Policy Since World War II,* edited by Michael L. Krenn, 255–75. New York: Garland, 1999.

————. *Martin Luther King, Jr.* Athens: University of Georgia Press, 1990.

Farrell, James J. *The Spirit of the Sixties: The Making of Postwar Radicalism.* New York: Routledge, 1997.

Feagin, Joe R. *Racist America: Roots, Current Realities, and Future Reparations.* New York: Routledge, 2000.

Fisher, Frederick B. *That Strange Little Brown Man: Gandhi.* New York: Ray Long & Richard R. Smith, 1932.

Flewelling, Ralph Tyler. *Personalism and the Problems of Philosophy: An Appreciation of the Work of Borden Parker Bowne.* New York: Methodist Book Concern, 1915.

Forman, James. *The Making of Black Revolutionaries: A Personal Account.* New York: Macmillan, 1972.

Gandhi, M. K. *Nonviolent Resistance,* edited by Bharatan Kumarappa. New York: Schocken Books, 1961.

Gardner, E. Clinton. *Biblical Faith and Social Ethics.* New York: Harper & Row, 1960.

Garrow, David J. "The Intellectual Development of Martin Luther King, Jr.: Influences and Commentaries." In *Martin Luther King, Jr. and the Civil Rights Movement,* edited by Garrow, 2:438–51. New York: Carlson Publishers, 1989.

———. *Bearing the Cross: Martin Luther King, Jr. and the Southern Christian Leadership Conference.* New York: William Morrow, 1986.

Gibbs, Jewelle Taylor. "The New Morbidity: Homicide, Suicide, Accidents, and Life- Threatening Behaviors." Chapter 8 in *Young, Black, and Male in America: An Endangered Species,* edited by Gibbs. New York: Auburn House, 1988,

Giddings, Paula. *When and Where I Enter: The Impact of Black Women on Race and Sex in America.* New York: William Morrow, 1984.

Gilson, Étienne. *God and Philosophy.* New Haven, Conn.: Yale University Press, 1941.

———. *The Spirit of Medieval Philosophy.* New York: Scribner's, 1936.

Gossett, Thomas F. *The History of an Idea in America.* Dallas: Southern Methodist University Press, 1963.

Grant, Joanne. *Ella Baker: Freedom Bound.* New York: Wiley & Sons, 1998.

Gyekye, Kwame. *An Essay on African Philosophical Thought: The Akan Conceptual Scheme.* 1987. Revised edition, Philadelphia: Temple University Press, 1995.

Hacker, Andrew. *Two Nations: Black and White, Separate, Hostile, Unequal.* 1992. Reprint, New York: Ballantine Books, 1995.

Handy, Robert T., ed. *The Social Gospel in America: Gladden, Ely, Rauschenbusch.* New York: Oxford University Press, 1966.

Hartshorne, Charles. *Omnipotence and Other Theological Mistakes.* New York: State University of New York Press, 1984.

Haskins, Lotte, ed. *"I Have a Dream": The Quotations of Martin Luther King, Jr.* New York: Grossett & Dunlap, 1968.

Hatcher, William E. *John Jasper: The Unmatched Negro Philosopher and Preacher.* New York: Fleming H. Revell, 1908.

Headley, Joel Tyler. *The Great Riots of New York, 1712–1873.* E. B. Treat, New York, 1873. Reprint, Indianapolis: Bobbs-Merrill, 1970.

Heschel, Abraham J. *The Prophets.* New York: Harper & Row, 1962.

———. *God in Search of Man.* New York: Harper Torchbooks, 1955.

Hine, Darlene Clark, and Kathleen Thompson. *A Shining Thread of Hope: The History of Black Women in America.* New York: Broadway Books, 1998.

Hopkins, Charles Howard. *The Rise of the Social Gospel in American Protestantism.* New Haven, Conn.: Yale University Press, 1940.

Humphrey, Zephine. *The Beloved Community.* New York: E. P. Dutton, 1930.

Ivory, Luther D. *Toward a Theology of Radical Involvement: The Theological Legacy of Martin Luther King, Jr.* Nashville, Tenn.: Abingdon, 1997.

Johnson, Paul. *Christian Love.* Nashville, Tenn.: Abingdon-Cokesbury Press, 1951.

Jones, Major J. *The Color of God: The Concept of God in Afro-American Thought.* Macon, Ga.: Mercer University Press, 1987.

Jones, William R. *Is God a White Racist?* Garden City, N.Y.: Doubleday, 1973. Reprint, Boston: Beacon Press, 1998.

Kant, Immanuel. *Critique of Practical Reason.* 1788. Translated with an introduction by Lewis White Beck. Indianapolis: Bobbs-Merrill, 1956.

———. *Lectures on Ethics.* Translated by Louis Infield, with an introduction by J. Macmurray. New York: Century Company, 1930.

Kaufmann, Walter. "Existentialism from Dostoevsky to Sartre" in *Existentialism from Dostoevsky to Sartre*, 11–51. New York: World Publishing, 1969.

King, Coretta Scott. *My Life with Martin Luther King, Jr.* 1969. Revised edition, New York: Holt Rinehart & Winston, 1969.

King, Henry Churchill. *Seeing Life Whole: A Christian Philosophy of Life.* New York: Macmillan, 1925.

———. *The Moral and Religious Challenge of Our Times.* New York: Macmillan, 1911.

———. *The Ethics of Jesus.* New York: Macmillan, 1910.

———. *Theology and the Social Consciousness.* New York: Macmillan, 1902.

King, Martin Luther Jr. *The Autobiography of Martin Luther King, Jr.* Edited by Clayborne Carson. New York: Warner Books, 1998.

———. "A New Sense of Direction." *Worldview* (April 1972): 5–12.

———. *The Trumpet of Conscience.* New York: Harper & Row, 1968.

———. *Where Do We Go From Here: Chaos or Community?* Boston: Beacon Press, 1967.

———. "Thou Fool." Sermon, preached at Mount Pisgah Missionary Baptist Church, Chicago, August 22, 1967. King Library and Archives.

———. "A Knock at Midnight." Sermon, preached at All Saints Community Church, Los Angeles, June 25, 1967. King Library and Archives.

———. "The Prodigal Son." Sermon, preached at Ebenezer Baptist Church in Atlanta, September 4, 1966. King Library and Archives.

———. "Lost Sheep." Sermon, preached at Ebenezer Baptist Church, Atlanta, September 18, 1966. King Library and Archives.

———. "What Is Man?" Sermon, preached April 17, 1966. on WAAF-AM, Chicago. King Library and Archives.

———. "The Un-Christian Christian." *Ebony* (August 1965): 77–80.

———. "Is the Universe Friendly?" Sermon, preached at Ebenezer Baptist Church in Atlanta, December 12, 1965. King Library and Archives.

———. *Why We Can't Wait.* New York: Harper & Row, 1964.

———. "The Social Organization of Nonviolence: A Reply to Robert F. Williams." In *Seeds of Liberation*, edited by Paul Goodman, 282–86. New York: George Braziller, 1964.

———. *Strength to Love.* New York: Harper & Row, 1963.

———. *Stride Toward Freedom.* New York: Harper & Row, 1958.

———. "Desirability of Being Maladjusted." Sermon, preached in Chicago, January 13, 1958. King Library and Archives.

———. *The Measure of a Man.* 1959. Reprint, Philadelphia: Fortress Press, 1988.

———. "A Comparison of the Conceptions of God in the Thinking of Henry Nelson Wieman and Paul Tillich." Ph.D. dissertation, Boston University, 1955.

King, Martin Luther, Sr. *Daddy King: An Autobiography.* With Clayton Riley. New York: William Morrow, 1980.

Knudson, Albert C. *The Principles of Christian Ethics.* New York: Abingdon Press, 1943.

———. *The Philosophy of Personalism.* New York: Abingdon Press, 1927.

Lewis, David L. *King: A Critical Biography.* 1970. Reprint, New York: Praeger Publishers, 1978.

Ling, Peter, and Sharon Monteith, eds. *Gender in the Civil Rights Movement.* New York: Garland, 1999.

Ling, Peter. *Martin Luther King, Jr.* New York: Routledge, 2002.

Lloyd, Roger. *The Beloved Community.* London: Nisbet and Company, 1937.

Long, Michael. *Martin Luther King, Jr. on Creative Living.* St. Louis: Chalice Press, 2004.

———. *Against Us, But For Us: Martin Luther King, Jr. and the State.* Macon, Ga.: Mercer University Press, 2002.

Lotze, Rudolph Hermann. *Microcosmus: An Essay Concerning Man and His Relation to the World.* First published in 3 vols., 1856–64. Fourth edition translated by Elizabeth Hamilton and E. E. Constance Jones. Edinburgh: T & T Clark, 1885.

Luker, Ralph. *The Social Gospel in Black and White: American Racial Reform, 1885–1912.* Durham: University of North Carolina Press, 1991.

Lyght, Ernest Shaw. *The Religious and Philosophical Foundations in the Thought of Martin Luther King, Jr.* New York: Vantage Press, 1972.

Malcolm X. In *The Negro Protest: James Baldwin, Malcolm X, and Martin Luther King Talk with Kenneth Clark*, 17–32. Boston: Beacon Press, 1963.

Marable, Manning. *Black Liberation in Conservative America.* Boston: South End Press, 1997.

———. *Speaking Truth to Power: Essays on Race, Resistance, and Radicalism.* Boulder, Colo.: Westview Press, 1996.

———. "Grounding with My Sisters: Patriarchy and the Exploitation of Black Women." Chapter 4 in *How Capitalism Underdeveloped Black America*. Boston: South End Press, 1983.

Marshall, L. H. *The Challenge of New Testament Ethics.* New York: Macmillan, 1947, chapter 1.

Mathews, Shailer. *New Faith for Old: An Autobiography.* New York: Macmillan, 1936.

Mays, Benjamin E. *The Negro's God: As Reflected in His Literature.* 1938. Reprint, New York: Atheneum, 1969.

——— and Joseph William Nicholson. *The Negro's Church.* New York: Institute of Social and Religious Research, 1933. Reprint, Salem: Ayer Company, 1988.

———. *Seeking to Be Christian in Race Relations.* Revised edition. New York: Friendship Press, 1952.

Mbiti, John. *African Religions and Philosophy.* 1969. Second edition. Oxford: Heinemann Educational Publishers, 1989.

McConnell, Francis J. *Borden Parker Bowne: His Life and His Philosophy.* New York: Abingdon Press, 1929.

———. *The Christlike God.* New York: Abingdon Press, 1927.

———. *Is God Limited?* New York: Abingdon Press, 1924.

———. *Personal Christianity.* New York: Fleming H. Revell, 1914.

McDowell, John Patrick. *The Social Gospel in the South: The Woman's Home Mission Movement in the Methodist Episcopal Church, South, 1886–1939.* Baton Rouge: Louisiana State University Press, 1982.

McKelway, Alexander J. *The Systematic Theology of Paul Tillich: A Review and Analysis.* Richmond, Va.: John Knox Press, 1964.

Mikelson, Thomas Jarl Sheppard. "The Negro's God in the Theology of Martin Luther King, Jr.: Social Community and Theological Discourse." Th. D. dissertation, Harvard University, April 1988.

Miller, Keith D. *Voice of Deliverance: The Language of Martin Luther King, Jr., and Its Sources.* New York: Free Press, 1992.

Muelder, Walter G. "Communitarian Dimensions of the Moral Laws." In *The Boston Personalist Tradition in Philosophy, Social Ethics, and Theology,* edited by Paul Deats, Jr., and Carol Robb, 237–52. Macon, Ga.: Mercer University Press, 1986.

———. "Martin Luther King, Jr.'s Ethics of Non-Violent Action." Lecture, King Center for Social Change, Atlanta, March 2, 1985.

———. "Martin Luther King, Jr., and the Moral Laws." Lecture, given at Morehouse College, March 24, 1983.

———. *Moral Law in Christian Social Ethics.* Richmond, Va.: John Knox Press, 1966.

Mueller, Carol. "Ella Baker and the Origins of 'Participatory Democracy.'" In *Women in the Civil Rights Movement: Trailblazers and Torchbearers, 1941–1965,* edited by Vicki L. Crawford, Jacqueline Anne Rouse, and Barbara Woods, 51–70. Bloomington and Indianapolis: Indiana University Press, 1993.

Murray, Pauli. *Song in a Weary Throat.* New York: Harper & Row, 1987.

Newhall, Jannette. "Edgar Sheffield Brightman." *Philosophical Forum* 12 (1954): 9–28.

Niebuhr, Reinhold. *The Nature and Destiny of Man: A Christian Interpretation.* 1941. Reprint, New York: Charles Scribner's Sons, 1949.

———. *Moral Man and Immoral Society.* New York: Charles Scribner's Sons, 1932.

Oates, Stephen B. *Let the Trumpet Sound: The Life of Martin Luther King, Jr.* New York: Harper & Row, 1982.

Olson, Lynne. *Freedom's Daughters: The Unsung Heroines of the Civil Rights Movement from 1830 to 1970.* New York: Simon & Schuster, 2001.

Ottley, Roi, and William J. Weatherby, eds. *The Negro in New York: An Informal History, 1626–1940.* New York: Praeger Publishers, 1969.

Pappas, Theodore. *Plagiarism and the Culture War: The Writings of Martin Luther King, Jr., and Other Prominent Americans.* Tampa: Hallberg Publishing, 1998.

Parks, Rosa, with Jim Haskins. *Rosa Parks: My Story.* New York: Dial Books, 1992.

Pobee, John S. *Toward an African Theology.* Nashville, Tenn.: Abingdon Press, 1979.

Ransby, Barbara. *Ella Baker and the Black Freedom Movement: A Radical Democratic Vision.* Chapel Hill: University of North Carolina Press, 2003.

Ransom, Reverdy. *The Pilgrimage of Harriet Ransom's Son.* Nashville, Tenn.: Sunday School Union, 1949.

Rauschenbusch, Walter. *The Righteousness of the Kingdom.* Edited by Max L. Stackhouse. Nashville, Tenn.: Abingdon Press, 1968.

———. *A Theology for the Social Gospel.* New York: Macmillan, 1917.

———. *The Social Principles of Jesus.* Edited by Henry H. Meyer. New York: Methodist Book Concern, 1916.

———. *Dare We Be Christians?* Cleveland: Pilgrim Press, 1993, 1914.

———. *Christianizing the Social Order.* New York: Macmillan, 1913.

———. *Christianity and the Social Crisis.* New York: Macmillan, 1907.

Reddick, Lawrence D. *Crusader without Violence: A Biography of Martin Luther King, Jr.* New York: Harper & Brothers, 1959.

Roberts, J. DeOtis. *A Black Political Theology.* Philadelphia: Westminster Press, 1974.

———. "Black Consciousness in Theological Perspective." In *Quest for A Black Theology,* edited by Roberts and James J. Gardiner, chapter 4. Philadelphia: Pilgrim Press, 1971.

Roberts, Samuel K. *An African American Christian Ethics.* Cleveland: Pilgrim Press, 2001.

Robinson, Jo Ann Gibson. *The Montgomery Bus Boycott and the Women Who Started It.* Edited by David J. Garrow. Knoxville: University of Tennessee Press, 1987.

Robnett, Belinda. *How Long? How Long?: African American Women in the Struggle for Civil Rights.* New York: Oxford University Press, 1997.

Royce, Josiah. *The Problem of Christianity.* Two vols. New York: Macmillan, 1913.

———. *The Philosophy of Loyalty.* New York: Macmillan Company, 1908.

Sartre, Jean-Paul. "Existentialism Is a Humanism." Translated by Philip Mairet. In *The Existentialist Tradition: Selected Writings,* edited by Nino Langiulli, 391–419. Garden City, N.Y.: Anchor Books, 1971,

———. *The Age of Reason.* Translated by Eric Sutton. New York: Bantam Books, 1968.

———. *Being and Nothingness: An Essay on Phenomenological Ontology.* Translated and with an Introduction by Hazel E. Barnes. New York: Philosophical Library, 1965.

Sharpe, Dores. *Walter Rauschenbusch.* New York: Macmillan, 1942.

Singer, Peter. *Animal Liberation: A New Ethics for Our Treatment of Animals.* New York: Avon Books, 1975.

Smith, Ervin. *The Ethics of Martin Luther King, Jr.* New York: Mellen Press, 1981.

Smith, H. Shelton, Robert T. Handy, and Lefferts A. Loetscher. *American Christianity: An Historical Interpretation with Representative Documents.* Vol. 2. New York: Charles Scribner's Sons, 1963.

Smith, Kenneth L., and Ira G. Zepp, Jr. *Search for the Beloved Community: The Thinking of Martin Luther King, Jr.* Valley Forge, Pa.: Judson Press, 1974.

Sniderman, Paul M., and Thomas Piazza. *The Scar of Race.* Cambridge, Mass.: Harvard University Press, 1993.

Taylor, Paul W. *Respect for Nature: A Theory of Environmental Ethics.* Princeton, N.J.: Princeton University Press, 1986.

Terrell, Mary Church. *A Colored Woman in a White World.* Introduction by Nellie V. McKay. New York: G. K. Hall, 1996.

Thelen, David, ed. "Becoming Martin Luther King, Jr.—Plagiarism and Originality: A Round Table." *Journal of American History* 78, no. 1 (June 1991): 11–123.

Thurman, Howard. *With Head and Heart: The Autobiography of Howard Thurman.* New York: Harcourt Brace Jovanovich, 1979.

———. *The Search for Common Ground: An Inquiry into the Basis of Man's Experience of Community.* New York: Harper & Row, 1971.

———. "The New Heaven and the New Earth." *Journal of Negro Education* 27, no. 2 (Spring 1958): 115–19.

———. "The Christian Minister and the Desegregation Decision." *Pulpit Digest,* 37, no. 229 (May 1957): 13–19.

Tillich, Paul. *Systematic Theology.* 3 vols. in one. Chicago and New York: University of Chicago Press and Harper & Row, 1967.

———. *Theology of Culture.* Edited by Robert C. Kimball. New York: Oxford University Press, 1959.

———. *Dynamics of Faith.* New York: Harper & Brothers, 1957.

———. *Biblical Religion and the Search for Ultimate Reality.* Chicago: University of Chicago Press, 1955.

———. *The Protestant Era.* Translated by James Luther Adams. Chicago: University of Chicago Press, 1948.

Trimiew, Darryl M. "The Social Gospel Movement and the Question of Race." In *The Social Gospel Today,* edited by Christopher H. Evans. Louisville, Ky.: Westminster John Knox Press, 2001.

Walker, Alice. *In Search of Our Mothers' Gardens: Womanist Prose.* New York: Harcourt Brace Jovanovich, 1983.

Ward, B., and T. Badger, eds. *The Making of Martin Luther King and the Civil Rights Movement.* Basingstoke: Macmillan, 1996.

Warren, Mervin A. *King Came Preaching: The Pulpit Power of Dr. Martin Luther King, Jr.* Downers Grove, Ill.: InterVarsity Press, 2001.

Washington, James M., ed. *A Testament of Hope: The Essential Writings and Speeches of Martin Luther King, Jr.* New York: Harper & Row, 1986.

Westin, Alan F., and Barry Mahoney. *The Trial of Martin Luther King.* New York: Thomas Y. Crowell, 1974.

White, Ronald C. *Liberty and Justice for All: Racial Reform and the Social Gospel (1877–1925).* New York: Harper & Row, 1990.

Williams, Preston. "The Social Gospel and Race Relations: A Case Study of a Social Movement." Chapter 10 in *Toward a Discipline of Social Ethics: Essays in Honor of Walter George Muelder,* edited by Paul Deats, Jr. Boston: Boston University Press, 1972.

Williams, Robert F. "Can Negroes Afford to Be Pacifists?" In *Seeds of Liberation*, edited by Paul Goodman, 270–77. New York: George Braziller, 1964.

Woodbey, George Washington. *What to Do and How to Do It, or Socialism vs. Capitalism.* In *Black Socialist Preacher*, edited by Philip S. Foner, 40–86. San Francisco: Synthesis Publications, 1983.

Zepp, Ira G. *The Social Vision of Martin Luther King, Jr.* 1971. Reprint, New York: Carlson Publishing, 1989.

Zinn, Howard. *SNCC: The New Abolitionists.* 1964. Reprint, Boston: Beacon Press, 1965.